THE RIAI CONTRACTS
– A WORKING GUIDE

THE RIAI CONTRACTS

A WORKING GUIDE | 4TH REVISED EDITION | DAVID KEANE

RIAI

THE ROYAL INSTITUTE OF THE ARCHITECTS OF IRELAND

THE RIAI CONTRACTS – A WORKING GUIDE
(4th revised edition)

DAVID KEANE
B.Arch. (NUI) FRIAI, MCI Arb, Barrister-at-Law
KMD Architecture

Published by the Royal Institute of the Architects of Ireland

First edition – October 1991
Second revised edition – September 1992
Third revised edition – May 1997
Fourth revised edition – October 2001

ISBN 0946846 588

Design – John O'Regan (© Gandon, 2001)
Production – Nicola Dearey
Produced by Gandon Editions, Kinsale, for the RIAI
Printing – Betaprint, Dublin

THE ROYAL INSTITUTE OF THE ARCHITECTS OF IRELAND
8 Merrion Square, Dublin 2
tel: 01-6761703 / fax: 01-6610948
e-mail: info@riai.ie

Contents

FOREWORD   *by Brian O'Connell*   11

PREFACE   13

PREFACE TO FOURTH EDITION   15

REFERENCES   16

STATUTES REFERRED TO   18

INTRODUCTION   19

ARTICLES OF AGREEMENT – RIAI and GDLA   43

CLAUSES

1	RIAI	Definitions	48
	GDLA	Definitions	50
2	RIAI	Scope of Contract	53
	GDLA	Scope of Contract and Architect's Instructions	65
	SF 88	Clause 1 – Contractor's Obligation	67
	SF 88	Clause 2 – Employer's Obligation	67
	SF 88	Clause 3 – The Architect (Agent/Instructions/Inspection)	68
	SF 88	Clause 9 – Dismissal of Workers	72
3	RIAI/GDLA	Drawings and Bill of Quantities	75
	RIAI	Drawings and Bill of Quantities	76, 80
	GDLA	Bill of Quantities: Schedule of Rates	80, 82
	SF 88	Clause 3 – The Architect (general)	84
4	RIAI	Variations arising from Legislative Enactments	86
	GDLA	Cost adjustments arising from Legislative Enactments	86
	SF 88	Clause 15 – Fluctuations	87

5	RIAI	Contractor to Provide Everything Necessary	88
	GDLA	Contractor to Provide Everything Necessary	88
6	RIAI	Local and Other Authorities Notices and Fees	90
	GDLA	Local and Other Authorities Notices and Fees	96
	SF 88	Clause 16 – Statutory obligations, notices, fees and charges	97
7	RIAI	Setting out of Works	99
	GDLA	Setting out of Works	100
8	RIAI	Materials and Workmanship to Conform to Description	101
	GDLA	Materials and Workmanship to Conform to Description	109
9	RIAI	Work to be opened up	111
	GDLA	Work to be opened up	112
10	RIAI	Foreman	114
	GDLA	Foreman	114
	SF 88	Clause 10 – Supervision	115
11	RIAI	Access for Architect to Works	116
	GDLA	Access for Architect to Works	116
	SF 88	Clause 11 – Site Safety	117
12	RIAI	Clerk of Works	120
	GDLA	Clerk of Works	123
13	RIAI	Ascertainment of Prices for Variations	125
	GDLA	Ascertainment of Prices for Variations, and Omissions	129
14	RIAI	Omissions	131
	GDLA	Clause 13 – Omissions	132
		Clause 14 – Vesting of Materials and Plant	134
15	RIAI	Assignment or sub-letting	138
	GDLA	Assignment or sub-letting	140
	SF88	Assignment	140
16	RIAI	Nominated Sub-Contractors	142
	GDLA	Nominated Sub-Contractors	157
17	RIAI	Nominated Suppliers	161
	GDLA	Nominated Suppliers	163

18	RIAI	Provisional Sums	165
	GDLA	Provisional Sums	166
	SF 88	Clause 3 – The Architect (Provisional Sums)	166
19	RIAI	Prime Cost Sums	167
	GDLA	Prime Cost Sums	169
20-27		The Insurance Clauses	172
20	RIAI	Liability and Indemnity for Damage to Persons and Property	178
	GDLA	Artists and Tradesmen	242
21	RIAI	Insurance against Damage to Persons and Property	181
	GDLA	Liability for Damage to Persons and Property and Public Liability and Employer's Liability Insurance by the Contractor	183
	SF 88	Clause 17 – Liability, Indemnity, and Insurance for Damage to Persons and Property	185
22	RIAI	All Risks Insurance	187
	GDLA	All Risks Insurance by the Contractor	192
	SF 88	Clause 18 – All Risks Insurance	193
23	RIAI	Insurance Policies	195
	GDLA	Contractor's Insurance Policies	202
	SF 88	Clause 20 – Production of Insurances	202
24	RIAI	Damage due to Excluded Risks	204
	GDLA	Loss or Damage to the Works and Ancillary Items due to Excluded Risks	205
25	RIAI	Damage due to Design	207
	GDLA	Loss or Damage to the Works due to Contractor's or Sub-Contractor's Design	207
26	RIAI	Responsibility for Existing Structures	209
	GDLA	Responsibility for Existing Structures	212
	SF 88	Clause 19 – Insurance of Existing Structures	213
27	RIAI	War Damage	214
	GDLA	War Damage	214

28	RIAI	Dates for Possession and Completion	215
	GDLA	Dates for Possession, Practical Completion and Final Completion	216
	SF 88	Clause 4 – Practical Completion	220
29	RIAI	Damages for Non-Completion	222
	GDLA	Non-Completion	226
	SF 88	Clause 6 – Liquidated Damages	226
30	RIAI	Delay and Extension of Time	229
	GDLA	Delay and Extension of Time	235
	SF 88	Clause 5 – Extension of Time	236
31	RIAI	Practical Completion and Defects Liability	237
	GDLA	Defects Liability	239
	SF 88	Clause 4 – Practical Completion	240
	SF 88	Clause 7 – Defects Liability	240
32	RIAI	A – Independent Contractors, Artists and Tradesmen	241
		B – Partial Possession	244
		C – Damage due to Use, Occupation, Possession by Employer	247
	GDLA	Clause 20 – Artists and Tradesmen	242
		Clause 32 – Partial Possession	246
33	RIAI	Determination of Contract by Employer	249
	GDLA	Determination of Contract by Employer	257
	SF 88	Clause 21 – Determination by Employer	258
34	RIAI	Determination of Contract by Contractor	260
	GDLA	Determination of Contract by Contractor	262
	SF 88	Clause 22 – Determination by Contractor	263
35	RIAI	Certificates and Payments	265
	GDLA	Certificates and Payments	282
	SF 88	Clause 12 – Payments	285
		Clause 13 – Payments on Practical Completion	286
		Clause 14 – Final Certificate	286
36	RIAI	Wage and Price Variations	289
	GDLA	Wage and Price Variations	293
	SF 88	Clause 15 – Fluctuations	297

37	RIAI	Collateral Agreements	298
	GDLA	Disputes Resolution	312
38	RIAI	Disputes Resolution	302
	SF 88	Clause 23 – Arbitration	312
	GDLA	Clause 37 – Disputes Resolution	312
		Clause 38 – Copies of Drawings and Specification the Employer's Property	313
39	GDLA	Fair Wages Clause	314
40	GDLA	Ministers and Ministers of State	316
41	GDLA	Receipt of Notices	316

SUPPLEMENT	RIAI Version	317
	GDLA Variations	319
SUB-CONTRACT FORMS		320
THE APPENDIX – RIAI and GDLA		322
INDEX		327

STANDARD DOCUMENTS		337
1	Collateral Agreement between Employer and Nominated Sub-Contractor	339
2	Sub-Contract Form – RIAI	345
3	Sub-Contract Form – GDLA	365
4	Building Contract (Plain Language Contract)	383
5	GDLA – Supplement (A): Clause 36 – Definitions	395
6	GDLA – Supplement (B): Retention Bond	397
7	GDLA – Supplement (C): Conciliation Procedures	399

Foreword

The RIAI Standard Forms of Building Contract, themselves an institution, are so widely used that they may be said to ground the administration of the construction process in Ireland. The Contract fixes the net agreement between the parties, and is the sole basis for the administration of the works. It is imperative that the documents which will establish the cost and direct the production of the works, be derived from the terms of the Contract which they incorporate and that the policies on those documents are consistent with the policies of the contractual terms. A full understanding of the Standard Forms is necessary to ensure this. On this basis alone any work which consolidates and elaborates the Standard Forms is to be welcomed.

The terms usually known as the Conditions of Contract lay down the principles by which the conflicting interests of the parties are to be resolved throughout the variable process of construction. The terms of the Standard Forms incorporate the wisdom of generations and are constantly up-dated to take account of changing practices and anomalies resulting from their composite construction. The terms are binding on the parties: in the event of a dispute which is referred to the adjudication of a Court, the Court is called on to interpret the facts in relation to the Contract as a whole within the matrix of the general law. The Court's interpretation casts a light on the meaning of the Contract, and matures and deepens understanding adding a dimension of certainty to its application in like circumstances.

The study of the Standard Forms and their application has always been a matter of first importance in the professional education of architects; until now the learning process in this area has been by the difficult process of assimilation from scattered sources; it has been equally difficult for practicing architects to keep up to date with developments. In this Working Guide to the RIAI Conditions of Contract, David Keane has set out each Form in an easily referable way, and set each clause within the context of the general law supported by relevant judicial interpretations with case citations and cross reference to the material provisions of other clauses. This work provides a valuable reference and source on the Standard RIAI Forms and fills a long awaited need. Mr Keane's work has not only provided students and practitioners and that wide range of persons whose interests are regulated either directly or indirectly by the Standard Forms, with a readily understandable commentary on the Conditions, but in bringing together all of the relevant interpretative elements to each clause, he has sharpened the focus of interpretation and so clarified the meaning and application of the Conditions in the administrative process, and in this he has made a substantial contribution to the law and practice of Building Contracts in Ireland for which he deserves the gratitude of both the Profession and the Industry.

The Forms of Contract are living institutions – they grow with the society they serve, and any definitive work is soon out of date. To overcome this limitation the book is designed to be updated by supplement. In an area when current knowledge is critical, this makes this work an indispensible companion to all who have responsibilities in the area of Building Contract Administration in Ireland. I have pleasure in expressing the compliments and gratitude of the Council of the RIAI to David Keane and recommending this book without reservation.

BRIAN O'CONNELL
B.Arch (NUI) FRIAI, RIBA, Barrister-at-Law
President, Royal Institute of the Architects of Ireland, 1991

Preface

Over the years, a number of books and articles have been written examining and commentating on the standard forms of contract, but there is not in existence, as far as I am aware, a comprehensive guide to those contracts that are published by the Royal Institute of the Architects of Ireland which would examine each clause and provide a view as to the meaning of the clause, the consequences of the operation of the clause, or the duties, powers, responsibilities, and liabilities of all those affected by the operation of those contract forms. In view of the widespread use of these forms, it appeared as if there was a gap to be filled.

The book is set out in a clause by clause format, with a commentary on each clause, or sub-clause, as it occurs. The extracts from the contract forms are printed in bold type. The clauses are, obviously, all numbered and all sub-clauses similarly so, but at times separate paragraphs are not numerically defined, and it is suggested that future editions of the contract forms might be broken down into, perhaps, a numbered sentence by sentence format.

This is not a legal text-book, but a practical guide for architects, engineers, surveyors, contractors, sub-contractors, suppliers, and, dare it be said, lawyers and even accountants, but it would not be possible, or sensible, to set the scene for the various interpretations of the contract forms without reference to the legal decisions which buttress these views. It must be pointed out, though, that the comments on the cases will of necessity be very concise and a reading of the full case can be very useful in appreciating why the court came to the eventual decision. Very often it appears that the decisions in similar cases differ, but it is very seldom that the facts in one case, while being similar, are identical to the facts in another.

The legal reference that is given in preference is that of the BUILDING LAW REPORTS (BLR published by Longman) whenever this is available, as these reports are the most accessible to those who work in the construction industry. Readers will suspect that building law is very complex, and the fact that the BUILDING LAW REPORTS now run to over fifty volumes testifies to that suspicion. For this reason cases are grouped with the clauses that they most impinge on. It will be seen that the majority of cases referred to are ones which have featured in the courts in Britain, or other common law countries. This is, naturally, because the greater scale of the construction industry there will inevitably lead to a greater number of cases, but the similarity both of the legal systems and the essence of the forms of contract in those countries makes them relevant. Decisions in these countries are not, of course, binding on the Irish courts but may be pleaded in them and can be taken as being 'persuasive'.

An introductory essay on the background to standard forms, and on the constantly shifting relationships between all the parties to the building process, together with a view on possible future developments has been included as it is felt that the proper interpretation of the standard forms must be informed by an appreciation of the overall scene, and a knowledge of the framework which covers the complex world of construction.

I am indebted to the Royal Institute of the Architects of Ireland, the Construction Industry Federation and the Society of Chartered Surveyors in the Republic of Ireland for permission to reproduce the Contract, Sub-Contract, and Collateral Warranty forms. John Graby, the General Secretary of the RIAI has been unfailingly helpful and encouraging. I am indebted to Judge Ronan Keane of the High Court, and the Law Reform Commission, for throwing a brotherly eye on the work, but the mistakes are all mine. To the partners of Keane Murphy Duff I owe a special debt for offering me the not inconsiderable resources of that organisation, and to Ian Duff in particular for the invaluable use of his country hideaway. My former secretary for over twenty years, Hilary Kirk, has dealt with the typing and word-processing tasks with patience and good humour. Finally my wife, Dr Maureen Keane, showed me that research and writing had their own rewards, and for that, and much besides, I thank her.

The information contained in the book is up to date, as far as I am aware, to the 1st October 1991.

DAVID KEANE
October 1991

Preface to Fourth Edition

A number of factors led to the decision to produce a fourth edition of this book. The first was the rewriting of the insurance clauses numbers 21 to 27 in the RIAI form by the Liaison Committee; the second was the alteration of the GDLA form in a number of ways by the State, and, thirdly, the decisions of the Forum for the Construction Industry. The recommendations of this body have altered both the RIAI and the GDLA forms. The Forum has also somewhat confused the role of the Liaison Committee, which was set up to agree alterations to the contract form and which comprises representatives of the Royal Institute of the Architects of Ireland, the Society of Chartered Surveyors in the Republic of Ireland, the Construction Industry Federation, and, latterly, the Association of Consulting Engineers of Ireland. No doubt time will resolve any problems arising from the relationship, or the lack of it, between the Liaison Committee and the Forum.

Some clause numbers have changed in the RIAI form. The previous clause 20 has become 32A, clause 21 has been split into clauses 20 and 21, and clause 32 has split into 32A (formerly 20), 32B and 32C.

The Forum has, in addition, set up two sub-committees to produce two national forms of contract for use by both the public and private sectors. The first contract will deal with civil engineering works, and the second one with building works. It would be hoped that final versions of both these contracts would be available before the end of the year 2001.

Finally, I have included the proposed introduction of a formula fluctuations method of dealing with inflation in the GDLA contract in place of the complex wage and price variations procedures presently in place (RIAI and GDLA Clause 36) even though negotiations to implement them are not yet complete. It is hoped that they will conclude shortly.

DAVID KEANE
October 2001

References

Two books are referred to on a number of occasions. The first of these is HUDSON'S BUILDING AND ENGINEERING CONTRACTS, edited by IN Duncan Wallace, the eleventh edition, published by Sweet & Maxwell in 1995. This is the standard work on building contracts and is invaluable. The second work is ENGINEERING LAW AND THE ICE CONTRACTS by Max W Abrahamson (4th edition), published by Elsevier Applied Science Publishers in 1979. Though written as a commentary on the engineering contracts, it is applicable in many respects to the RIAI forms. The RIAI has also published, in 1997, a third edition of BUILDING AND THE LAW, which deals with all the legislation affecting building up to 1997. A new edition is due shortly.

A legal reference normally contains firstly the year in which the case occurred, secondly the volume of the reference work in question, thirdly the identification of the reference work itself, and lastly the page number, i.e. [1973] 9 BLR 20. The abbreviations and legal references throughout the book are:

AC	Appeal Cases
AER	ALL ENGLAND REPORTS, published by Butterworths
ALJ (Aus)	AUSTRALIAN LAW JOURNAL
ALJR	AUSTRALIAN LAW JOURNAL REPORTS
BLISS	Building Law Information Subscription Services
BLR	BUILDING LAW REPORTS, published by Longmans
CA	Court of Appeal
Ch	Chancery Division
CIF	Construction Industry Federation
CLD	CONSTRUCTION LAW DIGEST
CLR	CONSTRUCTION LAW REPORTS
CLR	COMMONWEALTH LAW REPORTS
EX	Court of Exchequer
Fed. Rep.	FEDERAL REPORTS, United States

GDLA	Government Departments and Local Authorities
H&N	Hurlestone and Norman (1856–1862)
ICE	Institution of Civil Engineers
IEI	Institution of Engineers in Ireland
ILRM	IRISH LAW REPORTS MONTHLY, published by the Round Hall Press
ILTR	IRISH LAW TIMES REPORTS (1867–1980)
ILT	IRISH LAW TIMES, published by the Round Hall Press
IR	IRISH REPORTS, published by Butterworths
JCT/RIBA	The standard forms of contract produced in Britain by the Joint Contracts Tribunal and formerly referred to as the RIBA forms
KB	King's Bench Division
LGR	Local Government Reports
LT	LAW TIMES (1859–1847)
LQR	LAW QUARTERLY REVIEW
NI	Northern Ireland Reports published by the Incorporated Council of Law Reporting for Northern Ireland
NIJR	NEW IRISH JURIST REPORTS (1900–1905)
RIBA	Royal Institute of British Architects
RIAI	Royal Institute of the Architects of Ireland
SCS	Society of Chartered Surveyors in the Republic of Ireland
Unrep.	Unreported
WLR	WEEKLY LAW REPORTS, published by the Incorporated Council of Law Reporting for England and Wales

(The judgements in unreported cases can usually be obtained from the High Court or Supreme Court offices.)

Statutes referred to

	pars
Arbitration Acts 1954, 1980, 1998	– 35.14, 38.01, 38.03, 38.06
Arbitration Act 1957 (Northern Ireland)	– 38.01, 38.08
Arbitration Act 1979 (UK)	– 38.03
Bank Holidays Act 1871 Ch.17	– 1.02
Bank Holiday (Ireland) Act 1903	– 1.02
Bankruptcy Act 1988	– 33.06
Building Control Act 1990	– 6.01, 6.02, 6.03, 6.04, 6.05, 6.07, 8.02
Companies Act 1963	– 16.15
Companies (Amendment) Act 1990	– 33.06
Copyright and Related Rights Act 2000	– 3.13
Courts Act 1981	– 35.14
Environmental Protection Agency Act 1992	– 6.05
European Communities Act 1972	– Int.17
Holiday Employees Act 1973	– 1.02
Holiday Extensions Act 1875 Ch. 13	– 1.02
Housing Act 1966	– 6.08
Industrial Relations Act 1946	– 1.03
Local Government (Multi-storey buildings) Act 1988	– 6.05
Local Government (Planning and Development) Acts 1963–1990	– 6.01, 6.02
Planning and Development Act 2000	– 6.01
Prompt Payment of Accounts Act 1997	– 16.17, 19.03
Public Health (Ireland) Act 1878	– 6.02
Public Health Acts, Amendment Act 1907	– 6.04
Public Holidays Act 1924	– 1.02
Safety, Health and Welfare at Work Act 1989	– 6.05, 11.03
Sale of Goods Act 1893	– Int.10, 8.02, 8.03, 8.05, 8.06, 8.08
Sale of Goods and Supply of Services Act 1980	– 8.02, 8.03, 8.04, 8.06, 8.08
Sale of Goods Act 1979 (UK)	– 35.05
Single European Act 1978	– Int.17
State Property Act 1954	– 41.01
Statute of Frauds 1695	– Int.05
Statute of Limitations 1957	– Int.06, Int.15
Town and Regional Planning Act 1934	– 6.02
Treaty of Rome 1958	– Int.17

Introduction

Int.01   The standard forms of contract which are published by the RIAI are four in number.

The basic, and original, form is described in this book as the RIAI form. It is issued by the Royal Institute of the Architects of Ireland in agreement with the Construction Industry Federation and the Society of Chartered Surveyors in the Republic of Ireland. It is suitable for the whole range of building contracts, but is now primarily used for substantial contracts in the private sector. The latest edition was published on 30th August 1996.

The second form is described as the GDLA form. These initials stand for Government Departments and Local Authorities. This form is based on the RIAI form and is similar in most respects. It is intended for use by Government Departments, Local Authorities, and by other bodies 'the placing of whose contracts is subject to approval by a Government Department or Local Authority when the work is to be paid for wholly or partly from Exchequer Funds'. The GDLA form is published by the RIAI, after consultation with the Construction Industry Federation and the Royal Institution of Chartered Surveyors, but only after approval by the Department of Finance. The first edition, which is still current, was published on 1st March 1982. (At that date the name of the Royal Institution of Chartered Surveyors had not been changed to the Society of Chartered Surveyors in the Republic of Ireland.) Both the RIAI and GDLA forms are available in two slightly different versions, depending on whether or not a Bill of Quantities is one of the contract documents (see par. 3.01).

The third form dealt with in this book is the form known as SF 88, which are the initials referring to Shorter Form, and which is intended for small or simple contracts. The first edition was published on 1st November 1988.

Finally, in March 1997, the RIAI produced what is described as a plain language contract. This version, which is not intended to replace the standard form and has not been submitted to the Liaison Committee, was produced in response to requests from quite a large number of people, many of whom quoted the New Engineering Contract published in 1991 by the Institution of Civil Engineers. The new RIAI form is intended to have exactly the same legal effect as the standard form, but is written in a simple style and has the clauses arranged in a more logical sequence. It is reproduced at the end of this book in the Standard Documents section.

Int.02   The dramatis personae in the book are five in number, described in alphabetical order. The Architect, though not a party to the contract, has very wide powers under it and in effect controls it. He would normally be a member of the Royal Institute of the Architects of Ireland, though Ireland unlike many other countries, does not at the moment legally require a practising Architect to be properly qualified. This is likely to change soon. However, merely by describing himself as an architect, a person holds out that he has the appropriate skills and can be sued for negligence if he does not provide the appropriate standard of skill, whether he is qualified or not. An architect has been defined by Myles na gCopaleen as 'a chap who puts up artificial shelters'.

The next player is the Contractor. He would normally be a member of the Construction Industry Federation, but not necessarily so for the carrying on of his business. He is a party to the contract. His duties are well described in Clause 1 of the SF 88 form: 'The Contractor shall carry out and complete the Works in a good and workmanlike manner.' He is closely associated with the fourth player, the Sub-Contractor. Thirdly we have the Employer, who is the other party to the contract. The main requirement of the Employer is that he would have enough money to pay all concerned in the process. 'The Employer shall pay or allow to the Contractor such sums of money as shall from time to time become due...' (SF 88 Clause 2). Fourthly we have the Nominated Sub-Contractor (and the Nominated Supplier) who has a contract with the Contractor which is separate from the main contract and who normally would not have a contract with the Employer, unless what is called a Collateral Warranty is signed (see the notes to Clause 37 – Collateral Warranty). Lastly we have the Quantity Surveyor who, like the Architect, is named in both the RIAI and GDLA forms but who again like the Architect is not a party to the contract. He would normally be a member of the Society of Chartered Surveyors in the Republic of Ireland. His duties are to assist the Architect in performing his duties under the contract in the area of cost and value.

Int.03   There are a number of topics which should be examined before dealing with the intricacies of the standard forms, and a knowledge of these topics is necessary in order to understand the background to, and the reasons for, the provisions contained in the various standard forms. It is proposed to deal with the following areas:

1   The general law affecting contracts

2   The history and development of standard forms

3   The duties and responsibilities of

    a)   the Architect

    b)   the other Consultants

        (NOTE: It is not proposed to deal at this point with the duties and responsibilities of the Employer, the Contractor or the Sub-Contractors, as these are covered throughout the book on a clause by clause basis.)

4   The liabilities of the parties

The notes are all, necessarily, of a general nature and are only intended to give a broad view of the areas involved and to provide a frame work for further reading.

1 – LAW OF CONTRACT

Int.04   There have been many definitions of a legal contract, and possibly an equal number of criticisms of these definitions. An agreement which the law will enforce becomes a contract. A contract is primarily an agreement, and while all contracts are agreements, not all agreements are contracts. An agreement to meet someone is not a contract. The three basic requirements of all contracts are well known, those of offer, acceptance and consideration. The Contractor 'offers' by way of tender to construct the building in question for a certain sum of money – the 'consideration'. The Employer 'accepts' the offer, usually by way of letter and ultimately by signing the Articles of Agreement. There are few difficulties in the construction field with these three requirements, but some points should be noted. The acceptance of the offer cannot qualify the original subject of the contract, that is, the Employer cannot, in his acceptance, make any changes that would affect the contract. Equally, the Contractor in making the offer, should not attempt to alter the original terms. If he wishes to vary any items, or make alternative proposals, this should always be done by way of supplemental prices or conditions, so that the original terms of the contract are identifiable. This is important because the law regards it as fundamental that any parties to a contract must be certain as to the details and intention of the contract.

Consideration causes few problems for while it would be possible to enter into a building contract where the Contractor would perform the works for a consideration other than money, such as say part ownership of the building, this is very rare. In the case of *O'Neill v Murphy and Others* [1936] NI 16, the Architect was offered prayers instead of fees. The Court held that prayers were not a sufficient consideration in law. This was a Northern Irish case. Contract law over the years has dealt with many cases in the fields of offer, acceptance and consideration and, like nearly all aspects of law, differing and contradictory results have occurred but practitioners in building can rely on the words of Professor Harrison over fifty years ago: 'Consideration, offer and acceptance are an indivisible trinity, facets of one identical notion which is that of bargain' [1938] 54 LQR 233.

Int.05   In addition to the three requirements mentioned above there are other aspects of a contract which should be present in order to ensure validity. The first, and possibly most important, is certainty. This means that both parties must be of one mind, and must intend the same outcome. It will be seen in the notes to Clause 2 (par. 2.10) that an architect, despite his wide powers under the contract, cannot order a variation of the kind that would not have been contemplated by the Contractor when making his tender bid. Secondly, there must be what is called the necessary formality, which in some contracts require that they be in writing. Generally speaking contracts need not be in writing, but the futility of trying to prove the contents of an oral contract will be obvious, and all building contracts no matter how minor or insignificant should be confirmed in writing. A contract that must be in writing is a contract for the sale of land, and this is required by the Statute of Frauds 1695 which was introduced in Ireland shortly after equivalent legislation in England. The political and social uncertainty in England at the time, and in particular the Penal Laws in Ireland, led to the introduction of this statute which had as one of its objects 'the prevention of many fraudulent practices which are commonly endeavoured to be upheld by perjury and subornation of perjury.' Those in touch with the law to-day will observe that little has changed.

Finally, it is necessary that the parties to the contract have the capacity to enter into a contract, i.e. they must not be under age; the contract must not be for an illegal objective, or be tainted by illegality by, for instance, building in contravention of the planning laws (see par. 6.01); and the object of the contract must be capable of performance.

It might be appropriate at this stage to mention letters of intent. It is common practice for some projects to start on this basis, and indeed for some of them to be completed without any formal contract ever having been signed. This can cause great difficulties and it is suggested if a letter of intent is issued that several basic points be referred to. A court will often infer the existence of a contract in the absence of a concluded agreement but it would be prudent for the letter of intent to refer to the proposed contract form, the tender sum, the basis of payment, and the time for completion. It would also be sensible to suggest a limit to the amount that might be paid under a letter of intent.

Int.06   Having seen how a contract is entered into, it is logical now to see how a contract can be ended. The normal, and non contentious, way of ending a contract is when the parties have performed, or carried out, the contract. In a building contract this will happen when the Architect issues the final certificate (see par. 35.11) but the parties will have ongoing responsibilities for a number of years afterwards. This depends on whether the contract is a 'simple' contract or is a contract 'under seal'. The Articles of Agreement (A.01) allow for either. It is the normal practice for the State, government departments, large companies, etc, to sign under seal, i.e. to affix an official seal to the contract agreement. Contracts not under seal are 'simple contracts'. The distinction can be important. The Statute of Limitations 1957, sets out the time within which an action must be brought after the date of the occurrence of the act which gave rise to the cause of action. In a simple contract this is six years, but in the case of a contract under seal it is twelve years. It would tend to be in the interest of the Employer to conclude a contract under seal as this would give him a longer period within which to commence any action for defects, but this distinction has become somewhat academic because of the development of the law of tort in the field of building. This is discussed in par. Int.15.

The standard forms of contract provide for circumstances which would entitle one party to the contract to, in effect, end it. The process is called 'determining the employment of the Contractor' and it is defined in that way because the contract itself is not ended, but the employment of the Contractor is ended. The contract must remain in being so as to give effect to the provisions which deal with the tidying up process after determination. The circumstances which allow the Employer to determine the employment of the Contractor are contained in RIAI and GDLA Clauses 33, and SF 88 Clause 21, and the comparable provisions which allow the Contractor to determine his own employment are contained in RIAI and GDLA Clauses 34, and SF 88 Clause 22.

Int.07   In ordinary law, however, there are a number of circumstances which could give rise to the ending of the contractual relationship. These would be if a contract is either void, voidable, or unenforcable. In the first case if a contract is void there is in law no contract at all. A contract may be void as far as the majority of building contracts would be concerned because of either 'mistake' or 'illegality'. As far as mistake is concerned it must be a basic and fundamental mistake such as to destroy the certainty requirement of the contract referred to in par. Int.05. The word 'misapprehension' might give a better idea of the situation required to render a contract void, but it must be a misapprehension as to the fundamental nature of the contract and not merely to some aspect of interpretation or performance. As far as illegality is concerned, this would normally affect a building contract where either planning permission or building regulation consents had not been obtained, but the deliberate contravention of any statute would be sufficient to render the contract void (see par. 6.01).

If a contract is voidable it means that one of the parties to the contract may treat it as being at an end, though he may continue if he wishes. In building contracts most of the voidable situations arise because of mis-representation. This misrepresentation must have induced the innocent party to enter into the contract, and it must also be positive, and a fact. Failure to disclose a fact might not be a sufficient ground to render a contract voidable, and misrepresentation of an opinion would be no ground. If the innocent party continues to perform his part of the contract after becoming aware of the misrepresentation he loses his right to rescind the contract. In the case of a voidable contract, the innocent party is entitled to treat the contract as being at an end, and to obtain damages. This right is in addition to any rights to damages which are mentioned in the contract forms (see par. 29.01) and explains why the contract forms refer to 'without prejudice to any other rights or remedies' (Clause 33 RIAI and GDLA).

An 'unenforceable' contract is one where some statute, such as the Statute of Frauds, has not been complied with. This particular contract results in a situation where a positive action, such as claiming damages, cannot be taken but where a passive action, such as making a defence, can be relied on. An unenforceable contract has been defined as 'a shield, not a sword' (FR Davies, CONTRACT, p.81).

2 – THE STANDARD FORMS

Int.08   The development of a standard form of contract appears to date from the middle of the nineteenth century when many large and powerful organisations such as the railway companies, and trading houses found it useful to adopt a series of standard forms. Up till that time, each contract form, from the very beginning, was the subject of some suspicion, mainly on the not unreasonable ground that it was normally produced by a substantial organisation to its potential customers as an accomplished fact. The French have a name for it:

> The term *contract d'adhesion* is employed to denote the type of contract of which the conditions are fixed by one of the parties in advance and are open to acceptance by anyone. The contract, which frequently contains many conditions, is presented for acceptance en bloc and is not open to discussion (Amos and Walton, INTRODUCTION TO FRENCH LAW, p.149).

If the parties to the contract are equals, no problem arises but this is not often the case, and the fact that the standard forms came to be regarded almost as the law could be of disadvantage to the weaker parties to the contract. In this case of *ABC Ltd v Waltham Holy Cross UDC* [1952] 2 AER 452 (which is referred to later in the book at par. 30.15 dealing with extensions of time) the comment was made: 'This form is used in a great many building contracts and, like other standard forms, it has come to resemble a legislative code.' This reference was to the then current JCT/RIBA form.

On the other hand, the advantage of using a standard form is that the provisions contained in it should be well understood and case law should have by now interpreted nearly all the difficult areas. While this is largely true, cases are constantly coming before the courts as to the meaning of various clauses. A problem with standard forms is that those awarded the task of revising them very often use previous versions as drafts and this can result in some rather confused words:

> There is no wholly satisfactory interpretation or explanation of the third part of the clause, and one must choose between two almost equally unsatisfactory conclusions. In a case like this, where a clause in common use has simply been copied, one cannot try to find what the parties intended. They almost certainly never thought about things happening as they did (*Compania Naviera Aeolus v Union of India* [1962] 3 AER 670).

However, the temptation to change a standard form often results in even greater confusion, as the changing of one clause can affect others in the same contract form, or even in subsidiary sub-contract forms, and this is frequently overlooked by those making the changes. The results of such changes can be seen in the cases of *HA O'Neil v John Sisk and Son* [1984] Supreme Court, unrep. 28th July (referred to in par. 19.01) and that of *Irishenco v Dublin County Council* [1984] High Court, unrep. 21st March (referred to in par. 36.03). This latter case is particularly interesting as far as standard forms are concerned, because the court held that it was entitled to look at a clause that had been struck out, as well as looking at the one that replaced it, when trying to interpret the intentions of the parties.

The development of the standard form has led to the importation of the doctrine of *contra preferentem* into the construction industry. This doctrine provides that the least favourable interpretation of a document should be adopted against the person who has published or provided the document, on the grounds that he had the benefit of framing the document, as opposed to the other party who had to take it or leave it – *a prendre ou a laisser*. This factor is reflected in the differences between the RIAI and the GDLA standard forms. The GDLA form, deriving as it does from the Government, tends to favour the Employer in all those cases where the two forms differ. The doctrine is referred to at par. 2.14 with regard to the interpretation of the different contract documents and at par. 16.11 with regard to the use of a standard sub-contract form. But the use of a standard form will bind the parties to that contract very precisely and the courts will not look for implied terms or unusual meanings:

> The basic principle is that the court does not make a contract for the parties. The court will not even improve the contract which the parties have made for themselves however desirable the improvement might be. The courts function is to interpret and apply the contract which the parties have made for themselves. If the express terms are perfectly clear and free from ambiguity there is no choice to be made between different possible meanings; the clear terms must be applied even if the court thinks that some other terms would have been more suitable. An unexpressed term can be implied if and only if the court finds that the parties must have intended that term to form part of their contract; it is not enough for the court to find that such a term would have been adopted by the parties as reasonable men if it has been suggested to them, it must have been a term that went without saying, a term necessary to give business efficacy to the contract, a term which, though tacit, formed part of the contract which the parties made for themselves (*Trollope and Colls Ltd v North West Metropolitan Regional Hospital Board* [1973] 9 BLR 60).

Int.09   The history of the standard form in Ireland is obscure. There is a reference in 1857 to the use of a standard form in relation to the '*Phibsboro Church Case*'. At around the same time, a standard form was being developed in Britain, probably as a result of the rebuilding contract involving the Houses of Parliament. The original contract for that project was for £700,000 and was to take six years. In the event, the works cost £2,000,000 and took thirteen years to build. The ensuing disagreements seemed to focus the minds of those concerned in the construction field, and by 1870 the Builder's Society and the RIBA had produced a standard form for use in the London area. In Ireland, by 1899, the RIAI had come to a decision to produce a standard form, but differences with the Dublin Master Builders Association led to many delays, and it was not until 1910 that the first RIAI standard form was published, in agreement with the Master Builders. Meanwhile, in Britain, a revision of the standard form in 1909 saw the introduction of the nominated sub-contractor, while by 1922 the Quantity Surveyors Association had produced the first Standard Method of Measurement. The Joint Contracts Tribunal was established in the 1930s and has been subsequently responsible for the revisions in 1939, 1952, 1963, culminating in the present 1980 edition.

The development in Ireland was much the same. The RIAI first edition of

1910 seems to have been in general use up to around 1939, and at that time a revised draft of a new edition was circulated. An extremely long and unseemly row now broke out between the Federation of Building Contractors and Allied Employers of Ireland (now the Construction Industry Federation) and the RIAI. Without going into the details of the dispute it can be said that it derived from the mutual suspicion of the two bodies, the architects seeing the contractors as being only concerned with obtaining more favourable terms to themselves, and the contractors seeing the architects as being little more than the lapdogs of the employers. It was not until 1950 that matters were finally resolved. At the same time, to smooth the path to further revisions, a Liaison Committee was set up to interpret and review the standard form. This committee is representative of the RIAI, the CIF, the Society of Chartered Surveyors, and, latterly, the Association of Consulting Engineers of Ireland. The latest edition of the contract is dated 1996.

In concluding this section, the hopeful words of the Chairman of the Contract Conference in Britain in 1928 would still hold:

> It is my considered opinion that it is difficult to measure the advantage that will flow from the general adoption of this standard form of contract. The elimination of uncertainties and ambiguities and the certainty introduced by standardisation on fair and just lines in clear and simple language must necessarily create confidence throughout the building industry and I cannot doubt will by reason of equitable and known conditions result in closer prices and in reducing building costs.

3 – THE DUTIES AND RESPONSIBILITIES OF:

Int.10   a) the Architect

The words 'duty', 'power', and 'responsibility' are used very widely in relation to the position of the parties to the contract, and with regard to those advising the parties. The meaning of these words should be understood. They are discussed in some detail in the case of *Dutton v Bognor Regis UDC* [1971] 3BLR 11, which is a case we will hear more of later on. A 'power' confers on someone the authority to decide or control specified matters. A 'duty' arises in the carrying out of the power to see that it is exercised properly, and a 'responsibility' evolves from the consequences of both the power and the duty. It would be difficult to improve on HUDSON (p.284) for a definition of the Architect's duty which, he says, is to secure:

1   a design which is skillful, effective to achieve his purpose within any financial limitations he may impose or make known and comprehensive,

in the sense that no necessary or foreseeable work is omitted;

2   the obtaining of a competitive price for the work from a competent Contractor, and the placing of the contract accordingly in terms which afford reasonable protection to the Employer's interest both in regard to price and the quality of the work;

3   efficient supervision to ensure that the works as carried out conform in detail to the design; and

4   efficient administration of the contract so as to achieve speedy and economical completion of the project.

While this extract covers the general areas which the Architect will be responsible for, it is important to examine the precise level of skill that the Architect will be expected to achieve. It is generally accepted that the Architect's duty is to use reasonable skill and care in the course of his employment. This was laid down for professionals generally in a well known medical case, *Bolam v Friern Hospital Management Committee* [1957] 1 WLR 582, and expanded on in the case of *Chin Keow v Government of Malaysia* [1967] 1 WLR 813: 'Where you get a situation which involves the use of some special skill or competence, then the test as to whether there has been negligence or not is not the test of the man on top of the Clapham Omnibus, because he has not got this special skill. The test is the standard of the ordinary skilled man exercising and professing to have that special skill; it is well established law that it is sufficient if he exercises the ordinary skill of an ordinary competent man exercising that particular art.' A later case, *Wimpey Construction UK Ltd v DV Poole* [1984] – Lloyd's Rep 499, confirmed the Bolam test and added, very interestingly, that even if the Employer had paid for someone with specially high skills the basic negligence test did not alter. The Bolam test was approved in Ireland in the case of *Ward v McMaster and Others* [1989] ILRM 400, which concerned a house valuation. There is, however, an important exception. What was known as 'the State of the Art' defence was quite widespread in professional negligence actions, and meant, in brief, that what was considered acceptable on a general scale by a profession would not be held to be negligent. This was upheld in the case of *Flanagan v Griffith* [1981] High Court, unrep. 25th January, when the Court held that 'an architect cannot be liable in negligence for forming a judgement which conforms with the considered judgement of men prominent in his profession.' However, all this was qualified by what is known as the rule in *Roche v Peilow* [1986] ILRM 189 which was first set out in *O'Donovan v Cork County Council* [1967] IR 173:

If there is a common practice which has inherent defects, which ought to be obvious to any person giving the matter due consideration, the fact that it is shown to have been widely and generally adopted over a period of time does not make the practice any the less negligent. Neglect of duty does not cease by repetition to be neglect of duty.

The Architect's design must be skillful, but he will not be expected to guarantee that the result will be reasonably fit for the purpose. The distinction may be a fine one but it exists. The law does not imply a warranty that a professional man will achieve a desired result, but it does assume that he will use reasonable care. In *Greaves v Baynham Meikle* [1975] 4 BLR 56 it was said: 'A surgeon does not warrant that he will cure the patient. Nor does the solicitor warrant that he will win the case.' The concept of 'Fitness for purpose' is borrowed from the Sale of Goods Act 1893, which Act is concerned with 'products' and which is dealt with in detail in pars. 8.02 to 8.06. The reason why this concept is mentioned here is because it is suggested in a report on Defective Premises published by the Law Reform Commission in 1982 that all buildings should measure up to this requirement. The layman might be pardoned for thinking that every building should, as a matter of course, be fit for its particular intended purpose but this in a strict legal sense is a concept demanding a higher acceptance of design responsibility for the building than the prosaic meaning that the words suggest. It is a warranty stopping just short of an absolute assurance against defect in any circumstance. The important point is that a building is not a product and the same rules should not apply. In a paper to a joint RIAI/SCS Conference in 1987, John O'Connor put it very well:

> Building is an attempt to place an untested, hand-crafted cube made of materials which expand, contract, shrink, creep and warp unilaterally on to foundations laid in a mosaic of erratic geological conditions owing its nature to the caprice of the ancient ice. It can never be the tested product of the laboratory, and legislation governing defective products should have no application in building.

If however it can be shown that it was the common intention that a building should be fit for a particular purpose, then the Architect would be liable for this higher duty. Obviously a house must be fit for human habitation and the Architect will be responsible for this (*Hancock v BW Brazier (Anerley Ltd* [1966] 1 WLR 1317) but each building must be judged on the basis of the parties intentions.

The extent to which the Architect should be aware of the law and of the legal consequences of his various actions is fairly well defined. An architect should have a sound working knowledge of the general law as regards planning, building regulations, building contracts, and safety, but he is not of course expected to be able to offer a service which would be more properly the role of a solicitor with regard to advice in purely legal matters. In *BL*

Holdings v Wood [1978] 10 BLR 48 it was held that an architect is required to know enough law to be able to protect his client against bad advice from a planning authority. 'It may be thought "hard" by some to require of an architect that he know more law than the planning authority or at least have sufficient awareness of what may be bad law enunciated by such an authority as to make him advise his clients to check up on it.' An architect should always advise the Employer when he feels that formal legal advice should be sought. Equally, an architect should be aware that *ignorantia juris neminer excusat* – ignorance of the law is no excuse.

Int.11   b) the other Consultants

The Quantity Surveyor, and the Engineers, will be bound by the standards set out above with regard to the Architect. The expectation of skill will be the same. However, the Architect must be careful as far as the selection and appointment of other consultants is concerned. The Architect should always ensure that the appointments of these consultants are made directly by the Employer and that any professional advice from them is conveyed to the Employer in such a way as to make the Employer fully aware of the view of all the consultants concerned. In *Quinn v Quality Homes (Ltd)* [1975] High Court, unrep. 21st November, it was pointed out that the Architect could not act merely as a postman, and pass on to the Employer the advice of other consultants without any comment. He had a duty to point out to the Employer what his views were on the advice being offered, even if it were only to say that he was relying entirely on the Consultant's advice. This was confirmed in *Chesam Properties v Bucknall Austin* [1997] 82 BLR 92.

4 – THE LIABILITIES OF THE PARTIES

Int.12   It is difficult to know where to start. At one time, the various parties, Employer, Architect, Contractor, Sub-Contractor, Supplier, etc, all had a contractual relationship, and a contractual relationship only, with some or most of the other parties. The Architect had a contract with the Employer but had no other legal relationship with the Employer, and had no legal relationship of any sort with the Contractor. Similarly, the Sub-Contractor had a contractual relationship with the Contractor but no relationship with anyone else. There was a clear and distinct division in law between contract, and particularly, tort. A contract was a voluntary obligation, freely entered into. Tort was an involuntary relationship which arose from events not generally intended. A tort has been defined as a civil wrong, the remedy for which is damages. Injuries received in a motor accident would come under this heading. For any party to become involved with another party in tort, there are three basic requirements. Firstly, one party must owe a duty to the other party, such as to drive carefully or, in any event, not negligently. Secondly, this duty must be breached, and, thirdly, the innocent party must suffer some damage. It is the interaction between tort and contract, initiated by the courts, over the last thirty years in particular that have resulted in the rather unsatisfactory and uncertain position that exists to-day. If the Architect, or the Engineer, or Builder were liable in tort, as well as in contract, then he might be liable to a wide range of persons, and over a very long period of time. If he were liable only in contract he would be liable only to the other party to the Contract and for a period of six (or sometimes twelve) years.

Int.13 It is generally thought that the boundaries between contract and tort only began to unravel in this century, but as far back as 1370 the case of *Waldon v Marshall* dealt with the overlapping areas on contract and tort (see Cheshire and Fifoot, LAW OF CONTRACT, for a detailed history of this topic). The real expansion of tort was, of course, the 'snail in the bottle' case of *Donohue v Stevenson* [1932] AC 562 where it was held that a person whose actions injured another person was liable in tort if it could be reasonably contemplated that such a result would occur as had happened. This, however, did not affect architects, and as recently as 1970 HUDSON could state with authority (p.123): 'But the duty owed by an Architect or Engineer to his employer arises in contract and not in tort.' HUDSON based this view on, amongst others, the then recent case of *Bagot v Stevens Scanlon and Co* [1964] 2 BLR 67. The relevant part of the judgement read:

> It seems to me that, in this case, the relationship which created the duty on the part of the Architects towards their clients to exercise reasonable skill and care arose out of the contract and not otherwise. The complaint that is made against them is of a failure to do the very thing which they contracted to do. That was the relationship which gave rise to the duty which was broken. It was a contractual relationship, a contractual duty, and any action brought for failure to comply with that duty is in my view, an action founded on contract. It is also, in my view, an action founded on contract alone.

This was clearly a very definite position. But in the case of *Esso Petroleum v Mardon* [1976] 2 BLR 82 the following comment was made:

> A professional man may give advice under a contract for reward; or without a contract in pursuance of a voluntary assumption of responsibility, gratuitously without reward. In either case he is under one and the same duty to use reasonable care. In the one case it is by reason of a duty imposed by law. For a breach of that duty he is liable in damages, and those damages should be, and are, the same whether he is sued in contract or in tort.

This particular view was then followed in a whole series of cases. Recently, however, this view has been questioned more and more in Britain and other common law countries, and the principle of combined liability in both contract and tort is now in considerable doubt. In *Sealand of the Pacific v McHaffie* [1974] 2 BLR 74 it was held that 'duty and liability ought to be discovered in the contract. If additional duties and liabilities are to be attached it will have the effect of changing the bargain made by the parties' More emphatically in *Tai Ming Cotton Hill Ltd v Liu Chong Ming* [1986] AC 80 the Privy Council did 'not believe that there was anything to the advantage of the law's development in searching for a liability in tort where the parties are in a contractual relationship'. One Judge said: '...but as far as I know it has never been the law that the plaintiff who has the chance of suing in contract or tort can fail in contract yet nevertheless succeed in tort; and, if it ever was the law it has ceased to be the law since *Tai Hing Cotton Mill v Liu Chong Hill'* – *National Bank of Greece v Pinios Shipping* [1989] 3 WLR 195. Again, in *Edgeworth Construction Ltd v ND Lea and Associates Ltd* [1991] 7CLJ 238 it was held that a consulting engineer had no duty towards a contractor for inaccuracies in contract documents but only owed such a duty towards his client, with whom he was in a contractual relationship. The latest case that seems to have considered the matter in principle is *Arbuthnott v Fagan & Feltrim* [1994] 69 BLR 26. In this case the House of Lords had no doubts: '...unless the contract precludes him from doing so, the plaintiff who has available concurrent remedies in contract and tort, may choose that remedy which appears to him to be most advantageous.' It was pointed out in *Holt v Payne Skillington and de Groot Collis* [1995] 77 BLR 51 that the duty under tort could be wider than the duty under contract, depending on the facts and circumstances in each case.

There is a typically informative and entertaining comment in the judgement of the late and much lamented Judge McCarthy of the Supreme Court in the case of *Ward v McMaster* [1989] ILRM 400 when he was dealing with these various developments 'With the able assistance of counsel, we have travelled well charted legal seas seeking, for my part, to find a well marked haven, whether it be in Australia, Canada, Northern Ireland or England. Certainly, the judicial complements manning the several ports are not marked by unanimity.' He goes on to say with regard to an argument as to the different standings of the various cases that 'such a proposition, however, suffers from a temporal defect – that rights should be determined by an accident of birth.' If a Judge of the Supreme Court has difficulty with the subject the practitioner can be excused a certain amount of confusion.

However, these cases separating tort and contract were unfortunately not followed in Ireland, and it can be taken that the established law here, following the case of *Finlay v Murtagh* [1979] IR 249 which was a case involving alleged negligence against a solicitor, is that a professional man owes a duty both in contract and tort to his clients. It would, of course, be possible for a professional to insist in his terms of engagement that no liability would result in tort but it is difficult to see a client accepting this. It was, nonetheless, proposed by the Judge in *Conway and Another v Crowe Kelsey and Partners* [1994] 11 CLD-03-01, where he held fast to the traditional view that a professional was liable in tort as well as contract unless he stipulated otherwise. It is to be hoped that this position might eventually change because the consequences of the double jeopardy of tort and contract can place an extremely heavy burden on the practitioner. The same case confirmed the now accepted view that the Statute of Limitations begins to run from the date on which the damage was suffered.

Int.14   Back in the 1960s, even if the Architect owed a duty in tort and in contract, it was still considered that he owed that duty only to the Employer, but this view was in turn upset, particularly by the case of *Hedley Byrne v Heller* [1964] AC 465. This held that a negligent misstatement which resulted in financial loss gave rise to actions by persons who had no contractual relationship with the person who made the misstatement, provided that they were persons who, it might have been anticipated, would rely on that statement. This widened the field of liability considerably, and brought into the Architect's area people such as borrowers from financial institutions such as building societies, or tenants of buildings, and so on. Until that point it was the position that pure economic loss was not recoverable in tort and that there must have been physical damage present to sustain a claim. It was felt that economic loss was the domain of contract alone. However the case of *Junior Books v The Veitchi Co* [1982] 21 BLR 66 amongst others allowed the recovery of pure economic loss but this position was reversed by the decision in *D and F Estates v Church Commissioners* [1988] 41 BLR 1 which held that recovery for pure economic loss, as opposed to damage to property, was solely a matter for contract and not for tort.

The most recent twist in the economic loss saga is the case of *Invercargill City Council v Hamlin* [1996] THE TIMES, 15th January. In this case, the Privy Council was considering a decision of the Court of Appeal of New Zealand and agreed that the New Zealand Court was correct in awarding economic loss against a local authority for defects in a building that had been examined by the authority, despite the decisions taken in the *D and F Estates* and *Murphy* cases. The basis of the decision was a difference in practice in New Zealand where more reliance was placed on local authority building inspections.

The distinction that case law made between economic loss occurring as a result of an negligent act or as a result of a negligent statement was so fine as to be almost perverse. If a defective drawing was an act then no economic loss is recoverable, but if a defective drawing was a statement comparable to, say, an auditor's statement then economic loss was recoverable. Is a drawing an act or a statement? While it has been held that an architect's drawing is not a 'negligent misstatement' ('It would be artificial to treat the submission of drawings and designs by an architect to his client as some form of implied statement as to the technical adequacy of the proposed building' – *Lancashire and Cheshire v Howard and Seddon* [1991] 65 BLR 21), the opposite view is taken in *Edgeworth Construction Ltd v ND Lea* [1993] 66 BLR 56. The *Arbuthnott* case mentioned before also dealt with economic loss, and the Court comment was fairly strong:

> In recent years there have been several cases which deal with situations where no physical damage has resulted from the carelessness in question, but where the claimant has sustained financial loss or expense. To my mind the law draws no fundamental difference between such cases and those where there is damage to persons or property.

The position in Ireland is now fairly clear. The cases of *Ward v McMaster* [1989] ILRM 400 and *Sweeney v Duggan* [1991] 2 IR 274 were both approved in the recent case of *McShane Fruit v Johnston Haulage* [1997] 1 ILRM 86. Three rules have been established:

1   A sufficient relationship of proximity must exist between the alleged wrongdoer and the person who has suffered damage. A misleading advertisement which anyone can read is not sufficient to establish this link (*Bank of Ireland v Smith* [1966] IR 646) whereas a statement made directly to one person is specific enough to establish the link (*McAnerney v Hanrahan* [1994] 1 ILRM 210).

2   It must be in the reasonable contemplation of the alleged wrongdoer that carelessness on his part will be likely to cause damage to the other party.

3   The quality of the damage does not arise. It can be damage to property, to the person, financial or economic.

In all cases an exception can be made to these rules for compelling reasons of public policy.

At the same time the range of those affected by tortious responsibility was widening, and cases such as *Dutton v Bognor Regis UDC* [1971] 3 BLR 11 and *Anns v London Borough of Merton* [1977] 5 BLR 1 brought local authorities into the net of liability, and this is discussed in the book at par. 6.09.

Int.15   The real problem, though, as far as the construction industry was concerned, lay in the field of limitation. If a person was liable only in contract, that liability ended six years after the contract had been performed (or twelve years in the case of a contract under seal). But a number of cases (including the *Anns* case mentioned above) began to move the period until *Sparham-Souter v Town and Country Developments* [1976] 3 BLR 70 decided that the statute of limitations only began to run when the plaintiff knew of the defects or 'with reasonable diligence could have discovered them'. This extended the time indefinitely and led an exasperated commentator in the BUILDING LAW REPORTS to observe: 'The six year period (for limitation) begins to run afresh for all eternity with every new purchaser ... Is this really what Parliament intended?' At this time the exposure of professionals in the construction industry was extreme, both as far as the spread of liability in time and to various parties. The pendulum then began to move very slowly back.

In *Pirelli General Cable Works v Oscar Faber* [1982] 21 BLR 99 it was held that the time began to run when the damage occurred, whether it was observed or not. This case was not followed in Ireland in *Morgan v Park Developments* [1983] ILRM 156 when the old view was taken that time began to run when the defects were observed, on the grounds that otherwise 'it may have the effect of depriving an injured party of a right of action before he knows he has one.' However, the next case as far as this jurisdiction is concerned is *Hegarty v O'Loughran* [1990] ILRM 403 which is of considerable importance to practitioners as it concerned professional negligence relating in this instance to the field of medicine.

It is worthwhile examining this case in some detail as the appearance of defects in buildings occur on a varying time scale ranging from one day to up to fifty years afterwards, and any case or precedent which might indicate to a practitioner or Contractor when his liability might end would be very welcome. The Statute of Limitations 1957 says at section 11(2)(b):

> *An action claiming damages for negligence, nuisance or breach of duty (whether the duty exists by virtue of a contract or of a provision made by or under a statute or independently of any contract or any such provision) where the damages claimed by the plaintiff for negligence, nuisance or breach of duty consist of or include damages in respect of personal injuries to any person shall not be brought after the expiration of three years from the date on which the cause of action accrued.*

The Supreme Court considered three possible interpretations of this section:

1   the cause of action would be deemed to have accrued when the wrongful act was committed;

2   the cause of action would be deemed to have accrued at the time when the personal injury, allegedly arising from the wrongful act, manifested itself; or

3   the cause of action would be deemed to have accrued only when the injured party not only has suffered the committing of a wrongful act but has also suffered damage (personal injury) and could, by the exercise of reasonable diligence, have discovered that such personal injury was caused by the wrongful act complained of (i.e. objective discoverability).

The Court held that the first possibility was the correct one. The various judgements make it clearer:

> The time limit commenced to run at a time when a provable personal injury, capable of attracting compensation, occurred to the plaintiff which was the completion of the tort alleged to be committed against her.

Another judgement said:

> The period of limitation therefore begins to run from the date on which the cause of action accrued, i.e. when a complete and available cause of action first comes into existence. When a wrongful act is actionable per se without proof of damage as in for example, libel, assault or trespass to land or goods the statute runs from the time at which the act was committed. Where, however, when the wrong is not actionable without actual damage, as in the case of negligence, the cause of action is not complete and the period of limitation cannot begin to run until that damage happens or occurs.

And finally:

> The fundamental principle is that words in a statute must be given their ordinary meaning and I am unable to conclude that a cause of action occurs on the date of discovery of its existence rather than on the date on which, if it had been discovered, proceedings could lawfully have been instituted. I recognise the unfairness, the harshness and the obscurantism that underlies this rule but it is there and will remain there unless qualified by the legislature or invalidated root and branch by this Court.

The Court recognised that it was very difficult to strike a balance between the position of a plaintiff who might lose the right to take an action because of the passage of time in circumstances not due to his own fault against the position of a person being called on to defend an action many years after the event when his recollection, the availability of witnesses and documentary evidence might have disappeared, but the Court was satisfied that the 1957 Act was reasonable.

The perceived unfairness of the *Hegarty* case gave rise to an amendment to the 1957 Act but only as far as personal injuries were concerned. The 1991

Amendment added the words: *'or the date of the knowledge (if later) of the person injured'* to the phrase *'shall not be brought after the expiration of three years from the date on which the cause of action accrued'.*

Much the same arguments regarding the balance of fairness arose in the case of *Tuohy v Courtney* [1994] 2 ILRM 503. This was another professional negligence case, this time involving solicitors but is of even more interest in that it was not concerned with personal injury but with the conduct of professional duties and would, therefore, be more relevant to practitioners in the construction field. The Court the same view as was taken in *Hegarty v O'Loughran*, and this was that the cause of action accrued when the act complained of had occurred and not when the damage was discovered.

The 'six-year rule' can now be taken as being the law in this jurisdiction and it is a cause of considerable comfort to practitioners. The last word should be left to the Supreme Court: 'The counter balance to the objectives of the Statute of Limitations 1957 is the necessity for the State, as far as is practicable or as best it may, to ensure that the time limits do not unreasonably or unjustly impose hardship ... Viewed objectively, the limitation period of six years was a substantial period.'

As has been seen, liability for personal injury has a different time scale but can be tied to a building defect. The normal time within which to make a claim for personal injury would be three years from the date of the injury. This of course means that a defective building or structure which injures somebody even 30 years after construction would still give rise to an action. This was the position in *Cowan v Faghaule and Others* [1991] High Court, 24th January, where a defective wall which had been built in Croke Park in 1958 fell and injured a spectator in 1985. The original contractors were still liable.

At the time of writing, a paper has been published by the Law Reform Commission which proposes that, as far as construction is concerned, a) the limitation period should commence when the claimant first knew or, in the circumstances, ought reasonably to have known of the defect; b) that the date of the cause of action should accrue, as far as contract only is concerned, at the date of purported completion, and most importantly for construction professionals, a 'long stop' should be introduced in tort actions so that no claim could be brought after ten years from the date of the issue of the Certificate of Practical Completion. It is to be hoped that such a proposal will shortly be imported into law.

Int.16   The saga of all these cases can sometimes confuse the position as it relates to Ireland. Readers will probably be aware that English legal precedents are not binding on the Irish Courts but they are 'persuasive' and are being constantly pleaded. Some of the later ones referred to are not embodied in Irish decisions. The position as it appears to be at the moment is:

1   Professionals are liable in both contract and tort (*Finlay v Murtagh*).

2   The Statute of Limitations runs from the latest time that damage could have occurred, whether discovered or not (*Hegarty v O'Loughran* and *Tuohy v Courtney*).

3   Local authorities and contractors are liable if defects constitute imminent danger to health and safety of those occupying the building (*Anns v Merton* as approved in *Siney v Dublin Corporation*).

4   Economic loss is no different to any other form of loss (*McShane v Johnston*).

Int.17   The overall position with regard to liability in the construction industry could change drastically under legislation being considered by the European Community. It might be useful to give a very brief outline of the way in which the EC operates. The primary law of the European Community is contained in the Treaties, and in particular in the originating Treaty of Rome (Jan 1, 1958). Under this primary law is the secondary legislation which consists mainly of Regulations and Directives. The Treaties and the Regulations made under them are binding in their original form on the whole community. A Directive binds only in that the objective set out in the Directive must be achieved, but each member state can decide the details as to how the objective may be achieved. A Directive can be brought into force in Ireland by Ministerial Regulation as provided for in the European Communities Act 1972. One of the objectives of the Treaty of Rome, amended by the Single European Act 1987, is to ensure the free movement of goods, services persons, and capital, together with the guarantee of free and fair competition. (A Directive affecting construction products has already been issued; par. 8.03.)

To this end, a draft Directive was issued on 9th November 1990 with regard to liability for the Supply of Services which was to cover financial, transport, management, tourist, legal, and many other services. It was understood that construction services would be excluded but that did not occur. The proposals were radical and included:

1   A reversal of the onus of proof, placing the burden on the designer or contractor to prove that no fault of his caused the damage, in other words, guilty until proved innocent if the injured party can prove damage and cause.

2   An endorsement of the principle of joint and several liability, that is, if the damage is caused by a number of parties, the injured party can recover

from all or any of them depending on their resources.

3   A ban on the exclusion of liability, or even on the limitation of liability.

4   The person providing the service shall be liable for a period of 20 years from the date of the service, and an injured party shall have a period of 10 years in which to start proceedings, the 10 years commencing when the damage was observed. This meant, in effect, a possible 30 years exposure.

5   A definition of damage as being that of death or injury to persons, damage to property, and what was called 'financial material' damage, which is financial damage resulting from the first two classes of damage.

The production of this Directive caused something of a storm because of the inclusion of construction related services in this scope of the directive. The Community acceded to the representation from almost every member state and agreed to set up advisory panels to make proposals to the Commission with regard to construction related services. The RIAI has a representative on one of the panels. It is to be hoped that the final proposals from the EC will be more realistic and will show more understanding of the practicalities of the building process.

Int.18   The extent of the Architect's liability had become so wide that Max Abrahamson was able to write in 1991:

> The exact list of persons to whom the Architect owes a duty of care depends on the application of somewhat confused legal tests to the particular circumstances. But there have been decisions in various places at various times holding or suggesting that an architect might owe a duty of care to:
>
> a)   his client
>
> b)   a builder employed by his client
>
> c)   a purchaser, tenant or other user of the whole or part of a a building which he designed or supervised
>
> d)   an investor in such a building
>
> e)   buyers and investors who rely on his valuation of the building made for another party (e.g. a Building Society)
>
> f)   members of the public who suffer injury or damages because of his negligence
>
> g)   those who lose in any way due to his negligence where, for example, a telephone cable is cut through and neighbouring businesses lose orders.

But the cases listed in Int.15 and 16 were causing this liability to contract, and while this reduction of liability might have been seen to be a good thing by professionals and contractors, employers (who become building owners) did not like this trend and set about redressing the balance by widespread use of the collateral warranty. Collateral warranties exist already in the construction industry and are provided for in the RIAI form (see Clause 37). A collateral warranty is a contract, and one that exists in conjunction with another, or 'principal' contract with one party common to both contracts. The word 'collateral' means alongside, or together with. Put simply, building owners were concerned that the previous widespread liability of their advisors or contractors was being eroded and they endeavoured to copper-fasten in contract what seemed to be disappearing in tort. Employers were, in effect, forcing their professional advisors to go back to the bad old days of liability to 'everyone and for ever'. It was, to a large extent, a force that could not be resisted, for the advisors needed the work and somewhere there would be an architect or engineer who would accept the employer's conditions. But not only were professional institutions concerned at this development, so also were the insurance companies who very quickly put limits on the kind of warranties that they would be prepared to back. Needless to say, an architect signing a collateral warranty without informing his insurers would have no cover for the extended risk. The scene that the Employer was trying to create was that any subsequent claim against him, by a tenant of the building, by a financial institution, by a subsequent purchaser and so on, could be deflected towards the professional advisors, or the contractor. At the moment, the view of the RIAI is that if a collateral warranty must be signed, it should:

1   be signed by all members of the design team, main contractor, and nominated sub-contractors, and should only operate when all have signed;

2   be assignable by a client only to the beneficiary named and not be capable of being passed on to subsequent owners, lessees, tenants, etc;

3   be limited to six years;

4   be limited to a Schedule of Services based upon the RIAI Conditions of Engagement.

Int.19   The ideal solution to the wide and confusing range of duties and liabilities of all the participants in the building process set out in the preceding nine paragraphs would seem to be a form of single comprehensive insurance, possible decennial such as is discussed briefly at par. 20.02. This form of insurance would provide cover for the building itself, not for the consultants or contractor involved. The scope of the defects which might appear, known as 'latent defects', would be agreed in advance and would broadly cover repairing, renewing or strengthening the structural or water-proofing elements of the building. The policy would also provide cover for site clearance, and professional fees. It would, in short, cover any loss which occurs as a result of a design or construction problem. The cover would not require proof of fault, would be non-cancellable and would be freely assignable. It would be instituted by a single premium. The ideal length of time for the cover would appear to be 10 years for two reasons. Firstly, it has been estimated by the insurance industry itself that 95% of all latent defects appear within 10 years, and, secondly, 10 year or decennial insurance is a common concept in Europe and it is clear (see par. Int.17) that our involvement in Europe is becoming closer and closer.

This insurance is readily available and the cost of obtaining the cover has been estimated at around 1% of the contract value of the building, although it can be, as low as 0.5% depending on the technical survey which will be carried out by the insurers. This might seem expensive, but the overall protection provided to the building owner, and the removal of the time-consuming legal recovery route should be attractive. Not only that, but in a competitive property market, a new development which has decennial latent defects cover should have an advantage over the development without it, particularly as far as overseas buyers are concerned.

Int.20   CASES REFERRED TO

ABC Ltd v Waltham Holy Cross UDC [1952] 2 AER 452 — par. 08
Anns v London Borough of Merton [1977] 5 BLR 1 — pars. 14, 15, 16
Arbuthnott v Fagan & Feltrim [1994] 69 BLR 26 — pars. 13, 14
Bagot v Stevens Scanlon and Co [1964] 2 BLR 67 — par. 13
Bank of ireland v Smith [1966] IR 646 — par. 14
BL Holdings v Woods [1978] 10 BLR 48 — par. 10
Bolam v Friern Hospital Management Committee
    [1957] 1 WLR 582 — par. 10
Cavan v Faghaule and Others [1991] Hight Court, 24th January — par. 15
Chesam Properties v Bucknall Austin [1997] 82 BLR 92 — par. 11
Chin Keow v Government of Malaysia [1967] 1 WLR 813 — par. 10
Compania Naviera Aeolus v Union of India
    [1962] 3 AER 670 — par. 08
Conway v Crowe Kelsey [1994] 11 CLD-03-01 — par. 13
D & F Estates v Church Commissioners [1988] 41 BLR 1 — par. 14
Donohue v Stevenson [1932] AC 562 — par. 13
Dutton v Bognor Regis UDC [1971] 3 BLR 11 — pars 10, 14
Edgeworth Constuction Ltd v ND Lea and Associates Ltd
    [1991] 7 CLJ 238 — pars. 13, 14
Esso Petroleum v Mardon [1976] 2 BLR 82 — par. 13

Finlay v Murtagh [1979] IR 249   pars. 13, 16

Flanagan v Griffith [1981] High Court, unrep. 25th January   par. 10

Greaves v Baynham Meikle [1975] 4 BLR 56   par. 10

Hancock v BW Brazier (Anerley Ltd) [1966] 1 WLR 1317   par. 10

HA O'Neil v John Sisk and Son
[1984] Supreme Court, unrep. 26th July   par. 08

Hedley Byrne v Heller [1964] AC 465   par. 14

Hegarty v O'Loughran [1990] ILRM 403   pars. 15, 16

Holt v Payne Skillington [1995] 77 BLR 51   par. 13

Invercargill City Council v Hamlin
[1998] THE TIMES, 15th January   par. 14

Irishenco v Dublin County Council
[1984] High Court, unrep. 21st March   par. 08

Junior Books Ltd v The Veitchi Co [1982] 21 BLR 66   par. 14

Lancashire and Cheshire v Howard and Seddon
[1991] 65 BLR 21   par. 14

McAnerney v Hanrahan [1994] 1 ILRM 210   par. 14

McShane v Johnston [1977] 1 ILRM 86   pars. 14, 16

Morgan v Park Developments [1983] ILRM 156   par. 15

Murphy v Brentwood District Council [1990] 50 BLR 1   par. 14

National Bank of Greece v Pinios Shipping [1989] 3 WLR 195   par. 13

O'Donovan v Cork County Council [1976] IR 173   par. 10

O'Neill v Murphy and Others [1936] NI 16   par. 04

Pirelli General Cable Works v Oscar Faber [1982] 21 BLR 99   par. 15

Quinn v Quality Homes Ltd [1975] High Court, unrep. 21st Nov   par. 11

Roche v Peilow [1986] ILRM 189   par. 10

Sealand of the Pacific v McHaffie [1974] 2 BLR 74   par. 13

Siney v Dublin Corporation [1980] IR 400   par. 16

Sparham-Souter v Town and Country Developments
[1976] 3 BLR 70   par. 15

Sweeney v Duggan [1991] 2 IR 274   par. 14

Tai Hing Cotton Hill Ltd v Liu Chong Hing [1986] AC 80   par. 13

Trollope and Colls Ltd v North West Metropolitan Regional
Hospital Board [1973] 9 BLR 60   par. 08

Tuohy v Courtney [1994] 2 ILRM 503   pars. 15, 16

Waldon v Marshall [1370]   par. 13

Ward v McMaster and Others [1989] ILRM 400   pars. 10, 13, 14

Wimpey Construction UK Ltd v DV Poole [1984]
Lloyd's Ref. 49   par. 10

Articles of Agreement

This form is applicable where quantities form part of the Contract

made the .... day of .... 19......
between* ....
of (or whose Registered Office is situated at) ....
(hereinafter called 'the Employer') of the one part and* ....
of (or whose Registered Office is situated at) ....
(hereinafter called 'the Contractor') of the other part.

Whereas the Employer is desirous of ....
(hereinafter called 'the Works') at ....
has caused drawings (hereinafter called 'the Contract Drawings'), a Specification
and a Bill of Quantities describing the work to be done to be prepared by or under
the direction of .... of .... his Architect.

And whereas the Contractor has made an estimate of the sum which he will
require for carrying out the said Works as shown on the tender dated
.... and has furnished a Bill of Quantities fully priced in ink;

And Whereas the said contract drawings numbered ....
and the said Specification and the said priced Bill of Quantities have been signed
by or on behalf of the parties hereto:

Now it is Hereby Agreed as Follows:
1   For the consideration hereinafter mentioned the Contractor will upon and sub-
    ject to the Conditions annexed hereto execute and complete the Works shown
    upon the Contract Drawings and/or described in the Specification, Bill of
    Quantities and Conditions all of which together with this Agreement are here-
    inafter referred to as 'the Contract Documents'.
2   The Employer will pay the Contractor the sum of .... (IR£ ....)
    (hereinafter referred to as 'the Contract Sum') or such other sum as shall
    become payable by virtue of the said Conditions at the time and in the manner
    specified in the said Conditions.
3   The term 'the Architect' in the said Conditions shall mean the said
    .... of ....
    or, in the event of his death or ceasing to be the architect for the purpose of
    this Contract, such other person as shall be nominated for that purpose by the
    Employer, not being a person to whom the Contractor shall object for reasons
    considered to be sufficient by the Arbitrator mentioned in the said Conditions.

Provided always that no person subsequently appointed to be Architect under this Contract shall be entitled to disregard or overrule any certificate or instruction or decision or approval given or expressed by the Architect for the time being.

4   The term 'the Quantity Surveyor' in the said Conditions shall mean .... of .... or, in the event of his death or ceasing to be the Quantity Surveyor for the purpose of this Contract, such other person as shall be nominated for that purpose by the Employer or the Architect on his behalf, not being a person to whom the Contractor shall object for reasons considered to be sufficient by the Arbitrator mentioned in the said Conditions.

In witness whereof the parties hereto have set their hands (or the Common Seals of the parties hereto have been affixed, or the Common Seal of the Employer has been affixed and the Contractor has set his hand hereto, or the Employer has set his hand and the Common Seal of the Contractor has been affixed hereto) the day and year first above written.

Signature of Employer*..

Signature of Contractor*..

Signed by the above-named Employer in the presence of:
Name ....
Address ....   Occupation ....

Signed by the above-named Contractor in the presence of:
Name ....
Address ....   Occupation ....

or

Common Seal of the above-named Employer: Common Seal of the above-named
Employer affixed in the presence of:
Director ....
Director ....
and Secretary ....

Common Seal of the above-named Contractor: Common Seal of the above-named
Contractor affixed in the presence of:
Director ....
Director ....
and Secretary ....

---

* Where any of the parties to this Agreement is a partnership, the parties shall be described as .... and .... (the names of the individual partners) trading as .... (the partnership name) and all the partners shall sign the Agreement.

A.01   This is the basic contract. The Conditions which follow are the detailed arrangements which the parties have agreed will be used during the course of the Contract. The Agreement specifies seven (in some cases eight) items – the Employer, the Contractor, the Works, the Architect, the Contract Sum, the Quantity Surveyor if appropriate, the date of the agreement, and the Contract Documents. The filling in of the Articles of Agreement is very straight forward. 'The Works' can be quite simply described as, say, 'Building a house' or 'Building an office block', etc.

Care must be taken, however, to ensure that the names of the contracting parties are entered correctly. This can be important where large and complex organisations with many separate companies are the contracting parties. The problems that can arise in this situation are seen in the cases of *Badgerhill Properties Ltd v Cottrell* [1991] 54 Blr 23 and *Contronic (UK) Ltd v Dezonie T/A Wendeland Builders Ltd, Osborne* [1991] THE TIMES, 8th March.

The Articles differ depending on whether or not a Bill of Quantities is included in the Contract Documents. On some occasions even where a Bill of Quantities has been prepared it is not made a Contract Document although this is very rare (see pars. 3.01 and 3.02 – Drawings and Bill of Quantities). If no Bill of Quantities has been prepared, or if it is not to be made a contract document, the Contractor will submit a Schedule of Rates or the rates in the Bill of Quantities will be used as the Schedule of Rates. The 'Blue' version of both the RIAI and GDLA forms is used where quantities do not form part of the contract, and the 'Yellow' version is used if they do form part. Apart from the colour, the forms are identical.

The basic duty of the Contractor is defined in Article 1 as to 'execute and complete the Works'. The basic duty of the Employer is set out in Article 2 where he 'will pay the Contractor'. Articles 3 and 4 identify the Architect and, if appropriate, the Quantity Surveyor. In the RIAI form the Contractor is entitled to object to a re-nomination as far as the named Architect or Quantity Surveyor is concerned, but the reasons given must be considered sufficient by the Arbitrator referred to in Clause 38 (see par. 38.05). If there is no Bill of Quantities there will be no Quantity Surveyor. There is no mention of the Quantity Surveyor in the RIAI Conditions of Contract, except with regard to copying and confidentiality in Clause 3(b), and in reference to valuing in Clause 13. The Architect is required to consult with the Quantity Surveyor in the GDLA form [Clause 2(e)].

The provision in Article 3 that the re-nominated Architect cannot disregard or overrule any certificate or instruction or decision or approval given by the original Architect merely restates what the ordinary law would apply. Any valid instruction given by the Architect, acting as the Employer's Agent (see par. 2.05 for details of 'Agency') would be binding on any successor. The doctrine of 'estoppel' would preclude anyone from denying a fact which by his words or conduct he has led others to believe in.

The last part of the Articles of Agreement is where the parties sign or seal the Contract. A contract that is signed is a 'simple' contract. One that is sealed is a contract 'under seal'. The primary difference is that a simple contract binds the parties, as far as actions arising from it are concerned, for six years after completion of the contract, and a contract under seal binds them for twelve years. This, and the implications which follow, is discussed in pars. Int.6 and Int.15.

A.02   The GDLA Articles of Agreement are similar except for the following:

1   In Article 1, the Contractor's obligation to complete the Works is made subject to 'the said tender and the Employer's acceptance thereof'. This would be understood in the RIAI form. It defines the 'offer' and 'acceptance' requirements of any contract which are referred to in par. Int.04.

2   The wording of Article 2 is different from the RIAI form, but the meaning is identical.

3   The right of the Contractor to object to the re-nomination of the Architect and/or Quantity Surveyor as provided for in Articles 3 and 4 of the RIAI form is not contained in the GDLA form. Not only that, but the provision in the RIAI form that 'no person subsequently appointed to be Architect under this Contract shall be entitled to disregard or overrule any certificate or instruction or decision or approval given or expressed by the Architect for the time being' is not contained in the GDLA form. As has been pointed out in par. A.01, the Employer would in any event be bound by the valid decisions of his agent at the time and cannot afterwards change his mind.

SF 88

A.03   The Articles of Agreement in the shorter form are largely the same as the larger forms. There is, obviously, no mention of a quantity surveyor or of the Bill of Quantities in the Articles. The SF 88 contract form does not envisage any major variations, but provision is made in Clause 3 of the Conditions for any variations which might occur to be measured on a 'fair and reasonable basis, using where relevant prices in the priced specification / schedules / schedules of rates unless a price has been previously agreed'.

Because the shorter form contains no appendix (where a number of variable items are agreed and defined in the longer forms – see Appendix), there is provision in the Articles of Agreement for specifying a number of dates. References are given in brackets where the notes referring to these items may be found. The dates are:

1   Date for possession of the site (28.01 and 28.03)

2   Date for commencement of the Works (28.03)

3   Date for Practical Completion (28.02 and 28.04)

Provision is allowed for arbitration if the Contractor objects to the re-nomination of the Architect.

A.04   CASES REFERRED TO

Badgerhill Propereties Ltd v Cotterell
        [1991] 54 BLR 23   par. A.01
Contronic (UK) Ltd v Dezonie T/A Wendeland Builders Ltd,
        Osborne [1991] THE TIMES, 8th March   par. A.01

RIAI – Clause 1

DEFINITIONS

1.01   **(a) For the purposes of these conditions and of their application to any nominated sub-contract under Clause 16 or 17, the 'Designated Date' shall in each case mean the date ten days prior to the latest date set for the receipt of relevant tenders (whether the tenders be submitted by the Contractor, a nominated Sub-Contractor or a nominated Supplier) or the latest revision of such date.**

Where no date is set for the receipt of tenders the designated date for each tender shall mean the date of its receipt.

The Designated Date for the tender of the Contract is that set out in the appendix hereto.

The purpose of having a 'Designated Date' is to provide a base date from which any increase or decrease in materials or wages can be measured. Clause 36(b) and (c) establishes that the prices contained in the Bill of Quantities, or the Schedule of Rates, referred to in Clause 3, are deemed to be based upon the rates of wages and the prices of materials which obtained at the Designated Date. Clause 36 further provides at (a)(ii) that the Supplement referred to in Clause 36 is the Supplement last issued before the Designated Date. This Supplement sets out the meanings to be given to certain wordings of Clause 36, and it is now printed as part of the Contract Form on page 25. It was formerly issued as a separate document.

While fixed price contracts, that is, contracts with no wage or price variation clause, are quite common, particularly in times of low inflation, the more standard practice is to allow the Contractor to recoup any increases to wages and materials during the course of the contract. Taking a date ten days prior to the date set for the receipt of tenders as the designated date, is to allow for any increases in wages and materials that occur immediately before tenders are due to be included in any calculations made pursuant to Clause 36(b) and (c).

1.02   **(b) Where in these conditions any act, matter, or thing is to be done in a stated period of working days the following days shall not be counted, namely, Saturdays, Sundays, Holidays and Good Friday.**

RIAI – Clause 2

SCOPE OF CONTRACT

2.01   **The Contractor shall carry out and complete the Works in accordance with the Contract Documents and with the directions and to the reasonable satisfaction of the Architect who may in his absolute discretion and from time to time issue further drawings, details and/or written or oral instructions (hereinafter referred to as 'Architect's Instructions') in regard to:**

This is the introduction to the clause that defines the Architect's overall role in the contract. The Architect is not, of course, a party to the contract but he regulates considerable areas of the contract, and his judgement and opinion gives him very wide powers, duties and responsibilities. This clause also sets out the basic responsibility of the Contractor, which is to 'carry out and complete the Works in accordance with the Contract Documents'.

2.02   The general purpose of the building contract could be said to be to provide a mechanism for controlling the variables of the contract. It is assumed that the contract will vary. It must, though, be stated that many employers do not expect the contract to vary, and will often blame the Architect for his inability to carry out the work without variations. Employers often feel that the introduction of a Project Manager will control the problem, though this is not always the case. The fact remains that very many contracts will indeed vary. A contract would normally be broken if the terms originally agreed were departed from without consent by one of the parties, but in a building contract, by the very nature of the process, change is almost inevitable. A later clause (no.13) opens with the sentence: 'No variation shall vitiate this Contract', that is, no change shall invalidate the contract. The variables in the contract are The Works, the Contract Sum, and the Time. Strictly speaking, the Contract Sum is not changed, but is either added to or subtracted from. It is normally a variation in the works [as provided for in Clause 2(a)] which leads to a change in the contract sum or the time but there are other circumstances where the cost or the time could vary without any change occurring in the original 'Works'.

2.03   Clause 2 opens by requiring the Contractor to carry out and complete the Works in accordance with the Contract Documents. This is the Contractor's prime responsibility. If he fails in this, he is in breach of contract, and an Architect's action in, say, failing to observe or condemn faulty work, does not lessen this obligation or relieve the Contractor of any liability in respect of the Employer. The Contract Documents are defined at Item 1 of the Articles of Agreement, and are the numbered drawings, the specification, and, where appropriate, the Bill of Quantities. The carrying out and completion of the Works by the Contractor shall be subject to 'the directions and to the reasonable satisfaction of the Architect who may in his absolute discretion and from time to time issue further drawings, details and/or written or oral instructions (hereinafter referred to as 'Architect's Instructions')'.

2.04   This phrase 'in his absolute discretion' is not as all-embracing as it might appear. The Architect is the agent of the Employer and has authority to act on his own discretion where the contract is specific about his powers, and so to bind the Employer. He has no authority to bind the Employer to decisions which exceed his contractual powers, or to decisions which would commit the Employer to expense not originally contemplated, or authorised by, the Employer. What might be described as 'normal' instructions and which would be considered as the usual practice and custom would be binding on the Employer. It must be a matter of judgement for the Architect to decide whether his instruction would be considered a reasonable one for an agent to make. An instruction which resulted in an extra cost of £1,000 in a contract of £1M value would be reasonable; an extra of £100,000 would have to be authorised by the Employer. Somewhere in between is the watershed.

2.05   Agency arises whenever one person acquires authority to act as the representative of another. In the building contract, the Employer is the 'Principal' and the Architect is the 'Agent'. It is obvious that the principal is bound by any decision of his agent made within the scope of the agent's authority. Even where the act is not expressly authorised by the principal, the authority will extend to acts which are 'necessary' or 'ordinarily incidental' to the express authority and to acts which are within the agent's 'ostensible authority', ie, acts which the principal would normally delegate to a person in the agent's position. The reverse is equally true: where an agent exceeds his authority, the principal is not bound by any consequence of that excess of authority and a third party who suffers as a result may be entitled to recover damages for 'breach of warranty of authority' from the agent. So the Architect must remember that he will be personally liable in damages to a Contractor who was led to believe by the Architect that he had specific authority which in fact he lacked (*Vigers Sons and Co Ltd v Swindell* [1939] 3 AER 590).

The Architect should always make it clear that he is accepting sub-contracts, ordering supplies, etc, on behalf of the Employer, and to ensure that, at all times, both the Employer and the Contractor are made aware of any decisions which might affect his role as 'Agent' acting on behalf of the Employer.

Architect's Instructions under Clause 2 may be issued under any one of nine headings.

2.06   **a) The modification of the design, quality, or quantity of the works or the addition, omission, or substitution of any work (hereinafter referred to as 'variations')**

This could be described as the Architect's 'catch-all' power. While it reads as conferring extremely wide powers on the Architect, it must be read in the context of the observations set out above with regard to the Architect's position as the Employer's Agent. Further powers are conferred on the Architect in the clauses set out below:

Clause 3	Power to decide if re-measurement is necessary
Clause 5	Power to interpret Contract Documents
Clause 6	Power to instruct re Local and other Authorities' Notices and Fees
Clause 8	Power to vary materials used
Clause 9	Power to order work to be opened up
Clause 10	Power to instruct the Foreman
Clause 12	Power to direct the Clerk of Works
Clause 13	Power to deal with prices for variations
Clause 14	Power to deal with omissions
Clause 15	Power with regard to assignment
Clause 16	Power to nominate Sub-Contractors
Clause 17	Power to nominate Suppliers
Clause 18	Power to deal with Provisional Sums
Clause 19	Power to deal with Prime Cost Sums
Clause 28	Power to delay certain minor works
Clause 29	Power to certify re completion
Clause 30	Power to deal with delays and extension of time
Clause 31	Power to decide re practical completion
Clause 33	Power to initiate determination
Clause 35	Power to deal with certificates

It must be pointed out, however, that all these powers have concomitant duties and responsibilities.

2.07   Sub-clause 2(a) is necessary because an architect would normally have no power to vary or depart from a concluded contract, and this provision enables him to do so without referring every single variation to the Employer for approval. Only the Architect can order a variation. The Employer is not entitled to order variations, and the Contractor is entitled to refuse to carry out any such order from the Employer.

It is difficult to over-emphasise the importance of the legal position which restricts to the Architect the right to order variations or issue instructions. Of course the Architect may, if certain circumstances make it seem appropriate, delegate this power to Site Architects, Clerks of Works, other Consultants, etc, but this should only be done where unusual situations arise, and where the Employer is aware of the Architect's decision. While the Architect under this clause has the authority to vary the works, he has no authority to alter the contract, and only by agreement between the Employer and the Contractor can the terms and conditions of the contract itself be varied (see *Kinlen v Ennis UDC* [1916] 2 IR 299 at par. 2.12).

2.08   It follows from the above paragraphs that this sub-clause requires the most careful control by the Architect. It will be seen in Clause 13 (par. 13.01) that the contract intends that all variations shall be in writing, and the RIAI publishes a standard form which might be used as a model. If every variation is properly recorded, and if the effect of the variation of the cost and programme of the works is accurately recorded at the time of the instruction, then the agreement of the final account should be straight-forward. Nothing causes so much trouble at the conclusion of a contract as a list of alleged or unconfirmed instructions issued several months, or even years, before. There seems to be no clear legal precedent with regard to the right of a contractor to claim for a variation where the contract requires the variation to be in writing, and no such written confirmation exists. In ENGINEERING LAW AND THE ICE CONTRACTS by Max Abrahamson, 4th edition, p.178, he is of the view that an arbitrator may award payment, where no written confirmation exists.

2.09   In *Donovan v South Dublin, Guardians* [1905] 5 NIJR 106 it was held that extras, which had not been ordered in writing, had to be paid because they had been certified, but the position had they not been certified was not discussed. In *Quinn v Stranorlar RDC* [1907] 4I LTR 290, extras had not been confirmed in writing, but it was held that payment could be withheld as the contract provided for extra works to be ordered in writing, and countersigned by the chairman of the Council. In general it can be said that a written order would be necessary for payment to be made only if the clause is so worded as to make a written order a condition precedent to payment.

2.10   While the wording of sub-clause 2(a) appears to confer very wide discretion on the Architect as to the kind of variation that he can order, it is the case that the variation must be of the kind that would have been contemplated by the parties to the contract. 'If the additional or varied work is so peculiar, so unexpected and so different from what any person reckoned or calculated upon, it may not be within the contract at all, and he could refuse to go on or claim to be paid upon a *quantum meruit*' (*Thorn v London Corporation* [1976] 1 AC 120). Again in *Salt Lake City v Smith* [1990] 104 Fed. Rep. 457, it was held that a variation clause 'is limited to the subject matter and intention of the parties when it was made, to such modifications of the work contemplated at the time of making the contract as to not radically change the nature or cost of the work or materials required. For all other work and materials required by the alterations, the Contractors may recover the reasonable value, notwithstanding the agreement.'

It is generally accepted that an Architect has no authority to order a variation after the issue of the certificate of practical completion, although the contractor can always agree to the order.

2.11   A variation may result in changes to the cost of the Works, or to the time taken to complete the Works. Some variations will have no effect on either of these matters, and it is easy to see that an architect's instruction to, say, alter a colour scheme should not affect either the cost or the time. Similarly an omission may result in the cost being reduced, but an architect has no power to reduce the time taken to complete the works no matter how extensive the omission. A contractor may at any time agree to such a reduction. Omissions may also result in Clause 14 (Omissions) being brought into effect. Generally speaking, variations seem to result in extra costs, and claims for an extension of time. The extra cost of these variations is dealt with in Clause 13, unless the variation results from an instruction which will involve the Contractor in loss or expense not provided for or reasonably contemplated by the Contract. In this case the fourth paragraph of Clause 2 may be invoked.

2.12   A variation ordered under Clause 2(a) may not only entitle the Contractor to extra payment, but may also entitle him to claim for an extension of time as provided for in Clause 30(f) and (g). In the notes dealing with Clause 30, the various headings under which the Contractor may become entitled to an extension of time are examined in detail. Sub-clause 30(f) provides for an extension of time 'by reason of any Architect's Instructions given in pursuance of Clause 2 of these conditions' and sub-clause 30(g) allows an extension 'because the Contractor has not received in due time necessary instructions from the Architect for which he has specifically applied in writing'.

2.13   **(b) Any discrepancy in or between any of the Contract documents**

Some provision is required to enable any discrepancy in the contract documents to be resolved, and the Architect is the obvious person to decide in case of a dispute.

The Architect is not empowered, and in any case would hardly be competent, to construe the intent and meaning of the contract. In *Kinlen v Ennis UDC* [1916] 2 IR 299 it was held that the Architect had no function in deciding the meaning of the contract itself: 'There is no clause remitting to the arbitrament of this gentleman a decision as to the meaning of the contract itself.' The Architect is not expected to have any general legal knowledge, but he is assumed to have a working knowledge of the contract, and of the usual consequences of any contract provision as well as having a reasonable working knowledge of the law relating to his own job as an architect (see par. Int.10). Indeed he holds himself out as having this knowledge by accepting his naming in the Articles of Agreement.

The Architect should, however, be aware that any contract that is affected by illegality is void, and unenforceable. This is dealt with in the notes to Clause 6 (pars. 6.01–6.04).

The Architect must take note of the consequences of rectifying any such discrepancy in the Contract Documents. It could well be that extra costs or claims for delay could result but the Architect should be aware that he can certify expenses under this clause only if there is a genuine discrepancy. 'If the contract documents are clear they must be generally applied even if they produce a result which the parties obviously did not intend.' (Abrahamson p.41)

2.14 There is a provision in Clause 3 (Drawings and Bill of Quantities) which provides that 'nothing contained in the said Bill shall override, modify or affect in any way whatsoever the application or interpretation of that which is contained in these conditions.' The notes to Clause 3 (par. 3.03) deal in greater detail with the standing of this particular phrase as far as the interpretation of the Contract is concerned. The instructions to the Quantity Surveyor by the Architect should say that it is intended to use a specific form of contract and that form should be identified in the Bill of Quantities itself.

Some further general points which architects should be aware of as far as interpreting the Contract Documents is concerned, would be:

1 When amounts are given in words and figures, the words have precedence.

2 Written dimensions take precedence over scaled dimensions (Clause 5) – *Patman and Fotheringham Ltd v Pilditch* [1904] HUDSON, 4th edition, vol.2 p.368.

3 If differing documents cannot be reconciled, they must be interpreted in the least favourable way against the Employer because the Employer had

control over the drafting of the documents (*contra preferentem* – see par. Int.08 and 16.11).

There is also a reference in Clause 5 (par. 5.02) to discrepancies in the Contract Documents, but in a different context, and Clauses 2 and 5 must be read together.

2.15 **(c) The removal from the site of any materials or goods brought thereon by the Contractor and the substitution of any other materials or good therefore**

The contract does not state that the materials or goods which are to be removed must differ from those specified, but the assumption is there. The wording of the ICE form is perhaps preferable and removes any doubt: 'The Engineer shall during the progress of the Works have power to order in writing the removal from the Site within such time or times as may be specified in the order of any materials which in the opinion of the Engineer are not in accordance with the Contract.' [ICE, 6th edition, Clause 39(1)(a) and (b)]

The Architect has the power only to order the removal of materials which depart from the specification, and if he orders goods or materials to be removed because he has changed his mind, or because there is, perhaps, an improved or modified version now available, he must allow any extra expense to the Contractor. If the specification contains a phrase such as 'All materials to be the best of their respective kinds', it might give the Architect some extra power, but general phrases of this sort are becoming ousted by more specific reference to recognised codes or standards. Clause 8 (Materials and Workmanship to Conform to Description) describes the procedures to be adopted when materials (or workmanship) are being examined so as to determine if they conform to the Contract Documents.

If materials of a lesser quality than that specified are produced by the Contractor and accepted by the Architect, the Employer is required to pay only the reduced cost, and can even refuse to pay the retention money if he was not aware of the reduction in quality (*McKee v McMahon* [1935] 69 ILTR 180).

2.16 **(d) the opening up for inspection of any work covered up**

This is dealt with in detail in Clause 9 (Work to be opened up – par. 9.01).

2.17 **(e) the removal and/or re-execution of any works which in his opinion are not in accordance with the Contract**

The 'opinion' of the Architect is the key to this sub-clause. To some extent, this will be a subjective judgement; what will satisfy some architects will clearly not please others. It has been said that Contractors, when pricing, have been known to add a sum to their tender to allow for the strict interpretation by some architects as to what constitutes work in accordance with the contract.

A problem will obviously arise if the Contractor disputes the Architect's decision in this area. The Architect has authority (under paragraph 5 of this clause – see par. 2.28) to employ others to carry out his instructions if the Contractor will not comply, but invoking this provision will place a considerable strain on the contract, and on the relations between the Architect and the Contractor. On the other hand, if the Architect refuses to certify such work, the Contractor can seek arbitration under Clause 38 but again such a procedure during the course of a contract can be very disruptive.

The Architect, and through him, his site staff, should attempt to identify such defective work at as early a stage as possible so as to minimise any adverse effect on the course and progress of the works. It is not necessary for the Architect, however, to condemn such work immediately, and there is authority for the proposition that the Architect can condemn at any time during the contract, and that he can even change his mind, and condemn what has previously been approved. It is important to remember that the Architect's duty of supervision is owed to the Employer and not to the Contractor. If the Architect does not condemn defective work immediately the work has been completed, he can still condemn it at any later stage of the contract. It has been argued on behalf of the Contractor that if the defective work was visible at the time of the Architect's inspections, then the Employer has waived the right to claim damages at a later stage, but if this were so then it would imply that the Architect's inspections are to protect the Contractor rather than the Employer and this is clearly not so. 'It is essential to realise that the Architect's duty of supervision is owed to the Employer and not to the Contractor.' (HUDSON, 11th Edition, p.343)

'It seems to me most unlikely that the parties to the contract contemplated that the builder should be excused for faulty work at an early stage merely because the Architect failed to carry out some examination which would have disclosed the defect. Even if the Architect was in clear breach of his duty to his Client, the building owner, I can see no reason why this should enable the builder to avoid liability for his defective work; the Architect owes no duty to the builder.' (*East Ham BC v Sunley* [1966] AC 406). This particular quotation emphasises the basic duty of the Contractor as set out at the start of Clause 2, i.e. 'The Contractor shall carry out and complete the works in accordance with the contract documents.'

2.18 It was mentioned above that the Architect can change his mind, and condemn work which had previously been approved. If the Contractor specifically brings some matter to the Architect's notice, and requests approval, then the Employer would be bound by this, though not if some concealed defect were involved of which the Architect was unaware. In other cases however, where specific approval is not sought by the Contractor, it has been argued that the Architect can, at a later stage, condemn previously approved work, on the principle that the Architect has no power to alter the contract itself, and that if the specific defect infringes the contract, then the contract provisions prevail. 'But it seems to be quite clear from ... the reference to previous tests, etc, here that the Engineer's powers are not normally affected merely by a previous approval by him. On general principles, too, it does not seem that the Engineer has any power to alter the contract requirements by giving binding approval of work which infringes a specification.' (Abrahamson, p.127)

The finality of the Architect's decisions is also considered in the notes on Clause 35 (Certificates and Payments). In addition, the Disputes Resolution Clause (no.38) allows the review of such decisions, and is also discussed in the notes to that clause.

2.19 **(f) The postponement of any work to be executed under the provisions of this Contract**

This power of the Architect under this sub-clause is provided to deal with circumstances which might have altered since the commencement of the contract. The Architect must, however, be aware of the possible consequences of any such decision, and in particular, to the possibility of a claim under paragraph 4 of this clause ('loss or expense' – par. 2.26).

2.20 **(g) The dismissal from the Works of any person employed thereupon who may in the opinion of the Architect be incompetent or guilty of misconduct**

This provision is seldom invoked, and it is suggested that any circumstance that might give rise to such a situation be dealt with informally if at all possible. It is obvious that any order from the Architect in respect of a dismissal could give rise to disputes, and the possibility of industrial action. Quite apart from this, the employee in question will undoubtedly have rights in relation to his employment. Furthermore, if the instruction from the Architect was not well founded, an action for defamation from the dismissed employee is possible.

2.21   **(h) The amending and making good of any defects under Clause 31 of these Conditions**

Clause 31 (Practical Completion and Defects Liability) deals with defects which arise during the Defects Liability Period, and is a power in addition to those which arise under Clause 2(c) and 2(e). It is discussed in detail under the notes to Clause 31.

2.22   **(i) Any other matters appertaining to the proper execution of this Contract**

This sub-clause is inserted so as to give the Architect the power to issue instructions with regard to any matters which would not arise under the previous eight sub-clauses, (a) to (h).

2.23   Effect of sub-clauses (a) to (i) on the Contract, as regards time and cost:

The invocation of sub-clauses
(e) – removal and re-execution of work
(g) – the dismissal of persons
(h) – the making good of defects
(numbered as (v), (vii) and (viii) in the GDLA form), will not have any effect on the contract sum or on the date of practical completion.though the time taken to complete the Works may, indeed, be affected.

Whether the invocation of the other sub-clauses will have any such effect will depend on the facts in each particular case, but the Architect should always be aware when issuing instructions, of any possible claims with regard to either extra cost, or delays, or both.

2.24   **The Contractor shall forthwith comply with and duly execute any work comprised in such Architect's Instructions.**

The Contractor must carry out the Architect's Instructions, and paragraph 5 of this clause empowers the Employer to have any such instructions carried out by other persons if the Contractor does not comply (par. 2.28). In the case of persistent refusals by the Contractor to carry out the Architect's Instructions, the Architect can invoke Clause 33, which deals with the determination of the contract by the Employer.

2.25   **If compliance with an Architect's Instruction involves a variation, such variation shall be dealt with under Clause 13 of these Conditions and the value thereof shall be added to or deducted from the Contract Sum as the case may be.**

The rules for dealing with the cost of variations are set out in Clause 13 (Ascertainment of Prices for Variations) and these provisions will cover most of the situations which arise under Clause 2. However it is possible that unforeseen matters will arise and this difficulty is dealt with in paragraph 4 of this clause, dealt with in the next section (par. 2.26).

2.26 **If compliance with an Architect's Instruction will involve the Contractor in loss or expense beyond that provided for in or reasonably contemplated by this Contract the Contractor shall so inform the Architect; then, unless such instruction was issued by reason of some breach of this Contract by the Contractor the amount of such loss or expense shall be ascertained by the Architect and be added to the Contract Sum.**

It will be recalled that in the Introduction it was stated that a valid contract is based on agreement and that the parties to the Contract must contemplate the same intention and result. In the case of building works, however, unforeseen events or factors often intervene and this paragraph allows for the extra payment which might be involved.

It will be seen in paragraph 3 of this clause (par. 2.25) that an Architect's Instruction which can be valued under Clause 13 will so be dealt with. This paragraph (4) is to deal with circumstances which arise outside the provisions of Clause 13. It has been pointed out that it is the loss and expense that must be unforeseen, not the Architect's Instruction. It is a matter for the Architect's judgement as to whether or not the loss or expense could not reasonably have been contemplated, or whether or not it was provided for under the Contract.

Claims of this nature are very often difficult to resolve, and the Architect will consider the advice and expertise of the Quantity Surveyor in coming to a decision. Several books have been written on this subject alone, and the Architect cannot reasonably be expected to be conversant with all the detail, but he should be aware of some basic rules:

1   The claim should be made at the time the loss or expense is occasioned, and not at the final account stage.

2   The claim should be specific, and not an all-embracing claim.

3   The claim must relate to items of loss and expense that could not be claimed under Clause 13.

4   'Loss' would relate normally to preliminaries, head office, overheads, on costs and profit margins which the Contractor would have assumed to be protected under the contract provisions, and 'expense' would relate to an unexpected item in performing a variation.

2.27   There have been a number of cases in relation to this subject of loss and expense, although since most of them are cases referring to the JCT/RIBA Contracts the phrase being examined is '*direct* loss and expense'. The word 'direct' does not occur in the RIAI forms. A number of English cases have examined the difference between 'direct' loss and 'consequential' loss.

Where contracts have an exclusion clause to exclude the recovery of consequential loss, the Courts will look very closely at the sequence of events. If the damages result directly and naturally from the event in question, the Courts will hold that the loss is direct and any consequential or indirect loss will not be recoverable.

The various cases have established; that interest would be payable on a loss and expense claim if payment were delayed (*FG Minter Ltd v Welsh TSO* [1981] 13 BLR 1); that the phrase 'loss and expense' can be equated to damages at common law (*Wraight Ltd v PH&T (Holdings) Ltd* [1968] 13 BLR 26); that an allowance can be included for office overheads (*Tate & Lyle Food and Distribution Ltd v GLC* [1982] 2 AC 509),and finally, that loss of profit would be a permissible item for loss and expense claims, but only if the Contractor could prove that he could have employed his resources profitably elsewhere (*Peak Construction v McKinney Foundations* [1971] 1 BLR 114).

2.28   **If within five working days after receipt of a written notice from the Architect requiring compliance with the Architect's Instructions, the Contractor does not comply therewith the Employer may employ and pay other persons to execute any work whatsoever which may be necessary to give effect to such instructions and all costs incurred in connection therewith shall be recoverable from the Contractor by the Employer as a debt or may be deducted by him from any money due or to become due to the Contractor under this Contract.**

This paragraph authorises the Employer to have any work carried out by others if the Contractor refuses to comply with an Architect's Instruction. If there is no alternative to invoking this paragraph, the Architect should be careful to ensure that the costs incurred are reasonable and are, as far as is practicable, comparable to the costs contained in the Contract. It will be noted that the costs incurred by the Employer 'may be deducted by him from any money due or to become due to the Contractor under this Contract'.

This wording is almost identical to that in Clause 29(a), which wording was discussed in detail in *P Elliott & Co Ltd v The Minister for Education* [1987] ILRM 710. This case held that the final certificate referred to in Clause 35 was not 'conclusive' in respect of any claim made under Clause 29 (Damages for non-completion) because the wording of Clause 29 did not refer to the 'Contract Sum but merely to any money due ... under this Contract'. It would appear to follow that any adjustment made under this paragraph of Clause 2 would fall into the same category. The *Elliott* case is discussed more fully in the notes to Clause 29 at par. 29.05.

GDLA – Clause 2

2.29   This clause is very similar to the RIAI form Clause 2 except for the following three variations, and one additional sub-clause:

1   Paragraph 1: The phrase 'who may in his absolute discretion' is omitted. This is a sensible amendment. See the notes to paragraph 1, RIAI form Clause 2 (par. 2.04).

2   The substitution of the word 're-erection' for the word 're-execution' in paragraph 1(v) numbered as (e) in RIAI. This is not of any significance.

3   In paragraph 4, dealing with loss or expense, a timetable is provided. This is an improvement, because, as has been pointed out in the notes on paragraph 4, RIAI (par. 2.26) the claim must be made promptly, and this particular sub-clause removes any doubt as regards the timing of a claim. The paragraph requires the Contractor to notify the Architect within five working days of receiving the instruction, of the nature of the loss and expense claim, and in addition, to provide within twenty-five further working days, the details and value of the claim.

The Architect is required to deal with this claim 'as soon as possible' and this is not stated in the RIAI form. There is also provision for an extension of the time within which the original claim must be made, if the Architect considers this reasonable.

2.30   The recommendations issued by the Forum for the Construction Industry in February 2001 included an addition to GDLA Clause 2(c). The first two existing paragraphs are numbered (i) and (ii), and a third sub-clause is added, as follows:

(iii) Where the Contractor has exercised his right to provide a retention bond in accordance with the provision of Clause 35(o)(ii) and if within fifteen (15) working days after issue of a written notice from the architect requiring compliance with any Architect's instruction the Contractor does not comply therewith, the Employer shall have the right to claim payment against the retention bond for all costs incurred in employing or paying other persons to execute any work whatsoever which may be nec-

essary to give effect to such instruction provided that the requirements specified in Supplement (B) hereof have been complied with. Any shortfall that arises between the amount of the Employer's entitlement under the retention bond and all costs incurred in connection with such work shall be deducted by the Employer from any monies due or to become due to the Contractor under this contract or any other contract made between the Employer and the Contractor or may be recoverable from the Contractor by the Employer as a debt.

The reference to Supplement (B), which is reproduced at the end of the book in the Standard Documents section, is to the standard form of retention bond for dealing with retention money (see par. 35.15). This new provision is a protection to the Employer where financial difficulties might arise as far as the Contractor is concerned.

2.31   Clause 2(c) refers to the right of the Employer to deduct money which has been spent in employing other persons to carry out work which the Contractor has failed to carry out, resulting from an Architect's Instruction, but unlike the RIAI form adds the very significant words 'from this or any other Contract made between the Employer and the Contractor', which is known as a right to 'set-off'. This procedure whereby a party to one contract is entitled to deduct monies due to the other party under a separate contract can occur where the parties are in a position of mutuality, i.e. bear the same relation to one another. (For a review of the law of 'set-off', see *Freaney v Bank of Ireland* [1975] IR 376.)

A right of set-off is particularly useful for many of the employers who would use the GDLA, as they would tend to be engaged in a multiplicity of contracts at any one time, and several of these could be with the same Contractor. The situation is less likely to occur in the private sector where the RIAI form prevails, although cases involving 'set-off' have, of course, occurred. Some of these are inconclusive, but the latest one involving building works (*Rohan Construction Ltd v Antigen Ltd* [1989] ILRM 783) reperesents the present state of the law. In that particular case it was held that a right of set-off was inconsistant with the terms of the RIAI form, though it is clearly allowable in the GDLA form (see par. 35.04).

2.32   Clause 2(d) in the GDLA form does not occur in the RIAI form. It reads:

If the Quantity Surveyor is retained to advise during the currency of the Contract the Architect shall consult him on all matters of cost adjustment arising under these Conditions. Such consultation may be deemed by the Contractor to have taken place before the issue by

the Architect of any instruction, direction, decision or certificate concerning any such matter.

In the notes to paragraph 4 of the RIAI form (par. 2.26), the importance of consultation with the Quantity Surveyor was stressed. This sub-clause makes it a contractual requirement, and is a prudent addition. This clause, however, does not relieve the Architect of any responsibility for making the necessary decisions under Clause 2. The question of the Architect's liability in the matter of certification, and his relationship with the Quantity Surveyor, is discussed in the notes to Clause 35 (Certificates and Payments – par. 35.02).

SF 88 – Clause 1

CONTRACTOR'S OBLIGATION

2.33 **The Contractor shall carry out and complete the Works in a good and workmanlike manner and in accordance with the Contract Documents and to the reasonable satisfaction of the Architect.**

This is generally the same wording as the first paragraph of Clause 2 of the longer forms; apart from the phrase 'in a good and workmanlike manner' which has been added.

SF 88 – Clause 2

EMPLOYER'S OBLIGATION

2.34 **The Employer shall pay or allow to the Contractor such sum of money as shall from time to time become due by virtue of these conditions.**

This is the obverse of SF 88 Clause 1. The two clauses taken together can be paraphrased as follows, and constitute the essence of the contract: the Contractor shall build and the Employer shall pay.

SF 88 – Clause 3

2.35 **The Architect shall act as agent of the Employer for the purposes of the Contract.**

This paragraph defines clearly what is understood in the RIAI and GDLA contracts, where agency is not specifically identified. Agency has been discussed above in the notes to RIAI Clause 2 – pars. 2.04 and 2.05. Acting as agent does not, however, diminish the Architect's responsibility to act fairly and impartially towards both parties in dealing with any matters under the contract.

2.36 **The Architect shall issue any further information necessary in his opinion for the proper carrying out of the Works, and shall issue all directions, instructions and certificates properly required by virtue of these Conditions.**

This paragraph is the equivalent of paragraph 1, Clause 2 RIAI, and Clause 2(a) GDLA, but is more restrained than the RIAI provision referring to the Architect's 'absolute discretion'.

The following paragraph in SF 88 covers the general area of RIAI Clause 2 and GDLA 2(a) and (b). It reads as follows:

2.37 **Without invalidating the Contract, the Architect may instruct the Contractor in respect of any alteration or any addition or omission to the Works or as to the order or period in which the Works due to be carried out, any such instruction shall form part of the Contract and shall where appropriate be valued by the Architect on a fair and reasonable basis, using where relevant prices in the priced specification / schedules / schedules of rates unless a price has been previously agreed. Oral instructions shall not constitute instructions for the purposes of valuation unless confirmed to or by the Contractor within seven working days of issue.**

This is a paraphrase of most of what is contained in Clause 2 of the longer forms. The only new item is the reference to 'the order or period in which the Works are to be carried out'.

The right of the Architect to instruct the Contractor as to the order of carrying out the Works can only be on a general basis. As is discussed below (par. 2.39), the Architect has no right to instruct the Contractor as to the method of work and it should generally be a matter for the Contractor to decide on the order of the work. Unless provision is made in the tender documents for such instructions, or unless the Contractor's attention is directed to this clause, a claim might well be founded on such an instruction.

The right to instruct with regard to the 'period in which the works are to be carried out' must be regarded with similar discretion. Again unless the tender documents identify such a possibility, a claim is possible.

2.38 **The Architect shall issue instructions as to the expenditure of any Provisional Sums. A Provisional Sum shall be any amount included in the Contract Sum and so described to be expended on the direction of the Architect. Provisional Sums not expended shall be deducted from the Contract Sum.**

Provisional Sums (and Prime Cost Sums) are discussed in the notes to Clauses 18 (Provisional Sums) and 19 (Prime Cost Sums) of the RIAI and GDLA Contracts.

2.39 **The Architect shall carry out periodic inspections of the Works to satisfy himself on behalf of the Employer that the Works are proceeding generally in accordance with the Contract; these inspections shall not in any way relieve the Contractor of his sole obligation to carry out the Works in accordance with the Contract. The Contractor shall attend on such inspections and shall provide all facilities required for this purpose.**

The Architect's power and duty to inspect or supervise or observe is not referred to in the longer forms (although it is both implied and inferred), but it does form part of the RIAI Conditions of Appointment (par. 1.07): 'The Architect shall visit the site at intervals appropriate to the stage of construction to inspect the progress and quality of the work and to determine on behalf of the Employer that the work is being executed generally in accordance with the contract. Frequent or constant inspection of the work is not the responsibility of the Architect. Where such frequent or constant inspection is considered necessary separate arrangements will be agreed between the Architect and the Client.'

The whole area of the Architect's responsibility as regards inspection is one that requires continuing vigilance by the Architect. The employment of site staff does not relieve the Architect of any responsibility. It has been said that the act of inspection can be delegated but that the responsibility of inspection can not. In other words, site staff can do the inspecting and will report to the Architect, but it is always a matter for the Architect whether or not he will accept these reports without a personal check for himself (see par. 12.05 – Clerk of Works).

The view of the frequency of inspection referred to in the RIAI Conditions of engagement is supported by many cases, going back to the last century in some instances: 'If an Architect is entrusted with the general direction and superintendence of the work, his duties could not be performed if he were expected to go over individually every matter of detail, and if his certificate were to be held bad by a court of law because he has not himself gone into every detail.' (*Clemence v Clarke* [1880] HUDSON'S BC, 4th edition, vol.2, p.58.) This would still be the correct view, and the Architect will inspect those parts of the works which require, in his opinion, a personal inspection. There is a full judgement on this subject in Abrahamson at pp.353–54, from the case of *Florida Hotels Pty Ltd v Mayo* [1965–66] 39 ALJ 50 (Aus).

HUDSON, 11th edition, p.348, says: 'There is no doubt that there is a tendency at the present day for the Courts to demand a standard of care from Architects in detecting defective work which particularly in major contracts seems somewhat unrealistic. An architect may have other many important problems demanding attention and decision when visiting a site and may well, it is suggested, decide to rely on the builder to do his work properly on that particular occasion while dealing with the problems. The view that he should make a thorough examination of every part of the building in a large contract on each site visit seems somewhat perfectionist.'

It will be recalled that HUDSON says that an architect should provide 'efficient supervision'. There is an on-going debate about the appropriate word. 'Supervision' was widely used, but is now being replaced by words like 'inspection', as in the RIAI Architect's Appointment and in the shorter form of the RIAI Contract (SF 88). It was felt that the use of the word supervision imposed an unreal level of responsibility on the Architect and diluted the primary responsibility of the Contractor to build correctly. This is an area where there seems to be considerable doubt as to what is appropriate, building owners tending towards requiring a substantial level of supervision. The RIAI Architect's Appointment (par. 1.7) leaves the level to the Architect's discretion.

It has been held that an architect is entitled to use his judgement as to how frequently he inspects. The decision in *East Ham Corporation v Bernard Sunley* [1966] AC 406 has been much quoted and is worth repeating: 'As is well known, the Architect is not permanently on the site but appears at intervals, it may be of a week or a fortnight, and he has, of course, to inspect the progress of the work. When he arrives on the site there may be very many important matters with which he has to deal: the work may be getting behind-hand through labour troubles; some of the suppliers of materials or the sub-contractors may be lagging; there may be physical trouble on the site itself, such as, finding an unexpected amount of underground water. All these are matters which may call for important decisions by the Architect. He may in such circumstances think that he knows the builder sufficiently well and can rely upon him to carry out a good job; that it is more important that he should deal with urgent matters on the site than that he should make a minute inspection on the site to see that the builder is complying with the specifications laid down by him. It by no means follows that, in failing to discover a defect which a reasonable examination would have disclosed, in fact the Architect was necessarily thereby in breach of his duty to the building owner so as to be liable in an action for negligence. It may well be that the omission of the Architect to find the defect was due to no more than error of judgement, or was a deliberately calculated risk which, in all the circumstances of the case, was reasonable and proper.'

This overall view was quoted with approval by the Judge in *Corfield v Grant* [1992] 59 BLR 102: 'What is adequate by way of supervision and other work is not in the end to be tested by the number of hours worked on site or elsewhere, but by asking whether it was enough. At some stages of some jobs exclusive attention maybe required to the job in question (either in the office or on site): at other stages of the same jobs, or during most of the duration of other jobs, it will be quite sufficient to give attention to the job only from time to time. The proof of the pudding is in the eating. Was the attention given enough for this particular job?'

2.40   There is a disturbing (from an architect's point of view) passage in Wallace, CONSTRUCTION CONTRACTS (Sweet and Maxwell 1986) at p.66: 'There is no subject about which there is more misunderstanding than that of the role of the supervising professional in construction contracts. For this, the professionals themselves are largely to blame by reason of the terms in which they have chosen to frame their own contracts of employment, and also the construction contracts themselves. These, with their constant references to the approval, directions, opinions and decisions of the professional strongly suggest to the uninitiated that the professional is in such close and effective control of a construction site that even temporary works and the overcoming of unexpected difficulties during construction are within his jurisdiction and responsibility.'

I think that this view is rather alarmist but it does point to a danger. The Architect has a very wide range of powers, duties and responsibilities and it would be understandable if a third party took the view that the Architect should accept a measure of responsibility that would seem to be in sympathy with such an overall sense of control. It is for the Architect to make it clear from the very outset to the Employer what exactly is being offered by way of a professional service, and to ensure that the Employer accepts the position as proposed.

2.41   The reference to 'temporary works' is more relevant to engineering con-
        tracts, where it is quite common for the engineer to design temporary works
        and so, to some extent, to become involved in the Contractor's method of
        work. This is something which the Architect must avoid. The Architect is
        entitled to define the finished work which he requires, but he is not required
        to and should never, advise the Contractor on how to achieve this result.
        'That case, in both courts further establishes that an Architect has no right to
        instruct a builder how his work is to be done or the safety precautions to be
        taken. It is the function and right of the builder to carry out his own building
        operations as he thinks fit.' (*Clayton v Woodman & Sons (Builders) Ltd*
        [1962] 4 BLR 65)

        The danger of the Architect appearing to offer advice to the Contractor in the
        matter of operations on the site is well illustrated in case law. In *AG Clay v
        Crump and Sons Ltd* [1963] 4 BLR 80, an architect was held liable for
        injuries suffered by a workman because the Architect had offered an opinion
        about the safety of a wall, which subsequently collapsed. It is particularly
        important now, in view of the developments in health and safety legislation,
        that the Architect, in his role as Architect, never offers any safety advise to
        the Contractor.

        (See the notes to Clause 12 for some further comments on inspection and
        supervision – pars. 12.05–12.07.)

SF 88 – Clause 9

DISMISSAL OF WORKERS

2.42   **The Architect may issue instructions requiring the dismissal from
        the Works of any person employed thereon in any capacity whatso-
        ever who in the opinion of the Architect is incompetent or guilty of
        misconduct.**

        This is the provision that is contained in RIAI Clause 2(g) and GDLA Clause
        2(vii). See the notes to Clause 2(g) – par. 2.20.

2.43   A   ARCHITECT'S RESPONSIBILITIES UNDER CLAUSE 2
           RIAI and GDLA

1   Issue instructions as required.

2   Ensure that valuation under Clause 13 is carried out without 'undue delay'.

3   Ascertain any loss or expense involved following compliance with instructions.

Additional responsibilities under GDLA

1   Ensure that proper notice is received of any claim for loss or expense.

2   Consult with the Quantity Surveyor on matters of cost adjustment.

2.44   B   EMPLOYER'S RESPONSIBILITIES UNDER CLAUSE 2
           RIAI and GDLA

1   Employ others in default of the Contractor obeying Architect's instructions, and recover any costs.

2   Deal with retention bond matters (GDLA only).

2.45   C   CONTRACTOR'S RESPONSIBILITIES UNDER CLAUSE 2
           RIAI and GDLA

1   Carry out and complete the Works.

2   Comply with Architect's Instructions.

3   Provide details of any claims as soon as possible. In the case of GDLA, conform to the timetable set out.

2.46   CASES REFERRED TO

AG Clay v Crump & Sons Ltd [1983] 4 BLR 80   par. 2.40
Clayton v Woodman & Sons (Builders) Ltd [1962] 4 BLR 65   par. 2.40
Clemence v Clarke
      [1880] HUDSON'S BC, 4th edition, vol.2 p.38   par. 2.38
Corfield v Grant [1992] 59 BLR 102   par. 2.38
Donovan v South Dublin Guardians [1905] 5 NIJR 106   par. 2.09
East Ham BC v Sunley [1966] AC 406   pars. 2.17, 2.38
P Elliott & Co Ltd v The Minister for Education
      [1987] ILRM 710   par. 2.28

Florida Hotels Pty v Mayo [1956–66] 39 ALJ 50 (Aus) par. 2.38

Freaney v Bank of Ireland [1975] IR 376 par. 2.30

Kinlen v Ennis UDC [1916] 2 IR 299 pars. 2.07, 2.13

McKee v McMahon [1935] 69 ILTR 180 par. 2.15

FG Minter Ltd v Welsh T S O [1981] 13 BLR 1 par. 2.27

Peak Construction v McKinney Foundations
 [1971] 1 BLR 114 par. 2.27

Patman & Fortheringham Ltd v Pilditch
 [1904] HUDSON, 4th edition, vol.2 p.368 par. 2.14

Quinn v Stranorlar UDC [1907] 4 ILTR 290 par. 2.09

Rohan Construction Ltd v Antigen Ltd [1989] ILRM 783 par. 2.30

Salt Lake City v Smith [1990] 104 Fed. Rep. 457 par. 2.10

Tate and Lyle Food and Distribution Ltd v GLC
 [1982] 2 AC 509 par. 2.27

Thorn v London Corporation [1876] 1 AC 120 par. 2.10

Vigers Sons & Co Ltd v Swindell [1939] 3 AER 590 par. 2.05

Wraight Ltd v PH&T (Holdings) Ltd [1968] 13 BLR 26 par. 2.27

RIAI and GDLA – Clause 3

DRAWINGS AND BILL OF QUANTITIES – INTRODUCTION

3.01   Both the RIAI and GDLA contracts forms are available in two distinct versions, depending on whether or not the Bill of Quantities forms part of the
Contract Documents. The printed form of both RIAI and GDLA are identical
except as far as the distinction with regard to the quantities is concerned.

In the RIAI form a phrase appears on the front cover: 'This form is applicable where quantities form part of the Contract' or 'This form is applicable
where quantities do not form part of the Contract.' The words used on the
GDLA form are different: 'GDLA 82 for use when Quantities form / do not
form part of the Contract'. In both the RIAI and GDLA forms the 'blue' version is for use without quantities, and the 'yellow' version for use when
quantities are part of the Contract. The Articles of Agreement also differ in
both RIAI and GDLA by referring to a Bill of Quantities or Schedule of
Rates as appropriate (see Articles of Agreement notes).

The effect on the contract as to whether the Bill of Quantities forms part of
the contract or not is important. If the Bill of Quantities is a contract document then the quantities shown are those required under the contract and any
variation from the quantities shown in the Bill will be adjusted in the final
account under Clause 13 as if it were a variation.

If the Bill of Quantities is not part of the Contract, then the quantities are
provided only as a guide to the extent of the work (but also, of course, to
form in effect a Schedule of Rates) and the Contractor, or indeed the
Employer, must bear any loss which might result from differences in the bill
and in the actual work carried out. The practice of having a Bill of Quantities
not forming part of the Contract is unusual now and if a Bill of Quantities is
prepared it is almost always made a contract document.

3.02   Originally, quantities were taken out by the Contractors themselves when
tendering, or the Contractor employed a quantity surveyor to do this work.
Naturally, under those arrangements the responsibility for the accuracy of the
quantities fell entirely on the Contractor. Over the years, however, the role of
the quantity surveyor changed, and more and more he became employed by
the building owner. It seemed reasonable in these changed circumstances

that the Employer accept responsibility for the accuracy of the bill since he had ordered the preparation of the bill and his agent, the Quantity Surveyor, had prepared it. This area was a profitable source of litigation until the case of *Patman and Fotheringham Ltd v Pilditch* [1904], HUDSON's BC, 4th edition, vol.2, p.368 where it was held: 'If the quantities in the bills were less than those required by the drawings the Contractor was entitled to be paid an appropriate addition to the contract sum, since the quantities were introduced with the contract as part of the description of the contract work, and if the Contractor was required to do more, it was an extra.'

But genuine mistakes may be rectified even if the Bill of Quantities is not part of the Contract. Cases must be judged on the facts, but the general rule which applies is that one party to a contract cannot effectively accept an offer if he knows that the terms of the offer were not intended by the other party. About the same time as the Patman case above, this was examined in the case of *Collen Bros v Dublin Co Council* [1908] 1 IR 503. This was a case where the quantities did not form part of the contract, but a mistake had been made in a Bill of Reductions which had been prepared by the defendant employer's quantity surveyor. The court held that the mistake could be rectified because 'the meaning of rectification of a written instrument is to carry out the real intention of the parties which had been erroneously expressed.' The Contractor never got paid however, because this is one of those legal cases where even though the plaintiff won the main point, there was a secondary pitfall which undid the claim. Here, a Local Government law about the time of payments protected the County Council.

RIAI

3.03   **3(a)(i) If the Articles of Agreement provide for the inclusion of the Bill of Quantities as a Contract Document the Contract Sum shall be deemed to provide for the quality and quantity of work set out in the description and qualities in the Bill. The Bill unless otherwise expressly stated shall be deemed to have been prepared in accordance with the Method of Measurement of Building Works last before issued or approved by the Society of Chartered Surveyors in the Republic of Ireland and the Construction Industry Federation but save as aforesaid nothing contained in the said Bill shall override, modify or affect in any way whatsoever the application or interpretation of these Conditions.**

This sub-clause is the base on which the principles set out above are founded. The Bill is 'deemed' to provide the quantities to be supplied.

The Method of Measurement of Building Works is an agreed way of preparing quantities and of describing work to be done. It is agreed between the Society of Chartered Surveyors and the Construction Industry Federation, representing the employers and contractors respectively. It is constantly reviewed and updated. The current version is known as the Agreed Rules of Measurement (ARM), and the latest edition is Issue 3, 1999. In the case of any doubt, the provisions of the standard Method of Measurement will be assumed to apply to any descriptions, etc, in the bill.

This sub-clause also states 'nothing ... in the Bill shall override ... these Conditions'. It is important that the Architect check with the Quantity Surveyor before the contract documents are issued for tender (or for negotiation or agreement) to ensure that no discrepancies exist. Some disquiet has been expressed at this wording on the grounds that some important requirements might be contained only in the Bills, but this unease only serves to highlight the importance of liaison between Architect and Quantity Surveyor. In addition, the difficulty that this phrase causes has been the subject of judicial criticism. Normally a contract will be construed by looking at the overall provisions of the various documents involved.

A phrase such as 'nothing contained in the said Bill shall override, etc,' makes this overall view difficult. Lord Denning, in *English Industrial Estates Corporation v George Wimpey and Co Ltd* [1972] 7 BLR 122, took the view that provisions which had been specially typed in a Bill of Quantities must take precedence over a standard printed form, but this is an unusual view. Most judges seem to have taken the view that the phrase in Clause 3 was clear and unambiguous and must be followed, but one judge was so irritated by the problems caused by this approach that he referred to the Contract Conditions as a 'farrago of obscurities' (Davies LJ in the *English Industrial Estates* case). However, this case upheld the view that the contract conditions have precedence over the Bill of Quantities.

The possibility of some difference occurring in the various Contract documents is contemplated in the Contract Conditions in Clause 2(b) which provides for the Architect to decide on the correct interpretation (see notes to Clause 2). Whether or not a document is part of the Contract will depend on the facts, and both parties to the Contract should be clear as to what is intended. The contract documents must be clearly listed. In the case of *Kinlen v Ennis UDC* [1916] 2 IR 299, tender documents were not incorporated into the contract and the Contractor failed to obtain payment for building a wall that had been provided for in his tender, but was not mentioned in the contract document. HUDSON, at pp.441–442, deals with cases touching on this problem.

3.04 **No error in description or quantity in the Bill of Quantities nor any omission of items therefrom shall vitiate this Contract but such error or omission shall be rectified and the rectification treated as a variation under Clause 13 hereof.**

This is the sub-clause which provides the method of dealing with errors which may have occurred, and which are discussed above. The phrase 'vitiate this Contract' also occurs in Clause 13, and means that no such error shall affect the validity of the Contract. This protection, as has been stated before, is necessary in a Contract of this nature, which assumes deviations from the outset.

The correction of errors will be dealt with under the rules set out in Clause 13, but it is also possible that the error might be of such a scale or nature as to justify the invoking of paragraph 4 of Clause 2, which refers to 'loss or expense beyond that ... reasonably contemplated by this contract'.

The error may also be of such a fundamental nature as to render the contract voidable. A contract, generally speaking, is 'void' when it never had any legal effect in the first place. A contract may also be 'voidable', ie, it may be of legal effect when entered into but liable to be set aside at the instance of one of the parties. This may happen where the parties contracted under a common mistake as to a fundamental matter. 'A contract is ... liable in equity to be set aside if the parties were under a common misapprehension either as to facts or as to their relative and respective rights, provided that the misapprehension was fundamental and that the party seeking to set it aside was not himself at fault' – *Solle v Butcher* [1950] 1 KB 671.

A party to a 'voidable' contract may continue with the contract if he so wishes but cannot be forced to do so, provided he takes action promptly, and does not by his conduct appear to have accepted the contract.

Illegality may also affect the validity of a contact, and this is discussed in the notes to Clause 6 at pars. 6.01 to 6.04.

3.05 **When remeasurement is claimed by the Contractor under this Clause and the result in the opinion of the Architect proves such remeasurement to have been in whole or in part unnecessary the Contractor shall be liable for the fees involved by such part of the remeasurement as was in the opinion of the Architect unnecessary. This stipulation shall not apply to variations.**

This is a straight-forward provision and is intended to ensure that the Contractor will question the accuracy of the Bill of Quantities only in genuine cases. The 'opinion' of the Architect is important here, and the Architect could very well decide that no fees should be paid even if the Bill is found to be accurate, provided he feels that there were genuine grounds for believing that a mistake had been made. The provision does not apply to variations, as these result from an instruction by the Architect, and the Contractor is clearly entitled to discover whether the Contract Sum has been affected by the instruction given.

The alternative part to sub-clause 3(a)(i) reads as follows, and is relevant where Bills of Quantities do not form part of the Contract:

3.06 **3(a)(ii) If the Articles of Agreement do not provide for the inclusion of the Bill of Quantities as a Contract Document the Contract Sum shall be deemed to provide for the quality and quantity of the work set out in the Drawings and Specification and the Contractor shall before signing the Articles of Agreement furnish the Architect with a Schedule of Rates.**

The Schedule of Rates shall be deemed to mean:

> **a copy of the fully priced and detailed estimate upon which the Contractor's tender is based priced in ink, or**

> **where a Bill of Quantities is provided for tendering purposes the Rates therein contained.**

The Bill of Quantities unless otherwise stated shall be deemed to have been prepared in accordance with the Method of Measurement of Building Works last before issued or approved by the Society of Chartered Surveyors in the Republic of Ireland and the Construction Industry Federation. Nothing contained in the Contractor's estimate or the Bill of Quantities (except as a Schedule of Rates) shall confer rights or impose any obligations beyond those conferred or imposed by the Contract Documents.

This sub-clause is to take effect when the Bill of Quantities does not form part of the Contract and where, as it set out above, the accuracy of the quantities is not guaranteed by the Employer. The prime function of the Bill of Quantities in this case is to provide the rates from which variations can be valued under Clause 13.

In sub-clause 3(a)(i) the Bill of Quantities is deemed to provide for the quality and quantity of the work; in sub-clause 3(a)(ii) the drawings and specification are to perform this function.

The Contract Conditions at this point include the following:

NOTE: In sub-clause 3(a) either Section (i) or Section (ii) but not both will apply according to whether a Bill of Quantities is or is not included as a Contract Document. Article No.1 in the Articles of Agreement indicates whether or not a Bill is so included.

GDLA – Clause 3(a)

3.07   The wording of Clause 3(a)(i) and (ii) in GDLA is identical to that in the RIAI form, with the exception that the GDLA was prepared before the change of the title of the Society of Chartered Surveyors in the Republic of Ireland. The institution is described in GDLA as the Royal Institution of Chartered Surveyors (Republic of Ireland Branch).

RIAI

3.08   **3(b) The Contract Documents (together with the Schedule of Rates if supplied in accordance with the terms of Section (ii) of sub-clause (a) of this clause) shall remain in the custody of the Architect and by him be produced at his office during office hours when so required by the Contractor. The Architect shall furnish to the Contractor one copy of the Articles of Agreement and the Conditions of Contract, two copies of the Contract Drawings and Specification, and, if a Bill of Quantities is provided, two copies of the Bill. He shall also furnish the Contractor with two copies of all further drawings and instructions issued during the progress of the Works. All such drawings and documents shall be supplied free of cost to the Contractor. Upon final payment to the Contractor he shall forthwith return all drawings to the Architect.**

In practice, contractors often require further copies of Contract Documents and these would be supplied. The Contractor would be required to pay for the cost of supplying these extra copies. The signed Contract Documents are often retained in the custody of the Employer, and this is specifically provided for in the GDLA form.

The requirement that the Contractor return all drawings to the Architect (or as is required under Clause 38 of GDLA that they be returned to the Employer) has been the subject of a court dispute. In *Necap and Irishenco*

Ltd v Gas Unie Engineering and Kenny International Ltd [1983] High Court, unrep., a sub-contractor was required by injunction to return 'as-built' drawings to the main Contractor.

In the case of larger contracts, it is important that the Architect ensure that an accurate schedule of Contract Documents is prepared and updated. Lists of drawings issued by the Architect and any other consultants must be kept, and also related to Architect's Instructions issued during the course of the Contract.

3.09   **The Contractor shall keep one copy of all drawings and the specification on the Works and the Architect or his representative shall at all reasonable times have access to them. The Contractor and the Quantity Surveyor shall each be entitled to make one copy of the priced Bill of Quantities or Schedule of Rates which copies shall remain in their custody.**

This paragraph calls for no comment.

3.10   **The priced Bill of Quantities or the Schedule of Rates and all copies thereof shall be deemed to be the property of the Contractor and shall be confidential. Neither the Architect, the Employer nor the Quantity Surveyor shall divulge any information contained in such documents otherwise than for the purposes of this contract.**

There are sound commercial reasons for this provision. A building Contractor will obtain work if his rates are competitive, but will be at a serious disadvantage if these rates are known to his competitors. It is to protect the Contractor that a Bill of Quantities submitted with a tender is always contained in a separate envelope, which envelope is only to be opened on obtaining the Contractor's consent.

Similarly, the Architect, Quantity Surveyor and Employer (and their representatives) are required under this contract to preserve the confidential nature of the Contractor's prices and rates.

3.11   **All documents the property of the Contractor shall be returned to him on request after the final payment has been made.**

Such requests are seldom made.

GDLA – Clause 3(b)

3.12 This is largely similar to the RIAI form. The differences are:

1 The Contract documents shall remain 'in the custody of the Employer (or the Architect on his behalf) ... The RIAI form provides that the Architect alone shall have custody. This provision in GDLA reflects a widespread tendency, particularly in larger contracts for the documents to be retained by the Employer no matter which contract form is used. Similarly, the Employer (or the Architect on his behalf) shall furnish copies of documents as may be necessary.

2 There is a provision as follows, obviously not relevant to the RIAI form:

In cases where the Works are to be paid for wholly or partly from Exchequer funds through or in the control of a Government Department and the same Government Department is not the Employer but nevertheless retains its own technical and professional advisors the Government Department shall likewise be entitled to make one (1) copy of the priced Bill of Quantities or Schedule of Rates which copy shall remain in its custody.

3 The paragraph referring to confidentiality includes the Government Department referred to above in 2).

4 There is no provision for the return to the Contractor of documents which are his property. GDLA does have a later provision (Clause 38) for the return of documents to the Employer, which requirement is made in the first paragraph of Clause 2(b) of RIAI.

3.13 It might be appropriate at this point to make a few remarks about the copyright of Architect's drawings, in view of the provisions in the contract forms for the return of drawings (RIAI) and specifications (GDLA).

'The primary function of copyright law is to protect from annexation by other people the fruits of a man's work, labour, skill or taste' (White and Jacob, PATENTS, TRADE MARKS, COPYRIGHT AND INDUSTRIAL DESIGN [Sweet and Maxwell]). An architect's copyright of his design lasts for the architect's lifetime and for a period of seventy years after his death. It is not enough for the Architect to prove that he has designed the building in question in order for him to be protected by copyright. The Architect must be able to prove that his particular design is unusual or original to such an extent that it is unlikely that any other Architect would have come to the same design solution. This is difficult to establish in practice. Many designs produced by Architects are generic. This can apply to all classes of buildings but most of the disputes that arise in this particular field deal with houses. If an architect can show that the design derived from a well know example of the house type, then similarity to other designs also so derived would not constitute infringement of copyright.

A question often asked is whether a person is entitled to build from a set of drawings which were prepared only for planning purposes without the payment of a further fee to the Architect. The answer is yes. This point was specifically decided in *Blair v Osborne and Tomkins* [1970] 10 BLR 96, where an architect, who had obtained planning permission and had been paid, tried unsuccessfully to obtain damages for infringement of copyright. Having paid for the design stage the client would be entitled to have the working drawings prepared by another Architect and no further duty or responsibility would devolve onto the original Architect for that portion of the work. This was confirmed in an Irish case, *Burke v Earlsfort Centre Ltd* [1981] High Court, unrep. 24th February, which held, generally, once the appropriate fee had been paid that copyright had passed to the client. However, if the fee for the original sketch plan was very small, it has been held that there is no right or licence implied for the client to proceed to build without payment of a further fee. *Stovin-Bradford v Volpoint Properties* [1971] 10 BLR 105. A largely similar case, *Hunter v Fitzroy Robinson and Others* [1977] 10 BLR 81, held that where the Architect has been paid a substantial fee there was an implied licence for purchasers of the drawings to proceed without payment any further fee. The original Architect would, however, be liable for any damages that might result from an infringement of the planning code resulting from his drawings in the unlikely event of a planning authority not adverting to the infringement at the application stage. A planning authority is not empowered to overrule its own development plan.

A point to be watched in this area is the possible use of drawings which were originally prepared for planning application purposes being used for fire safety certificate applications without the original Architect being aware of this. All drawings for planning application purposes should state clearly that the drawings were prepared for that purpose and for that purpose alone.

The client would not be entitled to build more than once from the same design without payment of an additional fee unless this was agreed at the appointment stage. This point could be important in house design particularly but could also arise in the case of office parks, industrial estates or any other project where repetition is possible.

If copyright can be established, the only remedy available to the Architect after construction has commenced is damages. An injunction to prevent construction starting could be sought otherwise (The Copyright and Related

Rights Act, 2000). The Architect's claim for damages would relate to the size of his design fee. In this regard, White and Jacob referred to above says: 'Architects work for modest scale fees.'

3.14 ## SF 88 – Clause 3

This clause in the SF 88 form deals with a number of items which occur in different clauses in the other forms. Matters dealt with are: a) Agency – see pars. 2.05 and 2.34; b) Architect's instructions, par. 2.35; c) Variations. par. 2.36; d) Provisional sums, par. 18.01; and e) Inspection, par. 2.38.

3.15   A   ARCHITECT'S RESPONSIBILITIES UNDER CLAUSE 3
         RIAI and GDLA

1   Decide on the necessity or otherwise of the Contractor's claims for remeasurement.

2   Retain custody of the Contract Documents (in the case of GDLA, only if they are not retained by the Employer).

3   Furnish copies of drawings, specifications, instructions to the Contractor.

4   Return documents to the Contractor (not in GDLA).

5   Ensure confidentiality of the Bill of Quantities or Schedule of Rates.

3.16   B   EMPLOYER'S RESPONSIBILITIES UNDER CLAUSE 3 GDLA

1   Retain custody of Contract Documents

3.17   C   CONTRACTOR'S RESPONSIBILITIES UNDER CLAUSE 3
         RIAI AND GDLA

1   Decide whether or not to seek re-measurement.

2   Furnish a Schedule of Rates if there is no Bill of Quantities.

3   Return all drawings to the Architect on completion. (RIAI only; this requirement is contained in Clause 38 GDLA.)

4   Keep copies of the Contract Documents on site.

3.18   CASES REFERRED TO

Blair v Osborne and Tomkins [1976] 10 BLR 96	par. 3.13
Burke v Earlsfort Centre [1981] High Court, unrep 24th Feb	par. 3.13
Collen Bros v Dublin County Council [1908] 1 IR 503	par. 3.02
English Industrial Estates Corporation v George Wimpey & Co Lt d [1972] 7 BLR 122	par. 3.03
Hunter v Fitzroy Robinson [1977] 10 BLR 81	par. 3.13
Kinlen v Ennis UDC [1916] 2 IR 299	par. 3.03
Necap and Irishenco Ltd v Gas Unie Engineering and Kenny International Ltd [1988] High Court, unrep.	par. 3.08
Patman and Fotheringham v Pilditch [1904] HUDSON'S BC, 4th edition, vol. 2, p.368	par. 3.02
Solle v Butcher [1950] 1 KB 671	par. 3.04
Stovin-Bradford v Volpoint [1971] 10 BLR 105	par. 3.13

RIAI – Clause 4

VARIATIONS ARISING FROM LEGISLATIVE ENACTMENTS

4.01 **When after the Designated Date the cost of the performance of this Contract is increased or decreased as a result of any legislative enactment, rule or order or the exercise by the government of powers vested in it, whether by way of the imposition of new duties or tariffs or the alteration of existing duties or tariffs or the restriction of licences for the importation of any commodity, or by way of affecting the cost of labour or otherwise, the amount of such increase or decrease as certified by the Architect shall be added to or deducted from the Contract Sum as the case may be.**

This is a straightforward provision to deal with extra or reduced costs which may be due, as an example, to a change in the rate of VAT. In short, any change in a government duties or charges which occur after the Designated Date would come within the scope of this clause.

GDLA – Clause 4

4.02 This is very similar to the RIAI wording. The words 'instruments, rules, or orders' are added in line 2. The only other difference is that the reference to the 'cost of labour or otherwise' in the RIAI form is omitted and the following sentence is added to the end of the clause:

Such increases or decreases shall not be recoverable under this Clause if they come within the scope of Clause 36.

This is obviously provided so as to ensure that a wage claim arising from a government act, etc, is not paid for twice.

SF 88 – Clause 15

4.03 This clause in the shorter form says that no account will be taken of increases or decreases in the cost of wages or materials but that variations arising from Legislative Enactments, Statutory Instruments, or Ministerial Orders will be taken into account.

4.04 A ARCHITECT'S RESPONSIBILITIES UNDER CLAUSE 4
RIAI AND GDLA

1 Certify any increase or decrease in the Contract Sum.

RIAI and GDLA – Clause 5

CONTRACTOR TO PROVIDE EVERYTHING NECESSARY

5.01 **The Contractor shall provide everything necessary for the proper execution of the Works according to the true intent and meaning of the Contract Documents taken together whether the same may or may not be particularly shown or described provided that the same is reasonably to be inferred therefrom, and if the Contractor shall find discrepancy herein he shall immediately and in writing refer the same to the Architect who shall decide the course to be followed. Figured dimensions are to be followed in preference to scaled dimensions.**

The clauses are identical in both forms. (Sharp-eyed readers will notice that the RIAI clause has three sentences, and the GDLA clause has only two, requiring the use of the word 'and'.)

The burden of the consequences of this clause falls mainly on the Contractor. It is important for him to ensure that the tender documents are sufficiently explicit so as to remove the possibility of argument at a later stage. If there is a dispute it is for the Architect to decide. An early case in 1858 held that flooring must be inferred in a contract to construct a house. The plans showed floor joists but made no reference to the flooring boards themselves, but the court found that 'it was the intention of the contract' for the flooring to be included (*Williams v Fitzmaurice* [1858] 3 H&N, 844).

While the flooring case is perhaps an extreme example, and portrays a contractor who is clearly trying to exploit a loophole in a contract, there can be cases where the items to be inferred are not so obvious. The Architect will decide having examined the documents in question, and having considered the general custom and practice of the Building Industry in relation to the particular matters in dispute.

5.02 Examples where items might be inferred, if not specifically mentioned, would be the provision of wall ties in a cavity wall, or appropriate formwork for fair-faced concrete. As a general rule, the best course is to ensure that the documents are as detailed and as explicit as possible. The use of the Agreed Rules of Measurement will greatly assist in this area. To some extent, this clause overlaps Clause 2(a) which refers to discrepancies in the Contract Documents (see par. 2.13). Taking both clauses together, the Architect clearly decides the issue.

The reference to figured dimensions has been referred to in the notes to Clause 2 at par. 2.14.

5.03   A   ARCHITECT'S RESPONSIBILITIES UNDER CLAUSE 5
RIAI AND GDLA

1   Decide on any matter raised by the Contractor.

5.04   C   CONTRACTOR'S RESPONSIBILITIES UNDER CLAUSE 5
RIAI AND GDLA

1   Refer any discrepancy to the Architect for his decision.

5.05   CASE REFERRED TO

Williams v Fitzmaurice [1858] 3 H&N 844   par. 5.01

RIAI – Clause 6

LOCAL AND OTHER AUTHORITIES' NOTICES AND FEES

6.01 **The Contractor shall pay and indemnify the Employer against liability in respect of any fees or charges legally demandable under any Act of the Legislature, any Instrument, Rule or order made under any Act of the Legislature and any Regulations and Bye laws of any Local Authority or Public Service Company relating to the work and any fees and charges, if not the responsibility of the Contractor or expressly included in the Contract Sum by way of a Provisional Sum shall be added to the Contract Sum.**

This, Clause 6, is the first of the clauses to have been altered by the 1996 revision and the effect is considerable. The GDLA contract has not been changed (see par. 6.09). The old RIAI Clause 6 required the Contractor both to comply with any notices and to take account of the cost of these notices. While the monitory provisions of the old clause remain, it was felt that it was no longer appropriate for the Contractor to have to undertake in this contract that the law would be complied with. The corpus of law dealing with building is now so extensive and ranges from planning and building regulations to health and safety, and each of these pieces of legislation identifies the responsibilities of the various parties. When the previous editions of this work were being written, the clause, as it then existed, was specific with regard to compliance, and the notes in those editions reflected this fact. As, however, the basic responsibilities of the parties have not changed, and as the GDLA contract is, in any event, unchanged, the notes have been retained and are altered where necessary.

Any contract is void if it is affected by illegality, that is, if the contract is carried on in the face of some statutory restraint or prohibition. There are other forms of illegality in contracts, but they are not relevant here. In most building contracts, the 'Works' would require planning permission, and would require to conform to the Building Regulations and procedures, and failure to obtain these consents would, *prima facie*, import an element of illegality into the contract. Apart from planning and building regulations all relevant statutes must be obeyed (see par. 6.05).

As far back as 1692 it was held that 'Every contract made for or about any matter or thing which is prohibited and made unlawful by statute is a void contract, though the statute itself does not mention that it shall be so, but only inflicts a penalty on the offender because a penalty implies a prohibition though there are no prohibition words in a statute.' (*Bartlett v Vinor* [1692] Carth. 251)

The notices that Clause 6(a) GDLA refer to primarily relate to Planning Permissions, Building Regulations, and Health and Safety at Work. The Architect should be aware as to whether or not planning permission is required for the Works in question, and he should ensure that it has been obtained if it is required. Works which are exempted under the Planning Acts 1963 to 1993 are set out in Section 4 of the Local Government (Planning and Development) Act 1963, and the regulations contained in S.I.86 of 1994, S.I.69 of 1995, and S.I.181 of 2000.

It is expected that the Planning and Development Act 2000 and the Regulations made under that Act, will be in force when this edition appears, but no basic changes are expected that would affect this particular situation.

In practice the vast majority of all projects require planning permission and the existence and validity of the permission must be established by the Architect. If the Planning Permission has been obtained by the Employer, or was obtained by another Architect, the Architect should ensure that it is the grant of permission which has been issued (or a Bord Pleanála Order) and also ensure that the permission is still valid under the time limits set out in the Local Government (Planning and Development) Act 1982.

6.02   In June 1991 national building regulations came into force. They were a long time coming. Powers to introduce such regulations were first given to the Minister for Local Government (as the office was then called) in Sections 86, 87 and 88 of the Local Government (Planning and Development) Act 1963. Since 1878 the only form of building control operating in Ireland was the system of building bye-laws that derived from the Public Health (Ireland) Act of that year. That Act empowered local authorities, in their capacity as Sanitary Authorities, to make bye-laws 'with respect to the structure and description and quality of the substances used in the construction of new buildings for securing stability and the prevention of fires, and for purposes of health' (Section 41). The 1878 Act was similar to the Town and Regional Planning Act (1934) in that it was up to each local authority to decide whether or not to adopt the powers available under the Act. In the event, very few did. Only Cork City and County, Dublin City and County, and the Borough of Dun Laoghaire introduced bye-laws covering the full range of powers set out in the 1878 Act. Some other local authorities adopted limited bye-laws covering certain areas of building works.

While draft building regulations were, in fact, issued in 1969 as a result of the powers contained in the Local Government (Planning and Development) Act 1963, there was no further action until the Stardust fire tragedy occurred in February 1981. Forty-eight people were killed and 126 seriously injured in this disaster at the Stardust nightclub in Dublin. Immediately afterwards the Department of the Environment circulated revised draft regulations, but there was a further delay until 1990 when the Building Control Act was introduced.

6.03 The Building Control Act, as far as it affects the building contract, has two separate areas. The first of these is the building regulations themselves. They are contained in the Statutory Instrument no. 497 of 1997 and are very concise. As an example, part F, which deals with ventilation reads: 'Adequate means of ventilation shall be provided for people in buildings.' That is the full statement, and that is the legal requirement. However the Department of the Environment has published what are described as Technical Guidance Documents which go into some detail as to how the various requirements of the regulations might be met, and lists standards from various countries and organisations which would be acceptable. S.I. 497 of 1997 at article 7 says that 'where works are carried out in accordance with any guidance contained in a technical guidance document this shall, prima facie, indicate compliance with the relevant requirements of these regulations.'

The second area of the Building Control Act which affects the contract is the control mechanism that is set out in S.I.496 of 1997. There are, basically, two procedures which affect 'a person who intends to carry out any works, or to make a material change in the use of a building'. The first is the requirement to inform the building control authority that the works are about to start. This is the 'Commencement Notice'. It would appear that the Contractor would be the proper person to issue the Commencement notice. This is because the notice must be sent to the 'Building Control Authority' which is the guise the local authority adopts for this particular purpose, not less that fourteen days and not more than twenty-eight days before the commencement of the works and the Contractor is best placed to know the precise starting date. No reaction is required from the authority. The second procedure is the 'Fire Safety Certificate'. The application for the fire safety certificate would be made by the Architect (or, in large contracts, a Fire Safety Consultant) as it involves the submission of detailed plans and specifications. The procedure mirrors that in the planning acts in that drawings and specifications are submitted to the building control authority; they must give a decision (with or without conditions) to grant or refuse the certificate within two months; and there is an appeal to Bord Pleanála.

6.04 Because the introduction of building regulations has been so recent, there are still some areas of uncertainty as to details, but after some years of operation, the practical procedural problems should disappear. There are some pitfalls, however, of which the person responsible for complying with the procedures should be aware:

1   The exemptions from the building regulations, from the need to provide a commencement notice, and from the requirement to obtain a fire safety certificate can all be different. While any building works which result in the use of an RIAI standard form will almost certainly be covered by all three requirements (with the exception of single houses as far as a fire safety certificate is concerned) the Architect must be vigilant.

2   The concept of a material change of use is very different as between planning legislation and the building regulations and the Architect must be satisfied if an exemption from the need to obtain a fire safety certificate is concerned.

3   The transition provisions of the Building Control Act and the position of proposals which have already obtained bye-law approval must be noted. The Act provides that any building that had been completed before December 13th, 1989 shall be assumed to be in compliance with the bye-laws unless the building control authority takes appropriate action before December 1st 1992 [Section 21(7)]. Any proposal that has obtained bye-law approval before June 1st 1992 does not need to be subjected to the procedures as set out in the Building Control Act, and this means that no fire safety certificate need be sought. It must be remembered, however, that a local authority has the power to revoke a bye-law approval if work is not commenced within three years from the date of the application for approval (Public Health Acts, Amendment Act 1907, section 15). It is possible that local authorities will use this power as a tidying-up exercise.

4   The provisions of the Local Government (Multi-storey Buildings) Act 1988 have been very significantly altered by the Building Control Act 1990 at section 23. This provides that section 4 of the multi-storey buildings act shall no longer apply to multi-storey buildings whose construction commences after the coming into operation of the Building Control Act. Section 4 of that Act had required a certificate with regard to building codes and standards. This particular area of design is now regulated by Part A (Structure) of the building regulations.

6.05   A further area which the Architect should check is whether or not an Environmental Impact Assessment is required. Under the provision of the European Communities (Environmental Impact Assessment) Regulations, 1989 to 1999 an environmental impact statement is required in respect of a wide variety of industrial and agricultural projects. What might be described as ordinary building projects are also covered and those of most concern to architects would be industrial-estate development projects exceeding 15 hectares, and urban development projects exceeding 50 hectares in new or extended urban areas, or exceed 2 hectares in existing urban areas (First schedule to S.I.349 of 1989).

There is, in addition, a further layer of control that has been imposed by the provisions of the Environmental Protection Agency Act 1992. This Act brings together all the statutes and regulations which dealt with the environment into one all embracing Act, as a form of integrated pollution control. An architect dealing with any industrial project in particular should check as to whether or not the proposed activity requires a licence under the Act, and he should note that the relevant planning authority is precluded in these circumstances from dealing with any matters relating to environmental pollution resulting from the activity, as far as a planning application is concerned.

Finally, in this list of statutory control of the building process is the issue of the Statutory Instrument no.138 of 1995, The Safety, Health and Welfare at Work (Construction) Regulations issued under the Safety, Health and Welfare at Work Act 1989. This is dealt with in detail at par. 11.04. Revised regulations are expected to be introduced in the last quarter of 2001.

6.06   It is not only planning and building regulation requirements that are covered by this clause. Any Act of the Legislature must be observed. In *McIlvenna v Ferris and Green* [1955] IR 318 it was held that work done without a licence which was required under the Emergency Powers (no.358) Order 1945 was part of an illegal contract and that a claim under that contract would not be enforced. Interestingly, during the course of the contract the order was revoked, and claims for work done after the revocation were upheld.

6.07   The Architect must be aware of his responsibility with regard to the obtaining of any necessary approvals or consents. It is the practice and custom of the construction industry for the Architect to obtain these approvals and the courts recognise this. In *Townsend Ltd v Cinema News* [1959] 1 WLR 119, extra work was necessary because a bye-law had been infringed. It was held that the Employer could recover from the Contractor (the wording of the contract was similar to Clause 6 GDLA), but the court also held that the Architect was liable in tort to the Contractor, and would have to indemnify the Contractor against the Employer's claim.

Some concern had been expressed about the inclusion of the former clause in the contract and in particular over making the Contractor responsible for compliance. It was felt, certainly by contractors, that since almost all dealings with any statutory authority are undertaken by the Architect then the logical way of dealing with responsibility would be to transfer it to the Architect. This concern has been heightened since the Building Control Act 1990 came into force. The continued retention of the old clause in the GDLA contract is now in obvious contrast to the provisions of the RIAI form.

6.08   The liability of local authorities for decisions taken by them in furtherance of their statutory powers and duties has been the subject of many legal decisions, and the position has very recently been completely altered. The famous case of *Dutton v Bognor Regis UDC* [1972] 3 BLR 13 can be taken as the starting point as far a modern developments go. The case decided that a local authority in carrying out its functions (in this case the passing by a building inspector of foundations which turned out to be defective) had a duty not only to the building owner but to subsequent parties who might reasonably have been foreseen as being affected by the Council's actions. This duty was not to be negligent. Dutton also held that a Council would be liable for physical damage to the property whether it endangered others or not but not liable for pure financial loss.

The case of *Anns v Merton* [1978] 5 BLR 1 brought the matter further. It decided that a local authority was not obliged to inspect every building as far as building bye-laws were concerned but that they must properly exercise their discretion in deciding what to inspect, and that if they did inspect, it must not be negligent. The case further held that no cause of action arose until such time as the defects which had appeared would constitute 'imminent danger to the health and safety of persons occupying the building'.

Finally in this section is the rather extraordinary case of *Murphy v Brentwood District Council* [1990] 50 BLR 1. Ever since the *Dutton* case, it had been accepted, and case after case confirmed it, that local authorities (and builders) were liable for damage to property if caused by their negligence. The Murphy case decided that this only applied to ensure that no physical injury occurred either to occupiers or to any other property, and that damage to the property in question did not create a liability except for the injuries mentioned above. In other words, *Dutton*, *Anns*, and all the other cases were wrong. A footnote with regard to the unfairness of the law would be that the unfortunate Mr Murphy, despite winning in the High Court and Court of Appeal, and despite the House of Lords rulings in Anns and other cases, had to pay all the costs because the House of Lords changed the law. The New Zealand case mentioned above (par. Int.14 – *Invercargill*) has taken a different view again, but which route the Irish Courts might take is not yet clear.

In Ireland the case of *Siney v Dublin Corporation* [1980] IR 400 also dealt with the obligations of local authorities. The case did not deal with building bye-laws but was concerned with the Corporation's duty to provide housing under the requirements of the Housing Act 1966. A tenant sued the Corporation on the grounds that the house which had been let to him by the Corporation was not fit for human habitation. The Supreme Court examined the distinction between the duties and the powers which arose under statute as far as a local authority was concerned. It had always been accepted that breach of a duty would result in liability whereas breach of a power might not, and the Court confirmed that failure to exercise a power could not automatically guarantee immunity to a local authority. The Court's decision was in line with *Anns v Merton*, and it remains to be seen what effect *Murphy v Brentwood* will have on future decisions. The Court specifically approved of *Anns v Merton*. A later case (*Sunderland v Louth County Council* [1990] ILRM) seemed to be a warning that the Courts might not be as ready in the future to recompense for pure economic loss, but this line of argument has now been abandoned (*McShane v Johnston* [1997] 1 ILRM 86).

6.09 ## GDLA – Clause 6(a)

The Contractor shall comply with and give all notices required by any Act of the Legislature, and instrument, rule or order made under any Act of the Legislature and any regulations and bye-laws of any local authority and/or any public service company or authority relating to the Works or with whose systems the same are or will be connected and he shall pay and indemnify the Employer against any fees or charges demandable by law thereunder in respect of the Works. The said fees and charges if not expressly provided for in the Contract Sum shall be added to the Contract Sum.

Clause 6(a) of the GDLA form, which remains unchanged, is almost identical to the old Clause 6(a) which has been changed in the new RIAI form. In par. 6.01 it was pointed out that it was no longer felt appropriate for the Contractor to be specifically held responsible for complying with all the laws and regulations pertaining to the building process, but this is the situation which is retained in the GDLA form.

6.10 ## GDLA – Clause 6(b)

Upon the receipt of any such notice the Contractor shall immediately send a copy thereof to the Employer and a second copy thereof to the Architect and if compliance therewith would involve a variation the

Contractor in writing shall advise the Architect accordingly specifying and giving the reason for the variation and applying for instructions in reference thereto. If the Contractor does not receive such instructions within ten (10) working days thereafter he shall proceed to make the variation which shall then be measured and valued in accordance with Clause 13 of these conditions and the value thereof added to or deducted from the Contract Sum as the case may be.

This sub-clause is straightforward and requires no comment.

6.11 ## SF 88 – Clause 16

The Contractor shall comply with, and give all notices required by, any Statute, any Statutory Instrument, Rule or Order or any Regulation or Bye-Law applicable to the Works and shall pay all fees and charges in respect of the Works.

This clause deals with the matters set out in the notes to Clause 6 of both the RIAI and GDLA forms.

6.12 A   ARCHITECT'S RESPONSIBILITIES UNDER CLAUSE 6 GDLA

1   Issue any instructions following the Contractor's notice.

6.13 C   CONTRACTOR'S RESPONSIBILITIES
         UNDER CLAUSE 6 RIAI AND GDLA

1   Pay and indemnify the Employer.

2   Comply with, and give, all necessary notices (GDLA only).

3   Give copies of notices to the Employer and Architect (GDLA only).

4   Apply for instructions by way of written notice (GDLA only).

6.14 CASES REFERRED TO

Anns v Merton [1978] 5 BLR 1   par. 6,08
Bartlett v Vinor [1692] Carth 251   par. 6.01
Dutton v Bognor Regis UDC [1972] 3 BLR 13   par. 6.08

Invercargill City Council v Hamlin
    [1988], THE TIMES, 15th January   par. 6.08
McIlvenna v Ferris and Green [1955] IR 318   par. 6.06
McShane v Johnston [1997] 1 ILRM 86   par. 6.08
Murphy v Brentwood District Council [1990] 50 BLR 2   par. 6.08
Siney v Dublin Corporation [1980] IR 400   par. 6.08
Sunderland v Louth County Council [1990]   par. 6.08
Townsend Ltd v Cinema News [1959] 1 WLR 119   par. 6.07

RIAI – Clause 7

SETTING OUT OF WORKS

7.01   **The Architect shall furnish to the Contractor either by way of fully dimensioned drawings or by personal supervision and instructions at the time of setting out the Works, such information as shall enable the Contractor to set out the Works. The Contractor shall be responsible for and shall at his own cost amend any errors arising from his own inaccurate setting out unless the Architect shall otherwise direct.**

This is a straightforward provision. It can be summed up by saying that the Architect is responsible for supplying the Contractor with the information that is required to set out the Works; the Contractor is responsible for the actual setting out.

If the information supplied by the Architect is not accurate, the Employer will be required to pay any additional costs (which he may, in turn, seek to recover from the Architect) which may arise in order to correct any mistakes in the actual setting out unless 'the Architect shall otherwise direct'. This latter provision is somewhat odd. On the face of it, it would appear to give the Architect authority to agree to the Contractor being paid additional remuneration for remedying the Architect's own inaccuracies. This wording does not occur in the GDLA form.

The Architect should not get involved in, or approve the setting-out. The ICE form contains the stipulation 'The checking of any setting out or of any line or level by the Engineer or the Engineer's Representative shall not in any way relieve the Contractor of his responsibility for the correctness thereof.' While this warning does not occur in the RIAI or GDLA forms, it would hardly protect the Architect even if it were incorporated into the Contract in view of the well established widening of tortious liability of the various parties involved in the Contract. This is discussed in the introduction at pars. Int.12 seq.

GDLA – Clause 7

7.02   The first sentence is identical to that in the RIAI form. The second sentence differs:

The Contractor shall be responsible for any errors arising from his inaccurate setting out and shall amend such errors to whatever extent and in such a manner as the Architect will direct. All such amendments shall be carried out at the Contractor's expense.

This wording places the responsibility for the cost of errors much more clearly on the Contractor than in the RIAI form, and removes from the Architect the wider discretion given in that form.

7.03   A   ARCHITECT'S RESPONSIBILITIES UNDER CLAUSE 7
             RIAI AND GDLA

1   Provide the information to set-out the Works.

2   Direct the Contractor as to the rectifying of errors.

7.04   C   CONTRACTOR'S RESPONSIBILITIES UNDER CLAUSE 7
             RIAI AND GDLA

1   Set out the Works.

RIAI – Clause 8

MATERIALS AND WORKMANSHIP TO CONFORM TO DESCRIPTION

8.01 **All materials and workmanship, unless otherwise authorised by the Architect, shall be of the respective kinds described in the Contract Documents and the Contractor shall upon the request of the Architect furnish him with vouchers to prove that the materials comply therewith. The Contractor shall arrange for and/or carry out any test of any materials and/or workmanship which the Architect may in writing require. If no provision is made in the Contract Documents therefor by way of a Provisional Sum for payment of fees and charges for the carrying out of such tests then such fees and charges shall be added to the Contract Sum except where the test shows that the said materials and/or workmanship are not in accordance with this Contract.**

This clause is straightforward as regards the three basic requirements set out:

1   Materials and Workmanship are to conform to the Contract Documents.

2   The Contractor may be asked for proof of this conformation.

3   Fees and charges shall be dealt with as set out in the clause.

The second and third requirements set out above require very little commentary. The Contractor will in the ordinary course of business provide evidence that the materials which he is using are those which are specified under the Contract. He will normally supply this information to the Quantity Surveyor where one is retained.

The provision with regard to charges for tests is similar in intent to the charges referred to in Clause 9 (Work to be opened up). The principle in Clauses 8 and 9 is that any tests which are not provided for in the Contract Documents will be paid for by the Employer if the tests prove that the materials or workmanship do conform to the contract requirements, and will be paid for by the Contractor if they do not conform.

Provision is usually made in contracts for tests of various materials, the best known being the regular 'cube' tests for concrete.

8.02 The first requirement set out above needs some examination. Since the first edition of this guide was published in October 1991, the Building Control Act 1990 has introduced national building regulations (see pars. 6.02–6.04). Part D of the First Schedule to the Building Regulations (S.I.497 of 1997) now requires all building works to conform to the regulations as follows:

D1 – Materials and Workmanship

All works to which these regulations apply shall be carried out with proper materials and in a workmanlike manner.

D2 – Definition for this part

In this part, 'proper materials' means materials which are fit for the use for which they are intended and for the conditions in which they are to be used, and includes materials which:

a) bear a CE Mark in accordance with the provisions of the Construction Products directive (89/106/EEC); or

b) comply with an appropriate harmonised standard, European techni- cal approval or national technical specification as defined in article 4(2) of the Construction Products Directive (89/106/EEC); or

c) comply with an appropriate Irish Standard or Irish Agrément Board Certificate or with an alternative national technical specification of any Member State of the European Community which provides in use an equivalent level of safety and suitability.

The Technical Guidance Document published by the Department of the Envir- onment goes into further detail as to how these requirements may be met.

8.03 The Directive mentioned above is the Council Directive of 21st December 1988 (89/106/EEC). Par. Int.17 gives a brief description of the EC structures and legislation. This particular directive is to deal with 'the approximation of laws, regulations and administrative provisions of the Member States relat- ing to construction products'. While the primary aim of this Directive is to achieve the free movement of construction materials in the Single Market, and to harmonise standards, it will also have a considerable effect on con- struction liability. 'Construction Products' are defined in Article 1 of the Directive as being 'any product which is produced for incorporation in a per- manent manner in construction works, including both building and civil engineering works'. Article 2 of the Directive deals with the matters dis- cussed pars. 8.02–8.08. It requires that products intended for use in construc- tion works may be placed on the market 'only if they are fit for this intended use'. It goes on to define this as 'having such characteristics that the works in which they are to be incorporated ... can, if properly designed and built satisfy the essential requirements referred to in Article 3'. These Article 3 requirements deal with standards relating to:

– stability
– fire-safety
– hygiene, health and environment
– use-safety
– noise protection
– energy economy and heat retention

It will be the intention of the Community to have conforming products provided with an EC mark. What were previously known as National Standards will now be called Technical Specifications or Harmonised Standards. The European Committee for Standardisation has been given the task of producing these specifications. The various member states are in the process of producing harmonised standards for their own products and when this has been done the relevant national standard will be withdrawn, so that eventually all products will be assessed on a European basis. If building products which are not covered by harmonised standards are to gain access to the Single Market, they just obtain a European technical approval which is much the same as Agrement Certificate procedure.

Further details with regard to the EC requirements can be obtained from either the EC office in Molesworth Street, Dublin 2, or from the Environmental Research Unit of the Department of the Environment.

It is intended that the Directive will apply only to materials which are covered by National Regulations and the Directive came into effect in Ireland on 1st of January 1993.

8.04   Before the introduction of the Building Regulations with the included references to the EC legislation, the legal position was very complex. It is not yet clear how exactly these new developments will affect the traditional position. It was generally the case that if the contract did not set out specific standards, such as the IIRS or BSS requirements, then there was implied in the contract a condition that the Contractor must carry out the work in accordance with the standards which govern contracts of this sort. The law requires that the Contractor carry out the work in a good and workmanlike manner and that he supply materials which are, firstly, reasonably fit for the purpose for which they shall be used, and secondly, that the materials are of good quality. Those requirements, however, can vary in degree depending on the circumstances, and a summary of the development of the law in this area is useful in coming to an understanding of the overall position. SF 88 Clause 1 is very specific in requiring the Contractor to carry out the works 'in good and workmanlike manner'. It will, ultimately, be for the courts either in Ireland or in Europe to decide, in cases of dispute what exactly 'fit for intended use' (as set in the Directive) means, but it would certainly seem that the stricter requirement of 'fitness for the purpose' (as defined in the Sale of Goods Act 1893) as set out in previous domestic legislation will now be the norm.

As the law developed during the nineteenth century, contracts for the supply only of goods were distinguished from contracts which required goods to be both supplied and fixed. The former were known as 'contracts for the sale of goods' and the latter as contracts for 'work and materials'. Differences did exist as between the two sorts of contracts but by a series of judgements the point was reached where it was not thought that there was any great difference between these two sorts of contract. Originally a buyer purchased at his own risk – *caveat emptor* - let the buyer beware. But the law came to recognise the unfairness of this absolute rule, and eventually in 1893, the Sale of Goods Act was passed and this laid down the rules governing contracts for the sale of goods. This Act was in force in Ireland until 1980 when the Sale of Goods and Supply of Services Act 1980 was passed. This later Act incorporated many of the provisions of the 1893 Act but was different in some significant areas. The 1893 Act and the 1980 Act must be construed as one. These two Acts dealt only with the sale of goods, but it will be seen later that the courts generally took the view that contracts for work and materials could also be affected by the rules set out in the 1893 and 1980 Acts.

The following pars. 8.05–8.10 give a resume of the law as it has developed up to the point of the introduction of the Building Regulations and the EC Directive.

8.05 It is worth while setting out the provisions of the 1980 Act as far as the sale of goods is concerned. These would be the provisions that might affect the building contract. Section 14 of the 1893 Act is changed in the 1980 Act at Table 14 – Section 10, and reads as follows:

1 Subject to the provisions of this Act and of any statute in that behalf, there is no implied condition or warranty as to the quality or fitness for any particular purpose of goods supplied under a contract for sale.

2 Where the seller sells goods in the course of a business there is an implied condition that the goods supplied under the contract are of merchantable quality, except that there is no such condition – (a) as regards defects specifically drawn to the buyer's attention before the contract is made, or (b) if the buyer examines the goods before the contract is made as regards defects which that examination ought to have revealed.

3 Goods are of merchantable quality if they are as fit for the purpose or

purposes for which goods of that kind are commonly bought and as durable as it is reasonable to expect having regard to any description applied to them, the price (if relevant) and all the other relevant circumstances and any reference in this Act to unmerchantable goods shall be construed accordingly.

4   Where the seller sells goods in the course of a business and the buyer, expressly or by implication, makes known to the seller any particular purpose for which the goods are being bought, there is an implied condition that the goods supplied under the contract are reasonably fit for that purpose whether or not that is a purpose for which such goods are commonly supplied, except where the circumstances show that the buyer does not rely, or that it is unreasonable for him to rely, on the seller's skill or judgement.

5   An implied condition or warranty as to quality or fitness for a particular purpose may be annexed to a contract for sale by usage.

6   The foregoing provisions of this section apply to a sale by a person who in the course of a business is acting as agent for another as they apply to a sale by a principal in the course of a business, except where that other is not selling in the course of a business and either the buyer knows that fact or reasonable steps are taken to bring it to the notice of the buyer before the contract is made.

8.06   A summary of this part of the Act, taking into account recent case law, would be as follows:

14(1)   Normally there is no implied warranty either as to fitness for purpose or as to quality according to the 1980 Act. It does, however say that this exclusion is subject to the provisions of the Act. This reference to later provisions allows the first finding of the House of Lords (in the leading case on the matter – *Young and Marten v McManus Childs* [1969] 9 BLR 86) to co-exist with this initial statement (see par. 8.05). That finding was: 'Unless the circumstances of a particular case suffice to exclude it, there will be implied into a contract for the supply of work and materials, a term that the materials used will be of merchantable quality and a further term that the materials used will be reasonably fit for the purpose for which they are used.' The two separate requirements of quality (merchantable quality) and fitness for purpose are dealt with in sub-sections 14(2) and 14(4).

14(2)   Merchantable quality is required under this sub-section, and it is now generally felt that this requirement is absolute, and independent of any fault on the part of the buyer. It is necessary that the goods be bought from a seller who 'sells goods in the course of a business'. This means a seller who deals in goods of that description, whether he be a manufacturer or not. An examination of the goods which reveals defects which ought to have been seen, or the indication by the seller of defects in the goods, would defeat the implied warranty and protect the seller. However, latent defects may exist, and the seller would be responsible for the cost of replacement.

The position is different if the supplier is a Nominated Supplier under Clause 17. The notes to that clause at par. 17 set out the position with regard to nomination. Merchantable quality is defined in sub-section (3).

14(3)   'Goods are of merchantable quality if they are as fit for the purpose or purposes for which goods of that kind are commonly bought and as durable as is reasonable to expect having regard to any description applied to them, the price (if relevant) and all other relevant circumstances, and any reference in this Act to unmerchantable quality shall be construed accordingly.' This, it is submitted, is an unfortunate definition. By using the phrase 'as fit for the purpose for which goods of that kind are commonly bought' the distinction between quality as required in sub-section (2) and fitness for purpose as required under sub-section (4) is blurred. Various other definitions have been given over the years as to the meaning of 'merchantable'. Fundamentally, it means 'capable of being sold'. Subject to various factors such as price, purpose, etc, almost anything is merchantable to somebody at some price. As Lord Pearce said in the case of *Henry Kendall and Sons Ltd v William Lillico and Sons Ltd* [1969] 2 AC 31: 'Merchantability is concerned not with purpose but with quality.' It really establishes a much lower standard than 'fitness for purpose'. The *Young and Marten* case explains the distinction between quality and fitness (par. 8.06).

There is no necessity, as far as the requirement of merchantability is concerned, of the buyer relying on the seller's skill and judgement. This is required only as far as fitness for purpose is concerned.

14(4)   This sub-section deals with the more strict requirement of fitness for purpose, and it arises when the buyer relies on the skill and judgement of the seller. The various degrees of reliance, and the relative skill and knowledge of the buyer and seller are relevant, particularly in the building industry where the relationship of Architect, Contractor and Supplier brings into contact parties who all have specialised skill and knowledge, and where the particular skill and and knowledge required to satisfy the requirements of this sub-section might not be such as to negative the requirements.

Again the *Young and Marten* case is relevant. Reliance on a contractor's skill and judgement can readily be inferred where ordinary members of the public request that certain work should be done for them, but in this case the parties were all knowledgeable, and could not be said to be relying on the other's skill and judgement.

Latent defects are the responsibility of the seller. 'By getting the seller to undertake to use his skill and judgement the buyer gets under section 14(4) an assurance that the goods will be reasonably fit for his purpose and that covers not only defects which the seller ought to have detected but also defects which are latent in the sense that even the utmost skill and judgement on the part of the seller would not have detected them.' *Kendell v Lillico* [1969] 2 AC 31.

8.07   It will be seen, therefore, that there are two different requirements under the act – the first is 'fitness for purpose' or suitability, and the second is 'merchantability'. The distinction between these two descriptions is not always very clear. There is an example of the distinction in the *Young and Marten* case referred to in par. 8.06. This case dealt with a roofing sub-contractor who had been instructed to supply and fix a particular type of roof-tile. The work was done apparently satisfactorily, but there were latent defects in the tiles, and the tiles had to be replaced. It was held that in such a circumstance, there was no implied warranty as to fitness for purpose, but that there was an implied warranty as to merchantability. The Contractor had contended that the tiles were chosen by the Employer and that since there was only one manufacturer, no implied warranty as to fitness or quality existed. But the Contractor was, nevertheless, held liable because 'there were good reasons for implying such a warranty if it were not excluded by the terms of the contract, because the Employer would generally have no redress if he could not recover damages from the Contractor.'

This is the concept of the chain of liability. The judgement goes on to say: 'But if the Employer can recover damages the Contractor will not generally have to bear the loss; he will have bought the defective material from a seller who will be liable under Section 14(2) of the Sale of Goods Act because the material was not of merchantable quality. And if that seller had in turn bought from somebody else there will again be liability so that there will be a chain of liability from the Employer who suffers the damage back to the author of the defect.'

Lord Reid, in his judgement in *Young and Marten*, said: 'The loss was not caused by the tiles being unsuitable for the contract purpose; it was caused by the tiles which were supplied being of defective quality.' In other words, there was no warranty implied that the goods would be suitable for that par ticular job (because the Employer had relied on his own skill and judgement, and not that of the sub-contractor) but that there was an implied warranty that the materials would be of good quality.

8.08   It was pointed out above that the Sale of Goods Act 1893, and the Sale of Goods and Supply of Service Act 1980 referred to 'contracts for the sale of goods'. *The Young and Marten* case establishes that the same requirements of these Acts apply to contracts for 'work and materials'. The commentary in 9 BLR 80 says: 'As the present case makes clear, in the absence of some effective term excluding the implication, similar terms are to be implied in contracts for work and materials.' In his judgement in the same case Lord Upjohn said with regard to the two sorts of contract: 'It would be most unsatisfactory, illogical and indeed a severe blow to any idea of a coherent system of common law, if the existence of an implied obligation depended upon such a distinction.' He adds: 'So I cannot see any logical distinction between the obligations which ought in general to be implied with regard to quality and fitness between a sale of goods and a contract for work and materials.'

8.09   At the same time as the *Young and Marten* case, a similar question was raised in *Gloucestershire CC v Richardson* [1969] 9 BLR 86. Whereas in *Young and Marten* the items being supplied were roof tiles, in the *Gloucestershire* case the items were precast concrete columns. The House of Lords held in this second case (9 BLR 85) that the Contractor was in a different position.

'The situation thus created was one of a special and complex character, differing greatly from that which arose in *Young and Marten v McManus Childs Ltd*. There the Employer nominated a brand article to be supplied by the manufacturer with no limitation on the Contractor's freedom to contract with the manufacturer as he thought fit. The Contractor could, and it would be the expectation that he would, or at least it would be his responsibility if he did not, deal with the manufacturer on terms attracting the normal conditions or warranties as to quality or fitness.

But here the design, materials, specification, quality and price were fixed between the Employer and the sub-supplier without any reference to the Contractor; and so far from being expected to secure conditions or warranties from the sub-supplier, he had imposed upon him special conditions which severely restricted the extent of remedy. Moreover as reference to the main contract shows, he had no right to object to the nominated supplier though by contrast, the contract does provide a right to object to a nominated sub-contractor if the latter does not agree to indemnify him against his liability under the contract.'

The reference in this last sentence of the judgement to the absence of any form of objection to a nominated supplier refers to the JCT/RIBA 1957 form. The GDLA form at Clause 17 provides for such a right, but this is not yet incorporated into the RIAI form.

8.10   Both the *Young and Marten* and the *Gloucestershire* cases are referred to extensively in the well-known case of *Norta Wallpapers (Ireland) Ltd v John Sisk (Dublin) Ltd* 14 BLR 49. This case, which is discussed in detail in the notes to Clause 16 (Nominated Sub-Contractors) and Clause 37 (Collateral Warranties) deals primarily with the questions that arose when defects are discovered in a sub-contractor's design. It was held, much as in the Gloucestershire case, that as the Contractor had no opportunity to examine or comment on the sub-contractor's design , that he should have no liability. The case should be read, however in relation to Clause 8, as it gives the views of the High Court and the Supreme Court on the problems raised by 'sale of goods' and 'contracts for work and materials'.The case also refers to Section 10, Table 14(4) of the Sale of Goods and Supply of Services Act 1980 (formerly Section 14 of the Sale of Goods Act 1893), and holds that it would be necessary for the Employer to prove that he had relied on the 'skill and judgement' of the Contractor in regard to the sub-contractor's design work, in much the same way as a buyer would have to prove in relation to a sale of goods.

8.11   An architect is responsible for the suitability of any material which he selects and he cannot rely on representations made or guarantees given by the manufacturers of any product. This was so held in *Sealand of the Pacific v McHaffie* [1974] 2 BLR 74. The Architect must make his own enquiries. In this regard, architects should always endeavour to use materials, where they are comparatively new and untried, which have obtained some recognised 'agrément' or 'mark'.

GDLA – Clause 8

8.12   The wording is slightly different to that of the RIAI form, but the differences are of no significance. It, perhaps, makes it clearer that the Employer pays all charges if any tests show that materials and workmanship conform to the Contract requirements.

SF 88

8.13   There is no specific clause in SF 88 dealing with the suitability of materials. The requirement in SF 88 Clause 1 that 'the Contractor shall carry out and complete the Works in a good and workmanlike manner and in accordance with the Contract Documents' obviously requires the Contractor to provide whatever materials are specified and for him to ensure that these materials are of the appropriate quality. The Defects Liability clause of SF 88 – Clause 7 – refers to materials which are not in accordance with the Contract, and which must be replaced. In general, the notes to RIAI Clause 8 can be taken as applying to the SF 88 Contract.

8.14   A   ARCHITECT'S RESPONSIBILITIES UNDER CLAUSE 8
             RIAI AND GDLA

        1   Obtain vouchers, if required, confirming the correctness of materials.

        2   Order any necessary tests of workmanship or materials.

        3   Adjust the Contract sum if required to allow for the cost of tests.

8.15   C   CONTRACTOR'S RESPONSIBILITIES UNDER CLAUSE 8
             RIAI AND GDLA

        1   Ensure the workmanship and materials conform to the Contract Documents.

        2   Supply any vouchers required by the Architect.

        3   Carry out, or arrange for, any tests ordered by the Architect.

8.16   CASES REFERRED TO

        Gloucestershire Co Council v Richardson
            [1969] 9 BLR 85   pars. 8.09, 8.10
        Henry Kendall and Sons Ltd v William Lillico and Sons Ltd
            [1969] 2 AC 31   par. 8.06
        Norta Wallpapers (Ireland) Ltd v John Sisk & Son (Dublin) Ltd
            [1978] 14 BLR 49   par. 8.10
        Sealand of the Pacific v McHaffie
            [1974] 2 BLR 74   par. 8.11
        Young and Marten v McManus Childs
            [1969] 9 BLR 86   pars. 8.06, 8.07, 8.08, 8.09, 8.10

RIAI – Clause 9

WORK TO BE OPENED UP

9.01 **The Contractor shall at the request of the Architect and within such times as the Architect shall name open for inspection any work covered up and should the Contractor refuse or neglect to comply with such request the Employer may employ other workmen to open up such work. If the said work had been covered up in contravention of an Architect's Instruction or if on being opened up it be found not in accordance with the Contract Documents or any Architect's Instruction the expenses of opening it and covering it up again, whether done by the Contractor or other such workmen shall be borne by or be recoverable from the Contractor or may be deducted from any money due or to become due to him. If the work had not been covered up in contravention of an Architect's Instruction and is found to be in accordance with the said Contract Documents or with an Architect's Instruction then the expenses aforesaid shall be borne by the Employer and added to the Contract Sum.**

Provided always that in the case of foundations or of any other urgent work so opened up and requiring immediate attention the Architect shall, within a reasonable time after receipt of notice from the Contractor that the work has been opened up, make the inspection or cause it to be made. At the expiration of such time if such inspection has not been made the Contractor may cover up the said work and shall not be required to open it up again for inspection except at the expense of the Employer.

This clause is an expanded version of Clause 2(d): 'the opening up for inspection of any work covered up'. The power to employ other workmen is also referred to in Clause 2. It can be seen that the principle that applied in Clause 8 is applied here: If the work is defective, the Contractor pays, if it is not the Employer pays.

Since an instruction to open up work is an 'Architect's Instruction' as defined in Clause 2, it may lead to a claim for delay and extension of time as provided for in Clause 30(f). The Architect must be reasonably satisfied that there is good reason to ask the Contractor to open up work already completed, or otherwise he may be costing the Employer considerable sums in claims both for unnecessary work and for delay. The general performance of the Contractor should be a guide to the Architect in deciding whether or not to act under this clause. He will also be helped considerably by observant site staff.

9.02 The Architect is empowered under Clause 2(e) to order the 're-execution' of the works, where the original work did not conform with the Contract Documents or with an Architect's Instruction. The omission of this specific power from the JCT/RIBA forms has caused difficulty and has been the subject of judicial comment. In *Fairclough Buildings v Rhuddlan Borough Council* [1985] 30 BLR 26 the commentary states: 'There is a strong case for amending the JCT forms so as to confer on the Architect a power which is found in other standard forms requiring the investigation and rectification of defective work at the Contractor's expense, even though it may not entail the physical removal from the site of work not in accordance with the Contract.'

9.03 The references to 'time' in the second paragraph of Clause 9 could, it is suggested, be more precise. The Architect shall 'within a reasonable time, etc'. This next sentence refers to the 'exploration of such time'. Whether or not a thing is 'reasonable' is a source of much work for lawyers. It might be better if a specific period of working days were provided for instead.

GDLA Form – Clause 9

9.04 The wording of the GDLA form is very similar to that of the RIAI form. It contains, however, the reference to 'moneys due or to become due to him on foot of this or any other contract made between the Employer and the Contractor...' This right of 'Set-off' first appears in Clause 2(c) of the GDLA form and is dealt with in the notes at that point (par. 2.30).

SF 88

9.05 No reference to opening up.

9.06   A   ARCHITECT'S RESPONSIBILITIES UNDER RIAI AND GDLA

   1   Order work to be opened up if he is satisfied that there are good grounds for so doing.

   2   Inspect work 'opened up' within a reasonable time.

9.07   B   EMPLOYER'S RESPONSIBILITIES UNDER RIAI AND GDLA

   1   Open up work if instructed.

   2   Notify the Architect that foundations or other urgent work is available for inspection.

9.08   C   CONTRACTOR'S RESPONSIBILITIES UNDER RIAI AND GDLA

   1   Employ other workmen in case of the Contractor's default.

9.09   CASE REFERRED TO

   Farclough Building v Rhuddlan Borough Council
       [1985] 30 BLR 26   par. 9.02

RIAI – Clause 10

FOREMAN

10.01 **The Contractor shall constantly keep upon the Works a competent general Foreman and any instructions given to him by the Architect shall be deemed to be given to the Contractor in pursuance of Clause 2 of these Conditions.**

The number of site staff that any Contractor may provide will be governed by the size and complexity of the Contract, but in all contracts it is a requirement that the Contractor be represented by an 'agent' who is identifiable. In small contracts it may be the traditional 'foreman'. In the larger contracts there may be Site Agents, Site Engineers, and other personnel representing various aspects of the Contractor's operations.

It is important that the Architect establishes who is the person that represents the Contractor, in view of the last phrase of this clause, which states that 'instructions given to him ... shall be deemed to be given to the Contractor'. Architect's Instructions given under Clause 2 are valid if given to the appropriate site staff. This is made very clear in Clause 13 where reference is made to 'instructions given to the Contractor or his Foreman'.

It is understood from this clause that the Foreman must be competent to be in charge of the Works. In the ICE form, the person in charge is specifically required to have 'adequate knowledge of the operations to be carried out'.

While Architect's Instructions in the normal course may be given to the Foreman (or the Site Agent), formal notices which the Architect may issue under say, Clause 29 or 33, should always be delivered to the registered office of the Contractor.

GDLA – Clause 10

10.02 The GDLA form wording is almost identical to that of the RIAI form, but it recognises the fact that larger contracts may have a hierarchy of staff on site by referring specifically to a 'foreman or site agent'.

SF 88 – Clause 10

10.03 **The Contractor shall secure the proper execution of the Works and provide supervision at all times.**

This clause, to some extent, in the first phrase reflects what Clause 1 requires, i.e. 'shall carry out and complete the Works in a good and workmanlike manner'.

The second phrase referring to 'supervision at all times' confers on the Contractor the responsibility set out in RIAI and GDLA Clauses 10.

10.04   C   CONTRACTOR'S RESPONSIBILITY UNDER
RIAI AND GDLA (10) AND SF 88 (10)

1   Provide a competent person in charge of the Works.

RIAI and GDLA – Clause 11

ACCESS FOR ARCHITECTS TO WORKS

11.01 **The Architect and any person authorised by him shall at all reasonable times have access to the Works, the workshops of the Contractor, or other places where work is being prepared for the Contract.**

This clause is identical in both forms of contract. It might seem unnecessary for the contract to have to specify that the Architect be given stated right of access to the site, and to other designated places. However, a contractor is normally entitled to exclusive possession of the entire site in the absence of any express stipulation to the contrary, though he holds possession only by way of licence.

The Employer may at any time revoke the licence, though he will have to pay damages to the Contractor if the revocation is not justified. The possession of the licence means that persons coming on to the site must do so either by way of right under the Contract, or by permission of the Contractor. Not even the Employer has an unrestricted right of access. This was so held in *Nabarro v Cope and Co* [1938] 4 AER 565. A rather confusing case, *Hounslow LBC v Twickenham Garden Developments* [1971] Ch.233, seems to throw some doubt on the Contractor's exact position and while referred to in a number of other cases is now generally regarded as having being wrongly decided.

While there might be implied a right for the Architect to have access to the site, for he could hardly carry out his duties under the contract otherwise, most contracts of a construction nature identify this right, and in the case of the RIAI and GDLA Contracts, extend this right to the Contractor's workshops, or any other place where work is being prepared for the contract. This right of access would include the premises and workshops of nominated subcontractors and suppliers who on notice, would have imported the conditions of the main contract into their own agreements with the Contractor. The right of access is also extended to other contractors who would be required to enter on to the site to carry out work which the Contractor refuses to do (Clauses 2 and 9), and to artists and tradesmen (Clause 20 GDLA and Clause 32A RIAI).

11.02   The reason why the Contractor is given such exclusive possession of the site has mainly to do with working methods and with safety. The Contractor has the right to carry out the work in whatever manner he chooses, but he is responsible for the consequences of his actions on the site and for the safety of persons involved: 'I have already cited from *Clayton v Woodman and Sons Ltd* [1962] 1 WLR 585 the general proposition that an Architect has no right to instruct a builder how his work is to be done or the safety precautions to be taken.' (Lord Upjohn, *East Ham BC v Sunley* [1966] AC 406). This theme is discussed in pars. 11.03 and 11.04.

SF 88 – Clause 11

SITE SAFETY

11.03   **Site safety shall be the responsibility of the Contractor.**

This is the logical sequence in SF 88 to both RIAI and GDLA Clauses 11. While there is no mention of site safety in the other forms, it has been pointed out that one of the reasons why access to the site is restricted is because the operations, and therefore the safety of the operations, being carried out on the site are under the control of the Contractor.

Safety at work generally is controlled by the Safety, Health, and Welfare at Work Act 1989. While the Act is mainly concerned with the duties of employers, there is a section (no.11) which deals with those who design places of work. In sub-section 11(a) it says: 'It shall be the duty of any person who designs places of work to design them so that they are, so far as is reasonably practicable, safe and without risk to health.'

Section 8 of the same Act should also be noted as this deals with the duties of those who have control of places of work. While the reference, as far as building sites is concerned, must relate to the Contractor, it again emphasises the importance of the Architect making it clear that he is not involved in methods of work. The relevant section 8(2) reads:

> It shall be the duty of each person who has control, to any extent, of any place of work or any part of any place of work to which this section applies or of the means of access thereto or egress therefrom or of any article or substance in such place of work to take such measures as is reasonable for a person in his position to take to ensure, so far as is reasonably practicable, that the place of work, all means of access thereto, or egress therefrom available for use by persons using the place of work,

and any article or substance in the place of work or, as the case may be, provided for use therein, is or are safe and without risks to health.

The case of *AMF International Limited v Magnet Bowling* [1968] 2 AER 789 says of this aspect of the building operation: 'That case, in both courts further establishes that an Architect has no right to instruct a builder how his work is to be done or the safety precautions to be taken. It is the function and the right of the builder to carry out his own building operations as he thinks fit.'

11.04 Site safety was specifically addressed in the Health, Safety and Welfare at Work (Construction) Regulations – S.I.138 of 1995 issued under the Safety, Health and Welfare at Work Act 1989. Revised regulations are expected to be introduced in the last quarter of 2001. While not referred to in either the RIAI or GDLA contracts, this new legislation contains many provisions which affect the responsibilities of the Employer, the Contractor and the Architect, and the regulations apply to virtually every type of building operation, including maintenance. A detailed commentary on the legislation is given in Chapter 5 of the 3rd edition of Building and the Law published by the RIAI, but it might be useful to give a summary of what is involved.

Site safety is, in effect, shared between the Employer (referred to in the safety legislation as the Client), the Architect or designer, and the Contractor. The Client has two main duties, firstly the appointment of project supervisors for both the design and the construction of any project, and secondly to compile a safety file. The project supervisor for the design stage is usually the Architect (or Engineer in a civil engineering project) and the project supervisor for the construction stage is usually the Contractor. The same person can act for both stages but there are usually two project supervisors and their combined duties are to take account of the general principles of prevention of accidents (S.I.44 of 1993), to prepare or update the safety file, to prepare a safety plan, to co-ordinate the work of others working on the project, to specify any particular visits which might exist (S.I.138 of 1995, Second Schedule) and to notify the Health and Safety Authority where necessary by way of a commencement notice.

The Safety plan referred to sets out the rules for the site and points out any potential dangers or hazards. It can be described as being the 'before' document. The Safety file, the 'after' document, contains all relevant information about the completed building. The Contractor, whether acting as a project supervisor or not, has a very wide range of responsibilities under the regulations in respect of any operation which might take place on the site. Recent or proposed developments in safety legislation and control make it necessary for Architects to consider the prudence of accepting appointments as Project Supervisor – Design Stage.

11.05   C   CONTRACTOR'S RESPONSIBILITY UNDER CLAUSE 11

    1   Provide access as required under the clause (RIAI and GDLA).

    2   Be responsible for site safety (SF 88).

11.06   CASES REFERRED TO

AMF International Limited v Magnet Bowling
    [1968] 2 AER 789   par. 11.03
Clayton v Woodman and Sons Ltd [1962] 1 WLR 585   par. 11.02
East Ham BC v Sunley [1966] AC 406   par. 11.02
Hounslow LBC v Twickenham Garden Developments
    [1971] Ch. 233   par. 11.01
Nabarro v Cope and Co [1983] 4 AER 565   par. 11.01

RIAI – Clause 12

CLERK OF WORKS

12.01 **The Employer shall be entitled at any stage of the Works to appoint a Clerk of Works whose duty shall be to act solely as Inspector under the direction of the Architect and the Contractor shall afford him every facility for the performance of that duty. The Contractor shall be notified before such appointment is made.**

No Clerk of Works shall be employed on the Works to whom the Contractor shall make objection for reasons which shall be considered sufficient by the Architect.

The Clerk of Works shall be paid by the Employer.

The primary duty of a Clerk of Works is to ensure that the work is carried out in strict accordance with the Contract Documents. He will be present on the site during all working hours, and his presence is intended to assist the Architect in the discharge of the Architect's duties of supervision and control of the work.

An architect is not, under the normal conditions of engagement, expected to provide constant inspection. 'Frequent or constant inspection of the work is not the responsibility of the Architect. Where such frequent or constant inspection is considered to be necessary, separate arrangements will be agreed between the Architect and the client.' (par. 1.07, RIAI CONDITIONS OF APPOINTMENT 1986 and par. 2.39)

In former years the word 'supervision' was used widely to describe the Architect's duties on site, but it is suggested that 'inspection' or even 'observation' is to be preferred. 'Supervision' implies an overall responsibility that is not appropriate to the Architect's appointment.

12.02 Apart from the primary duty referred to above in paragraph 1, the Clerk of Works will:

1 Condemn (subject to the Architect's later confirmation) work which does not conform with the requirements of the drawings or specification.

2   Keep a record of any work which is likely to be covered up, particularly in relation to items of a 'provisional' nature which will be required to be measured by the Quantity Surveyor.

3   Examine and agree day work sheets with regard to time and materials (see pars. 13.06 and 13.07).

4   Confirm any verbal instructions given to him by the Architect.

5   Report, in writing, on a weekly basis to the Architect.

While it will be seen from the above list of duties that the Clerk of Works has a very important role to fill, it should be remembered that his authority is limited and derives from the Architect. The Clerk of Works is generally appointed on the advice and recommendation of the Architect but he is paid by the Employer. He will take his instructions from the Architect but he is the servant of the Employer. While the Architect has to act impartially as between the Employer and the Contractor, the Clerk of Works is responsible only to the Employer.

12.03   The extent of the Clerk of Work's authority should be clearly understood from the outset. He has no power to give instructions. Only the Architect, as provided for in Clause 2, can issue what are defined in the Conditions as 'Instructions', and a Contractor who accepts directions from a Clerk of Works where his authority is not clearly set out, could find that he has no entitlement to extra payment for additional or varied works. It hardly seems necessary to state that a Clerk of Works cannot issue certificates, but this is what occurred in the case of *Mitchelstown Union v Doherty* (1897) 31 ILT 514. Needless to say, the certificate was held to be invalid.

12.04   Equally with regard to the method of carrying out the works, the Clerk of Works has no role. In the notes to Clause 2 (par. 2.41) it was pointed out that the Architect has no power to instruct the Contractor as to how, or in what manner, he should carry out the Works, and this applies also to the Clerk of Works. In *O'Donnell v Begley and Bord Telecom Éireann* [1987] ILRM 105, it was stated: 'It was not necessary for the Clerk of Works to be present when the work was being done as he simply conveys the direction and does not say how it is to be carried out.'

Often, though, an informal arrangement develops where Clerks of Works do give oral instructions even though these have no legal force, and the Architect may condone this practice. This type of arrangement can develop where the relationship on the site between the foreman and Clerk of Works is very constructive and helpful, but the Contractor should ensure that any such oral instructions are confirmed as provided for in Clause 13, otherwise he might lose his right to claim a variation.

It will be recalled that under the Clerks of Works' duties at a) above, reference was made to the condemning of work. There again, the Contractor must require the Architect to confirm such a course of action, as only the Architect by virtue of Clause 2(e) can authorise such action.

12.05 The employment of a Clerk of Works cannot relieve the Architect of the ultimate responsibility. An architect employed to inspect a project remains in the last resort personally responsible for seeing that the work is properly carried out and he cannot evade responsibility for matters which he should have seen to for himself by delegating them to the Clerk of Works. The various questions raised by the Architect's duty to inspect are considered in the notes to SF 88 Clause 3, which occurs in the section dealing with RIAI and GDLA Clause 2 (par. 2.38).

HUDSON, 11th edition, p.254, says: 'An Architect only visits a site at periodic intervals, so that the Clerks of Works may be in a position to see many things which the Architect would miss. Provided an Architect gives proper instructions to a Clerk of Works, it is submitted that it would be wrong to impose liability on an Architect for acts or omissions of the Clerk of Works in regard to matters which the Architect on his own weekly or other visits might not have reasonably seen for himself. In other words, the presence of a Clerk of Works who is not an employee of the Architect should not in principle either reduce or add to the Architect's personal responsibility.'

12.06 In larger contracts there has recently been a tendency to have staff with differing capabilities and responsibilities to those of the traditional Clerk of Works. These staff would normally be resident architects, and in such cases would occupy a different role. This development has spread from the world of engineering, where resident engineers have long been employed on large and difficult contracts. The ICE 6th edition form provides in great detail for this, and envisages four different levels of engineer's representative.

Resident architects are very often chosen from the Architect's staff, but even in that case are employed and paid by the Employer. When this is so he is held to be a servant of the Employer and not an independent professional like the Architect. He would, therefore, be in the same position as a Clerk of Works employed by the Employer.

12.07 It is vital, however, that the Contractor, Employer, and Architect are all very clear as to the duties, powers, and responsibilities of the resident Architect. It is possible, and quite proper for the Architect to arrange for the resident Architect to have the power to give instructions, and if this is communicated to the Contractor, then the Contractor would be bound by these instructions. It would be essential, in these circumstances, for the Architect to have clear written instructions presented to the resident Architect, with similar notification to the Contractor.

In the unusual event of the resident Architect being an employee, in the ordinary way, of the Architect, then the position changes, and the Architect would be fully responsible for all the actions of his own staff. The resident Architect in those circumstances would be required to be impartial in his dealings with the Contractor, just as the Architect is so required, whereas a resident Architect who is an employee of the Employer is not so bound and owes no such duty to the Contractor.

Finally, as was mentioned in the notes to SF 88 Clause 2, the employment of site staff does not relieve the Architect of any responsibility. The act of inspection can be delegated but the responsibility of inspection cannot.

GDLA – Clause 12

12.08   There are some significant differences in the GDLA form, as compared to the RIAI form.

Firstly, the persons whom the Employer is entitled to appoint are described as 'a Clerk or Clerks of Works and/or other supervisory representative(s)'. This provision is to enable the Employer to retain the services of, for instance, resident architects and engineers. While contractors invariably accept such appointments in contracts governed by the RIAI form, this provision removes any doubt as to the contractual standing of such staff.

Secondly, the provisions in the RIAI form that the Contractor shall be notified in advance of any Clerk of Works appointment, and that the Contractor has some rights of objection to a specific appointment, are not repeated in the GDLA form.

It has been pointed out in the introductory chapter on the standard forms that a considerable number of the differences that exist in the wording of the RIAI and GDLA forms reflect a tendency in the GDLA form to favour the Employer as compared to the comparable provisions in the RIAI form, and this is a good example.

SF 88

12.09 There is no provision in the short form for the employment of site staff. The reference in Clause 3, paragraph 5 to site inspections by the Architect are dealt with in the notes to SF 88, Clause 3 (par. 2.38).

12.10 A ARCHITECT'S RESPONSIBILITIES UNDER CLAUSE 12 RIAI AND GDLA

1 Recommend the appointment of a Clerk of Works (or others).

2 Direct the Clerk of Works as to his duties.

3 Notify the Contractor of any proposed appointment (not in GDLA).

4 Consider any objections from the Contractor to an appointment (not in GDLA).

12.11 B EMPLOYER'S RESPONSIBILITIES UNDER CLAUSE 12 RIAI AND GDLA

1 Appoint and pay the Clerk of Works (or others).

12.12 C CONTRACTOR'S RESPONSIBILITIES UNDER CLAUSE 12 RIAI AND GDLA

1 Afford facilities to the Clerk of Works (or others).

2 Consider the Architect's proposed appointment of a Clerk of Works (RIAI only).

12.13 CASES REFERRED TO

Mitchelstown Union v Doherty
    [1897] 31 ILT 514   par. 12.03
O'Donnell v Begley and Bord Telecom Éireann
    [1987] ILRM 105   par. 12.04

RIAI – Clause 13

ASCERTAINMENT OF PRICES FOR VARIATIONS

13.01   **No variation shall vitiate this Contract. Any oral instructions, directions or explanations given by the Architect upon the Works to the
Contractor or to his Foreman shall if involving a variation be confirmed in writing by the Contractor to the Architect within five
working days and if his dissent therefrom is not communicated by
the Architect to the Contractor in writing within a further five working days shall be deemed to be authorised in writing.**

A 'variation' is defined in Clause 2(a) as an instruction in regard to 'the
modification of the design, quality or quantity of the Works or the addition,
omission or substitution of any work'.

Clause 13 opens by stating that no variation shall vitiate the contract. Vitiate
means to render imperfect or faulty. It was pointed out earlier that contracts
cannot be varied once agreed upon (except, of course, by the joint agreement
of the parties to the contract) but the nature of the building process is such
that some change or other will inevitably occur and it is essential to provide
some mechanism to deal with these changes.

This clause, then, gives the Employer the right to order variations (through
the Architect) instead of relying on the agreement of the Contractor to the
proposed variations. The clause specifically authorises the foreman to accept
instructions, and these may or may not be variations. Furthermore, the
Architect would have no implied power to order variations unless the
Contract specifically conferred such power to him.

13.02   The position that results from the amount of work actually performed differing from that provided in the Bill of Quantities is a variation as provided for
in Clause 3, but only if the Bill of Quantities is part of the Contract
Documents. The notes to Clause 2 deal generally with the problems which
may arise because a variation might not have been properly authorised, or
because the variation in question was of an unforeseen nature. Clause 13, on
the other hand, deals with the various ways in which proper and foreseeable
variations are dealt with in relation to their effect on the Contract Sum. The
effect of variations of the time for completion of the Works is dealt with in
Clause 30(f).

The first paragraph of Clause 13 also deals with the procedure for ensuring that variations are properly recorded. It has been pointed out before (par. 2.08) that it is essential for the Architect to record all variations, and to ensure that any oral instructions are incorporated into the schedule of variations. Again the notes to Clause 2 deal with the importance of this area.

13.03 **All variations ordered or authorised by the Architect in writing or subsequently sanctioned by him in writing shall be measured and valued without undue delay by the Architect or Quantity Surveyor who shall give to the Contractor or his representative the opportunity to be present with him on the Works at the time and take such notes and measurements as the Contractor may require. The Contractor shall be supplied with a copy of the measured Bill of Variations on or before the issue of the Architect's certificate for payment in respect of such variations and the valuation thereof unless previously or otherwise agreed shall be made in accordance with the following rules:**

This paragraph requires any variation to be valued 'without undue delay'. The Contractor is entitled to prompt payment for variations properly authorised and carried out, and these payments should be included in the next certificate to be issued by the Architect. The requirement that the Contractor be allowed to be present and take notes when the Architect, or more likely the Quantity Surveyor, is valuing the variation is a sensible provision which should help to eliminate any dispute at a later stage as to the value of the variation. The completion of the final account will be rendered much more simple if variations are measured, agreed, and valued as the Works proceed.

The remainder of Clause 13 provides the framework under which the variations are measured. There are three rules:

13.04 **(a) The rates in the Bill of Quantities referred to in section (i) of sub-clause 3(a) or the Schedule of Rates mentioned in section (ii) of sub-clause 3(a) of these Conditions whichever applies to this Contract shall determine the value of work carried out as a variation where such work is of a character similar to that to which the aforesaid rates apply and is carried out under similar conditions. The aforesaid rates shall also determine the value of any work omitted provided that if in the opinion of the Architect such an omission varies the conditions under which any remaining items of work are carried out such remaining items shall also be deemed to be varied and shall be valued under rule (b) hereof.**

Put simply, this first rule provides that any variation which results in work of the same kind as that included in the contract is ordered, then the rates included in the Contract Documents shall be the basis of calculating the extra or the omission. The rule also provides that if the omission 'in the opinion of the Architect' affects the remaining work to be carried out, then the second rule of measurement in the clause shall be used for valuing the remaining works.

It was mentioned earlier when discussing Clause 2, par. 4, that the variation in question must be one which would not vary the works in such a way as could not have been foreseen when the contract was entered into, otherwise a separate claim for 'loss and expense' could arise.

13.05   **(b) The said rates where variations are not of a similar character or executed under similar conditions as aforesaid shall be the basis of prices for the same so far as may be reasonable; failing which a fair valuation thereof shall be made based upon rates for similar work in the locality current at the time the variations are executed.**

This rule deals with work which is of a different kind to that originally included in the contract. The Agreed Rules of Measurement referred to in the notes to Clause 3 will make it easier to determine whether the work is or is not 'of a similar character' or is 'executed under similar conditions'. The Quantity Surveyor will know from experience how to calculate the prices for these variations. The second paragraph of this clause provided for the possibility of a separate agreement for valuing variations, and this provision would undoubtedly be invoked in cases where conditions were anticipated, or suspected, which might lead to work of such a nature as to justify departing from the standard rules.

'Similar' does not mean 'identical'. It is a matter of judgement for the Quantity Surveyor or Architect as to whether or not the variation can be so described. The Architect, of course, accepts the responsibility for the decision even if his decision is founded on the judgement of the Quantity Surveyor. If the Contractor disagrees with the decision of the Architect he can invoke Clause 38 and seek arbitration on the matter, and if the amount in dispute is sufficiently large he may well do so. Arbitration on any matter would not be permitted under Clause 38 until after Practical Completion of the Works, but there are exceptions, and any reference to arbitration which would deal with certificates may be opened during the course of the Works.

13.06   **(c) Where in the opinion of the Architect variations cannot properly be measured and valued in the manner set out in rule (a) or rule (b) the Contractor shall be allowed daywork prices:**

i)   at the rates in any in the Bill of Quantities referred to in Section (i) of sub-clause 3(a) or in the Schedule of Rates referred to in Section (ii) of sub-clause 3(b) as the case may be; or

ii) where no such rates have been inserted at the rates in the Schedule of Daywork Charges agreed between the Society of Chartered Surveyors in the Republic of Ireland and the Construction Industry Federation and approved by the Royal Institute of the Architects of Ireland and current at the time the work is carried out; or

iii) where the work has been executed by a member of a sub-contracting trade at the rates agreed between the said Society and the appropriate body representing the sub-contracting trade or, where no such rates have been agreed, at the rates set out in Section (i) of this rule.

Daywork prices means a method of pricing work by recording the hours spent on it by various tradesmen and their hourly wages, and recording also the quantities of any materials and the hours of any plant used. A Schedule of Daywork Charges is published from time to time by the Society of Chartered Surveyors in the Republic of Ireland and the Construction Industry Federation. The current schedule was published in May 1976 and has been approved by the Royal Institute of the Architects of Ireland. This schedule defines the various terms which are used with reference to labour, materials, machinery, haulage and plant, and in addition sets out the agreed percentages which may be added to the original costs to cover profit, overheads, etc. These percentages vary from 5% to 35% depending on the nature of the original cost.

The use of daywork prices tends to be viewed with disfavour by architects (and employers), and this is based on the difficulty of establishing the correct amounts, particularly in relation to hours worked. Clause 13 attempts to deal with this in the last paragraph of the clause (par. 13.07).

13.07   **Vouchers specifying the time for each day (and if required by the Architect the workmen's names) and the materials used shall be delivered for verification to the Architect or his authorised representative at or before the end of the week following that in which the work was executed.**

These vouchers are commonly referred to as 'daywork sheets'. In the notes to Clause 12 (at par. 12.02) reference was made to the Clerks of Works duties, and in particular to that of checking daywork sheets. The Clerk of Works should agree these with the Contractor and should then sign and submit them to the Architect. It would be a condition precedent to payment for dayworks that the amounts be agreed in advance. It is not for the Clerk of Works to adjudicate as to whether or not a particular item is a variation; he is merely to ensure the accurate recording of the work carried out.

GDLA – Clause 13

13.08   The wording of the GDLA form is very similar to that of the RIAI form. The differences arc as follows:

1   The first paragraph refers to a site agent as well as to a foreman. This is consistent with the reference to a site agent in GDLA Clause 10.

2   Not only the Contractor but also the Employer if he so requests and the relevant Government Department if it so requests, shall be supplied with a copy of the Bill of Variations referred to in paragraph two.

3   In rule (b) at par. 13.05 the rates to be used shall be those current at the Designated Date. In the RIAI form the rates shall be those current at the time the variations are executed. There could be an advantage to the Employer in the GDLA rule, particularly in a contract which might be of some duration during a period of significant inflation. Both the RIAI and GDLA forms of contract at Clause 36(g) and (h) respectively, specifically exclude daywork charges from the provisions that deal with the price and wage variation clauses.

Clause 13 of the GDLA form then goes on in sub-clauses (d) and (e) to deal with the matters set out in Clause 14 of the RIAI form, that is, omissions. This is one of the occasions where the numbering of the two forms differs. The notes to Clause 14 (RIAI) should be consulted.

SF 88

13.09   There is no provision in the short form for variations, and therefore, no method of valuing them. It would however be prudent for the Architect to obtain from the Contractor a list of basic rates and daywork charges to enable any variations which do arise to be dealt with as simply as possible.

It has been mentioned before that where no express provision is included in a contract for a particular event, the Courts will import into the contract the normal custom and usage of the business in question.

13.10   A   ARCHITECT'S RESPONSIBILITIES UNDER CLAUSE 13
                RIAI AND GDLA

       1   Acknowledge and confirm (if appropriate) the Contractor's confirmation of a variation within five working days.

       2   Measure and value (or instruct the Quantity Surveyor) without undue delay any variation.

       3   Advise the Contractor if measuring and valuing is being undertaken.

       4   Provide the Contractor (and in the case of GDLA, the Employer and the relevant Government Department if they request) with a copy of the Bill of Variations.

       5   Decide under rule (a) if omissions vary subsequent works.

       6   Decide if daywork prices are appropriate, rule (b).

       7   Check on the providing of 'daywork sheets'.

       8   Ascertain after consultation with the Employer a reasonable sum for omitted work (GDLA only).

       9   Ascertain 10% of the value of the omitted work provided the credit exceeds 20% of the Contract Sum (GDLA only).

13.11   B   EMPLOYER'S RESPONSIBILITIES UNDER CLAUSE 13 GDLA

       1   Request a copy of the Bill of Variations if appropriate.

       2   Consult with the Architect in respect of the value of omissions.

13.12   C   CONTRACTOR'S RESPONSIBILITIES UNDER CLAUSE 13
                RIAI AND GDLA

       1   Confirm any variation within five working days.

       2   Attend at measuring and valuing, and take any necessary notes.

       3   Provide daywork sheets as required.

RIAI – Clause 14

Note: Clause 14 in the RIAI and GDLA forms deals with different subjects

OMISSIONS

14.01 **(a) Where a variation by way of omission is, as compared with the Works included in the Contract, of a character so extensive that in the opinion of the Architect the Contractor has sustained a loss by reason of, prior to the notification to him of such variation, having properly incurred expenses which in consequence of the variation have become wholly or in part unnecessary there shall be added to the Contract Sum a sum to be ascertained by the Architect as being in all the circumstances reasonable compensation for such loss.**

This sub-clause is, to some extent, derived from the provisions of Clause 2, firstly at sub-clause (a) and secondly at paragraph four. These references deal with, amongst other things, omissions and unforeseen expense.

It can readily be envisaged that a contractor might have ordered materials, or entered into employment contracts, or refused other work in anticipation of carrying out the Works that are now being omitted. The amount which he will be paid as recompense for the omitted work will be decided on a *quantum meruit* basis which means literally 'as much as he has earned or deserves'. The Contractor will have to provide evidence of the expense incurred and the Quantity Surveyor will have to advise on the reasonableness, or otherwise, of the sums claimed.

The Employer is not entitled to omit work, and then have it performed by another contractor, or by a sub-contractor. This, oddly enough, is specifically allowed in JCT/RIBA 80 at Clause 13.1.3, but the use of this provision must, it is suggested, lead to problems with the Contractor. If the Employer attempts to omit work under the RIAI or GDLA forms, he is in breach of contract and liable for damages. If the breach of contract is considered vital, the injured party may repudiate the contract as well as claiming damages.

The prohibition on the Employer in omitting work and having it performed by others is confirmed in *Carr v JA Berriman Pty Ltd* [1953] 27 ALJR 273, and in *Commissioner for Main Roads v Reed and Stuart Limited* [1974] 48 ALJR 461. The Architect is not required, however, to give extra work to the main contractor although it would be very unusual and could lead to claims for extras and delays if a second contractor were employed on the site at the same time as the original contractor.

14.02   **(b) if through variations and omissions the final measurement shows a credit on the Contract Sum the Contractor shall be entitled to an allowance of 10% of that credit. Adjustments arising from P.C. Sums, Provisional Sums, Provisional Work, Contingency Sums or any additions or deductions permitted under Clause 36 shall not be taken into account in arriving at the credit on which the allowance is based.**

This sub-clause must obviously be taken in conjunction with sub-clause (a). The provision that the Contractor be entitled to an allowance of 10% on omitted work must take account, of any payments made on a *quantum meruit* basis under sub-clause (a).

The purpose behind sub-clause (b) is to compensate the Contractor for the loss of anticipated profit and for under-productive use of overheads as a result of reduced workload.

Any provision in the Contract that clearly anticipated a possible credit is excluded from the requirement to pay a 10% allowance. This is why P.C. Sums, Provisional Sums, Provisional Work, Contingency Sums or any deductions under the wages and prices variation clause (36) are specifically excluded.

GDLA Form – Clause 13(d) and (e)

14.03   These sub-clauses are the equivalent of Clause 14 in the RIAI form. The provisions are largely similar, but two differences exist:

1   When the Architect at sub-clause (d) is ascertaining the reasonable compensation for an omission he must consult with the Employer.

2   The 10% credit allowance on omitted work is payable only if the overall credit on the Contract Sum exceeds 20% (sub clause [e]). The reasoning here seems to be that a contractor should be compensated for loss due to omitted work only if the size of the omissions is significant and the figure of 20%, though presumably arbitrary, was seen to be appropriate.

SF 88

14.04   There is no provision in the short form for dealing with omissions. But see
the notes to SF 88 under Clause 13.

14.05   A   ARCHITECT'S RESPONSIBILITIES UNDER CLAUSE 14
RIAI AND CLAUSE 13(D) AND (E) GDLA

1   Ascertain a reasonable sum for omitted work (in GDLA after consultation with the Employer).

2   Ascertain 10% value of omitted work.

14.06   CASES REFERRED TO

Carr v JA Berriman Pty Ltd
    [1953] 27 ALJR 273   par. 14.01
Commissioner for Main Roads v Reed and Stuart Ltd
    [1974] 48 ALJR 461   par. 14.01

GDLA – Clause 14

Note: Clause 14 in the RIAI and GDLA forms deals with different subjects

VESTING OF MATERIALS AND PLANT

14.07 **(a) All materials, goods, plant, tools and equipment owned by the Contractor or by any company in which the Contractor has a controlling interest shall when brought on to the site immediately be deemed to be the property of the Employer and the Contractor shall not remove the same or any part thereof without the consent in writing of the Architect, which consent shall not be unreasonably withheld. But the Employer will permit the Contractor the exclusive use of all such materials, goods, plant, tools and equipment in and for the completion of the Works until the happening of any event which gives the right to the Employer to exclude the Contractor from the site and proceed with the completion of the Works.**

(b) Upon the removal of any such materials, goods, plant, tools and equipment with consent as aforesaid the same shall be deemed to revest in and become the property of the Contractor. Upon final completion of the Works the said plant, tools, equipment and all surplus materials and goods shall be removed by the Contractor from the site and upon such removal shall be deemed to revest in and become the property of the Contractor. If the Contractor fails to remove any of said plant, tools and equipment and any such surplus materials and goods within such reasonable time after final completion of the Works as may be allowed by the Architect then the Employer may sell the same and after deducting from the balance the costs and charges of and in connection with such sale shall pay the balance (if any) to the Contractor.

The purpose of this clause is, in essence, to protect the Employer in the event of the bankruptcy of the Contractor. The 'event' referred to in sub-clause 14(a) is the determination of the employment of the Contractor by the Employer, and this will mainly be as a result of bankruptcy, although there are six other reasons (four in the RIAI form) why the Contract might be determined. The clause does not occur in the RIAI form, though reference is made in Clause 33(a) of the RIAI form to the Employer's right to a lien on plant and materials in the case of the determination of the employment of the Contractor, and at Clause 33(d) to the Employer's rights in protecting the site. (Lien is defined and discussed in the notes to RIAI Clause 33.)

The ownership of materials intended for use in the Works is also dealt with in Clause 35, both RIAI and GDLA. The property in materials which have been incorporated into the Works is clearly passed to the Employer. This is an old common law rule expressed by the phrase *quicquid plantatur solo, solo cedit*. i.e. whatever is fixed to the soil, belongs to the soil. Once the materials are fixed in the building works, they become the absolute property of the Employer, whether certified for payment or not. 'Materials worked by one into the property of another become part of that property. This is equally true whether it be fixed or movable property. Bricks built into a wall become part of the house, thread stitched into a coat which is under repair, or planks and nails and pitch worked into a ship under repair, become part of that coat or that ship.' (*Appleby v Meyers* [1867] 14 LT 549)

Even where a contract stated that materials would remain the property of the Contractor until paid for, the general rule prevailed and the court held that the materials fixed into the Works were the property of the Employer (*Re Yorkshire Joinery Co Ltd* (in liquidation) [1967] 111 S.J.701).

14.08　The common law also held, however, that materials which were brought onto the site but not yet fixed or attached to the works would remain the property of the Contractor, unless there was a specific agreement between the Contractor and the Employer to the contrary. Clause 14 provides this specific agreement. The position with regard to ownership of plant was exactly the same as that of unfixed materials, with the possible exception of 'attached' plant such as scaffolding where the ownership of the plant might pass to the Employer until the works are complete, or the plant is no longer required. Again, Clause 14(a) deals with this, and clearly passes or 'vests' ownership in the Employer.

The absence of any such clause from the RIAI form, it is suggested, reflects the different balance as between the Employer and the Contractor which occurs in the two forms of contract, and which is referred to in the Introduction.

14.09　HUDSON, 11th edition, at p.1,226 sums up the present position and says: 'The leading cases of *Brown and Bateman* [1867] LR 2CP 272 leave little doubt that the courts will give effect to the prime purpose of vesting clauses, namely, the provision of security for the due completion of the works, which may entail defeating the claims of third parties whether made through the Employer or the builder, at least until completion of the work.'

The sub-clauses (a) and (b) also ensure that the normal operations and procedure that occurs in the building process is protected. At various stages plant is no longer required and should be removed, possible surplus materials referred to in sub-clause (b) might be removed at an early stage, and so on. The Architect can permit the Contractor to manage the Contract in the normal way by agreeing in writing to such removals, but the provisions of Clause 33(a) override any such permission by the Architect where a determination occurs.

In the notes to Clause 35 (par. 35.06), there is a more detailed discussion with regard to ownership, and in particular to the position as far as retention of title is concerned.

The other provisions of these sub-clauses are quite straightforward and need no further commentary.

14.10 **(c) The Employer shall not at any time be liable for loss of or damage to any of the said material, goods, plant, tools and equipment nor for their maintenance operation or safeguarding.**

It would be prudent for the Architect to notify the Employer's insurers of any circumstance that led to the exclusion of the Contractor from the site, so as to ensure that the provisions of sub-clause (c) are not endangered or rendered invalid.

14.11 **(d) The operation of sub-clauses (a) to (c) of this Clause shall not be deemed to imply any approval by the Architect of the materials or goods or other matters referred to therein nor shall it prevent the rejection of such materials or goods at any time by the Architect.**

This sub-clause appears to be an over-cautious disclaimer in view of the very specific powers given to the Architect under Clause 2 and Clause 8 with regard to materials.

14.12 A ARCHITECT'S RESPONSIBILITIES UNDER CLAUSE 14 GDLA

1 Give consent, if appropriate, to the removal of materials, etc.

2 Decide on the time to be allowed to the Contractor to remove plant, etc, after completion.

14.13   B   EMPLOYER'S RESPONSIBILITIES UNDER CLAUSE 14 GDLA

    1   Permit the Contractor exclusive use of materials, plant, etc, which are under 'lien'

    2   Sell any materials, plant, etc, which are not removed after completion.

14.14   C   CONTRACTOR'S RESPONSIBILITIES UNDER CLAUSE 14 GDLA

    1   Keep all materials, plant, etc, on site until approval is obtained for removal.

    2   Remove all surplus materials, plant, etc, on completion.

14.15   CASES REFERRED TO

Appleby v Meyers [1867] 14 LT 549	par. 14.07
Brown v Bateman [1867] LR 2CP 272	par. 14.09
re Yorkshire Joinery Co Ltd (in liquidation) [1967] 111 SJ 701	par. 14.07

RIAI – Clause 15

ASSIGNMENT OR SUB-LETTING

15.01 **Neither the Employer nor the Contractor shall without the written consent of the other assign this contract. The Contractor shall not without the written consent of the Architect sub-let any portion of the Works.**

The clause has been altered in the 1996 edition of the contract form. The previous form restricted the right of the Contractor to assign, but did not mention the Employer. This clause deals with two separate aspects of Contract Law, i.e. assignment and sub-letting, which shall be dealt with in turn.

Every contract such as the normal building contract imposes on one of the parties both a 'benefit' and a 'burden'. A person who is entitled to the benefit of a contract can assign, or transfer, that benefit to a third party. In the case of the building contract, the benefit of the Contract to the Contractor is the Contract Sum. In Contract Law, it would not be necessary for the Contractor to either give notice to, or receive the consent of the Employer, if he wished to assign this benefit. A Contractor might wish to assign to, say, a bank his right to contract payments and in the absence of any prohibition, he would have an absolute right to do this. The ICE CONTRACT at Clause 3 specifically prohibits the Contractor from assigning 'any benefit to or interest therein'. Abrahamson, at p.34, questions the legal validity of any such prohibition.

The position with regard to the 'burden' of the contract is almost the direct opposite. The burden of the building contract is the Contractor's obligation to 'carry out and complete the works' (Clause 2). The reference in the RIAI form to assignment would primarily refer to the burden of the Contract. It is thought that the Contractor would not be entitled to assign this burden, and allow another contractor to take over, even if there was no specific prohibition, and there are very good reasons for this. The Contractor, in almost any building contract, will have been chosen by the Architect (possibly from a selected number of tenderers) because of his suitability and experience of the kind of work involved. A right of assignment would negative the skill and knowledge of the Architect in selecting a suitable contractor and would lead inevitably to difficulties.

Sometimes an assignment happens in fact, if not in law, when either of the parties to the contract is a limited company and where the shares in the company change hands, and new directors are elected. Neither of the parties to the contract can object to this, as the company is the contracting party and being a legal entity is unaffected by changes in shareholders or directors.

15.02   Only the parties to the Contract can agree to any assignment. In the case of *Tolhurst v Associated Portland Cement Manufacturers* [1903] 2 KB 660 it was stated: 'It is, I think, quite clear that neither at law nor in equity could the burden of a contract be shifted off the shoulders of a contractor onto those of another without the consent of the contractee. A debtor cannot relieve himself of his liability to his creditor by assigning the burden of the obligation to somebody else; this can only be brought about by the consent of all three and involves the release of the original debtor.'

Some of the commentaries on assignment refer to 'novation', which is a procedure whereby a new contract can be substituted for an existing one. This can be done only by agreement amongst all the parties concerned. Novation differs from assignment in that it involves a totally new contract, whereby in assignment the original contract remains in force.

15.03   The clause also refers to a 'sub-let'. This differs from assignment. A party to contract would normally be entitled to have the contract physically performed by someone else while remaining solely liable to the other party to the contract. This restriction on sub-letting is more honoured in the breach than in the observance. Large parts of most building contracts are now sub-let, very often without the knowledge, never mind the consent, of the Architect. On the other hand, most architects are aware of the fact that contractors sub-let, often on a wide scale, such items as demolition, form-work, blockwork, plastering, etc, and by raising no objection are assumed to have approved of the practice.

The sub-contractors who perform this work are known as 'domestic' sub-contractors, and have no contractual relationship whatsoever with the Employer. As far as the Employer is concerned, they do not exist, and the performance of their sub-contract is the total responsibility of the Contractor.

The position of sub-contracting generally is dealt with in the introduction to the notes to Clause 16.

GDLA – Clause 15

15.04 **The Contractor shall not without the written consent of the Employer assign this Contract or any share of interest therein nor shall he without the approval of the Architect sub-let any portion of the Works provided always that such consent or such approval shall not be withheld unreasonably.**

This clause is much the same as the 1988 RIAI version in that it does not attempt to restrict the right of the Employer to assign. The notes to par. 15.01 would still apply. It is somewhat surprising that the Employer is required to agree to an assignment if the Contractor can prove that his request is reasonable for, as has been stated before, the common law view of assignment, as far as the burden of the Contract is concerned, would seem to be that the Employer had an absolute right of refusal and would be entitled to insist on the carrying out of the Contract by the original party. There may, of course, be circumstances where it would benefit an employer to agree to an assignment and each case must be viewed on its merits. The Architect's approval, or otherwise, of any sub-letting is more straightforward contractually and should not cause any difficulty.

SF 88 – Clause 8

ASSIGNMENT

15.05 **Neither the Employer nor the Contractor shall, without the written consent of the other, assign this Contract.**

This was perhaps the best wording of the three clauses referring to assignment. It has validity and clarity, and has been used for the 1996 revision of the RIAI form.

15.06 A ARCHITECT'S RESPONSIBILITIES UNDER CLAUSE 15
RIAI AND GDLA

1 Consider any request from the Contractor for sub-letting.

15.07   B   EMPLOYER'S RESPONSIBILITY UNDER CLAUSE 15
        RIAI AND GDLA

  1   Consider any request from the Contractor for assignment.

15.08   C   CONTRACTOR'S RESPONSIBILITY UNDER CLAUSE 15
        RIAI AND GDLA

  1   Apply to the Employer for consent for assignment and to the Architect
      for assignment and sub-letting.

15.09   CASE REFERRED TO

Tolhurst v Associated Portland Cement Manufacturers
[1903] 2KB 660   par. 15.02

RIAI – Clause 16

16.01   **Where provision is made in the Contract Documents for work to be executed on site and for materials or goods to be supplied and fixed by a firm to be selected by the Architect such firm is hereby declared to be a Nominated Sub-Contractor employed by the Contractor.**

The concept of sub-contracting, or sub-letting, was generally examined in the notes to Clause 15, but it needs to be considered now in greater detail. The present position has become somewhat difficult and unsatisfactory, and this has arisen because of the concept of 'nomination', and for some other reasons, which are discussed below.

Up to, say, the middle of the nineteenth century the building contractor would have employed directly all those engaged in the building works. A building might be very large and extensive but it would be a basically simple and straightforward matter as far as the construction process would be concerned. The primary trades of mason, bricklayer, joiner, carpenter, plasterer and painter would deal with the majority of the works with such assistance from general labourers as might be required. But as buildings grew more complicated, and as central heating, plumbing, electrical works, and lifts came on the scene, the general contractor found that he could no longer carry out all these works directly, and that it was necessary for him to go to specialist firms who would deal with these parts of the works. Nowadays, the list of specialist firms has expanded to include sub-contractors who deal with piling, structural steel, precast concrete, special roofing and floors, curtain walling, air-conditioning, etc.

A further complication arises because many of these Nominated Sub-Contractors provide a considerable design input into their own specialist works, and this design responsibility has to be properly allocated.

In these notes to Clause 16 the use of the word Contractor means in all cases the main contractor. This latter description is not used in the main contract forms, although it does appear in the sub-contract forms.

16.02   The employment of these specialist firms as sub-contractors caused no difficulty as long as they were sub-contractors in the normal sense and where it was clearly understood that they had no contractual relationship with the Employer. However, contractual changes and developments in the law led to the rather involved position that exists today.

The most significant of these developments was the idea of nomination or selection of the sub-contractor by the Architect. This practice arose from the wish of the Architect to have a measure of control over the sub-contractors, who might be selected to carry out parts of the Works particularly in regard to quality of work and the cost of the work. The Architect would usually require the Contractor to obtain prices from a number of sub-contractors who would be selected by the Architect, and if a satisfactory price were received, the particular sub-contractor would be nominated by the Architect and the Contractor would be instructed to enter into a contract with the selected sub-contractor.

But a difficulty arises if this Nominated Sub-Contractor defaults in any way. The Employer has no privity of contract with the sub-contractor, that is he has no contractual relationship with him, so it is essential that the Employer be protected if such a default occurs, and that the Employer be entitled to recover any loss from the Contractor. This should cause no problem as far as the Contractor is concerned, because in the first place the Contractor is entitled to object to any nomination, and secondly, he can recover any loss which he suffers against the Employer, from the sub-contractor. Contracts which are not very clear on these points could result in the situation where the Employer could not recover his loss from either the Contractor, or the sub-contractor.

16.03   However, nomination of a sub-contractor was not viewed as clearly by the Courts as the writers of the contracts would like in as far as establishing that no privity of contract existed. The reasons for this are well advanced by HUDSON in the 10th edition (p.757): 'It is widely thought, particularly by lawyers and, it would seem, the draughtsmen of building contracts, that the system of nomination of specialists springs from the employer's desire or need to control the *quality* of specialist work. In fact this is frequently not the case and, on analysis, the system really springs from the employer's need to secure a *competitive price* for such work as is not normally carried out by main contractors or is outside the more familiar building processes ... By removing such unusual work from the main contractor's area of pricing, in the form of a P.C. or provisional sum (see Clauses 18 and 19 for notes on these) common to all the tendering main contractors and by retaining the right to select, the employer retains control over the price competition for the sub-contracted work, which he would lose if the right to select the specialist in question were to be exercised by the main contractor. It is vital to an understanding of the system of nomination to appreciate this, and it seems likely that many of the modern decisions, and some contractual provisions which have had the effect of modifying the no privety principle, have been based on the assumption that control over the personality, rather than the price of the sub-contractor is the principal object of the system. The true view in the majority of cases is that control over the personality is only necessary machinery in order to achieve the principal object, which is control over the price.'

Over the years, three principal areas of dispute arose. The first of these is now only of historical interest, but is worth setting out, because of numerous references to it in text books and commentaries:

16.04   (1) Previous versions of the RIAI contract, up to and including the 1977 Edition contained a provision that allowed the Contractor to claim for an extension of time if delayed by a Nominated Sub-Contractor – a delay which the Contractor should 'have taken all practicable steps to avoid or reduce'. This led to all sorts of anomalies such as the argument advanced in the case of *Westminster City Council v J Jarvis and Sons Ltd* [1971] 7 BLR 64. The sub-contractor involved in this case admitted, indeed, claimed that they had been guilty of 'delay on their part' because if the court accepted this position, then the Contractor would be entitled to claim for delay on the main contract, and in turn the sub-contractor would not have to compensate the Contractor for any damages for delay which the Contractor would have to pay to the Employer.

This sub-clause was eliminated in the RIAI 1988 Edition, and it does not appear in the GDLA form. Surprisingly, it still appears in the JCT/RIBA forms and is the ongoing source of numerous disputes. Any delay now caused by a nominated sub-contractor has to be absorbed and accepted by the Contractor. However, if the Contractor has to pay damages to the Employer, he can recover these sums from the sub-contractor. The standard sub-contract form for use with both the RIAI and GDLA form contains this specific provision. The details of this sub-contract form are dealt with in a later section of the notes to this clause (pars. 16.10 and 16.11).

16.05   (2) The next problem area of dispute arose in connection with re-nomination. It often happened that a Nominated Sub-Contractor would default for one reason or another (very often as a result of bankruptcy) and the question arose as to what procedure should be followed as far as obtaining a replacement is concerned, and equally important, who would bear any resultant increase in cost, and what would be the position if any extension of time were claimed. The provisions of sub-clause 16(e) set out the contract arrangements (see par. 16.16). The overall position was unclear until the case of *Bickerton v Northwest Metropolitan Hospital Board* [1970] 1 AER 1039, both parties to the contract claiming that responsibility lay with the other party. In this case, a Nominated Sub-Contractor went into voluntary liquidation before starting work, and the liquidator refused to carry out the sub-contract. Under the JCT/RIBA form of the time (and in the old wording of the RIAI 1977 Edition) the contract stated that the Employer 'may' re-nominate. In the event, the main contractor carried out the work directly, and claimed that the Employer was bound to re-nominate and was also liable for any extra costs. The Employer contended that the sub-contract was no concern of his, and that the Contractor was required to make whatever arrangements were necessary, but that no extra cost would be allowed. The House of Lords held that there was a duty to re-nominate. 'The Main Contractor has neither the right nor the duty to do prime cost work himself when the nominated sub-contractor drops out, any more than he had before the sub-contractor was nominated', per Lord Reid. The Lords looked at the wording of the clause referring to prime cost sums (Clause 27(a) in the JCT / RIBA form) which said that 'such P.C. sums shall be expended in favour of such persons as the Architect shall instruct', and held that this wording implied a duty on the Architect to re-nominate in case of default.

A previous Northern Ireland case – *Reilly Ltd v City of Belfast* [1970] NI 68 – was overruled. In that case the Northern Ireland Court of Appeal held that the Contractor had to bear the extra cost involved in the employment of a second sub-contractor, and also that the Employer had no duty to renominate as this duty was the responsibility of the Contractor. It can be taken, however, that the *Bickerton* decision is now the accepted law in Ireland and that, therefore:

1   Any extra cost arising from the necessity to nominate a second sub-contractor falls on the Employer.

2   It is the duty of the Employer to re-nominate the second sub-contractor.

16.06   The *Bickerton* case, however, did not decide another important matter, which was the question of any delay that might be involved in any re-nomination. It can readily be seen that if a sub-contractor defaults at a late stage in a contract, there might very well be delays caused to the Contractor, and it needed to be decided as to where the responsibility lay for any such delay. It will be recalled that at (1) above it was pointed out that delay on the part of a Nominated Sub Contractor is still a ground in the JCT/RIBA forms for an extension of time by the Contractor, whereas there is no such entitlement in the RIAI or GDLA forms. However, this difference does not affect the consequences of the leading case which deals with time delays. This is the case of *Percy Bilton Ltd v Greater London Council* [1982] 20 BLR 1.

In this case, Bilton (the Contractor) terminated the employment of a sub-contractor and requested a re-nomination. This was done, but lengthy delays inevitably ensued and the Contractor sought an extension of time. This was partially granted by the Architect but the Contractor was not satisfied with the extent of the extension granted and the Contractor commenced proceedings. The House of Lords held, in effect:

1 Any delay caused by the Employer would entitle the Contractor to an extension of time. The re-nomination must be made in a 'reasonable time' and the House held that this had not been done, and that an extension was due under Clause 23(b) of the 1963 JCT/RIBA form. This is the same as Clause 30(g) of both the RIAI and GDLA forms and allows for an extension of time where 'the Contractor has not received in due time necessary instructions from the Architect for which he has specifically applied in writing'.

2 Any delay caused by the fact of the nomination itself was the responsibility of the Contractor, and no extension of time would be due for this. The House held that the general rule was that the Contractor is bound to complete the Works by the date for completion stated in the contract. If he fails to do so he will be liable for liquidated damages to the Employer see Clause 29. Withdrawal of a Nominated Sub-Contractor is not caused by the fault of the Employer.

It has been pointed out by commentators that the *Bilton* case could result in an odd situation If the Contractor refuses to accept a second Nominated Sub-Contractor, as he is entitled to do under Clause 16(a), because of the second sub-contractor's inability to complete on time, an impasse occurs. It appears that the only resolution of this stalemate would be for the Employer and Contractor to agree a new arrangement which would vary the terms of the original contract.

16.07 This particular matter was dealt with in the case of *Fairclough Building Ltd v Rhuddlan Borough Council* [1985] 30 BLR 26. A Nominated Sub-Contractor stopped work, and the Contractor terminated the sub-contract. At this stage, the sub-contract works were late, and were also defective. The Architect instructed the Contractor to place an order with a second sub-contractor and the Contractor refused to accept the nomination on the grounds, firstly, that the new sub-contractor's programme was such that he would not complete until after the main contract completion date and, secondly, because the nomination did not include for remedial work which was necessary. The Court held that:

1 The Architect's instruction was invalid because the work could not be completed by the main contract date. The problem referred to in par. 16

was commented on: 'If no sub-contractor could be found to complete by the currently fixed date for completion the employer would be driven if he wanted the work done at all, to vary the main contract ... it seems to us possibly by an implied term that if the nomination were accepted, an appropriate extension would be granted.'

2   The re-nomination was also invalid because it did not include remedial works, and the Contractor was not obliged under the contract to do this work: 'I can find nothing anywhere to indicate that the principal contractor can ever have in any event either the right or the duty to do any of the prime cost work himself'.

16.08   (3) The third problem which arose as far as Nominated Sub-Contractors were concerned was in relation to the design input of a Nominated Sub-Contractor. It will be recalled that sub-contracting had tended to proliferate because of the increasing specialisation of the building process, and in a large number of areas, the sub-contractors themselves were providing a substantial design input. It can readily be appreciated that specialist areas such as lifts, air-conditioning, curtain walling, etc, were areas where the proposed sub-contractor would have a far greater experience of design and performance than would the Architect or any of the Consulting Engineers. The position then to be considered was that of the different parties if problems arose as to failure due to a sub-contractor's design. This problem was the basis of the well-known case of *Norta Wallpapers (Ireland) Ltd v John Sisk and Sons (Dublin) Ltd* [1983] 14 BLR 49.

The facts of the case were simple. Norta Wallpapers engaged Sisks to build a factory. Before Sisks had been appointed, a specialist roofing firm (Hoesch) had tendered for the design and supply of the roof, and when Sisks were appointed as Contractors, they were instructed to employ Hoesch as Nominated Sub-Contractors. Leaks developed in the roof, and the matter went to arbitration. The Arbitrator stated a case to the High Court (see the notes to Clause 38), which meant that the Arbitrator asked the High Court to decide matters of law which the Arbitrator felt should be so referred. The question which the High Court was asked was: Is the Contractor liable for the defective design of the Nominated Sub-Contractor, on the basis that there was an implied term in the contract that the materials and workmanship would be suitable for their purpose and that the Contractor was liable to the Employer for the defective workmanship and materials of his sub-contractor.

The High Court decided in favour of Sisks, and on appeal to the Supreme Court it was held:

1   The Contractor was liable to the Employer for the defective workmanship and materials of the Nominated Sub-Contractor. The Arbitrator had

previously held that 15% of the defects arose from defective workman-ship and materials. The case of *Brown v Norton* [1954] IR 34 was the basis of this decision.

2   There was no warranty implied in the main contract in respect of design by the Nominated Sub-Contractor and the Contractor was not liable for damage caused by the defective design on the part of the Nominated Sub-Contractor. The Arbitrator had held that 85% of the defects arose from defective design, and the Supreme Court's view was that since the sub-contractor, and his design, had been selected before the Contractor was appointed, that the Contractor had no option in the matter, and that the Employer had not relied on the 'skill and judgement' of the Contractor in approving the sub-contractor's design.

The Court quoted HUDSON, 10th edition, p.289: 'Unlike a warranty of good workmanship, a warranty that the work will answer the purpose for which it is intended is not implied in every contract for work. The essential element for the implication of such a term is that the Employer should be relying, to the knowledge of the Contractor, upon the Contractor's skill and judgement and not upon his own or those of his agents.'

The *Norta* case refers to the *Young and Marten Ltd v McManus Childs Ltd*, and the *Gloucestershire County Council v Richardson* cases mentioned in the notes to Clause 8. The case is worth reading in full as the judgements give a good review of the law in this area, and of some related problems which are not relevant to the contract clauses under discussion but which deal with other areas of building law.

The above notes are intended as a general review of the present law relating to nominated sub-contractors. Clause 16 goes on to say:

16.09   **(a) No Nominated Sub-contractor shall be employed upon or in con-nection with the Works against whom the Contractor shall make rea-sonable objection or (save where the Architect and Contractor shall otherwise agree) who will not enter into a sub-contract which shall indemnify the Contractor against the same obligations in respect of the sub-contract as those for which the Contractor is liable in respect of this contract.**

This sub-clause contains the justification for entitling the Employer to regard a default on the part of a sub-contractor as being entirely the responsibility of the Contractor, and that is the Contractor's right of objection to a sub-con-tractor. It may be that the Contractor is aware, either by direct experience or by repute, of difficulties which a particular sub-contractor might cause, and by being allowed to accept or reject the Architect's nomination, the Contractor thereby accepts responsibility for the sub-contractor's performance. The Contractor's objection, if any, must be 'reasonable'. The Architect would be very wise to examine most carefully any objection from a Contractor, for it would not benefit any party to the contract if the Contractor's objections were overruled and if they proved later to be well founded. *The Fairclough v Rhuddlan BC* case discussed at par. 16.07 is an example of this problem.

16.10   The nominated sub-contractor must enter into a sub-contract which will indemnify the Contractor against the same obligations in respect of the sub-contract as those for which the Contractor is liable in respect of the main contract. The Architect and Contractor can agree to waive this requirement. It is difficult to envisage a circumstance which would justify such a waiver. A standard form of sub-contract has been agreed between the Construction Industry Federation and the Sub-Contractors and Specialists Association. There are two versions depending on whether the main contract form is the RIAI version or the GDLA version. The forms are very much the same, and the differences are set out in a schedule to the Standard Documents.

The standard form of sub-contract (5th edition, October 1989) sets out the requirement with regard to indemnity as follows:

3   The Sub-Contractor agrees:

a)   To observe, perform and comply with all the provisions of the Main Contract on the part of the Contractor, to be observed, performed and complied with so far as they relate and apply to the Sub-Contract Works (or any portion of the same) and are not repugnant to or inconsistent with the express provisions of this Sub-Contract as if all the same were severally set out herein and

b)   Subject to Clause 4(b)(ii) to indemnify and save harmless the Contractor against and from:
   i)   Any claim, breach or non-observance or non-performance of the said provisions of the Main Contract or any of them due to any act, neglect or the default on the part of the Sub-Contractor only; and
   ii) Any act or omission of the Sub-Contractor, his servants or agents which involves the Contractor in any liability to the Employer under the Main Contract; and
   iii) Any damage, loss or expense due to or resulting from any negligence or breach of duty on the part of the Sub-Contractor, his servants or agents (inclusively of any wrongful use by him or them of the Contractor's property); and

iv) Any claim by an employee of the Sub-Contractor under the Employer's Liability Acts or other Acts of the Oireachtas of a like nature, respectively, in force for the time being.

This is obviously a comprehensive undertaking on the part of the Nominated Sub-Contractor (as far as the carrying out of his work is concerned), to indemnify the Contractor. Clause 4(b)(ii) referred to above at (b) deals with insurances and allows the Sub-Contractor to exclude the items from Insurance which are listed as permitted exclusions in Clause 23(d) of the main contract as far as Employer's Liability and Public Liability is concerned. The provisions of Clause 21(c) of the Main Contract are referred to in the second sentence of Clause 4(b)(ii) of the Sub-Contract. In a previous clause, the Sub-Contractor agrees to carry out his work as directed by the Contractor, and also by the Architect:

2   The Sub-Contractor shall execute and complete the Sub-Contract Works subject to an in accordance with this Sub-Contract in all respects to the reasonable satisfaction of the Contractor and of the Architect for the time being under the Main Contract (hereinafter called the Architect) and in conformity with the reasonable directions and requirements of the Contractor which shall be a programme agreed between the Contractor and the Sub-Contractor and approved by the Architect who in the case of default in carrying out the programme may himself direct the order in which the Sub-Contract Work shall be carried out.

These provisions are all fairly straightforward, although it is submitted that the language used might be simplified. The full text of the Sub-Contract form is given in the Standard Documents section at the end of the book.

16.11   Clause 3 of the Sub-Contract form ends with the paragraph:

Provided that nothing in the Sub-Contract contained shall impose any liability on the Sub-Contractor in respect of any negligence or breach of duty on the part of the Employer, the Contractor, his other Sub-Contractors or their respective servants or agents nor create any privety of contract between the Sub-Contractor and the Employer or any other Sub-Contractor.

This is a two-way protection. The Sub-Contractor should obviously be in no way liable for the misdeeds of either the Employer or the Main Contractor. Equally (and this has been discussed in detail earlier on) no privity of contract, i.e. contractual relationship will exist as between the Employer and the Sub-Contractor.

Reference has been made in pars. Int.08 and 2.14 to the doctrine of *contra preferentem*. This is the doctrine that would allow any interpretation of a standard form to be construed against the person who was responsible for drafting the contract. In the case of the RIAI and GDLA forms they would be construed against the Employer on the grounds that he would, through his agent, have had a significant influence of the wording of the form. The case of *County District Properties Ltd v C Jenner and Son and others* [1974] 3 BLR 38 held that the standard sub-contract form as used in conjunction with the JCT/RIBA form did not have to be construed against the Contractor, as the two organisations had worked out the form between themselves. It could be assumed that the same position would apply to the CIF/SCSA forms used in conjunction with the RIAI and GDLA forms.

16.12   **(b) The sums directed by the Architect to be paid to Nominated Sub-Contractors for work, materials or goods comprised in the sub-contracts shall be paid by the Contractor within five working days of receipt of payment on the Architect's certificate for the value of such work, materials, or goods less only any retention money and cash discount which the Contractor may be entitled to deduct.**

The sub-clause states that the amounts certified shall be paid in full, less only any retention money or cash discount. Retention is the procedure whereby an agreed percentage, defined in the appendix, is to be deducted from all payments due to the Contractor, up to an agreed limit. This is to ensure that if the Contractor defaults in remedying any defects, the Employer will have the money to pay another contractor to remedy the defects. This is dealt with fully in the notes to Clauses 31 and 35.

The reference to cash discount allows the Contractor claim 5% of the amount certified to the Sub-Contractor, and the standard sub-contract form at Clause 11(b) provides for this, but only if, firstly, the payment is made to the Sub-Contractor within seven days of the Contractor being paid and, secondly, the Main Contract has provision for this discount which the RIAI contract has.

16.13   **(c) before any certificate is issued to the Contractor he shall, if requested, by the Architect furnish to him reasonable proof that all Nominated Sub-Contractor's accounts included in previous certificates have been duly discharged, in default whereof the Employer may pay such accounts upon a certificate of the Architect and deduct the amount so paid from any sums due to or to become due to the Contractor.**

This clause raises the desirability of providing a Collateral Warranty (Clause 37). It will be recalled that the Employer has no privity of contract with the

Sub-Contractor. Separate contracts exist as between the Employer and the Contractor on the one hand, and between the Sub-Contractor and the Contractor on the other. By a device known as a Collateral Agreement (literally 'by the side of') parties to contracts can enter simultaneously into other contracts which then bind them.

In the Case of the Collateral Agreement published by the Royal Institute of the Architects of Ireland in agreement with the Society of Chartered Surveyors and the Construction Industry Federation (1988 Edition), the Employer and Sub-Contractor enter into a separate contract. This Collateral Agreement is set out in the Standard Documents. In this contract the Sub-Contractor will agree to exercise all reasonable skill and care in the design, execution, and completion of the sub-contract works. In return, the Employer guarantees direct payment to the Sub-Contractor if the Contractor defaults. The position of the bankruptcy of the main contractor in this situation is dealt with in par. 16.15. The subject of Collateral Warranties is dealt with in detail in the notes to Clause 37.

The Collateral Warranty referred to above contains much the same provisions as sub-clause 16(c) but with the advantage to the Sub-Contractor of a specific timetable and a guarantee of payment if the Contractor defaults.

The relevant sections read as follows:

B1 The Architect shall on a written request from the Sub-Contractor require the Main Contractor to furnish reasonable proof that he had duly discharged any sum in respect of the value of the works, goods, or services executed or supplied by the Sub-Contractor which is included in the total of a Certificate issued by the Architect under the Main Contract.

2 If in respect of the whole or part of such sum the Contractor fails for 5 working days from the Architect's requirement of proof of discharge either to furnish in writing reasonable cause for withholding payment, the Architect shall within 10 working days thereafter issue to the Employer a Certificate stating the sum wrongly withheld and naming the Sub-Contractor. The Employer shall deduct the sum so certified from any amount payable or which shall become payable to the Main Contractor (or part of the sum to the extent that the amount payable is less than the whole sum) and pay the sum so deducted direct to the Sub-Contractor within 10 working days of the Certificate or of the amount becoming payable to the Main Contractor (whichever is the later).

3 Any payment on foot of any Certificate issued under this clause

shall be deemed payment to the Main Contractor under the Main Contract.

It will be seen that these provisions are much the same in principle as Clause 16(c) of the Contract, but that the express times ensure prompt payment to the Sub-Contractor if the Contractor defaults, and more importantly, the Employer is required to pay the Sub-Contractors directly. The Contract itself says that the Employer 'may pay' amounts directly to Sub-Contractor if the Contractor defaults, whereas the Collateral Warranty says that the Employer 'shall ... pay'.

The same provisions with regard to retention money [Clause 16(d)] are optional in the Contract, but again are, in the case of the Collateral Agreement, mandatory.

16.14 **(d) If the Architect desires to secure final payment to any Nominated Sub-Contractor before final payment is due to the Contractor and if such Nominated Sub-Contractor has satisfactorily indemnified the Contractor against any latent defects then the Architect may in a certificate under Clause 35, of these Conditions include an amount to cover the said final payment and the Contractor shall forthwith upon receipt of payment on such certificate pay to such nominated Sub-Contractor the full amount so certified less the cash discount whereupon the 'Limit of Retention Fund' named in the Appendix hereto shall be reduced in proportion to the amount so certified and the Contractor shall be discharged from all liability for the work or materials covered by such certificate except for any latent defects.**

It frequently happens, particularly in large contracts, that a Nominated Sub-Contractor will have completed his work long in advance of the Contractor's final completion. Retention money, as explained at par. 35.07, will have been held by the Contractor, so that any defects in the sub-contract works can be remedied without further cost if the sub-contractor defaults. Under the main contract, the retention money will be held for an agreed time after practical completion. This agreed time in the 'Defects Liability Period' is set out in the appendix to the RIAI form and GDLA form. 'Practical Completion' is defined in Clause 31.

If a period of time has elapsed since practical completion of the sub-contract works which is equal to the retention period of the main contract, then the Sub-Contractor can ask the Contractor to apply for final payment of the sub-contract sum by way of a certificate from the Architect. The Sub-Contractor will be required to indemnify the Contractor against any latent, or hidden, defects in the sub-contract works, and the Contractor will then be discharged from any liability for the sub-contract works, except for any of the latent defects referred to above.

16.15 The status of the retention money held in connection with the sub-contract works has been the subject of debate. Clause 11(d) of the standard form of sub-contract says:

> Payments made to the Contractor in respect of work done and materials used by the Sub-Contractor shall until received by the Sub-Contractor be deemed to be money or moneys worth held in trust (but without obligation to invest) by the Contractor for the Sub-Contractor to be applied in or towards payment of the Sub-Contractor's account, subject always to the right of adjustment by the Architect in the event of his certifying that adjustment is necessary

The case of *Murphy Bros (Dublin) Ltd v Morris and Others* [1975] High Court, unrep. 6th October, dealt with this aspect of the contract in some detail. This case, and another referred to below, deal with a situation where the Contractor is in receivership or in liquidation and where money has been certified to the Contractor which contains specified amounts for Nominated Sub-Contractors, and where this money has not been passed on.

The Court held that money which had been paid into the contractor's account was, in fact, a trust, and that any such money which had been received by the liquidator must be passed on to the sub-contractor in question. The liquidator had argued that such a requirement would give the Nominated Sub-Contractors preference over other unsecured creditors and that this would be contrary to the provisions of the Companies Act 1963, but this argument was rejected by the Court in view of the clear statement in both the main contract form and the sub-contract form that retention money was held in trust. The Court also held that any money received by the Contractor (before the receiver or liquidator was appointed and of which the receiver has no notice) on behalf of the Sub-Contractors did not rank before the other unsecured creditors. The contract forms in this case were the RIAI 1966 Edition and the CIF/SCSA sub-contract form, 1971 Edition, but the relevant provisions of these clauses are similar to the present forms.

Much the same argument arose in the case of *Glow Heating Ltd v Eastern Health Board and Others* [1988] 6 ILT 237. This Contract was based on the form approved by the Department of Health, but the provision with regard to direct payment by the Employer to the Nominated Sub-Contractor was the same as that in the Collateral Agreement, i.e. the Employer 'shall pay'. Again, the Court rejected the liquidator's argument that such a clause was contrary to public policy as it would defeat the provisions of the 1963

Companies Act, and in particular section 275. The Court held that::

> ... the clauses in the main-contract and in the sub-contract which provid-
> ed for direct payment by the Employer to the Nominated Sub-Contractor
> did not reduce the property of the insolvent Main Contractor in contra-
> vention of section 275 of the Companies Act 1963 because the liquidator
> took the Main Contractor's property (i.e. the retention money) subject to
> such liabilities as affected it while it was in the Main Contractor's hands.

The provision in Clause 16(c) that the Employer 'may pay' raises the question as to what would happen in similar circumstances under the RIAI form,
and it is unclear as to what a Court might decide. It would be an argument
for concluding a Collateral Agreement, as the 'shall pay' provisions of that
document should ensure that the status of the retention money would be
clear, as in the *Murphy* and *Glow Heating* cases.

A recent Northern Ireland case (*B. McMullan and Sons v John Ross and
Malcolm London* [1996] 86 BLR 1) has distinguished, i.e. not followed, the
Glow Heating case and held that in accordance with the *pari passu* rule, an
Employer cannot make a direct payment to a nominated sub-Contractor following the bankruptcy of the Main Contractor. However, this case would not
effect the *Glow Heating* decision in this jurisdiction. *Pari passu* means 'with
equal step', and Section 275 of the Companies Act 1963 as amended by
Section 132 of the Companies Act 1990 confirms that the property of a company in a voluntary winding up is applied in satisfaction of its liabilities *pari
passu*.

16.16   **(e) Neither the existence nor the exercise of the foregoing powers nor
         anything else contained in these Conditions (subject to Clause 37)
         shall render the Employer in any way liable to any Nominated Sub-
         Contractor and (subject to Clause 25) the Contractor shall be
         responsible to the Employer for the execution of the said work
         and/or supply and fixing of the said materials or goods. Provided
         always that if the Contractor determines the employment of the
         Nominated Sub-Contractor in accordance with the provisions of the
         sub-contract then another sub-contractor (who shall be selected by
         the Architect and employed by the Contractor as a Nominated Sub-
         Contractor in accordance with the provisions of this clause) shall
         unless otherwise agreed be appointed to complete the sub-contract
         work. In such a case, unless the determination is set aside as a result
         of litigation or arbitration, the Contractor shall not be liable for any
         increase in the cost of the sub-contract work that may arise by rea-
         son of the necessity to have the work so completed.**

The first part of this sub-clause attempts to clarify the relationship of the Employer and the Nominated Sub-Contractor, and this particular area has been dealt with above, both in relation to various cases which have arisen, and in relation to the Collateral Agreement which the sub-clause refers to specifically, i.e. Clause 37. The reference to Clause 25 is directed at the insurance provisions of the Contract, and deals with damage due to design either on the part of the Contractor or on the part of a Nominated Sub-Contractor or Nominated Supplier. The *Norta* case at par. 16.06 deals with an aspect of this provision.

The second part of the sub-clause deals with re-nomination. The sub-contract agreement at Clause 20 allows the Contractor to determine the employment of the Sub-Contractor under seven headings. The first six are described as 'Default':

a) *Default*

If the Sub-Contractor shall make default in any of the following respects, viz:

1   without reasonable cause shall wholly suspend the works before completion, otherwise than in accordance with Clause 11(e) hereof;

(This is the sub-clause that allows the sub-contractor to suspend the works in the event of a non-payment by the Contractor.)

2   shall fail to proceed with the works with reasonable diligence;

3   refuses or persistently neglects after notice in writing from the Contractor to remove defective work or improper materials;

4   shall fail to commence the Sub-Contract Works within a reasonable period after receipt by him of an order in writing;

5   shall fail to execute the Sub-Contract Works in accordance with the Sub-Contract or shall be in serious breach of his obligation under the Sub-Contract;

6   where a trade dispute arises between the Sub-Contractor and the workmen engaged by him on or in connection with the Sub-Contract Works to whom a Registered Employment Agreement applies shall fail, neglect or refuse to comply with the settlement procedures set out in such Agreement;

If any of the six events listed above occur, then the Contractor may, subject to certain restrictions and notice, determine the employment of the Sub-Contractor.

The seventh heading refers to bankruptcy, and is as follows:

b) *Bankruptcy of Sub-Contractor*

If the Sub-Contractor commits an act of Bankruptcy or being company enters into liquidation whether compulsory or voluntary (except liquidation for the purpose of re-construction) or has a receiver appointed to it or has suspended work on the sub-contract or left the State, the Contractor without prejudice to any other rights contained herein may send by registered post to the Sub-Contractor a written notice determining the employment of the Sub-Contractor under this Contract.

When determination occurs, a re-nomination is mandatory (early printings of the contract form include the word 'may' in line 8 of this sub-clause. Later printings show the correct word 'shall'). The procedure and consequences of re-nomination are dealt with at par. 16.05 where the *Bickerton* and *Percy Bilton* cases are examined.

GDLA – Clause 16

NOMINATED SUB-CONTRACTOR

16.17   The clause is similar to that in the RIAI form with the following changes made (NOTE: The sub-clause references differ):

1   In sub-clause 16(a), the Nominated Sub-Contractor may be selected either by the Architect or the Employer. In the RIAI form only the Architect is mentioned.

2   The wording of sub-clause 16(b) has been slightly rearranged but with no change in meaning. The original GDLA form has been altered by the omission of the words 'and discount for prompt payment' in (c). This was occasioned by the passing of the Prompt Payment of Accounts Act 1997. Sub-clause (d) is the same as sub-clauses (b) and (c) in the RIAI form.

3   Sub-clause (e) is similar to sub-clause (d) RIAI, except for the reference to sub-clause 35(d), but there is no change in meaning or effect. Again, the words 'less only any discount for prompt payment that may be allowable' have been deleted.

4   Sub-clause (f) differs from sub-clause (e) RIAI in two important respects. Firstly, there is no reference to a clause dealing with a Collateral

Agreement. As pointed out in par. 37.05, the GDLA form contains no provision for a Collateral Agreement.

Secondly, the sub-clause does not require the Architect to re-nominate in case of default. Neither is any mention made of the possibility of a determination by the Contractor of the Sub-Contractor's employment. In this respect the GDLA form is inferior to the RIAI form in not making any provision for events which may very well occur. The Contract [at Clause 16(b)] refers to a sub-contract as between the Contractor and the Sub-Contractor, and this will be presumably, the standard form of sub-contract issued by the Construction Industry Federation and the Sub-Contractor and Specialists Association for use with GDLA 82. As this form refers to determination of the sub-contract on the same grounds as the sub-contract from used in the RIAI form, it clearly leaves an area of doubt with regard to the consequences of a re-nomination that is required by reason other than that of bankruptcy.

The sub-clause is clear on the point that the Contractor will not be liable for extra costs arising from re-nomination as a result of bankruptcy, and sooner or later, a Court will decide who is liable for any extra costs arising from re-nomination due to any other cause.

The fact that re-nomination is not made mandatory (as in the RIAI form) also raises some queries. It is quite likely that the decision in the *Bickerton* case would apply. It will be recalled that one of the decisions in that case was that there was an obligation on the part of the Employer to re-nominate another Sub-Contractor, and the Court reached this conclusion in part, because of the wording of the clause referring to P.C. sums (Clause 19 RIAI and GDLA) in the RIBA form in use at the time. These words were: 'Such P.C. sums shall be expended in favour of such persons as the Architect shall instruct.' The words in the RIAI and GDLA forms are: 'Such provisions/payments shall be expended only in accordance with the directions of the Architect.' Since these wordings are so similar it is likely that a Court would interpret them in the same way and come to the same conclusion as the Court did in *Bickerton*.

SF 88

16.18   There are no provisions in SF 88 for Nominated Sub-Contractors.

16.19 A ARCHITECT'S RESPONSIBILITIES UNDER CLAUSE 16
RIAI AND GDLA

1 Nominate any necessary Sub-Contractors.

2 Consider any reasonable objection by the Contractor to such nomination.

3 Endorse the certificates to the Contractor with any necessary list of payments due to Nominated Sub-Contractors.

4 Obtain from the Contractor any necessary proof of payment to Nominated Sub-Contractors.

5 Certify, if appropriate, final payment to a nominated Sub-Contractor.

6 Re-nominate if necessary in case of default on the part of the original Nominated Sub-Contractor (not in GDLA).

16.20 B EMPLOYER'S RESPONSIBILITIES UNDER CLAUSE 16
RIAI AND GDLA

1 Nominate, if appropriate, any necessary Sub-Contractors (GDLA only).

2 Pay directly the Nominated Sub-Contractor (see notes at par. 16.13 in relation to Collateral Agreement).

16.21 C CONTRACTOR'S RESPONSIBILITIES UNDER CLAUSE 16
RIAI AND GDLA

1 Employ any Sub-Contractor nominated by the Architect (or Employer – GDLA) or any re-nomination.

2 Make objection, if justified, against any proposed nominee.

3 Enter into sub-contract agreements with any Nominated Sub-Contractor who is acceptable.

4 Furnish proof, if requested, to the Architect of payment to Nominated Sub-Contractors.

5 Secure indemnity from any Nominated Sub-Contractor who is receiving final payments.

16.22 CASES REFERRED TO

*Bickerton v Northwest Metropolitan Hospital
Board* [1970] 1 AER 1039 line 2   pars. 16.05, 16.06, 16.16

Brown v Norton
    [1954] IR 34   par. 16.08

Percy Bilton Ltd v Greater London Council
    [1982] 20 BLR 1   pars. 16.06, 16.16

County District Properties Ltd v C Jenner & Sons
    [1974] 3 BLR 38   par. 16.11

Fairclough v Rhuddlan Borough Council
    [1985] 30 BLR 26   pars. 16.07, 16.09

Gloucestershire County Council v Richardson
    [1969] 9 BLR 85   par. 16.08

Glow Heating Ltd v Eastern Health Board and Others
    [1988] 6 ILT 237   par. 16.15

McMullan and Sons v Ross and London
    [1996] 86 BLR 1   par. 16.15

Murphy Bros (Dublin) Ltd v Morris and Others
    [1975] High Court, 6th October 1975   par. 16.15

Norta Wallpapers (Ireland) Ltd v John Sisk and Sons
    (Dublin) Ltd [1978] 14 BLR 49   pars. 16.08, 16.16

JM Reilly Ltd v Belfast Corporation
    [1970] NI 68   par. 16.05

Westminster City Council v J Jarvis and Sons (Ltd)
    [1971] 7 BLR 64   par. 16.04

Young and Marten v McManus Childs Ltd
    [1969] 9 BLR 86   par.16.08

RIAI – Clause 17

NOMINATED SUPPLIERS

17.01 **Where provision is made in the Contract Documents for materials or goods for the Works to be supplied by a firm selected by the Architect such firm is hereby declared to be a Nominated Supplier**

The role of Nominated Suppliers occupies a surprisingly varied position as far as the standard forms of contract are concerned. The 1980 JCT/RIBA form at Clause 36 deals with Nominated Suppliers by way of 27 sub-clauses. The ICE form, 6th edition, makes no mention of Nominated Suppliers as a separate concept. The RIAI form is deceptively simple a regards Nominated Suppliers, but on the other hand the JCT/RIBA form seems to enter into unnecessary detail with regard to P.C. sums and Provisional sums (see Clause 18 and 19) and with regard to quality and payment. The fact that the RIAI form does not refer to any of these matters does not, of course, mean that there are no conditions or obligations implied.

The first point to consider is the responsibility of the Nominated Supplier and of the Contractor. The Contractor is responsible to the Employer for the quality of the goods supplied, and no privity of contract exists between the Employer and the Nominated Supplier, nor is there any provision (unlike in the case of a Nominated Sub-Contractor) for any type of collateral warranty between the Employer and the Nominated Supplier. The use of collateral warranty for suppliers is, however, available under the JCT/RIBA forms by way of the JCT Standard form of tender by a nominated supplier (TNS/1 and 2). The purpose of this particular warranty is to ensure that the Employer has a right under the Contract against a supplier of defective materials, as it can happen that where a Nominated Supplier's terms of contract with the Contractor excluded liability, the Contractor would have no liability as against the Employer, who would then have to stand the loss. The case of *Gloucestershire County Council v Richardson* [1968] 9 BLR 85 referred to in par. 8.06 deals with this.

HUDSON comments on the use of the term Nominated Supplier as follows. After stating that the intention of nominating either sub-contractors or suppliers is to ensure that there is no privity of contract between them and the Employer, he goes on to say: 'The only doubt relates to the strange expression 'Nominated Suppliers' used in the JCT/RIBA forms, which by itself has, of course, no legal significance and is nowhere further defined or explained in the contract; nor is any indication given of its legal consequences other than in the purely accounting provisions of the contract, but its effect appears to be identical in fixing the Main Contractor with liability for the Nominated Supplier'.

Again, the ICE form, 6th edition, makes it equally clear as to the respective positions of the parties in Clause 59(3): 'Except as otherwise provided in Clause 58(3)' – which deals with design – 'the Contractor shall be responsible for the work executed or goods, materials or services supplied by a Nominated Sub-Contractor employed by him as if he had himself executed such work or supplied such goods, materials or services.' The ICE form does not have a separate provision for Nominated Suppliers, but this sub-clause makes it clear what the contractual provision is as regards suppliers of goods or materials.

17.02   The apparent simplicity of the RIAI Clause 17 referred to in par. 17.01 does not in any way alter the legal position. Nomination itself ordinarily demonstrates that there has been no reliance placed on the Contractor's skill and judgement as far as selection is concerned, so that the Contractor is not ordinarily liable if the goods of the Nominated Supplier of good quality are unfit for their intended purpose. However, the Contractor would be liable if the goods, even though suitable for the purpose for which they were supplied, were not of good quality, or as the Sale of Goods and Supply of Services Act 1980 says are not 'of merchantable quality'. Par. 8.04 deals in greater detail with this area.

It has been argued that the fact that the Contractor has no right of objection to a Nominated Supplier is important. It will be recalled that the Contractor has a right of objection to a Nominated Sub-Contractor, and this fact is of some significance in establishing liability as between the various contracting parties. Sub-clause 16(a) specifies the Contractor's right of objection. The case of *Gloucestershire County Council v Richardson* discussed at par. 8.07, is a good example of the changed circumstance that emerges if a right of objection exists. In that case, the Contractor was required to order from a Nominated Supplier, items that were of a very complex nature, and that had a considerable design input as well. The Contractor was not consulted at any stage, and the Court held that he could be in no way liable. Since the RIAI form has no right of objection, the Contractor has some protection. 'The essential protection of the implied terms (i.e. quality or fitness) would be absent in all cases where an express right to reject a nomination was not given in the Main Contract' (HUDSON, 10th Edition, p.764). These comments have been dropped from the 11th edition due to changes in the UK forms.

Right of objection as far as Nominated Suppliers are concerned would carry much the same consequences as a right of objection to a Nominated Sub-Contractor. Abrahamson on p.239 comments: 'Reasonable objection will relate typically to the sub-contractor's ability to do the work, the necessary skills, plant and other resources or his finances. Commercial facts of life may make it difficult for a main contractor to object to a sub-contractor, particularly as the roles of sub-contractor and main contractor are often interchanged.' This last comment on role reversal is more applicable to civil engineering contracts, but the other comments are relevant to building contracts generally. The GDLA form has a right of objection to a Nominated Supplier.

GDLA – Clause 17

NOMINATED SUPPLIERS

17.03 The GDLA form is different from the RIAI form in two respects:

1 The firm may be selected by the Employer or the Architect. In the RIAI form only the Architect can nominate a Supplier.

2 The Contractor has a right to 'make in writing objection which the Architect accepts as reasonable'. The importance of the right of objection is discussed in par. 17.02. Basically where a right of objection exists and is not availed of, the Contractor is liable if the Nominated Supplier defaults.

SF 88

17.04 There is no provision in the shorter form for Nominated Suppliers.

17.05 A ARCHITECT'S RESPONSIBILITIES UNDER CLAUSE 17 RIAI AND GDLA

1 Select and nominate required suppliers.

17.06 B EMPLOYER'S RESPONSIBILITIES UNDER CLAUSE 17 GDLA

1 Select and nominate required suppliers.

17.07   C   CONTRACTOR'S RESPONSIBILITIES UNDER CLAUSE 17 GDLA

    1   Object, if considered proper, to a nominated supplier.

17.08   CASE REFERRED TO

Gloucestershire County Council v Richardson
    [1969] 9 BLR 85   pars. 17.01, 17.02

RIAI – Clause 18

18.01 **Sums, items or quantities marked 'Provisional' included in the Contract Documents shall be at the entire disposal of the Architect and shall be expended in whole or part as he may direct. If the Architect's instructions under this clause involve the employment of Nominated Sub-Contractors or Nominated Suppliers then the amounts expended shall be treated as if they were Prime Cost Sums (Clause 19). If compliance with the Architect's Instructions under this clause involves work by the Contractor it shall be valued in accordance with Clause 13 of these Conditions.**

Neither the term 'Provisional Sum' nor the term 'Prime Cost Sum' (Clause 19) is defined in the Contract form but the general understanding of the terms is that a 'Provisional Sum' is included in the Contract Sum to cover some aspect of the work that cannot be foreseen or estimated. A good example would be where an architect might suspect the existence of dry rot but where there would be no opportunity before commencing the works of establishing the extent of the outbreak. The Architect would use his judgement, and, if appropriate, consult the Quantity Surveyor, to include in the contract documents a provisional sum of money to cover this possible expenditure.

If the work which is the subject of the provisional sum can be carried out by the Contractor, the actual cost will be determined in accordance with the provisions of Clause 13, which is the clause which deals with the ascertainment of prices for variations. If, however, the work required the nomination of a Sub-Contractor or Supplier, then the rules governing Prime Cost Sums in Clause 19 shall be used to assess the cost. A reduction in the Contract Sum after final measurement due to the omission in whole or part of any provisional sums will not entitle the Contractor to the 10% allowance on credit as far as that particular item is concerned, as directed by Clause 14(b).

GDLA – Clause 18

18.02   This Clause is identical to the RIAI form except for the words 'or not at all' after 'whole or part' in line 2.

SF 88 – Clause 3

18.03   Clause 3 of the SF.88 forms deals with Provisional Sums at paragraph 4. It reads:

The Architect shall issue instructions as to the expenditure of any Provisional Sums. A Provisional Sum shall be any amount included in the Contract Sum and so described, to be expended on the direction of the Architect.

Provisional Sums not expended shall be deducted from the Contract Sum.

This Clause is covered in the comments at par. 18.01.

18.04   A   ARCHITECT'S RESPONSIBILITIES UNDER CLAUSE 18
RIAI AND GDLA

1   Issue directions with regard to the expenditure of provisional sums.

RIAI – Clause 19

PRIME COST SUMS

19.01   **(a) Sums or rates included in the Contract Documents and marked 'Prime Cost' or 'P.C.' are provisions to meet payments by the Contractor to Nominated Sub-Contractors or Nominated Suppliers. Such payments shall be net of Value Added Tax and any commission or trade or other discount except a discount for prompt payment by the Contractor calculated at the rate of 5% of the payment. The Prime Cost or P.C. sums or rates included in the Contract Documents shall be deemed to include amounts to allow for such discounts for prompt payment.**

Any amount arising under Clause 36 for payment to or allowance by a Nominated Sub-Contractor shall be increased to make provision for the above discount for prompt payment.

In par. 18.01 it was pointed out that a Provisional Sum is included in the Contract to cover unforeseen, or unascertainable work. A Prime Cost Sum is included to cover work which is foreseen but which will be carried out by a Nominated Sub-Contractor or Supplier, and where the precise amount is not known at the time of signing the Contract. Examples of such items would be the installation of the electrical services, or the supply of sanitary fittings. The lack of definition in the Contract for the terms Provisional Sum and Prime Cost Sum has been the subject of criticism and has led to the terms being described as 'a distinction without a difference'. In the ICE form, 6th edition, Clause 58 attempts to make clear the distinction as between the two, but even in that form the two seem to overlap.

The cost to the Employer of the items covered by P.C. sums is set out in the clause. The Contractor must pass on to the Employer any benefit from trade discounts, or any other reductions in cost, with the exception of a 5% prompt payment discount. While 'prompt' is not defined in the contract, it is defined in the CIF/SCSA Sub-Contract agreement (referred to at par. 16.10) as being seven days.

The 5% prompt payment discount is also allowed to the Contractor in respect of any increases which might arise from the provisions of Clause 36, that is, any increases in the P.C. sum due to wage or materials increases (and, presumably, decreases).

A dispute concerning the 5% prompt payment discount illustrates the problems that arise in altering standard forms. This is shown in the case of *HA O'Neil Ltd v John Sisk and Son Ltd* [1984] Supreme Court, unrep. 27th July. A clause had been inserted in the main contract which differed from that in the sub-contract form, and the question arose as to which would have precedence. The Contractor deducted 5% from payment to the sub-contractor but no provision was made in the Architect's certificates for this amount to be made available to the sub-contractor. This would normally be done by adding one-nineteenth to the certified amount. The Court held that where two clauses were incompatible the main contract clause would apply. This case was an example of the law being imposed, even though the result might be unfair, and one of the judgements added: 'At the same time I think it right to add that in fairness the sums involved should have been paid to the plaintiffs (the sub-contractors) and I would hope that such payment would eventually emanate from the Employers'.

19.02 **(b) Payments as aforesaid shall be made only in accordance with the directions of the Architect as to the work to be executed by the nominated Sub-Contractors or the goods to be supplied by the Nominated Suppliers, the firms to which payments are to be made and the amounts to be paid. If any amount so authorised and properly paid is more or less than the relevant Prime Cost or P.C. Sum or rate included in the Contract Documents the difference shall be added to or deducted form the Contract Sum as the case may be.**

This Clause is self-explanatory. The certificates issued by the Architect under Clause 35 (Certificates and Payments) will specify the amounts payable to each nominated sub-contractor. Further details of payments to sub-contractors are provided in par. 16.13. It is important to note that the Architect has no authority to expend sums in excess of those set out in the Contract Documents, and contractors should ensure that an instruction is obtained from the Architect in cases where this occurs. Failure to obtain this instruction could result in the Employer refusing to pay the excess amounts.

As in the case of Provisional Sums, any decrease in the amount expended on a P.C. Sum is not allowable to the Contractor when calculating any payment due under Clause 14 (Omissions). See also par. 18.01.

GDLA – Clause 19

19.03   There are considerable differences between the RIAI and GDLA forms as regards Prime Cost Sum provisions. The overall effect of the clause is the same, but both the wording, and the sequence of the requirements differ, and there are four matters referred to which do not occur in the RIAI form. The clause reads as follows:

Money provisions in the Contract Documents described as 'Prime Cost' or 'P.C.' are net of Value Added Tax and are provided to meet payments for the execution of Work by Nominated Sub-Contractors or the supply of goods by Nominated Suppliers. Such provisions shall be expended only in accordance with the directions of the Architect as to the extent of the work to be executed or the goods to be supplied, the firms to which payments are to be made and the amounts to be expended.

The amounts to be expended in each case shall mean the net amount to be paid by the Contractor to the Nominated Sub-Contractor or Nominated Supplier before the addition of Value Added Tax and after deduction of any credits arising under Clause 36. It shall include the cost of the carriage of a Nominated Supplier's goods to the site of the Works and any additions arising under Clause 36. It shall not include any trade discount, commission or profit for the Contractor or other person either directly or through an agent nor any interest payable by the Contractor to the firm executing the Work or supplying the goods, nor, in the case of a Nominated Supplier, the cost of fixing or the materials required for fixing the goods supplied by him.

The Contractor shall when required produce invoices and other vouchers to prove that the amount to be paid has been computed in accordance with these requirements.

If the amount expended in accordance with the Architect's directions is more or less than the Prime Cost or P.C. Sum provided in the Contract Documents the difference shall be added to or deducted from the Contract Sum as the case may be.

Any amounts included in the Contract Sum separately from the P.C. sum for fixing, materials required for fixing, profit or any other charges in connection with the work of the Nominated Sub-Contractor or Nominated Supplier shall be adjusted equitably and any extra or credits arising therefrom shall be added to or deducted from the Contract Sum

The differences with the RIAI form are as follows:

1   The amount of any Prime Cost sum to be expended shall be adjusted to deal with any credit arising under Clause 36 (Wage and Price Variations). In other words, if the price of any materials or the wages of the work people involved in the particular activity covered by the prime cost sum is reduced then this credit shall be allowed to the Employer. Following the passing of the Prompt Payment of Accounts Act 1997, the phrase 'shall include a discount equal to 5% of itself for the Contractor for prompt payment by him' was deleted.

2   The amount expended shall also include 'the cost of the carriage of a Nominated Supplier's goods to the site'. This cost would be certainly charged in any event, either by the Contractor or the Nominated Supplier, but is presumably included to remind the Architect and the Contractor to ensure that any quotations for such goods will include this charge. The 5% prompt payment provision has been removed.

3   The Contractor is required to produce invoices when instructed, in order to prove that the sums expended as Prime Cost Sums have been calculated in accordance with the requirement of Clause 19.

4   The amount to be expended shall not include 'in the case of a Nominated Supplier, the cost of fixing or the materials required for fixing the goods supplied by him'. The purpose of this phrase is not clear, though it presumably emphasises the difference between a Nominated Sub-Contractor who does work on site, and a Nominated Supplier who only supplies materials. The standing of either party is now considered as being similar. Par. 8.02 explains that the law now views contracts for the 'sale of goods' and contracts for 'work and materials' as having the same requirements.

The last paragraph of the clause says that any amounts included in the Contract Sum separate from the P.C. Sum is to provide for any charges for fixing, etc, shall be adjusted equitably. The normal arrangement in the Bill of Quantities would be that a separate charge is allowed for fixing, attendance, etc, and the purpose of this clause is to specify that any such charge is adjusted depending on the circumstances in each case. This provision does not occur in the RIAI form, and can be seen as another, admittedly small, example of the advantage to the Employer in the GDLA form. Normally the amounts involved here would be minor and the overall effect on the Contract Sum would be negligible. If, on the other hand, very large credits arose because of the reduction of the amount of work by Nominated Sub-Contractors (or less likely the amounts provided by Nominated Suppliers) then Clause 2(c) dealing with loss or expense would be invoked.

SF 88

19.04 There is no mention of P.C. sums in the shorter form. Provisional sums are dealt with in Clause 3 of that form. See pars. 18.01 and 18.03.

19.05 A ARCHITECT'S RESPONSIBILITIES UNDER CLAUSE 19 RIAI AND GDLA

  1 Make directions with regard to payments to Nominated Sub-Contractors or nominated suppliers.

19.06 C CONTRACTOR'S RESPONSIBILITIES UNDER CLAUSE 19 GDLA

  1 Produce invoices, etc, if required to prove payments.

19.07 CASE REFERRED TO:

  HA O'Neil Ltd v John Sisk and Son Ltd
    [1984] Supreme Court, unrep. 27th July   par. 19.01

The Insurance Clauses – Nos 20 to 27

INTRODUCTION

20.01   The insurance provisions in the standard forms are viewed with some apprehension by many of those involved in the construction industry, and while this view may be partly justified, the overall concept can be quite easily grasped, once the various sections of insurance cover are separately understood. Insurance itself is a very old concept originating in the Western World at some time in the fifteenth century. In the OXFORD ENGLISH DICTIONARY the word 'insurance' is dated as having first appeared in 1553. Various changes and events in society provoked the development of the various branches of insurance. One of the best known of these events, the Great Fire of London, was responsible for the rapid spread of fire insurance in the later part of the seventeenth century. The first appearance of the word 'premium' is given in the OXFORD ENGLISH DICTIONARY as the year 1666, which is the date of the Great Fire. Initially, the words 'insurance' and 'assurance' were used interchangeably, but a distinction eventually emerged so that 'insurance' was taken out to provide for an event which *might* occur such as a fire, and hence 'fire insurance', whereas, 'assurance' was taken out for an event which *must* occur, such as death, and hence 'life assurance'. The first reference to insurance in the RIAI standard forms occurs in the 1910 edition at Clause 22.

Insurance has been defined as 'the equitable financial contribution of many for the benefit of an individual who has suffered loss'. The provisions of the RIAI forms are examined in a very clear and useful paper by Max Abrahamson, NOTES ON THE INSURANCE CLAUSES, issued by the Liaison Committee. The paper refers to the 1975 and 1977 editions, but the general comments would apply to the latest revisions. Naturally, the standard forms will deal with insurance only as it affects the contract itself.

The responsibility for insuring was generally placed on the Contractor. This had been criticised, as it was argued that the ultimate benefit of these clauses was to the Employer. 'If the insurance were to be of the owner alone, the principal purpose of the policy would be defeated, since the insurer would be in a position to subrogate in the name of the owner against the contractor, even in those cases where the fault was not the contractor's or a sub-contractor's fault, by reason of the contractor's breach of his unqualified obligation to complete if he failed to reinstate free of charge, and obviously, in cases of fault, for breach of workmanship or other contractual obligations. This would subvert the overriding object of the insurance, namely to safeguard the contractor from crippling liabilities.' HUDSON, 11th edition, p.1430. Some contractors endeavour to have all the insurance clauses struck out and a specially drafted one inserted. This might not be a bad way to approach the whole problem in view of some of the problems which exist, but on the other hand, as has been pointed out in the introduction (par. Int.08) standard forms have their uses.

The 2001 revisions to the RIAI Form by the Liaison Committee moved the previous Clause 20 (Artists and Tradesmen) to Clause 32A, and split the previous Clause 21 (Liability, Indemnity and Insurance for Damage to Persons and Property) into Clause 20 (Liability and Indemnity for damage to Persons and Property) and Clause 21 (Insurance Against Damage to Persons and Property). These revisions also give the parties the choice to decide whether the Contractor or the Employer would take out the insurance for damage to persons or property, and the All Risks Insurance. This change was introduced on the basis that an Employer might be able to arrange cheaper insurance.

There are three basic insurance requirements:

1   The Contractor or the Employer must insure against any loss to property (Clause 21(a)).

2   The Contractor or the Employer must insure against any injury to persons (Clause 21(a)).

3   The Contractor or the Employer must insure the Works themselves (Clause 22).

Other clauses in the insurance part of the standard form deal with risks which the Contractor can exclude from his cover (Clauses 23 and 27), the procedure to be followed if damage does occur as a result of excluded risks (Clause 24), damage resulting from the Contractor's design, as opposed to the Architect's design (Clause 25) and the requirements for insuring existing structures (Clause 26).

20.02   There are, in addition, certain areas of risk which the Contract does not deal with. The following notes are a very brief summary of the three main types of insurance which are not dealt with in the standard forms.

1   Non-Negligence Insurance: As will be seen later, the risks which the Contractor is required to insure against as far as damage to property is concerned, must be those relating to the Contractor's own negligence

[Clause 21(a)]. Circumstances can arise, however, where damage will be caused even if the Contractor is not negligent. The most obvious case would be where a new building is being erected between two older buildings, or where piling is being carried out near existing buildings. In these cases, even where the Contractor takes all care, damage to other property can result, and Clause 21(a) will not apply. This particular problem was highlighted in the case of *Gold v Patman and Fotheringham* [1958] 1 WLR, 697, where piling damaged an adjoining building. There were other insurance principles involved which are not relevant here, but the Court held that the Employer, and not the Contractor, was liable as no negligence had been displayed by the Contractor or (as was the case here) the Sub-Contractor. This case is viewed as having led the development of non-negligence insurance to the stage which it has reached to-day, where it is an almost standard requirement on contracts where any such non-negligence damage can be anticipated. The JCT/RIBA (1980 Edition) contains provision for such insurance at Clause 21.2. It is important to remember that non-negligence insurance is issued for the protection of the Employer. The Contractor is named in the policy as it is necessary for him to provide certain information, and a contract of insurance is, as is set out in par. 23.11, a contract of the utmost good faith – *uberrimae fidei*. Non-negligence insurance takes some time to arrange as the insurers normally require their own consulting engineer to inspect the site or affected buildings before they will issue a policy. The arrangements for this type of cover must be put in hand as soon as possible to avoid delay.

2   Professional Indemnity Insurance: As mentioned in the notes to Clause 16 (Nominated Sub-Contractors) at par. 16.01, there is often a considerable design input from sub-contractors and, to a lesser extent, from contractors. Under Clause 25 (Damage due to Design), this damage from design must be made good by the Contractor at his own expense, though not if the damage is caused by faulty design on the part of a Nominated Sub-Contractor (see par. 16.06 – the *Norta* case). Since the Contractor is entitled under the exclusions allowed by Clause 23 to exclude damage due to design from his insurance policies, there is a gap in the cover which would be available under the insurance policies. This gap could be closed in either of two ways. Firstly, it could be closed by both the Contractor and the Nominated Sub-contractor taking out Professional Indemnity Insurance if it is thought appropriate, but they cannot be forced to do so under the standard contract forms. Secondly, the Contractor or the Employer could agree not to exclude the risk from the All Risks Insurance (commonly referred to as CAR – Contractor's All Risks). It must be remembered, however, that damage due to design can affect areas outside the CAR policy, such as damage to persons or other

property and these risks should be kept in mind. Damage due to design on the part of the professional team is not relevant to the contract, and would be a matter for the contracts drawn up between the Employer and the Architect, and any other professional advisers who might be involved.

3   Decennial Insurance: This is a type of insurance that is being used more commonly, and it provides cover for the Employer for a period of ten years against any damage resulting from defective design, materials, workmanship or construction. It is a comprehensive umbrella, and is consequently very expensive but the very simplicity of the arrangement, from the Employer's point of view, in providing him with one overall protection from damage from almost any building defect, irrespective of the origin of the defect, is very attractive: Normal wear and tear would, of course, be excluded from such a policy.

The further imposition, nowadays, of collateral agreements between the design team and a wide variety of parties such as tenants of the building, gives a level of comfort and security to employers and others, while rendering even more liable to risk the architects and engineers who are, to some extent, forced to accept the collateral agreements. These agreements render the Architect and Engineer directly liable to tenants, financial institutions, subsequent owners, etc, for the exercise of due skill and care in the performance of their duties and cements in contract what might only have existed previously in tort (see par. Int.18).

20.03   At this point it would be helpful to define the more important words used in the insurance world:

1   Responsibility: While it has been said that this word is a general term with no specific technical meaning, it is generally taken that a person is responsible if he can fairly be held accountable and legally liable for the consequences of his actions.

2   Liability: A person is under a liability when he is legally obliged, or may be legally obliged, to perform some action. This can be voluntary, as in a contract freely entered into, or by law under a statute.

There is a passage in a book by Dr Nael Bunni (CONSTRUCTION INSURANCE AND THE IRISH CONDITIONS OF CONTRACT) which makes the distinction very clearly between 'Responsibility' and 'Liability': 'One could be responsible and also liable as a result of a certain action; one could also be responsible for an action but not liable for the damages that result; and finally one could be liable but not responsible. An example of the first situation would be the (Architect) who acts negligently causing damage. He is responsible for his actions and he is also liable for the damages towards the party who has suffered the loss. The second and third situations can be illustrated by the example of the employer who nowadays is held liable for the negligent acts of his servant even though the employer himself may have been completely without blame and thus not responsible for the negligent act.'

3   Indemnity: An undertaking, or contract, to compensate for loss or damage. A contract of insurance (for a non-fixed sum) is an indemnity.

4   Guarantee: A Contract whereby one party, the guarantor, undertakes to a third party to be liable for the default of another party, the guarantee. A guarantee differs from an indemnity in that a default must occur, whereas in an indemnity, the obligation is immediate once the loss occurs.

5   Subrogation: A right of substitution. The insurance company can be subrogated, i.e. substituted, for the insured in an action against a third party who has caused the loss which has been suffered by the insured.

20.04   Before dealing with the individual clauses in the contract forms, it is important to emphasise the Architect's overall responsibility with regard to insurance. In par. 2.13 it was stated that while the Architect is not expected to have any general legal knowledge, he is assumed to have a working knowledge of the contract and of the usual consequences of any contract provision, as well as having a reasonable working knowledge of the law relating to his own job as an architect. This assumption would apply to the insurance clauses, but it is submitted that no architect in practice would be expected to have the specialised knowledge that would be required to advise an Employer in respect of the insurance provisions, apart from advising the Employer as to the overall type of insurance required. Obviously, the Architect would point out to the Employer that the basic rule is that new buildings are generally the Contractor's responsibility to insure, and that existing structures are the responsibility of the Employer (Clause 26), but even here the two may overlap, as in the case of new additions to existing structures.

The Architect should also be aware of the meaning of the basic terms used in insurance, and these are set out in par. 20.03. In addition the terms 'excess' and 'average' as defined in par. 22.03 should be familiar to the Architect. The Architect will also need to be advised of the details of the insurance policies held by the Contractor as these may be of a general nature and not confined to any one project.

As a general rule, the Architect should ensure that the insurers acting for the Contractor and the insurers acting for the Employer are in contact either directly or through brokers, so as to ensure that there are no gaps in the cover, and to make sure that the insurers to both parties to the contract are aware at all times during the course of the contract what the position is in regard to any factor which might affect the insurance provisions.

Finally, the Architect must at all times remember that a contract of insurance is one of 'the utmost good faith' – *uberrimae fidei*. This means that the parties seeking insurance must reveal to the insurers every relevant fact, and if this is not done, the insurer can repudiate the policy. This was graphically illustrated in, amongst others, the case of *Chariot Inns v Assicurazioni Generali SPA* [1981] ILRM 173. In this case, very extensive damage was caused by fire to the Chariot Inn, Ranelagh, Dublin, and the fire insurance claim was successfully repudiated by the insurers on the grounds that it had not been disclosed to them that a director of Chariot Inns had made a successful fire claim, on behalf of another company of which he was also a director, two years previously.

An even more extreme example is the case of *Keenan v Shield Insurance Company Ltd.* In this case, the insurer was allowed to avoid a claim of £16,000 for fire damage to a house because the house owner had omitted to disclose a claim of only £53 in the proposal form the previous year

20.05   To conclude this section, it is suggested that the wording of these clauses (Clauses 20–27) could be simplified in future editions. The clauses in SF 88 (Clauses 17–20) are a considerable improvement in this regard. The clearest wording of any standard form would appear to be that of the New Engineering Contract (NEC) published by the Institution of Civil Engineers and referred to previously at par. Int.09.

Sample clauses would be:

80   Risk Allocation

80.1   The risks of loss of or damage to physical property and of personal injury and death which arise in connection with the Contract, except those allocated to the Employer, are allocated to and are the responsibility of the Contractor.

It then goes on to list the risks allocated to the Employer. There seems to be no reason why such simple language could not be imported into the RIAI and GDLA forms, as has been done in the RIAI plain language contract.

Dealing with the individual clauses has been complicated by the fact that the RIAI and GDLA forms are now substantially different in format, even if not much so in content. The option for insurances to be taken out either by the Employer or the Contractor is not imported into the GDLA form, and this is now the most significant difference between the forms. The GDLA version of each clause is now printed in full where substantial differences remain.

RIAI – Clause 20

LIABILITY AND INDEMNITY FOR DAMAGE
TO PERSONS AND TO PROPERTY

20.06 (a) **Subject to sub-clauses (b) and (c) and except for such loss, damage or expense as is at the risk of the Employer under Clauses 26, 32A or 32B (where applicable) the Contractor shall be liable for and shall indemnify the Employer against any liability, loss, claim or proceedings whatsoever arising under statute or common law in respect of:**

i) **any loss of or damage or injury whatsoever to any property real or personal; and**

ii) **any personal injury to or disease contracted by or death of any person whomsoever,**

insofar as any such loss, damage injury, disease or death arises out of or in the course of or by reason of the execution of the Works and provided that such loss, damage, injury disease or death is due to the negligence, omission, default or breach of statutory duty of the Contractor, its servants or agents or any sub-contractor, its servants or agents.

(b)[1] Notwithstanding the provisions of sub-clause (a) above the Contractor shall not be required to indemnify the Employer in respect of any damage, injury or death to the extent that such damage, injury or death is due to the negligence, omission, default or breach of statutory duty by the Employer, its servants or agents or any person for whom the Employer is responsible (including persons employed or otherwise enaged by the Employer to whom Clause 32A refers or persons who may have use, occupation or possession of the whole or part of the Works with the consent of the Employer subsequent to the issue of a Possession Certificate pursuant to Clause 32B).

[1] The Employer is advised to arrange appropriate Public Liability Insurance Cover against the consequences of any damage, injury or death, due to the negligence, omission, default or breach of statutory duty by the Employer

(c) The reference in Clause 20(a)(i) above to 'property real or personal' does not include the Works (or any part) or the Ancillary Items up to and including the date of Practical Completion as certified by the Architect or up to and including the date of determination of the employment of the Contractor under this Contract, whichever is the earlier. Provided however if Clause 32B has been operated then the Relevant Part from the date of the Possession Certificate shall not be regarded as the Works (or part thereof).

Clause 20 deals in effect with third party claims brought by those who have suffered damage to property [sub-clause (a)(i)] or injury [sub-clause (a)(ii)]. The 2001 revisions to the contract form removed the phrase '(whether or not also partly due to the negligence, omission or default of the Employer or of any person for whom the Employer is responsible)'. This revision separates the parties as far as responsibility is concerned but there may be cases of overlaps.

Earlier editions of the contract forms conformed to the position under ordinary law where the Employer and Contractor would have shared liability for damage or injury in proportion to their responsibility for the occurrence.

The case of *Roscommon County Council v Waldron* [1963] IR 407 allowed a contractor to escape liability from an indemnity because the injury was caused by negligence on the part of the Employer even though the requirement that the damage be caused 'solely' by the negligence of the Employer was not present.

In the case of *PJ Kelly Ltd v Ryder and the Minister for Posts and Telegraphs* [1980] ILTR 98, an indemnity was agreed whereby the Minister was protected whether or not the Contractor was negligent, but this case was not covered by the standard forms and was before the general use of the GDLA form.

However, when the case of *AMF (International) Ltd v Magnet Bowling Ltd* [1968] 8 BLR 1 decided that in such cases the indemnity clauses did not apply, editions of the standard form were changed to establish that the previous arrangements have been altered.

This clause can be simplified by saying that the Contractor shall be liable for any damage caused to property of persons by the Contractor's negligence in carrying out the Works, even though other parties may be involved. The exceptions referred to in line 2 are covered by Clause 26 (Responsibility for Existing Structures) which puts the onus for insurance on the Employer in the case of existing structures, Clause 32A dealing with Independent

Contractors, Artists and Tradesmen and Clause 32(b) which allows cover to be reduced in the case of a handover of part of the Works. Property is referred to as being 'real or personal'. Real property comprises land and buildings, whereas personal property includes goods and chattels. The cover required for this insurance would form part of the Public Liability policy.

RIAI – Clause 21

INSURANCE AGAINST DAMAGE TO PERSONS AND PROPERTY

21.01   (i)[2] **Subject to and in accordance with Clause 23, the Contractor shall take out before commencing the Works and maintain until the issue of the final certificate or eighteen months after Practical Completion, whichever is the earlier, insurances including but not limited to Public Liability, Employers' Liability and Motor Insurance covering any liability, loss, claim or proceedings in respect of the matters referred to in Clause 20. Provided however that if the Contractor is required to return to the Works, for whatever reason, after the issue of the final certificate or more than eighteen months after Practical Completion, the Contractor shall take out and maintain for the period that it remains on or about the Works the insurances as set out above.**

or

(ii)(a) Subject to and in accordance with Clause 23, the Employer shall take out before commencing the Works and maintain until the issue of the final certificate or eighteen months after Practical Completion, whichever is the earlier, Public Liability Insurance covering any liability, loss, claim or proceedings in respect of the matters referred to in Clause 20 other than in relation to any personal injury to or disease contracted by or death of any employee of the Contractor, its servants or agents or in relation to liability, loss, claim or proceedings required to be covered under the Motor Insurance polity to be maintained by the Contractor pursuant to Clause 21(ii)(b) below.

(b) Subject to and in accordance with Clause 23, the Contractor shall take out before commencing the Works and maintain until the issue of the final certificate or eighteen months after Practical Completion, whichever is the earlier, Employers' Liability Insurance covering any liability, loss, claim or proceedings relating to any employee of the Contractor and Motor Insurance covering any liability, loss, claim or proceedings in respect of the matters referred to in sub-clause (ii)(a) above. Provided however that if the Contractor is required to return

to the Works, for whatever reason, after the issue of the final certificate or more than eighteen months after Practical Completion, the
Contractor shall take out and maintain for the period that it remains
on or about the Works all the insurances as set out in sub-clauses
(ii)(a) and (b) above.

(c) Without prejudice to the Contractor's liability at Common Law
or by statute sub-clause (ii) above shall not apply to any liability, loss,
claim or proceedings which arise otherwise than in connection with
an accident or fall within an exclusion permitted by Clause 23(d) par.
(i) or (ii) as relevant and which is not covered by an Employer's liability or public liability insurance policy of the Contractor.

[2] Strike out sub-clause 21(i) or (ii) as required; should neither be
struck out, sub-clause 21(i) is deemed to apply

Whereas Clause 20 deals with indemnity, this Clause deals with the insurance to cover that indemnity, referring both to persons and property. The
Public Liability policy referred to in par. 21.01 would provide the cover for
persons who are not employees of the Contractor. Both forms require a minimum of £1,000,000 and this should be increased where circumstances
require. The Employer's Liability policy referred to provides cover for the
Contractor's employees. While the cover is not required by statute it is to
deal with injury or disease arising out of the employment. There is usually
no limit to the cover, as this is normal insurance practice.

A new provision is the requirement that this insurance be maintained until
the issue of the final certificate, or eighteen months after the issue of the certificate of practical completion whichever is the earlier. The position of the
Contractor if he has to return to the site after that is also covered.

The GDLA form requires the cover to remain in force 'until final completion
of the work' (see par. 21.02).

Contractors' insurance policies should make allowance for accidents which
occur after the building has been completed. A contractor would be liable, in
the case of personal injury, for three years after the accident occurred irrespective of the date when the building was finished. The case of *Cowan v
Faghaile and Others* [1991] High Court, unrep. 24th January, held a contractor liable for an accident which occurred in 1985, even though the building
works which had been negligently carried out, were completed in 1959. It
would obviously be wise for a contractor to have an on-going policy to cover
such eventualities.

GDLA – Clause 21

LIABILITY FOR DAMAGE TO PERSONS AND PROPERTY AND PUB-
LIC LIABILITY AND EMPLOYER'S LIABILITY INSURANCE BY THE
CONTRACTOR

21.02 **(a) Subject to sub-clause (c) the Contractor shall be liable for and
shall indemnify the Employer against:**

i) **(except for such loss or damage as is at the risk of the Employer
under Clause 26 or sub-clause 32b if applicable) and any liability,
loss, claim or proceedings in respect of such injury or damage
arises out of or in the course of or by reason of the execution of
the Works and provided that such injury or damage is due to any
negligence omission or default of the Contractor, his servants or
agents or any Sub-Contractor is servants or agents (whether or
not also partly due to the negligence omission or default of the Employer or of any person for whom the Employer is responsible):**

ii) **any liability, loss, claim or proceedings whatsoever arising under
any statute or at common law in respect of personal injury to or
disease contracted by or the death of any person whomsoever
arising out of or in the course of or caused by the execution of the
Works unless solely due to any act or neglect of the Employer or
any person for whom the Employer is responsible:**

**(b) Subject to and in accordance with Clause 23, the Contractor shall
take out before commencing the Works and maintain until final completion of the work is certified by the Architect. Public Liability
insurance and Employers Liability insurance covering any liability,
loss claim or proceedings in respect of the matters referred to in sub-
clause (a):**

**(c) Without prejudice to the Contractor's liability at common law or
by statute sub-clause (a) shall not apply to any liability, loss, claim or
proceedings which arise otherwise than in connection with an accident or which fall within an exclusion permitted by sub-clause 23(e)
section (i) or (ii) (as relevant) and are not covered by an Employers
Liability or Public Liability insurance policy of the Contractor.**

The GDLA form is much the same as the previous RIAI form. The differences are as follows:

1   Clause 21(b) requires the Contractor to maintain Public Liability and
    Employer's Liability insurance until 'final completion of the work is cer-

tified by the Architect'. The minimum level of Public Liability Insurance is set out in the appendix as £250.000. As suggested in par. 21.01 this is inadequate.

2   Sub-clause 21(d) did not occur in the RIAI form. It reads:

(d) Nothing contained in the foregoing shall avoid the liability of the Contractor within the terms of the Contract for defective workmanship or materials nor shall it avoid the responsibility for any fault, defect, error, or omission as set out in Clause 25 hereunder nor for damage to the Employer's property while in the Contractor's custody and control if caused by the negligence of the Contractor, his servants or agents or any other person on the site of the Works with the permission or on the invitation of the Contractor.

This sub-clause does not seem to add much to the protection of the parties to the contract. It is obvious that defective materials and workmanship would be dealt with in other clauses in the contract, principally Clauses 8 (Materials and Workmanship to conform to description) and 31 (Defects Liability). Similarly, Clause 25 (Loss or damage to the Works due to Contractor's design) is equally clear in defining responsibility.

The reference to 'damage to the Employer's property while in the Contractor's custody and control' is an addition, though again it is difficult to see how this might occur outside a contract dealing with an existing structure, and this is covered by Clause 26 (Responsibility for existing structures). It could, possibly, be intended to refer to goods and materials which have been paid for by the Employer, but which are still in the custody or control of the Contractor, either on site or stored elsewhere. Insurance for such goods is, however, required under Clause 35 (Certificates and Payments) at sub-clause (c)(viii). That clause also contains provisions with regard to safety and ownership of materials at sub-clauses (b) and (c)(viii). See par. 35. It is not clear if the word 'invitation' used in line sub-clause 21(d) is meant in the strict legal sense of an 'invitee'. Such a person is one who enters a premises (or site) with the express or implied invitation of the occupier, in this case the Contractor. It is necessary for the invitee to have a common interest with the occupier, e.g. a customer in a shop.

SF 88 – Clause 17

LIABILITY, INDEMNITY AND INSURANCE FOR DAMAGES
TO PERSONS AND PROPERTY

21.03 **(a) The Contractor shall be liable for and shall indemnify the Employer against:**

i) **any liability, loss, claim or proceedings or any injury or damage whatsoever to any property real or personal insofar as such injury or damage arises out or or by reason of the execution of the Works and is due to any negligence, omission or default of the Contractor, or any person for whom the Contractor is responsible, and**

ii) **any liability, loss, claim or proceedings whatsoever in respect of personal injury, disease or death sustained by any person whomsoever arising out of or in the course of or caused by the execution of the Works.**

(b) Without prejudice to the foregoing liability the Contractor shall prior to the commencement of the Works take out with a Registered Insurance Company and shall for the duration of the Works maintain Public Liability Insurance in the minimum sum of one million pounds and Employer's Liability Insurance sufficient to insure the said liability.

This is a concise summary of what is contained in Clause 20 and 21 of the two longer forms. The level of £1m Public Liability cover is appropriate, as opposed to the £200,000 minimum in the RIAI form and £250,000 in the GDLA form (see par. 21.01). A Registered Insurance Company is one that is registered under the provisions of the Insurance Acts 1909–1989.

21.04 B   EMPLOYER'S RESPONSIBILITIES UNDER CLAUSE 20

1   Take out and maintain until appropriate, the necessary insurance policies as set out in the clause.

21.05 C   CONTRACTOR'S RESPONSIBILITIES UNDER CLAUSE 21
RIAI AND GDLA

1   Take out and maintain until appropriate the necessary insurance policies as set out in the clause.

21.06   CASES REFERRED TO

AMF International Ltd v Magnet Bowling and GP Turtham Ltd
     [1968] 1 WLR 1028   par. 21.06
Chariot Inns v Assicurazioni Generali SPA
     [1981] ILRM 173   par. 21.04
Cowan v Faghaile and Others
     [1991] High Court, unrep. 24th January   par. 21.08
Gold v Patman and Fotheringham
     [1958] 1 WLR 697   par. 21.02
Keenan v Shield Insurance Co Ltd
     [1988] IR 89   par. 21.04
PJ Kelly v Ryder and the Minister for Posts and Telegraphs
     [1980] ILTR 98   par. 21.06
Roscommon County Council v Waldron
     [1963] IR 407   par. 21.06

RIAI – Clause 22

ALL RISKS INSURANCE

22.01   **(a) 'Ancillary items' shall in this Clause and Clauses 20, 23, 24, 25, and 30 mean temporary works and all unfixed materials and goods delivered to or placed on or adjacent to and intended for the Works except temporary buildings, plant, tools or equipment owned or hired by the Contractor or any sub-contractor.**

This definition is intended to make clear what must be insured under the Contractor's All Risks policy. (This is normally referred to as the CAR.) It is open to the Contractor, if he so wishes, to insure the items which are excepted under this sub-clause, and most contractors would insure these items. The words 'plant' and 'equipment' are used here, but not in the sense that they are understood in the insurance industry. 'Plant' is normally divided into 'equipment', which refers to stationary items such as concrete mixing plant, and 'machinery', which are items that can move, such as bulldozers, cranes, etc. The distinction is made because of the higher risk involved in machinery.

22.02   **(b)(i)[3] Subject to and in accordance with Clause 23, the Contractor shall before commencing in the Works take out and shall, until practical completion of the Works is certified by the Architect, maintain All Risks insurance covering any loss or damage to or destruction of the Works and Ancillary Items from any cause whatsoever for the full reinstatement cost including a provision for:**

(a) the percentage for Professional Fees and the Cost of Site Clearance stated in the Appendix; and

(b) value added tax, if the Employer is not registered for value added tax and not in a position to reclaim value added tax paid in respect of the Works.

Further the Contractor shall maintain All Risks Insurance covering any loss or damage to or destruction of the Works and Ancillary Items during the Defects Liability Period which.

(i) arises from a cause which occurred prior to the commencement of the Defects Liability Period; or

(ii) **if caused by the Contractor in the normal course of any opera-tions carried out by him for the prupose of complying with his obligations during the Defects Liabilility Period.**

or

(ii) **Subject to and in accordance with Clause 23 the Employer shall before commencement of the Works take out and shall until Practical Completion of the Works is certified by the Architect maintain All Risks insurance covering any loss or damage to or destruction of the Works and Ancillary Items from any cause whatsoever for the full reinstatement cost including a provision for:**

(a) **the percentage for Professional Fees and the Cost of Site Clearance stated in the Appendix; and**

(b) **value added tax, if the Employer is not registered for value added tax and not in a position to reclaim value added tax paid in respect of the Works.**

Further the Employer shall maintain All Risks Insurance covering any loss or damage to or destruction of the Works and Ancillary Items during the Defects Liability Period which:

(i) **arises from a cause which occurred prior to the commencement of the Defects Liability Period; or**

(ii) **if caused by the Contractor in the normal course of any oerations carried out by him for the purpose of complying with his obligations during the Defects Liability Period.**

[3] **Strike out sub-clause 22(b)(i) or (ii) as required; should neither be struck out, sub-clause 22(b)(i) is deemed to apply.**

This is the basic requirement to insure the Works. As in Clause 21, a change in the 2001 revisions to the RIAI form provides that the Employer or the Contractor can arrange the insurance. It will be seen that this insurance must be kept in force until the Architect has issued the Certificate of Practical Completion (Clause 31) at which point the responsibility for insuring the Works themselves passes to the Employer. Damage to the Works can occur in many ways such as fire, floods, winds, subsidence, defective workmanship or materials, negligent use of machinery, theft, etc. This list is not meant to be comprehensive, but the normal arrangement would be that all risks are covered, except for those allowed under Clause 23(d) to be excluded.

The appendix requires two items to be specified as far as cost is concerned.

These are referred to a Clause 22(b)(i)(c) and Clause 23(b)(ii)(c). The first is a sum for the professional fees that would result from the necessity to renew or repair any part of the Works. The figure of 12.5% suggested if no other figure is given, is to cover the cost of architectural, engineering and survey-ing services. The other figure given in the appendix is the cost of clearing the site, if this is required, after any damage has been caused. This sum would be agreed between the Architect (and the Quantity Surveyor if one is retained) and the Contractor.

22.03 **(c) The Contractor shall proceed with due diligence to make good any loss or damage to or destruction of the Works or the Ancilliary Items resulting from the occurrence of any risk required to be insured by sub-clause (b) subject to the following provisions**

(i) The monies received under the All Risks insurance policy (less the portion included to cover professional fees which shall be paid to the Employer) shall be paid into a bank account in the joint names of the Contractor and Employer. The monies shall be paid out to the Contractor by instalments under certificates of the Architect related to the proportion of the work done and materials and goods delivered upon the site for making good the damage or destruction. In respect of such payments Clause 35(a) and (b) shall apply mutatis mutandis and without any deduction of any amount to be retained by the Employer.

(ii) Where the Contractor is required to maintain the All Risks insurance pursuant to Clause 22(b)(i), the Contractor shall not be entitled to any payment in respect of the rebuilding, repair or replacement of the Works or Ancillary Items destroyed or dam-aged other than the money received (plus any interest earned thereon) under the All Risks insurance policy.

(iii) Where the Employer is required to maintain All Risks insurance pursuant to Sub-Clause 22(b)(ii) and in the event of the monies received under the All Risk Insurance policy not being adequate to provide for the full reinstatement cost of the Works the Employer shall pay the amount of any shortfall to the Contractor on foot of Architect's Certificates of the value of work done and/or materials supplied (less the amounts previously paid).

(iv) Where as a result of any variation by the Employer of the Works a balance remains in the said account after completion of making good by the Contractor as required by the Employer the balance shall be paid to the Employer together with the interest earned on that balance.

This sub-clause sets out the method of dealing with the money received under the All Risks policy. It is to be kept separately from all other moneys, and in a joint account. It can be released only when the Architect certifies that certain sums are due. Clause 35 (Certificates and Payments) sets out the rules for the issuing and calculating of certificates under normal circumstances. These same rules apply to the insurance payments – *mutatis mutandis* – literally, the necessary changes being made. If variations occur during the rebuilding, and some of the insurance money remains, the balance may be retained by the Employer. Any money certified by the Architect under this sub-clause will not contain any retention amount. Under the rules of Clause 35 (Certificates and Payments) the Employer is entitled to retain a percentage of the value of the Work done [sub-clause (c) and (e)], but in the case of certificates for the work required to repair damage to the works under this clause, the full value of the work done must be certified. Also the Contractor is not entitled to any payment for making good loss or damage to the Works, apart from money received under the policy, and this is because it is the primary duty of the Contractor to complete the Works for the original contract price. A new provision in the 2001 revisions is sub-paragraph (c)(iii), and provides that in the case of the insurance money not being sufficient to complete the works, the employer shall make up the difference, but only where the Employer takes out the insurance.

The amount of cover provided in the CAR will be the full contract sum. Even though the value of the Works themselves will increase from zero to the ultimate final account figure, it is the practice in the insurance industry to insure the full contract sum from day one. Incidentally, unlike the SF 88 form (Clause 17) there is no statement that the insurance policies under the contract be with a 'Registered' insurance company, but this is, in any case, unnecessary as all companies in the State carrying on insurance business must be registered. European Community legislation will ultimately allow free access to all insurance companies in member states being entitled to do business in Ireland, but this is at a transitional stage at the moment. This legislation may also affect the domestic law of insurance as it presently operates.

In the case of the Public Liability policy a maximum cover will be taken out, and it has been seen that this must be at least £200,000 (RIAI), £250,000 (GDLA) or £1m (SF 88). Under the Employer's Liability, no ceiling is allowed. In the All Risks policy, however, the sum to be insured is set by the Contractor or the Employer and while this is primarily a matter for the parties themselves, both the Employer and the Architect in respect of partial possession of the Works are required to ensure that sufficient cover is maintained (par. 23.11).

In this regard the Architect should be aware of at least two of the factors involved in setting the appropriate cover. The first of these is the 'excess'. In insurance terms, excess means the amount of any claim that the insured person will pay before calling on the insurer. The use of this word is odd, for, as has been pointed out, it means the opposite of what is intended. The Architect should be aware of the amount of the excess and be satisfied that the Contractor is capable of absorbing the amount of the excess as far as his finances are concerned. In the IEI Standard Form (3rd edition) the maximum permitted excess is stated in the Form of Tender. Secondly, the Architect should be aware of what is called the 'average clause'. Most policies of insurance contain a provision that where the sum insured is understated, the insurer will reduce the amount paid out by the proportion of the under-valuation. Accordingly, the Architect should be aware of, or should take advice relating to, the amount stated in the All Risks policy. This amount could very well vary, and in the case of larger contracts, will certainly do so far as the work proceeds the value of the 'Works' increases and some arrangement will be required to allow for this. Often, time is used as the basis of calculating an appropriate level of cover.

GDLA – Clause 22

ALL RISKS INSURANCE BY THE CONTRACTOR

22.04 **(a) 'Ancillary Items' shall in this Clause and Clauses 23, 24, 25 and 30 mean temporary works and all unfixed materials and all goods delivered upon the site of the Works for use thereon except temporary buildings, plant, tools or equipment owned or hired by the Contractor or any Sub-Contractor.**

(b) Subject to and in accordance with Clause 23 the Contractor shll before commencing the Works take out and shall until practical completion of the Works is certified by the Architect maintain All Risks insurance covering any loss or damage to the Works and Ancillary Items from any cause whatsoever for the full reinstatement value of the Works and Ancillary Items from time to time (plus the percentages stated in the Appendix for professional fees and the cost of site clearance).

(c) The Contractor shall proceed with due diligence to make good any damage to or destruction of the Works by any risk required to be insured against by sub-clause (b) and such extension of time for completion as shall be fair and reasonable (if any) shall be made therefore under clause 30 of these conditions. The moneys received under the policy (less the portion included to cover professional fees which shall be paid to the Employer) shall be paid into a bank deposit account in the joint names of the Contractor and the Employer. The moneys so deposited shall be paid out with the interest earned to the Contractor by instalments under Certificates of the Architect related to the proportion of the work done and materials and goods delivered upon the site for making good the damage or destruction. In respect of such payments sub-clauses 35(a) and (b) shall apply *mutatis mutandis* and without deduction of any amount to be retained by the Employer. The Contractor shall not be entitled to any payment in respect of the rebuilding, repair or replacement of the Works or Ancillary Items destroyed or damaged other than the money received under the policy. Where as a result of a variation made by the Employer a balance remains in the said account after completion of making good by the Contractor as required by the Employer the balance shall be paid to the Employer together with the interest earned on that balance.

This clause is much the same as in the previous RIAI form. The differences are:

1   In sub-clause (b) the word 'replacement' is inserted between 'full' and 'value' on line 4. This is of no significance.

2   In sub-clause (c) the phrase 'and such extension of time for completion as shall be fair and reasonable (if any) shall be made therefore under Clause 30 of these conditions' is inserted at the end of the first sentence. This, it is submitted is an unnecessary addition as Clause 30 (Delay and Extension of Time) at sub-clause (d) specifically allows for extension of time due to events covered by Clauses 21 to 26. The phrase '(if any)' would be better placed immediately after the word 'completion'.

3   In sub-clause (c) the word 'deposit' is inserted on line between 'bank' and 'account'. This presumably is to ensure that interest will accrue from the money deposited.

SF 88 – Clause 18

22.05   ALL RISKS INSURANCE

Except insofar as provided by Clause 19 the Contractor shall in the joint names of the Employer and Contractor insure the Works and all materials and goods on the site including unfixed materials and goods against loss and damage by fire, storm, flood, tempest and associated perils for the full value thereof plus 10% to cover professional fees.

Clause 19 in the SF 88 form refers to existing structures (see par. 26.04). There are no exclusions set out here as in the longer forms (see par. 23.04) and the policy itself will define the precise nature of the cover. The amount of the professional fees is set at 10% as opposed to 12.5% in the longer forms, as it is quite likely that there might be no Quantity Surveyor, or Engineer, retained for the project. The clause is admirably simple.

22.06   A   ARCHITECT'S RESPONSIBILITIES UNDER CLAUSE 22
RIAI AND GDLA

1   Ensure that the items relating to professional fees and site clearance are set out in the appendix.

2   Certify any monies due for making good damage to the Works under the All Risks policy.

22.07 B EMPLOYER'S RESPONSIBILITIES UNDER CLAUSE 22
RIAI AND GDLA

1 Take out and maintain All Risks Insurance if required.

2 Arrange the joint bank account with the Contractor.

3 Retain any money not expended after variations.

22.08 C CONTRACTOR'S RESPONSIBILITIES UNDER CLAUSE 22
RIAI AND GDLA

1 Take out and maintain All Risks Insurance if required.

2 Make good any damage to the Works.

3 Arrange the joint bank account with the Employer.

RIAI – Clause 23

INSURANCE POLICIES

23.01   **(a) The Contractor's policies under Clause 21 and 22 shall be with insurers approved by the Employer, which approval shall not unreasonably be withheld. Where applicable, the Employer's policies under sub-clauses 21(b)(i) or 22(b)(ii) shall be with insurers approved by the Contractor which approval shall not be unreasonably withheld.**

This requires very little comment, but it does give the Employer the right to be involved with the Contractor's insurers.

23.02   **(b) The All Risks policy under Clause 22 shall be in the joint names of the Contractor and the Employer.**

It is important when joint insurance is being sought to make that clear to the insurer. Naming the Employer on the policy is not sufficient for this purpose; it must be specifically stated that the two parties are joint insured. Assuming that the intention of sub-clause (c) is to provide joint insurance, it would seem that the provisions of sub-clause (b) are not necessary, for if both the Contractor and Employer are insured as far as the All Risks policy is concerned, then neither need be indemnified as against the other.

23.03   **(c) The Contractor shall comply (insofar as it is within its competence to do so) with all conditions in any policy or policies of insurance under Clauses 21 or 22. where the Public Liability and/or All Risks insurance is maintained by the Employer, the Employer shall comply with all conditions of the said policies.**

This sub-clause needs no comment.

23.04   **(d) The policies of insurance under Clauses 21 and 22 may contain only the exclusions from cover summarised below worded as specified in sub-clause (e).**

This sub-clause lists the risks that the Contractor may exclude from the three insurance policies referred to in Clauses 21 and 22. The procedure for dealing with damage caused by excluded risks is set out in Clause 24. The excluded risks are defined in detail in agreed wordings, as set out in sub-clause 23(e). This sub-clause (e) provides that these 'permitted wordings' shall be agreed from time to time between the Royal Institute of the Architects of Ireland, the Construction Industry Federation and the Society of Chartered Surveyors in the Republic of Ireland. The last agreed wordings were issued on the 22nd October 1976. They are contained in a supplement to the contract form at pages 22 and 23 of the RIAI form, but are not part of the GDLA form. They are, however, available separately, published by the Royal Institute of the Architects of Ireland. The exclusions added by the 2001 revisions have not yet been given agreed wordings.

For convenience of reference, the permitted wordings are given in brackets after each phrase used in Clause 23(i), (ii), (iii) or (iv).

i) EMPLOYER'S LIABILITY

Liability in excess of the sum stated in the Appendix to these conditions of contract for any one event

'Limited War Risk'

Limited War Risk: the company shall not be liable by virtue of this policy for any injury:
a) caused by
    i) the discharge of any missiles (including liquids and gas); or
    ii) the use of any weapon, explosive or other noxious thing; or
    iii) the doing of any other injurious act either by a belligerent or in combatting a belligerent or in repelling an imagined attack by a belligerent.
b) caused by the impact on any person or property of any belligerent aircraft or any aircraft used to combat a belligerent or to repel an imagined attack by a belligerent or any part of, anything dropped from such aircraft.

The term 'belligerent' includes any State or Nation engaged in hostilities with the Republic of Ireland or not, whether war has been declared or not, and any person or body acting on behalf of a belligerent.

'Offshore Work'

'Liability compulsorily insurable under Road Traffic Acts'

ii) PUBLIC LIABILITY

Liability in excess of the sum stated in the appendix to the conditions of contract for any one accident –

Liability in excess of the sum stated in the Appendix to any one claimant or any number of claimants in respect of or arising out of any one occurance or all occurances of a series consequent on one original cause.

'War Risks'

Liability for any consequence of War, Invasion or act of Foreign Enemy Hostilities [whether war be declared or not], Civil War, Rebellion, Revolution, Insurrection or Military or Usurped power.

'Radioactive contamination / nuclear explosion'

Any legal liability of whatsoever nature directly or indirectly caused by or contributed to by or arising from:

a) ionising radiations or contamination by radioactivity from any irradiated nuclear fuel or from any nuclear waste from the combustion of nuclear fuel.

b) the radioactive toxic explosive or other hazardous properties of any explosive nuclear assembly or nuclear component thereof.

'Sonic boom'

This insurance does not cover loss, destruction or damage directly occasioned by pressure waves caused by aircraft and other aerial devices travelling at sonic or supersonic speeds.

'Persons under a contract of service or apprenticeship with the insured'

Liability in respect of injury or disease to:

a) any person who sustains such an injury or contracts such disease arising out of and in the course of his employment by the Insured under a Contract of service or apprenticeship.

b) any labour-master [or labour only sub-contractor] or persons supplied by him and/or any self-employed person for labour only whilst engaged on behalf of the insured.

'Property belonging to the Insured or in the Insured's custody and control with exceptions'

Liability in respect of damage to:

a) property belonging to the insured

b) property held in trust by or in the custody or control of the Insured or of any employee or servant or agent of the insured other than:

    a) the personal effects of the Insured's employers provided that the liability of the company for loss or damage in this respect shall not exceed the sum of IR £500 for any one employee.

b) buildings [together with the contents thereof] temporarily occupied by or on behalf of the Insured for the purpose of cleaning, maintenance, alteration or repair.

'Defective workmanship and materials but not damage resulting therefrom'

The cost of repairing, replacing or reinstating defective work or materials or goods provided by or on behalf of the insured.

'Mechanically propelled vehicles to which the Road Traffic Act applies'

Lliability in respect of injury or disease, loss or damage caused by or in connection with or arising from the ownership or possession or use by or on behalf of the Insured of any mechanically propelled vehicle or airborne vessel or craft or the loading or unloading thereof or the delivery or collection of goods in connection with such ownership or possession or use but this exception shall not operate in respect of liability for injury or damage occasioned beyond the limits of any carriageway or thoroughfare in connection with the bringing of a load to or the removal of a load from any vehicles owned by or under the control of the Insured.

'Loss or damage due to design'

Bodily injury, loss or damage to property caused by defective design, plan or specification – see par. 25.

'Pollution or Contamination'

'Territorial Limits'

'Loss or Damage due to use, occupation or possession by or on behalf of the Employer.

iii) ALL RISKS

'War risks' (previously 'War risks, riot and civil commotion')

Any consequence of war, invasion, act of foreign enemy, hostilities [whether war be declared or not] civil war, rebellion, insurrection or military or usurped power and riot and civil commotion, confiscation, nationalisation or requisition or destruction of or damage to property by or under the Order of any Government or Public or Local Authority.

'Radioactive contamination / nuclear explosion'

a) loss or destruction of or any damage to any property whatsoever or any loss or expense whatsoever resulting therefrom or any consequential loss;

b) any legal liability of whatsoever nature directly or indirectly caused by or contributed to by or arising from ionising radiations or contamination by radioactivity from any nuclear fuel or from any nuclear waste from the combustion of nuclear fuels.

c) the radioactive toxic explosive or other hazardous properties of any explosive nuclear assembly or nuclear component thereof.)

'Sonic boom'

This insurance does not cover loss, destruction or damage directly occasioned by pressure waves caused by aircraft and other aerial devices travelling at sonic or supersonic speeds.

'Loss or damage due to design'

Loss, destruction or damage due to default, defect, error, or omission in design, plan or specification.

'Defective workmanship and materials but not damage resulting therefrom'

The cost of repairing, replacing or rectifying the property insured rendered necessary by defective material or workmanship but not the cost of making good any damage to other property insured resulting from such defective material or workmanship.

'Wear and tear'

Loss or damage due to wear and tear.

'Consequential losses'

Consequential loss of any nature whatsoever.

'Limited mechanically propelled vehicles'

Loss of and / or damage to any locomotive, waterborne vessel or craft, aircraft, or any mechanically propelled vehicle other than mobile cranes, mechanical navvies, shovels, grabs, excavators, site clearing and levelling plant and vehicles with plant permanently attached.

'Loss or damage due to use, occupation or possession by or on behalf of the Employer'

Damage arising from the use of occupation by the Employer of any portion of the Works.

'Inventory Losses'

23.05 The purpose of setting out in full the exclusions allowed from the insurance policies of the Contractor, together with the explanations of these exclusions (the 'permitted wordings') is primarily for reference purposes, and to enable those engaged in the building industry to have the details readily available. The Architect in particular, however, would be well advised to ensure that expert insurance advice is available both to himself and to the Employer as necessary in view of the complexity of the subject. It does not seem appropriate to attempt to cover such a wide area as exclusions in a standard building contract form and, indeed, the futility of attempting to be all-embracing can be seen from the fact that the consequences of a 'revolution' can be excluded under 'War Risks' that affect the Public Liability policy, but not under the 'War Risks' that affect the All Risks policy. What the difference between a rebellion, a revolution, or a civil war is, is not made clear. What has been established is that malicious fire damage is not a 'civil commotion' – *Craig v Eagle Star and British Dominions Insurance Co* [1922] 56 ILTR 145.

As an example of how the contract might be simplified, it is interesting to look again at the New Engineering Contract (see par. 20.05):

Employer's Risks 81

81.1   The following risks are allocated to the Employer (the Employer's risks):

(c) War (including Civil War) and radioactive contamination risks in common form exclusions in the Contractors' approved insurance policies.

Again, when dealing with the Contractor's policies, it states:

Insurance Cover 85

85.2   Insurance policies may exclude the following:

– the cost of correcting a Defect but not of correcting any other part of Works damaged as a result.
– consequential loss.
– payment of delay or low performance damages.
– wear and tear, shortages and pilferage.
– risks relating to vehicles for which insurance is required by law.

The redrafting suggested in par. 20.05 could make the clauses easier to understand for the layman while still retaining the proper legal meaning.

23.06   **(e) The Royal Institute of the Architects of Ireland, the Construction Industry Federation and the Society of Chartered Surveyors in the Republic of Ireland acting jointly shall publish from time to time permitted wordings of the exclusion from insurance cover permitted by sub-clause (d) and this clause shall take effect as if the permitted wordings of the authorised exclusions at the Designated Date were set out in sub-clause (d).**

The excluded risks and the permitted wordings are dealt with in pars. 23.04–23.05.

23.07 **(f) Each party shall, before commencing the Works, produce to the other party for inspection any policy or policies of insurance required by Clauses 21 and 22 together with the receipt in respect of premiums paid under such policy or policies and should either party make default in insuring or maintaining insurance the other party may itself insure against any risk with respect to which the default shall have occurred and may recover a sum equal to the amount paid in respect of premiums as a contract debt from the defaulting party and may set off such debt against any other payment which may be due under this contract to the defaulting party.**

This is worded in the New Engineering Contract (referred to in pars. 20.05 and 23.05) as follows:

87 If the Contractor does not insure.

87.1 If the Contractor does not submit any of the policies and certificates required, the Employer may effect the insurance for which the Contractor should have produced the policies and certificates. The premiums paid by the Employer are paid by the Contractor.

Sub-clause 23(f) has the same effect. The Architect should ensure, if he is taking over the responsibility allocated to the parties in this sub-clause, that he has sight of the policies themselves. Receipts without the policies are not sufficient. Many contractors have insurance policies of a general nature covering their overall responsibility with regard to insurance liability in respect of all the contracts which they may be engaged in at any one time. The Architect should ensure that the insurers or their brokers are satisfied with these policies.

GDLA – Clause 23

23.08   The GDLA clause is basically the same as the previous RIAI clause and is, therefore, not reproduced here, but the 'Note' after sub-clause (f) contains a number of important differences:

1   Line 2 has the phrase 'if the Employer does not intend to carry the risk himself without insurance'. It is the practice of large companies and of the State itself, in certain circumstances, to act, in effect, as their own insurers. They will do this in areas where they judge that the risk which they might carry is acceptable when compared to the cost of the premiums.

2   Whereas in the RIAI form the Architect's duty is to make certain that the necessary cover is provided, in the GDLA form he need only 'draw the Employer's attention to the necessity of obtaining such cover'. This lesser duty is to be welcomed by the Architect.

3   The last line has the phrase 'the policies ... must remain in the force until the Works are finally complete.' [See the definition of 'final completion' in sub-clause 28(e)]. Final completion is not defined in the RIAI form.

4   The reference to Clause 32 is omitted.

5   The last line of sub-clause (h) contains the phrase 'under this or any other contract made between the Employer and the Contractor'. This phrase, which occurs on a number of occasions in the GDLA form is discussed in par. 2.30.

SF 88 – Clause 20

PRODUCTION OF INSURANCES

23.09   **The Contractor shall produce evidence of insurance in accordance with the provisions of the Contract prior to the commencement of the Works and shall submit from time to time evidence to the Architect that these insurances are in force for the duration of the Contract. If the Contractor shall fail to produce evidence that such insurances are in force having been requested to do so, the Employer may take out equivalent policies of insurance to those the Contractor shall fail to prove are in force, and deduct the cost of the same from money due or which shall become due to the Contractor.**

See the notes to par. 23.07. This clause is much the same as RIAI Clause 23(f).

23.10   A – ARCHITECT'S RESPONSIBILITIES UNDER CLAUSE 23
RIAI AND GDLA

    1   To make certain that the necessary cover is in place if the Employer proposes to take possession of any part of the Works (RIAI). To draw the Employer's attention to the necessity to obtain such cover (GDLA) if he proposes to insure.

23.11   B – EMPLOYER'S RESPONSIBILITIES UNDER CLAUSE 23
RIAI AND GDLA

    1   Approve, if appropriate, the Contractor's insurance policies or produce the insurance policy for the Contractor's approval.

    2   Ensure that insurance cover is in place if he proposes to take possession of any part of the Works.

    3   Insure for any risk on which the Contractor has defaulted.

23.12   C – CONTRACTOR'S RESPONSIBILITIES UNDER CLAUSE 23
RIAI AND GDLA

    1   Approve, if appropriate, the Employer's insurance policies or produce the insurance policy for the Employer's approval.

    2   Insure for any risk on which the Employer has defaulted.

23.13   CASE REFERRED TO

Craig v Eagle Star and British Dominions Insurance
    [1922] 56 ILTR 145   par. 23.05

RIAI – Clause 24

DAMAGE DUE TO EXCLUDED RISKS

24.01 **The following provisions shall apply to any loss or damage to the Works or Ancillary Items from any risk which the Contractor or the Employer (as the case may be) is permitted to exclude by Clause 23 and is excluded from the All Risks insurance other than such design with in Clause 25 (without prejudice to any liability of the Contractor to the Employer for the negligence of the Contractor, his servants or agents):**

On the assumption that damage has occurred, and that the Contractor was entitled to exclude the risk under the provisions of Clause 23, then the rules in sub-clauses (a), (b) and (c) will apply.

24.02 **(a) Subject to sub-clause 22(c)(iii) the occurrence of such loss or damage shall be disregarded in computing amounts payable to the Contractor under this contract.**

In other words, no financial penalty shall attach to the Contractor for any damage or loss which occurs as a result of excluded risks, and no payment shall be made to him for making good such damage.

24.03 **(b)(i) If it is just and equitable to do so the employment of the Contractor under this Contract may within 20 (twenty) working days of the occurrence of such loss or damage be determined at the option of either party by notice sent to the other by registered post or recorded delivery to the principal place of business or last known address of the other party. Within (but not after) 5(five) working days of receiving such notice either party may give to the other a written request to concur in the appointment of an arbitrator under Clause 38 of these Conditions in order that it may be determined whether such determination would be just and equitable.**

It can readily be imagined that an event may occur which is an excluded risk, such as, say, 'War Risks', and which causes damage of such an extensive nature, that it appears sensible to end the contract, then, this may be done. Strictly speaking, the contract itself is not determined or ended, but the employment of the Contractor. This is so as to allow the contractual provisions after determination to subsist or continue. If the parties cannot agree that determination is appropriate, then an arbitrator may be appointed. The rules governing arbitration are dealt with in Clause 38 (Disputes Resolution).

24.04 **(b)(ii) upon the expiration of 7 (seven) working days of receipt of a notice of determination or, where reference to arbitration is made, upon the arbitrator upholding the notice of determination, the provision of sub-clause 34(b) except sub-paragraph (v) shall apply;**

Where the employment of the Contractor is determined, the provisions of Clause 34 will apply (Determination of Contract by Contractor). The exception is sub-paragraph (v) of sub-clause (b) of that clause, which would normally allow to the Contractor any loss or damage caused by the determination itself.

24.05 **(c) If no notice of determination is served or where a reference to arbitration is made, if the arbitrator does not uphold the notice of determination, then,**

    i)   **the Contractor with due diligence shall reinstate or make good such loss or damage and proceed with the carrying out and completion of the Works,**

    ii)   **the reinstatement and making good such loss or damage to the Works or Ancillary Items and (when required) the removal and disposal of debris shall be deemed to be a variation ordered by the Architect.**

If, for one cause or another, it is decided to proceed with the Works after damage due to an excluded risk, then this work is regarded as a variation and will be paid for under the rules governing variations (Clause 13 – Ascertainment of Prices for Variations) dealt with in pars. 13.03 to 13.06.

GDLA – Clause 24

24.06 This clause is still much the same as the RIAI clause except for the reference to the Employer.

SF 88

24.07   There is no provision for excluded risks in the shorter form.

24.08   B   EMPLOYER'S RESPONSIBILITIES UNDER CLAUSE 24
RIAI AND GDLA

        1   Decide whether or not to seek determination, and/or arbitration.

24.09   C   CONTRACTOR'S RESPONSIBILITIES UNDER CLAUSE 24
RIAI AND GDLA

        1   Decide whether or not to seek determination, and/or arbitration.

        2   Proceed, if appropriate, to reinstate and complete the Works.

RIAI and GDLA – Clause 25

DAMAGE DUE TO DESIGN

25.01 **Notwithstanding clauses 23(d)(iii) and Clause 24 the contractor shall proceed with due diligence to repair, rebuild or make good at his own expense any damage to or destruction of the works or ancillary items due to any fault, defect, error or omission in design by the contractor, his servants or agents (including sub-contractors and suppliers, other than nominated sub-contractors or nominated suppliers). The Contractor shall not be responsible to the Employer for any error or omission in:**

(a) any design provided to the Contractor by the Employer, its servants or agents; or

(b) design prepared by any Nominated Sub-Contractor or any Nominated Supplier

In previous editions of this book it was suggested that the overall provisions of the Contract Conditions with regard to design need some tidying up. Damage due to design will obviously be caused either by the Contractor, or his agents, or the Employer and his agents. The case of damage caused by negligent or defective design on the part of the Employer (this means in effect the Architect or Engineers) is quite clearly the responsibility of the Employer, and the cost of making good any damage caused must be borne by the Employer. The damage is dealt with as if it were an excluded risk.

This tidying up has now been done in sub-clauses (a) and (b) added in the 2001 revisions. These additions do not apply to the GDLA form. Sub-Clause (b) confirms the decision of the Supreme Court in *Norta Wallpapers (Ireland)Limited v John Sisk and Sons (Dublin) Limited* [1978] 14 BLR 49.

The Architect and Consulting Engineers will very often have Professional Indemnity Insurance cover, and the Employer is usually protected in this way, but it would be prudent for the Employer to check this.

25.02 Damage caused by the design default of the Contractor is dealt with in a number of ways. It was seen in par. 23.04 that 'loss or damage due to design' is a permitted exclusion under both the All Risks policy and the Public

Liability policy. This has been allowed because of the difficulty of obtaining such cover, but the Contractor must repair or make good any such damage under the provisions of this clause. The references in the clause to Clause 23(d)(iii) and to Clause 24 are to the permitted exclusion in regard to the All Risks Policy and to provisions for making good damage due to such excluded risk. The permitted exclusion under Clause 23(d)(ii) for damage due to design in connection with the Public Liability policy is not referred to here, but the provisions of this clause would also apply.

25.03 It will have been seen in par. 16.08 that the Contractor is not liable for damage caused by defective design on the part of a Nominated Sub-Contractor, and that the cost of making good any such damage must be borne by the Employer. However, as set out in par. 37.02, the Employer will be entitled to recover directly from the Nominated Sub-Contractor under the provisions of the collateral warranty which should, in all cases, be executed by the Employer and Sub-Contractor.

25.04 There is no requirement under the standard forms for the Contractor to be insured against liability for defective design, but it is recommended in any contract where there is a design input on the part of the Contractor that a separate policy be taken out by the Contractor to cover the risk. This policy would be similar to the Professional Indemnity policy of the Architect.

SF 88

25.05 There is no reference in the shorter form to damage due to design.

25.06 C   CONTRACTOR'S RESPONSIBILITIES UNDER CLAUSE 25

1   Repair any damage due to defective design.

26.07 CASE REFERRED TO

Norta Wallpapers (Ireland) Limited v John Sisk and Son
    (Dublin) [1978] 14 BLR 49   par. 25.01

RIAI – Clause 26

RESPONSIBILITY FOR EXISTING STRUCTURES

26.01 **(a) Subject to Clause 26(b) where the works involve the alteration or extension of existing structures,**
  (i) all existing structures
  (ii) together with the contents of existing structures.
shall be at the sole risk of the Employer as regards loss or damage caused by the undernoted perils (as defined in a standard policy of insurance in the insurance market)
  • **fire, storm, tempest, flood; or**
  • **bursting or overflowing of water tanks apparatus or pipes; or**
  • **explosion, impact, aircraft; or**
  • **riot, civil commotion or malicious damage**

(b) Where the contents of the existing structures are not the property of the Employer (or an associated or subsidiary company of the Employer) the Contractor shall indemnify the Employer (or an associated or subsidiary company of the Employer) against any liability which the Employer (or an associated or subsidiary company of the Employer) may incur to third parties by reason of any loss or damage to the said contents caused by the negligence omission or default of the Contractor up to an amount equivalent to the Minimum Sum for Public Liability Insurance stated in the Appendix but shall have no liability for any greater amount.

(c) The Employer shall maintain from the commencement of the Works until completion by the Contractor of the Works (including the making good of defects) under this Contract a proper policy of insurance against the said risks as referred to in Clause 26(a) above and such policy shall include, subject to Clause 26(b) a waiver of all rights of subrogation against the Contractor and/or its sub-contractors. The Employer shall before commencement of the Works produce such policy to the Contractor for inspection with the receipt for the last premium paid for its renewal and should the Employer make default in insuring or maintaining insurance the Contractor may himself insure against any risk with respect to which the default shall have occurred and for that purpose shall have such right of entry

and inspection as may be required to make a survey and inventory of the existing structures and contents and shall upon production of the receipt for any premium paid by him be entitled to have its amount added to the Contract Sum. If any loss or damage be caused to the existing structures by any of the said risks or by way, riot or civil commotion then the terms of Clause 24(b) shall apply.

(d) Further, the Employer shall have no right to recover from the Contractor any consequential loss howsoever and whatsoever incurred by it consequent on the occurrence of any of the perils referred to in this clause.

(e) If, after the issue by the Architect of the Certificate of Practical Completion, the Contractor is requested to carry our varied or additional Works, the provisions of sub-clauses 26(a) and (b) above shall apply mutatis mutandis as if the Works referred to in the said Certificate of Practical Completion are existing structures and the varied and additional works are alterations or extensions to such existing structures.

(f) For the purposes of this Clause, 'existing structures' shall mean
- all and/or any parts of a structure or building on, under, over or adjoining which the works are to be constructed; or
- all and/or any parts of a structure or building which gives structural support to such structure or building; or
- structures or building which are owned (whether in fee simple or under lease) by the Employer (or an associated or subsidiary company of the Employer) or for which the Employer (or an associated or subsidiary company of the Employer) is responsible.

This is a fairly straightforward provision. It is important to note however, that while the Employer is responsible for any damage which results to the existing structures, the Contractor must obtain the necessary Public Liability, Employer Liability, and All Risks insurances as would be the case in a contract dealing with a new building. The cover provided under Clause 26 is quite restricted. It must be remembered that the Employer's policy will pay for any damage, even if caused by the negligence of the Contractor – 'the existing structures ... shall be at the sole risk of the Employer'.

Sub-Clause (b) has been added in the 2001 revisions and needs no comment. However, it should be noted that many house or apartment insurance policies have a condition that the property must not remain unoccupied for more than a stated period and Architects should always ask Employers to have regard to this restriction if the Employer proposes to vacate the premises during renovations, alterations or extensions.

In addition, sub-clause (d) clarifies the position regarding consequential loss, and sub-clause (e) deals with works carried out after the issue by the Architect of the Certificate of Practical Completion. The final change is the inclusion of a definition of the phrase 'existing structures'.

The Architect's exposure as far as insurance matters are concerned was demonstrated recently in a case reported in the ARCHITECT'S JOURNAL of 23rd January 1991. The contract (under the JCT/RIBA Minor Works Contract) was for restoration and repair work to a church, and the Employer was liable for any damage to the structure and contents just as in the RIAI form, Clause 26. The Contractors caused damage to the extent of £100,000 to a valuable organ, whereas the church insurance policy provided cover of only £10,000. There was no question but that the responsibility for insuring lay with the Employer. The Architects were held to be negligent because they did not advise the Employer of the risk involved nor did they draw the Employer's attention to the need for obtaining adequate insurance cover. The judge said that it was common ground that the Architect was under a duty to draw the Employer's attention to the perils specified in the contract form and to the obligation to insure. (The case is *William Tomkinson and Sons Ltd and The Parochial Council of St Michael-in-the-Hamlet v Holford Associates.*)

26.02 Other provisions of this clause reflect the requirements of previous clauses:

1 The Employer must produce the insurance policy to the Contractor (23.07). The Contractor should ensure that the Employer has informed his insurers that building works are being carried out, for if this has not been done the cover would not be in place, and even though the loss would fall on the Employer it could well affect the Contractor if the loss reduced the Employer's financial ability to continue with, or repair, the works.

2 The Contractor may himself insure if the Employer defaults (par. 23.07).

GDLA – Clause 26

26.03   The wording in the GDLA form is the same as in the original RIAI form but the sentences have been rearranged. The effect of the clause is the same as the new RIAI clause.

(a) The existing structures together with the contents thereof shall be at the sole risk of the Employer as regards loss or damage by fire, storm, tempest, bursting or overflowing of water tanks, apparatus or pipes or explosion. If any loss or damage is caused to the existing structures by any of the said risks or by war, riot or civil commotion then the terms of sub-clause 24(b) shall apply.

(b) The Employer shall maintain from the commencement of the Works until the completion by the Contractor of all work (including the making good of defects) under the Contract a proper policy of insurance against the said risks. The Employer shall before com-mencement of the Works produce such policy to the Contractor for inspection with the receipt for the last premium paid for its renewal and should the Employer make default in insuring or maintaining insurance the contractor may himself insure against any risk with respect to which the default shall have occurred and for that pur-pose shall have such right of entry and inspection as may be required to make a survey and inventory of the existing structures and contents and shall upon production of the receipt for any pre-mium paid by him be entitled to have its amount added to the Contract Sum.

NOTE: The whole of Clause 26 shall be struck out unless the Contract is for the alteration or extension of an existing building. If the Contract is for the alteration or extension of an existing building and if the Employer intends to carry his own risk without insurance sub-clause (b) shall be struck out. Sub-clause (b) shall be retained if the Employer intends to insure against his risk.

In par. 23.08 it was noted that in some cases the State, and some other organ-isations and companies, carry the risk themselves without insurance. This note is to allow for that circumstance.

SF 88 – Clause 19

INSURANCE OF EXISTING STRUCTURES

26.04 **In the case of alterations or additions to existing buildings all existing structures, contents, the Works and unfixed materials except plant, tools and equipment shall be insured by the Employer for the full value thereof plus 10% to cover professional fees, from commencement to Practical Completion against loss or damage by fire, storm, tempest, lightning, flood, earthquake and associated perils. The Employer shall produce evidence of such insurance if so requested and if such evidence is not produced then the Contractor may take out insurance to cover such risks and the cost of same will become a debt due to the Contractor by the Employer.**

This is a paraphrase of Clause 26 in the longer forms. The only item not contained in the longer forms is the reference to professional fees, which is not of great significance, except that it will cover the Employer against these costs.

26.05 A ARCHITECT'S RESPONSIBILITY UNDER CLAUSE 26
RIAI AND GDLA

    1 Ensure that Clause 26 is struck out where appropriate (GDLA).

    2 Advise Employer as to occupancy.

26.06 B EMPLOYER'S RESPONSIBILITIES UNDER CLAUSE 26
RIAI AND GDLA

    1 Take out and maintain insurance (see 'Note' – par. 26.03).

    2 Produce insurance policies and receipts.

26.07 C CONTRACTOR'S RESPONSIBILITIES UNDER CLAUSE 26
RIAI AND GDLA

    1 Take out insurance if the Employer defaults.

26.08 CASE REFERRED TO

William Tomkinson and Sons Ltd and the Parochial Council of
St Michael-in-the-Hamlet v Holford Associates
[1991] (ARCHITECT'S JOURNAL, 23rd January)   par. 26.01

RIAI and GDLA – Clause 27

WAR DAMAGE

27.01 **No liability shall attach to the Contractor under this Contract for any damage to the Works or unfixed materials caused by war, invasion, act of foreign enemy, hostilities (whether war be declared or not), civil war, civil commotion, rebellion, revolution, insurrection or military or usurped power.**

This is a comprehensive exclusion which extends the exclusion allowed in Clause 23(e)(iii). In that clause any damage to the Works resulting from war, etc, would be covered by the provisions of Clause 24. This clause allows a total exclusion to the Contractor from any damage, and renders the provisions of Clause 23(e)(iii) superfluous in extreme circumstances.

RIAI – Clause 28

DATES FOR POSSESSION AND COMPLETION

28.01 **Possession of the site shall be given to the Contractor on or before the 'Date for Possession' stated in the Appendix. He shall thereupon begin the Works, regularly proceed with and complete same (except such painting, papering or other decorative work as the Architect may instruct him to delay) on or before the 'Date for Completion' stated in the Appendix subject nevertheless to the provisions for extension of time hereinafter contained. If the Date for Possession is deferred by the Employer then the Contractor shall be entitled to receive from the Employer compensation for any loss incurred due to dislocation of the Contractor's organisation and any time lost from this cause shall be ascertained and certified by the Architect.**

The appendix on page 20 of the RIAI form provides for the insertion of the two dates mentioned in this clause. The date for possession of the site will normally be agreed between the parties, or it might be stated in the tender documents. If any delay occurs in handing over possession of the site to the Contractor, then he may become entitled to both an extension of time [see Clause 30(b)] and to compensation under this clause.

As far as the extension of time is concerned, which might result from late possession, the Architect will take into account such factors as the time of year. It will be obvious that a builder's programme that is based on an assumed start in April will differ substantially from one where the start is taken as being in September. Other factors such as obtaining other work will also have to be considered. Similar factors will apply as far as compensation is concerned. The phrase states that this will apply to 'Dislocation of the Contractor's organisation' and this can be extensive depending on circumstances. There can also be cases, of course, where no real loss or delay is caused. The Architect must judge each case on the facts. The Architect will realise that such delays might adversely affect the Contractor's budget, create losses due to under-utilisation of company resources, and in some circumstances cause the lay-off of employees. On the other hand, a delay might benefit a contractor by bringing the start of the work into a better weather period.

The amount of compensation might also be affected by the provisions of Clause 2(f) which deals with the postponement of any works to be executed under the contract, and if the delay in obtaining possession of the site is extensive, it is submitted that the provisions of paragraph 4 of Clause 2 would apply, and that the Contractor might found a claim on that wording (see par. 2.26).

In cases of very long delay, the Contractor may be entitled to damages under ordinary law for breach of contract. It is obviously in the interests of all parties to ensure that the site is available (or as much of it as is necessary to allow a start to be made) before the contract is signed and a possession date agreed.

28.02   The date for completion stated in the appendix will either have been agreed between the parties, be fixed by the tender documents, or proposed by the Contractor. It is subject to change under the provisions of Clause 30. As stated before (par. 2.11) it cannot be brought forward by the Architect, although the Contractor is, of course, entitled to finish early. Provision is sometimes made as between the Employer and the Contractor for bonus payments to be made in the case of early completion, but they are not provided for in the standard forms. The consequences of late completion are dealt with in Clause 29.

GDLA – Clause 28

DATE FOR POSSESSION, PRACTICAL COMPLETION AND
FINAL COMPLETION

28.03   This clause in GDLA combines the provisions contained in RIAI Clause 28, some of the provisions of RIAI Clause 31, and some additional items. The clause is divided into five sub-clauses.

(a) Possession of the site will be given to the Contractor within ten (10) working days after issue by the Employer of his Acceptance of the tender provided that within that period he has received from the Contractor satisfactory evidence that the insurance required by these conditions (and any Contract Guarantee Bond that the Employer may require) have been obtained and that the Contractor has in writing given an undertaking to the Employer that he will within ten (10) working days of their issue to him sign the Articles of Agreement. The Contractor shall thereupon begin the Works and regularly proceed with and bring same to practical completion (as hereinbelow defined) within the period stated in the Appendix such

**period to commence on expiry of the above mentioned ten (10) work-
ing days subject nevertheless to the provisions for extension of time
contained in these Conditions. If through any fault of the Employer
possession is not given within the above mentioned ten (10) working
days or within such extended period as may be agreed between the
Contractor and the Employer the Contractor shall be entitled to
receive from the Employer compensation for any loss incurred due to
dislocation of the Contractor's organisation and any time lost from
this cause shall be treated as a delay under Clause 30.**

This sub-clause differs substantially from the provisions set out in the RIAI
form. Under GDLA, possession of the site is only given to the Contractor if
two or sometimes three conditions have been fulfilled. The conditions are as
follows:

1   The Contractor must produce evidence that the insurances required have
been obtained. The Contractor is already required to do this under
Clause 23(f) and under Clause 26(b) if appropriate, so this condition is
superfluous. It can possibly be justified on the grounds of emphasising a
very important requirement.

2   If required, a Contract Guarantee Bond, must be produced. If a bond is
required, it must be made a condition precedent in the tender documents.
It cannot be imposed without notice. A bond is an undertaking by a
financial institution, often an insurance company, to reimburse the
Employer for any loss or damage, which results from breach of contract.

The most frequent occasion when a bond is called in is in the case of
bankruptcy. A bond can only exist where a contract exists, and this is
why a Collateral Agreement is a pre-requisite to the obtaining of a bond.
The amount of the bond will be agreed between the Employer and the
financial institution (generally referred to as 'the Bondsman'). The bond
used to be for the full contract amount, but nowadays the bond will only
be required to cover from 10% to 25% of the contract sum. It is important to remember that the purpose of the bond is to reimburse the
Employer, and that the Bondsman is under no obligation to complete the
contract (see par. 33.09 for further notes on the bond).

3   The Contractor must undertake to sign the Articles of Agreement within
ten working days of their issue to him.

If these conditions have been fulfilled, the Employer will give possession of
the site to the Contractor within ten working days after the acceptance by
him of the Contractor's tender. These provisions, it is suggested, appear to be
somewhat involved and might cause unnecessary difficulties. The purpose
behind them is clear, but it is not clear why the obtaining of the required

insurances (or of the Bond) must be related to possession of the site rather than being made a general condition precedent for the commencement of the Works. The imposition of a rigid time-table could cause problems, particularly as it appears as if some of the periods of time allowed might be very short in the case of large and involved contracts. The notes in par. 28.01 cover the items with regard to compensation and delay.

28.04   **(b) 'Practical Completion' means that the Works have been carried to such a stage that they can be taken over and used by the Employer for their intended purpose and that any items of work or supply then outstanding or any defects then patent are of a trivial nature only and are such that their completion or rectification does not interfere with or interrupt such use. Such outstanding items and defects shall be proceeded with expeditiously and shall be finished or rectified within a reasonable time after practical completion.**

This sub-clause is the same as RIAI Clause 31, paragraph 2, with the addition of the last sentence. Previous forms of contract contained no definition of practical completion, which was a serious omission, as the consequences of the issue by the Architect of the notice of practical completion will show. The GDLA form uses the word 'notification' with regard to the Architect's decision that practical completion has occurred. The RIAI form requires the Architect to 'certify'. In any event, when practical completion has occurred, the following contractual provisions apply:

1   The All Risks insurance policy (Clause 22(b) can be terminated by the Contractor, and responsibility for insuring the Works falls on the Employer. The Public Liability and Employer's Liability policy on the other hand must be kept in force until 'final' completion of the Works, which is defined in sub-clause (e) of this clause.

2   The Defects Liability Period begins on the day after the Architect's 'Notice' of practical completion (see Clause 31).

3   Half of the 'Retention Fund' [see Clause 35(d)] which is the money retained during the course of the Works by the Employer as protection against the cost of employing others is released to the Contractor. The other half (moiety) is released as part of the final certificate.

4   The period of 'Final Measurement' stated in the appendix shall commence.

The last sentence in the sub-clause is self-explanatory.

28.05   **(c) When the Contractor is of the opinion that the Works are approaching practical completion he shall in writing notify the Architect accordingly. When the Architect is of the opinion that the**

**Works are practically complete he shall in writing notify the
Employer and the Contractor to that effect and at the same time
shall in writing draw the Employer's attention to the termination of
the Contractor's responsibility for insurance under Clause 22.
Practical Completion of the Works shall be deemed for all the purposes of this Contract to have taken place on the day named in the
Architect's notification.**

This sub-clause, which deals in essence with the matters in RIAI Clause 31,
paragraph one, provides the mechanism for the issue of the notice of practical
completion. It is up to the Contractor to initiate the process, and the Architect
must notify both parties to the Contract of his decision. The requirement that
the Architect draw the Employer's attention to the insurance position is sensible, and it is not contained in the RIAI form. The consequences of the issue
of the notice of practical completion are dealt with in par. 28.04.

28.06   **(d) Notwithstanding the provisions of sub-clause (b) of this Clause
the Architect at his discretion may instruct the Contractor to postpone the execution of all or any part of the painting, papering, decorative or other finishing work until after practical completion of the
Works. Such instructions shall be given in writing and they shall not
in any way invalidate or affect the notification issued or to be issued
under sub-clause (c) of this Clause.**

This sub-clause is to preserve the date of practical completion, and also to
protect the Employer as regards claims for an extension of time. Normally, if
an Architect's instruction under Clause 2(a) is issued after the issue of the
notice of practical completion, it has been argued that time is 'at large' and
that the final completion date is no longer binding. In that case, the
Contractor's obligation would be reduced to that of completing 'within a reasonable time'. This sub-clause gives the Architect the right to issue instructions with regard to these minor matters without any danger to the
Employer's position.

28.07   **(e) The Works shall be deemed to have been finally completed only
when all outstanding items of work as above described and all work
postponed on the written instructions of the Architect have been finished and all defects, shrinkages and other faults for which the
Contractor is liable under Clause 31 have been made good.**

The Defects Liability Period, which is set out in the appendix, is the period
allowed after practical completion during which all defects must be made
good (see Clause 31). At final completion all insurances may be terminated
by the Contractor as far as contractual provisions are concerned. However,

contractors will be advised by their insurers that they remain liable to the public, more or less indefinitely. If a person injured by say, portion of a building falling off, can prove that this was caused by the negligence of the original contractor then the contractor is liable. It does not matter if this accident occurs ten or twenty years after the building was completed. A person who is injured must bring an action against the person responsible within three years of the injury being suffered, but the length of time since completion of the contract is not relevant. Most contractors carry a general Public Liability policy to guard against this eventuality.

SF 88 – Clause 4

PRACTICAL COMPLETION

28.08 This clause is the same in basic content as Clause 28(b) GDLA and Clause 31 RIAI.

28.09 A ARCHITECT'S RESPONSIBILITIES UNDER CLAUSE 28

RIAI

1 Ascertain and certify any loss due to late possession

GDLA

1 Deal with any delay for late possession under Clause 30.

2 Notify the Employer and Contractor of the issue of the notice of practical completion.

3 Notify the Employer of the change in insurance responsibilities.

4 Instruct, if appropriate, the Contractor to delay finishing works.

28.10 B EMPLOYER'S RESPONSIBILITIES UNDER CLAUSE 28

RIAI

1 Provide possession of the site.

GDLA

1 Issue notice of acceptance of tender.

2 Insure the Works as necessary.

28.11   C   CONTRACTOR'S RESPONSIBILITIES UNDER CLAUSE 28

RIAI

1   Take possession of the site, proceed with, and complete the Works.

2   Apply for compensation and delay for late possession.

GDLA

1   Provide evidence of insurance cover (and bond if necessary).

2   Undertake to sign articles of agreement within 10 working days.

3   Take possession of the site, proceed with, and practically complete same.

4   Apply for compensation and delay for late possession.

5   Complete outstanding items.

6   Notify the Architect that the Works are practically complete.

7   Complete all defects as required under Clause 31.

RIAI – Clause 29

DAMAGES FOR NON-COMPLETION

29.01 **(a) If the Contractor fails to practically complete the works by the Date for Completion stated in the Appendix or within any extended time under Clause 28 or 30 of these conditions and the Architect certifies in writing, on simultaneous notice to the Employer and the Contractor that in his opinion the same ought reasonably so to have been completed the Contractor shall pay or allow to the Employer the sum named and at the rate stated in the Appendix as 'Liquidated or Ascertained Damages' for the period during which the said works shall so remain or have remained incomplete and the Employer may deduct such damages from any money due or to become due to the Contractor under this Contract.**

The conditions required for the implementation of this clause are:

1   There must be a completion date stated in the appendix.

2   The Architect must certify that, in his opinion, the Works should have been completed by that date or by any extended date.

3   The Architect must have adjudicated on the Contractor's claim for an extension of time (see pars. 30.12 and 30.14).

This is sometimes referred to as the 'Penalty Clause' but this is not a recommended or indeed accurate description. The law does not approve of penal conditions. The position is well set out in the case of *Dunlop Pneumatic Tyre Co Ltd v New Garage and Motor Company Ltd* [1915] AC 79 as follows:

1   Though the parties to a contract who use the words 'penalty' or 'liquidated damages' may *prima facie* be supposed to mean what they say, yet the expression used is not conclusive. The court must find out whether the payment stipulated is in truth a penalty or liquidated damages.

2   The essence of a penalty is a payment of money stipulated as *in terrorem* of the offending party; the essence of liquidated damages is a genuine covenanted pre-estimate of damage.

3   The question as to whether a sum stipulated is a penalty or liquidated damages is a question of construction to be decided upon the terms and

inherent circumstances of each particular contract judged as at the time of making the contract, not as at the time of the breach. (The sum must be an attempt to estimate the actual loss as far as this can be done at the time [*Finnegan v Community Housing* [1993] 65 BLR 103].)

Where there is an agreed damages clause in a contract, a plaintiff can recover the specified sum even if his actual loss is less. Similarly, if his actual loss is more he can still recover only the agreed amount. A party to a contract cannot hold a threat over the other party (to hold the party *in terrorem*) and if a court decides that a damages clause is indeed a 'penalty' it will be disregarded. The court will allow a plaintiff in that case to recover only his actual loss, but it is curious that in the unlikely event of the actual loss being more than the 'penal' amount then the plaintiff can recover in full. In *Lombank Ltd v Kennedy and Others* [1961] NI 192 it was held that the damages in a contract were in the nature of a penalty because the damages were not a genuine pre-estimate of the loss. It has also been held that if no loss at all has been suffered, then no damages will be paid (*Laird Bros v City of Dublin Steam Packet Co* [1900] 34 ILTR 9).

In the case of a building which is being built to be let, it is easier to relate the projected loss to the actual loss, basing it on the going commercial letting rates, and this computation should form the basis of the damages proposed. It is more difficult in the case of a building which is used for, say, residential, social, educational, use, etc, but the proposed damages should still relate as far as possible to the estimated damages. The liquidated and ascertained damages should be set out in the tender documents so that tenderers would be aware of the possible damages, and so that they could take this into account when making up their tender. The details of the proposed damages are generally included in the Bill of Quantities, where most of the appendix details are set out, but where there is no Bill of Quantities, the details should be contained in other tender documentation.

29.02   The appendix will state the date for completion, and this will have been agreed between the contracting parties, being derived from the Contractor's tender or agreed in some other way. The date for completion is obviously founded on the date for possession, and this clause refers to Clause 28, where the Contractor is protected if the date for possession is delayed by the Employer, and any loss to the Contractor will be compensated. A very early case where late possession of the site was held to be a breach of a condition precedent to the contract is *Arterial Drainage Co v Rathangan River Board* [1880] 6 LR IR 513. Clause 30 is also referred to, and this allows the Architect at 30(b) to allow an extension of time for late possession of the site.

29.03   The works must be practically complete on or before the date set out in the appendix. Practical completion is defined in Clause 31. The date for completion may, of course, be extended by the Architect under the provisions of Clause 30, and practical completion would then occur at the extended date.

If the works are not practically complete at the completion date as set out in the appendix, or as extended under Clause 30, then the Architect must notify both the Employer and Contractor that, in his opinion, the works should have been complete, and damages begin to run from the date of that certificate. Failure to issue this certificate invalidates the claim (*Bell and Son v CBF* [1989] 46 BLR 102). The phrase 'Liquidated and Ascertained' referring to damages due is tautologous, as 'liquidated' is legally defined as 'ascertained'. This is in contrast to 'unliquidated' damages which have to be determined by a court in the event of the parties not agreeing in advance to the extent of damages. It is obviously much more convenient to agree the rate and amount of damages in advance.

29.04   It is very important for the Architect to be aware of his duty to certify in full any works properly completed, whether or not damages are being paid under Clause 29(a). The two duties of the Architect in this sub-clause are to certify the monies due firstly, and then to certify that the building should have been completed by the completion date (or the extended completion date). It is the Employer who will deduct any damages which are properly due under the Contract.

Obviously, an employer is not entitled to liquidated damages if by his acts or omissions he has prevented the Contractor from completing the works by the completion date, and Clause 29(b) deals with the position that then arises. This is discussed in *Percy Bilton Ltd v Greater London Council* [1982] 20 BLR 1. This case is dealt with in detail at par. 16.05 in relation to delays caused by nominated sub-contractors. If an Employer deducts liquidated and ascertained damages, and an extension of time is subsequently certified by the Architect, the Contractor will then become entitled to interest or financing charges as a direct loss or expense. This was so held in *Department of Environment (NI) v Farrans (Construction) Ltd* [1982] NI 11.

The Employer is entitled to recover money which would normally form part of the retention fund where he is entitled to liquidated damages, even where these moneys would normally be part of a trust fund. It has been held that this is because of the provision in Clause 35(e)(i) where the Employer was entitled to have 'recourse thereto (i.e. the Retention Fund) from time to time for payment of any amount which he is entitled under the provisions of this contract to deduct from any sum due or to become due to the Contractor' (*Henry Boot Building Ltd v The Croydon Hotel and Leisure Company* [1985] 36 BLR 41).

29.05 **(b) If any act or default of the Employer delays progress of the Works then the Contractor shall within five working days of the Act or default give notice in writing to the Architect to this effect and any time lost from this cause shall be ascertained and certified by the Architect and the Employer shall pay or allow to the Contractor such damages as the Contractor shall have incurred by the delay.**

This is the reverse of Clause 29(a) where the Employer benefits. This clause, 29(b), allows the Contractor to recover any loss caused by the actions of the Employer (including of course any actions of the Employer's Agents) and also provides for extensions of time if appropriate. This is particularly set out in Clause 30(j).

It is important that the Contractor notify the Architect, as required, within five working days of the occurrence of the event which caused the delay. Failure to do so might not necessarily deprive the Contractor of his right, but it would be prudent to avoid the risk.

Clause 29(b) has been the subject of an important case, bearing on the conclusiveness or otherwise of the final certificate. The case is *P Elliott and Co Ltd v The Minister for Education* [1987] ILRM 710. The case in question involved a contract where the 1966 edition of the RIAI form was used, but the wording in the 1996 edition is identical, although the clause numbers are now different. Clauses 24(b), 29(g) and 31, referred to in reports of the case are now numbered 29(b), 35(j) and 38 respectively.

The issue in the case revolved around the wording of 29(g), now Clause 35: (i). 'The said final certificate shall be conclusive in any proceedings arising out of this contract (whether by arbitration under Clause 31 – now Clause 38 – of these conditions or otherwise) that the works have been properly carried out and completed in accordance with the terms of this contract and that any necessary effect has been given to all terms of this contract which require an adjustment to be made to the contract sum'.

The Supreme Court upheld the decision of the High Court that a claim under Clause 24(b) – now 29(b) – was not debarred because the final certificate had been issued. The judgement is based on the fact that the other 'money' clauses in the contract all refer to the 'contract sum' whereas 24(b) / 29(b) does not so refer, and any claim under this clause stands outside the 'contract sum' as determined by the final certificate.

GDLA – Clause 29(a)

29.06 The wording of the GDLA form is slightly different, but the intent and effect is the same, with the important exception of the last phrase – 'under this or any other Contract made between the Employer and the Contractor'. The meaning and the consequences of this phrase are discussed in par. 2.31 as it is in Clause 2 – GDLA that this phrase first occurs.

GDLA – Clause 29(b)

29.07 **If the Contractor claims that any act or default of the Employer has delayed or will delay progress of the Works, the Contractor shall within five (5) working days of the alleged act or default give notice thereof in writing to the Employer and the Architect and any time lost and treated as a delay under Clause 30. If the Contractor has incurred any loss as a result of such delay the Architect shall as soon as possible ascertain the amount of such loss and the Employer shall pay or allow such amount to the Contractor provided that the Contractor in the opinion of the Architect has taken all reasonable steps to minimise loss.**

This wording is largely the same as in the RIAI form, but with two additional requirements. The Contractor is firstly required to give notice of any alleged delay to the Employer in addition to notifying the Architect, and the Architect must consult with the Employer before agreeing on any extension of time which might be granted under Clause 30. Secondly, the Architect must be satisfied that the Contractor has taken all reasonable steps to minimise any loss which has occurred. The use of the word 'loss' as opposed to 'damages' in the RIAI form does not have significant effect.

SF 88 – Clause 6

29.08 **If the works are not completed by the date fixed for Practical Completion in the Articles of Agreement or any later date as fixed by virtue of these conditions then the Contractor will pay or allow by way of set-off to the Employer Liquidated Damages at the rate of £ per week for every week or part of a week during which time the work remains incomplete.**

This wording, though not as detailed as that in RIAI 29(a) or GDLA 29(a), is nevertheless an accurate paraphrase of the longer clauses. The use of the word 'set-off' in this clause is not the same as the right of set off mentioned in respect of GDLA 29(a). There the set-off refers to distinct contracts between the same parties; here, the use of the phrase is to describe the right of the Employer to set-off one sum of money as against other sums of money in the same contract.

29.09   A   ARCHITECT'S RESPONSIBILITIES UNDER CLAUSE 29 RIAI and GDLA

1   Ensure that the dates for Possession and Completion are set out in the appendix.

2   Certify that the building ought to have been complete on the date in the appendix.

3   Ascertain any delay caused by the Employer and (in the case of the RIAI form) certify the delay.

Additional Responsibilities under GDLA

1   Consult with the Employer before ascertaining any delay caused by the Employer

2   Decide if the Contractor has taken all reasonable steps to minimise any loss caused by the Employer.

29.10   B   EMPLOYER'S RESPONSIBILITIES UNDER CLAUSE 29 RIAI AND GDLA

1   Consult with the Architect and determine the appropriate rate of damages.

2   Deduct the Ascertained or Liquidated damages (if any) from the moneys due to the Contractor.

3   Pay or allow to the Contractor the loss or expense caused by his own act or default, after consulting with the Architect.

29.11   C   CONTRACTOR'S RESPONSIBILITIES UNDER CLAUSE 29 RIAI AND GDLA

1   To complete the works by the date in the appendix (or the extended date)

2   To pay or allow to the Employer the Liquidated or Ascertained Damages (if any).

3   To notify the Architect within five working days of any act or default of

the Employer which might lead to delay and expense.

Additional Responsibilities under GDLA

1   To notify the Employer, in addition to notifying the Architect, of any act or default of the Employer.

2   To minimise any loss or expense caused by the Employer's delay.

29.12   CASES REFERRED TO

Arterial Drainage Company v Rathangan River Drainage Board [1880] 6 LRIR 513	par. 29.02
Bell and Son v CBF [1989] 46 BLR 102	par. 29.03
Dept of the Environment (NI) v Farrans (Construction) Ltd [1982] NI 11	par. 29.04
Dunlop Pneumatic Tyre Co Ltd v New Garage and Motor Company Ltd [1915] AC 79	par. 29.01
P Elliott and Co Ltd v Minister for Education [1987 ILRM 710	par. 29.05
Finnegan v Community Housing [1993] 65 BLR 103	par. 29.01
Henry Boot Building Company v Croydon Hotel and Leisure Company [1974] 36 BLR 41	par. 29.04
Laird Bros v City of Dublin Steam Packet Company [1900] 34 ILTR 9	par. 29.01
Lombank Ltd v Kennedy and Others [1961] NI 192	par. 29.01
Percy Bilton Ltd v Greater London Council [1982] 20 BLR 1 line 11	par. 29.04

RIAI – Clause 30

DELAY AND EXTENSION OF TIME

30.01 This is one of the most significant, and perhaps contentious clauses in the contract. Clause 28 sets out the date by which the works must be practically complete, and Clause 29 sets out the damages which the Contractor must allow to the Employer if the works are not complete on that date, or on any extended date as decided by the Architect. Clause 30, in turn, controls the fixing of any extended date. It has been argued that this clause is primarily of benefit to the Contractor but in fact it is also of substantial benefit to the Employer since in the absence of a specific clause such as this the liquidated damages provisions might cease to have effect where the delay, or any part of it might be due to some act by the Employer or by his agents. In essence however, the clause is to the benefit of the contract itself for if there were no arrangements for extension of time on either side the other party could argue that a breach of contract had occurred and thereby seek a determination of the contract. The Contractor will normally produce a programme and it is generally held that this is for the Contractor's own benefit and is not enforceable. It has been held, however, that a builder is obliged under the JCT/RIBA contract to produce a programme (*Moody v Ellis* [1983] 26 BLR 39).

There are ten grounds (eleven in the case of GDLA) on which the Architect may allow to the Contractor an extension of time. It is proposed to define these grounds first and then to comment on the general position of the parties as far as the contract, and the law, is concerned.

If in the opinion of the Architect the Work be delayed:

30.02 **(a) by *force majeure***

Force majeure has been defined as something which is outside the control of the parties to the contract and implying the use of force of such strength that the works could be delayed or even stopped. Examples might be Acts of God, i.e. earthquakes or epidemics, Government actions such as a curfew, etc. A general strike, or even a prolonged electricity strike might rank as *force majeure* [but see sub-clause (e)].

30.03 **(b) because possession of the site was not given to the Contractor in accordance with the terms of Clause 28**

This is quite straightforward. See par. 28.01.

30.04 **(c) by reason of any exceptionally inclement weather**

Two factors are relevant here. Firstly, the weather must be 'exceptional' for the time of year, and the meteorological records for the area would form the basis of a decision as to whether the weather was indeed exceptional. The Contractor is assumed to have made allowances for both the time of year, and the area where the works are being carried out. Secondly, the stage which the works might have reached when the 'exceptional' weather occurred might be such that no adverse effect would be had on the Contractor's programme. If sufficient work were available internally, then an extension of time might not be justified.

30.05 **(d) by reason of loss or damage to the Works or ancillary items which is covered by Clauses 20 to 26 of these Conditions**

The Works may be delayed by a wide variety of causes, as has been seen in the notes to Clauses 20 to 26. It would be rare that an event would occur under these clauses which would justify the Architect granting an extension of time, other than as a result of the operation of sub-clause 24(c)(ii). In that case, the reinstatement and making good of damage to the Works or Ancillary Items is deemed to be a variation ordered by the Architect and, as such, would rank as an Architect's Instruction under Clause 2 (see par. 30.07).

30.06 **(e) by reason of civil commotion, local combination of workmen, strike or lockout affecting any of the trades employed upon the Works**

This category would include both those employed directly on the site, and also those employed indirectly, i.e. employees of transport companies, manu-facturers, suppliers, etc. Strikes would cover both official and unofficial strikes. It would be possible that a strike affecting artists and tradesmen employed under Clause 32A would entitle the Contractor to compensation as well as to extension of time (see par. 30.12).

30.07 **(f) by reason of Architect's Instructions given in pursuance of Clause 2 of these Conditions**

Par. 2.23 pointed out that of the nine items listed as Architect's Instructions in Clause 2, any one of six of these items, depending on the circumstances, might entitle the Contractor to claim for an extension of time. These are the items dealing with (a) modification, addition, etc, (b) discrepancy, (c) removal of materials, (d) opening up for inspection, (f) postponement, and (i) any other matters. The facts in each case will enable the Architect to decide.

30.08 **(g) because the Contractor has not received in due time necessary instructions from the Architect for which he has specifically applied in writing**

Again this is a straightforward provision, but architects must be vigilant in providing the Contractor with information. One of the first items which should be sought by the Architect on the signing of the contract is a Schedule of Information Requirements, which would set out in a timetable the latest date by which items of information are required by the Contractor. These dates must then be met, but architects must also ensure that such timetables are reasonable. Claims for delay and expense under this heading will not be viewed sympathetically by the Employer and might well result in a claim against the Architect.

30.09 **(h) because the Contractor or any Nominated Sub-Contractor or Supplier has been unable for reasons beyond his control to secure such labour and materials as may be essential to the proper execution of the Works**

The Architect will form a view as to whether or not the obtaining of materials and/or labour was beyond the control of the Contractor, etc. The Contractor must establish that this was so, and that this problem was unforeseeable at the time of tender.

30.10 **(i) by delay on the part of other contractors, artists or tradesmen engaged by the Employer in executing work not forming part of this contract**

This calls for little comment, but it is interesting to note that the JCT/RIBA 80 form at Clause 25.4.11 allows as a ground for extension of time any delay caused by 'the carrying out by a local authority or statutory undertaker of work in pursuance of its statutory obligations in relation to the Works, or the failure to carry out such Works'. Whether these would be 'other Contractors engaged by the Employer' has not been established.

30.11 **(j) by reason of any act or default of the Employer causing delay in the progress of the Works as provided for in Clause 29(b)**

The procedure in dealing with delays caused by the Employer is set out in par. 29.06.

30.12 These, then, are the headings under which the Architect may give an extension of time, and they are the only reasons which are allowable under the Contract. The granting of an extension of time can have two differing consequences, depending on the reasons for the granting of the extension. For this reason it is essential that the Architect identify the heading (or headings) on which he relies when making his decision on whether or not to allow an extension. Firstly, the granting of an extension of time will allow the Contractor, in the case of all ten headings, to escape the consequences of the provision for damages set out in Clause 29, as far as the newly-extended date is concerned. Secondly, if the extension of time is granted under sub-clause (b) late possession, (f) Architect's instructions, (g) late instructions, (i) delay by others, (j) default of the Employer, or (k) in the GDLA the Contractor will be entitled to payment for loss and expense in addition to avoiding the damages referred to in Clause 29(a).

The delays referred to in some of the sub-clauses are dealt with under other clauses, as far as loss or damage is concerned:

1   Sub-clause (b), late possession, is dealt with under Clause 28 where the Contractor is entitled to receive 'from the Employer compensation for any loss incurred due to dislocation of the Contractor's organisation'. This limitation would probably not protect the Employer from having to pay other costs which the Contractor could establish he had suffered as a result of the late possession. These costs are discussed below.

2   Sub-clause (i), delay by others, is covered by Clause 32A where 'the Employer shall indemnify the Contractor against all claims whatsoever arising from the employment of such specialists.'

3   Sub-clause (j), default of the Employer, is dealt with at Clause 29(b) where 'the Employer shall pay or allow to the Contractor such damages as the Contractor shall have incurred by the delay.'

Notwithstanding the three specific provisions set out above, the Contractor would be generally entitled to damages for delay resulting from any of the five sub-clauses mentioned above. The loss which a contractor suffers as a result of a delay would normally include:

1   Off-site overheads: While such costs are normally independent of actual site expenditure, they may be affected by a delay. It could be, for instance, that they may have to be recovered from a smaller annual turnover.

2   The loss of profit-earning capacity by not being able to take on other profitable work.

3   The cost of on-site overheads: These can often be calculated from items in the 'Preliminary' section of the Bill of Quantities (where one is supplied),

where the weekly or monthly cost of plant, equipment or personnel is often set out.

4   Loss of productivity: This is an unusually difficult heading to assess.

30.13   Damages under ordinary law are recoverable under what are called the *'Rules under Hadley v Baxendale'* [1854] 9 Ex.34. These rules are: a) damages are payable if the result is the usual consequence of the event, and one which would be presumed to be in the contemplation of the parties; b) damages are payable even if the result is unusual, where a reasonable man, knowing the circumstances, would have thought them liable to result.

It is normally only the first branch of the rule (a) which would apply to a building contract. In a number of standard forms the word 'direct' is used in connection with loss or damage, and in such a case, the first rule only would be taken to apply. Even where, as in the case of the RIAI and GDLA forms, the word 'direct' is not used, it is thought that the same position would apply.

30.14   Having set out the ten headings which cover reasons for delay and therefore extension of time, the clause goes on to say:

then in any such case the Architect shall, as soon as it is possible for him to do so, make a fair and reasonable extension of time for completion of the Works. Upon the happening of any such event causing delay the Contractor shall immediately give notice thereof in writing to the Architect but he shall nevertheless use constantly his best endeavours to prevent delay and to proceed with the Works. In determining what extension of time (if any) is fair and reasonable under paragraph (d) for loss or damage to the Works or Ancillary Items the Architect shall have regard in particular to any negligence, omission or default of the Contractor which caused or contributed thereto.

The procedural requirements of this paragraph are:

1   The Contractor is required to notify the Architect 'upon the happening of any event': This is essential, as it is necessary for the Architect to know immediately if an event has occurred which might occasion a delay so as to enable him to adjudge a fair and reasonable extension, if appropriate, before this delay becomes swallowed up in the general programme and, perhaps confused with other events which might have differing contractual consequences.

2   The Contractor must minimise any delay: It is a requirement in ordinary law that a person 'mitigate' his damages, and the Contractor must there-

fore ensure that he can show that he has taken all steps available to him to reduce any delays caused.

3   The Architect shall make a fair and reasonable decision as soon as possible: In this regard the Architect will not be acting purely as an agent of the Employer. He must decide the rights of the parties under the Contract according to his own opinion, both impartially and independently. It used to be thought that when acting in this capacity the Architect was performing a 'quasi-arbitral' role and that he was immune from any claims of negligence in that role. It was decided in the case of *Sutcliffe v Thackrah* [1974] 4 BLR 16 that this is not so, and that the Architect must display the usual standard of skill and care. The *Sutcliffe* case is dealt with in par. 35.03, for it dealt primarily with certification.

4   The Architect shall consider the conduct of the Contractor as far as paragraph (d) is concerned – the insurance clauses.

30.15   The Architect must be aware of the more important legal requirements and decisions with regard to the whole area of delay and extension of time. The first of these is the question of the timing of the Architect's decision, and this is tied up to the question of whether the delay is occasioned by an act of the Contractor, or by an act of the Employer. It has been established that where the default has been caused by an act of the Contractor, then the Architect may delay his decision on an extension of time until the Works have been completed, even though the Date for Completion has passed. This is allowed so as to give the Architect the opportunity to see how the remaining works are completed, and to enable him to reach an overall view. The leading case in this matter is *ABC Ltd v Waltham Holy Cross UDC* [1952] 2 AER 452, which established the principle.

On the other hand, if the delay has been caused by an act of the Employer and perhaps more importantly, his agents, then the consequences differ. Originally, when the delay was caused by acts of the Employer, time became 'at large' which means that the completion date becomes irrelevant, and damages no longer apply. In this event the Contractor's responsibility is to complete within a reasonable time (*Wells v Army and Navy Co-Operative Society Ltd* [1902] 86 LT 764). This position was altered by the case of *Peak Construction (Liverpool) Ltd v McKinney Foundations Ltd* [1971] July 1, CA unrep. which allowed for extensions of time where the delay was caused by acts of the Employer, but only where the contract specifically allowed for events which caused the delay: 'If the Employer wishes to recover liquidated damages for failure by the Contractor to complete on time, in spite of the fact that some of the delay is due to the Employer's own fault or breach of contract, then the extension of time clause should provide expressly or by necessary inference, for an extension on account of such fault or breach on the part of the Employer.' In any event, for delays caused by acts of the Employer, the Architect must decide on the extension before the completion date set out in the appendix.

However, even where the delay, or part of it, has been caused by acts of the Employer the right to liquidated damages to the Employer is preserved by the Architect awarding extensions of time for any of the acts or 'events' which have been the responsibility of the Contractor. Failure, on the other hand, to grant proper extensions of time for delay caused by acts of the Employer will remove the right of the Employer to obtain damages for other delays. In *Percy Bilton Ltd v Greater London Council* [1982] 20 BLR 1 this principle was established. The case itself dealt with the position where the bankruptcy of a nominated sub-contractor delayed the Contractor, and the case is referred to in par. 16.06 dealing with Nominated Sub-Contractors.

30.16   The requirement that the Architect take into account the Contractor's negligence, omission or default when deciding on an extension of time claim under paragraph (d) is touched on in par. 30.05. This provision makes the procedure clear.

GDLA – Clause 30

30.17   The clause is much the same as the RIAI clause except that one further reason for extension is given in GDLA:

(k) by reason of suspension of the Works as provided for in Clause 34

Clause 34 deals with the determination of the Contract by the Contractor and allows in sub-clause (a), the Contractor to suspend the Works. This sub-clause 30(k) makes provision to ensure that any such suspension ranks as an event for calculating delay and extension of time. Par. 30.12 identified the events which entitle the Contractor to payment for loss and expense, and this event would be included in that list.

GDLA Clause 30 also differs from the RIAI clause in some procedural respects:

1   it is for the Employer, not the Architect, to extend the time for practical completion 'by such a period, as the Architect, as soon as it is possible for him to do so, shall certify as fair and reasonable'.

2   the Contractor is required to give notice of any delay as soon as possible and 'at latest within twenty (20) working days of the happening of any of the aforesaid causes of delay'.

SF 88 – Clause 5

EXTENSION OF TIME

30.18 **If it becomes apparent that the Works will not be completed by the date of Practical Completion as set out in the Articles of Agreement for reasons beyond the control of the Contractor, then the Contractor shall so notify the Architect who shall make, in writing, such extension of time for Practical Completion as he may consider reasonable.**

This clause sets out simply what the main provisions of the clauses in the longer forms contain.

30.19 A ARCHITECT'S RESPONSIBILITIES UNDER CLAUSE 30
RIAI AND GDLA

1 Make a fair and reasonable extension of time. (Certify in GDLA.)

2 Note if any delay occurs under sub-clause (d).

30.20 B EMPLOYER'S RESPONSIBILITIES UNDER CLAUSE 30 GDLA

1 Extend the time, if appropriate, for practical completion.

30.21 C CONTRACTOR'S RESPONSIBILITIES UNDER CLAUSE 30
RIAI AND GDLA

1 Give immediate notice (within 20 days in GDLA) of any delay.

2 Minimise delay.

30.22 CASES REFERRED TO

ABC Ltd v Waltham Holy Cross UDC [1952] 2 AER 452	par. 30.15
Percy Bilton v Greater London Council [1982] 20 BLR 1	par. 30.15
Hadley v Baxendale [1854] 9 Ex 341	par. 30.13
Moody v Ellis [1983] 26 BLR 39	par. 30.01
Peak Construction (Liverpool) Ltd v	
McKinney Foundations Ltd [1974] July 1, CA unrep.	par. 30.15
Sutcliffe v Thackrah [1974] 4 BLR 16	par. 30.14
Wells v Army and Navy Co-Operative Socity Ltd	
[1902] 86 LT 764	par. 30.15

RIAI – Clause 31

PRACTICAL COMPLETION AND DEFECTS LIABILITY

31.01 **When in the opinion of the Architect the Works are Practically Complete he shall forthwith issue a certificate to that effect and Practical Completion shall be deemed for all the purposes of this Contract to have taken place on the day named in such certificates.**

'Practical Completion' means that the Works have been carried to such a stage that they can be taken over and used by the Employer for their intended purpose and that any items of work or supply then outstanding or any defects then patent are of a trivial nature only and are such that their completion or rectification does not interfere with or interrupt such use.

The matters dealt with in the first two paragraphs of RIAI Clause 31 have been dealt with in the notes to GDLA Clause 28, at pars. 28.04 and 28.05.

In the GDLA form the issue of practical completion has been incorporated into the clause dealing with possession of the site. A summary of the effect of the issue of the Certificate of Practical Completion is:

1   The Contractor's All Risks policy shall cease to have effect (Clause 22).

2   The Defects Liability period commences (see par. 31.02).

3   Half the Retention Fund is released to the Contractor [Clause 35(2)(f)].

4   The period of Final Measurement begins [Clause 35(h)(iii)].

The definition of practical completion is clear and requires no comment. The addition, in the GDLA form at Clause 28(b) of the sentence 'Such outstanding items and defects shall be proceeded with expeditiously and shall be finished or rectified within a reasonable time after practical completion' does not in reality add to the Contractor's liability, and the fact that it is omitted from the RIAI form is not of significance.

31.02 **'The Defects Liability Period' stated in the Appendix hereto shall commence on the day after the date of Practical Completion named in the aforesaid Architect's Certificate.**

Any defects, shrinkage or other faults which appear before the expiration of the Defects Liability Period which are in the opinion of the Architect due to materials or workmanship not in accordance with the Contract shall within a reasonable time after receipt of the Architect's written instructions be made good by the Contractor and (unless the Architect shall otherwise decide) at his own cost. The Architect may issue such written instructions from time to time during the Defects Liability Period and in any event shall issue a final list of defects not later than twenty working days after the expiration of the Defects Liability Period.

One of the more important decisions required from the Architect is the length of the defects liability period. The intended period should always be set out in the tender documents, so as to become an accepted limitation by the Contractor when the contract is being signed, and to remove any possibility of a dispute. It is obvious that an Employer will seek as long a period as possible, and that a Contractor will seek the minimum. It is a matter for the Architect's judgement as to what would be a reasonable time, but it is thought that the period should always include from say, November to March. A nine-month defects liability period commencing in February might not contain any bad weather, where heavy rain or strong winds would reveal defects, whereas such a period commencing in September would almost certainly test the weather-resisting qualities of the building.

The normal procedure in the average contract would be that the Architect would ask the Contractor to remedy any defects, during the defects liability period, if the defect was of such a nature as to inhibit or restrict the Employer's use of the building. After the expiry of the defects liability period, the Architect would prepare a 'snagging' list and this would be dealt with by the Contractor in the normal way. Problems sometimes arise where defects are of such a nature that the cost to the Contractor of rectifying them would be out of proportion to the loss to the Employer, and it is thought that in such a circumstance, the Architect would be empowered to deduct an appropriate amount from the final certificate in lieu of rectification.

There is a somewhat unusual provision in this clause that enables the Architect to allow to the Contractor the cost of making good defects. It seems odd that the Contractor might be paid for correcting his own bad work. This should be done only in exceptional circumstances and after consultation with the Employer. The phrase does not appear in the GDLA form.

31.03   The provision of Clause 31, paragraph 4, does not remove from the Employer his common law rights for remedies in respect of defective materials and workmanship. Abrahamson (p.163) says in relation to the equivalent areas in the ICE CONTRACTS: 'The Contractor's duties under this clause are in addition to, not substitution for, his lengthy liability under the general law for defective workmanship or materials.'

The notes to Clause 8 deal with with general position with regard to the standard of workmanship and materials required under the Contract, and these requirements must be read alongside the provisions of Clause 31.

31.04 In the GDLA form (see par. 28.06) there is a reference to the Architect being entitled to postpone certain minor items. This provision is contained in RIAI Clause 28, and is to protect the Employer and to allow him to issue instructions in these matters after the date of Practical Completion. Instructions given otherwise after this date could deprive the Employer of the right to liquidated damages by rendering time 'at large' (par. 30.15).

31.05 If the Contractor refuses, or unreasonably delays, the remedying of defects, the Architect may under Clause 2, paragraph 5, employ other contractors to complete the Works, and use the remaining moiety of the retention money to pay for this work.

GDLA – Clause 31

DEFECTS LIABILITY

31.06 As has been seen above (pars. 28.04 and 28.05), the matter of practical completion in the GDLA form is dealt with in Clause 28. The provisions with regard to defects liability are much the same except for:

1   The Architect 'notifies' rather than 'certifies'. This is because in Clause 28, he is required to 'notify' the Employer that practical completion has occurred. In the RIAI form, the Architect certifies without being required to consult, or notify, the Employer.

2   The requirement that defects which are due 'to negligence on the part of the Contractor' be made good does not appear in the RIAI form. It would not appear to add to the Employer's safeguards under this clause.

3   The Contractor must make good any defects at his own cost. The Architect has no authority to allow any such costs to the Contractor, and this seems sensible.

4   The time within which the defects must be made good is not 'reasonable' as in the RIAI form, but 'within such time as shall be determined by the Architect'.

SF 88

PRACTICAL COMPLETION (CLAUSE 4) AND
DEFECTS LIABILITY (CLAUSE 7)

31.07   **4. Practical Completion**
The Architect shall certify the date when in his opinion the Works have been substantially completed so that they can be taken over and used by the Employer for their intended purpose. This date shall be known as the date of Practical Completion.

7. Defects Liability
The Contractor shall complete forthwith any work outstanding at the date of Practical Completion and shall make good any defects which appear within six months of that date where these shall have been scheduled by the Architect and notified to the Contractor and are due in the opinion of the Architect to materials and workmanship not in accordance with the Contract. Such defects shall be made good by the Contractor entirely at his own cost.

There are only two points worth noting here. Firstly, the Defects Liability Period is fixed at six months, and is not an agreed duration as in the longer form. Par. 31.02 discusses the desirable length of a defects liability period, and the Architect should advise the Employer if he feels that the standard form should be changed, where it might seem appropriate to the Architect to seek a longer term. Notice, before tenders, must be given to the Contractor if it is intended to alter this clause. Secondly, the requirement that defects be remedied by the Contractor is emphasised by the use of the word 'entirely'.

31.08   A   ARCHITECT'S RESPONSIBILITIES UNDER CLAUSE 31
RIAI AND GDLA

1   Certify that the Works are practically complete.

2   Issue instructions to the Contractor to make good defects.

31.09   C   CONTRACTOR'S RESPONSIBILITIES UNDER CLAUSE 31
RIAI AND GDLA

1   Make good defects as instructed.

RIAI – Clause 32A

Clause 32 in the 1996 edition has now been altered and extended. Clause 20 in the 1996 edition now becomes Clause 32A with some changes; Clause 32B is the previous Clause 32 and Clause 32C is new and is part of the insurance revisions made by the Liaison Committee.

INDEPENDENT CONTRACTORS, ARTISTS AND TRADESMEN

32.01 **Provided that no objection is made by the Contractor the Employer may engage Independent Contractors, Artists, Tradesmen or others to carry out works not specified in the Contract. The cost of such work shall be paid by the Employer who shall indemnify the Contractor against all claims whatsoever arising from the employment of such specialists, etc, their servants and agents made against the Contractor. The Contractor shall in all circumstances be entitled to payment for attendance and the use of plant**

It is quite common in many types of buildings that the Employer would wish to have sculptures, murals or other works of art commissioned by artists so as to enhance and complete the Architect's design. For this purpose, separate arrangements will be entered into by the Employer in consultation with the Architect. Since these arrangements do not involve the Contractor, a separate contractual provision is required so as to place these particular works in an appropriate context.

The revisions of 2001 removed the phrase 'and which would not normally be part of a building contract'. It has been pointed out above (par. 14.01) that the Employer is not entitled to omit work that has been included in the original Contract Documents, and then have it performed by others. It must be clear and this clause makes it so, that it is intended from the outset to have work of this nature carried out by persons having no involvement in the contract itself.

The Clause opens by allowing the Contractor a right of objection. This objection need not (as in the GDLA form) be 'reasonable', but it is unlikely that any Contractor would raise, and insist on, an objection which would be seen to be unreasonable. The clause then goes on to say that the cost of this work will be paid by the Employer. These payments are in no way part of the Contract Sum. They are not certified by the Architect under this contract, nor is the Contractor entitled to any percentage or discount in respect of these payments. The payments are purely a matter between the Employer and the Artists in question.

The next point dealt with in the clause is that of insurance. In the RIAI form, the Employer is required to 'indemnify' the Contractor against any claims that may arise as a result of the artists working on the site. In other words, the Employer agrees to make good any loss suffered by the Contractor in this regard. (Indemnity is covered more fully in par. 21.03 in the notes to the insurance clauses.)

Lastly, the Contractor shall be entitled to be paid for any 'attendance' and the use of plant. 'Attendance' is the word used in the construction industry for any services provided by the Contractor to others working on the site, whether they be Nominated Sub-Contractors (Clause 16), independent con-tractors, artists and tradesmen, as in this clause. Attendance can include the provision of scaffolding, lighting, power, plant of any sort, and the services of any of the Contractor's own workmen or site staff. In the case of some artist's work, say the installation of stained glass windows in a church, this attendance might be considerable and provision should be made in the Contract Documents to cover these costs.

GDLA

32.02 The numbering of the Artists and Tradesmen clause has not been changed in the GDLA form and is still numbered 20.

The GDLA form is very similar to the RIAI 1996 edition. The differences are:

1   The Contractor's objection to any artist or tradesman employed directly by the Employer must be 'reasonable'. In addition, the intention of the Employer to use such artists or tradesmen must be written into the speci-fication. This is prudent, if only to ensure that provision is made in the Contract Documents for the cost of attendance and plant.

2   The arrangements for insurance are different from the RIAI provisions. In that form the responsibility was that of the Employer alone. Here, if the Employer so wishes, he may require the Contractor to take out insur-ance in the joint names of the Employer and the Contractor, to cover the cost of any such claims. If the cost of this insurance is not provided for in the Contract Sum, any such cost will be allowed.

SF 88

32.03   There is no provision in the shorter form for independent contractors, artists and tradesmen.

32.04   B   EMPLOYER'S RESPONSIBILITIES UNDER CLAUSE 20
              RIAI AND GDLA

        1   Pay all artists and tradesmen and indemnify the Contractor. (In the case of GDLA make provision in the specification for such artists and tradesmen.)

        2   Pay the Contractor for attendance and plant.

32.05   C   CONTRACTOR'S RESPONSIBILITIES UNDER CLAUSE 20
              RIAI AND GDLA

        1   Make objection, if justified, against any tradesman or artist.

RIAI Clause 32B

PARTIAL OR PHASED POSSESSION

32.06   **If at any time or times before practical completion of the Works the Contractor consents to the Employer taking into possession of any part or parts of the Works ('the relevant part') by or on behalf of the Employer then:**

This is the introduction to this clause, and the clause itself is provided to cover the situation where it is convenient for the Employer to take over some of the Works before the Contractor has completed. It might be that the overall contract covers a number of separate buildings, as in a hospital project, or less usually, a number of floors in a building might be available for the Employer's use. This situation requires clear contractual provisions because of the divided and overlapping responsibilities that might arise. Pars. 11.01 and 11.02 dealt with the Contractor's position in relation to possession of the site, and explains why this clause is necessary. The consent of the Contractor is required before any partial possession can be given to the Employer and the reasons for this are clear, as pars. 11.01 and 11.02 explain. It is possible, if the situation can be foreseen, to make provision for possession in stages in the tender documents, and the clause allows for this. There are six sub-clauses dealing with the situation which arises under partial possession.

32.07   **(a) at least 3 (three) days prior to such taking of possession by or on behalf of the Employer the Architect shall issue a certificate ('the possession certificate') describing the relevant part and certifying his estimate of the percentage which the value of the relevant part as at the date of possession bears to the value of the works including variations instructed or authorised by the Architect ('the relevant percentage')**

The importance of accurately defining what part, or parts, of the works are being taken over by the Employer is evident and this should be done by agreed drawings and description, signed by both parties. An example of what can occur when the Contract provisions are not exactly adhered to can be seen in the case of *English Industrial Estates Corporation v George Wimpey and Co Ltd* [1972] 7 BLR 122. The Employer had taken partial possession of the Works when a fire seriously damaged the building. The court held that the Contractor was still liable as the Architect had not issued the appropriate certificate. The Quantity Surveyor, if one is retained, will advise the Architect as to what proportion of the Contract Sum is represented by the parts being taken over. In addition to the building or parts of the building, it might be appropriate for the Employer to take over some site works, road-ways, etc, but here again, both parties must clearly define the works involved. In any event, the relevant percentage must be certified so as to allow the operation of some of the other sub-clauses.

32.08 **(b) without prejudice to Clause 23(d) and 32. C. the relevant part and contents thereof shall as from 2 (two) days after the date of the possession certificate be at the sole risk of the Employer as regards any of the contingencies required to be insured under Clause 22(b) and the reinstatement cost of the Works to be insured under sub-clause 22(b) shall be reduced by the relevant percentage.**

Insurance is the obvious area where partial possession could cause problems, unless these are specifically dealt with in the contract provisions. This sub-clause refers to the insurance provisions contained in Clauses 22 and 23. Clause 22 deals with All Risks Insurance, and sub-clause (b) of that clause requires the Contractor to insure 'the full value of the Works and Ancillary Items'. Sub-clause 32(b) allows this amount to be reduced in proportion to the value of the Works being handed over. Clause 23, also referred to here, deals with exclusions in sub-clause (d) and one of the permitted exclusions is 'loss or damage due to use, occupation or possession by or on behalf of the Employer. Sub-clause 23(d) makes it clear that the Employer will have no claim against the Contractor in the case of partial possession, even where such damage is caused by the Contractor's negligence. The importance of the Architect ensuring that both parties are aware of their responsibilities must be emphasised.

32.09 **(c) any sum to be paid or allowed by the Contractor under Clause 29 in respect of any period during which the Works may remain incom-plete after the date of the possession certificate shall be reduced by the relevant percentage;**

Any damages for non-completion which results in either money being deducted from, or paid to, the Contractor under Clause 29 shall be adjusted. If the relevant percentage is 50% then all damages due under Clause 29 would be halved.

32.10 **(d) when in the opinion of the Architect the relevant part is practical-ly complete he shall forthwith issue a certificate to that effect and the Defects Liability Period in respect of the relevant part shall com-**

mence on the day after the date of practical completion;

This is a clear requirement, and will have the consequences (for the relevant part) that are set out in par. 31.01.

32.11 **(e) when in the opinion of the Architect any defects, shrinkages or other faults in the relevant part which he may have required to be made good under Clause 31 shall have been made good he shall issue a certificate to that effect;**

The notes in par. 31.02 dealing with the overall contract defects arrangements, would be applicable here.

32.12 **(f) the Employer shall pay to the Contractor one half of the relevant percentage of the sum then retained under Clause 35 and the sum named in the Appendix as the Limit of Retention Fund shall be reduced by one half of the relevant percentage (i) 10 (ten) working days after the date of the Certificate of Practical Completion, of the relevant part and (ii) again on the expiration of the Defects Liability Period in respect of the relevant part or the issuing of the certificate of completion of making good defects in respect of the relevant part, whichever is the later;**

This sub-clause, again, imports the overall contractual arrangements with regard to retention into the provisions for partial possession (see par. 35.07).

GDLA – Clause 32

32.13 This is very similar to the RIAI form. The differences are:

1 Phased possession in accordance with contract provisions is not dealt with. Presumably it could be specially arranged and incorporated in the contract documents where required.

2 The Employer may 'take' possession, subject to the consent of the Contractor. In the RIAI form, the Contractor's role is active rather than passive – he 'consents'.

3 **NOTE: It may be necessary for the Employer to insure his responsibility under this Clause. See Note to sub-clause 23(f).**

This refers to the Employer's right under the GDLA Contract to carry his own insurance (see par. 23.08).

RIAI Clause 32C

DAMAGE DUE TO USE, OCCUPATION, POSSESSION
BY THE EMPLOYER

32.14 **If any damage loss or destruction should occur to the Works or Ancillary Items which is not effectively insured by the All Risks insurance policy under Clause 22(b) by reason of the use, occupation or possession of the whole or any part of the Works by or on behalf of the Employer, including the independent contractors, tradesmen or others appointed by the Employer (other than by the Contractor, his servants or agents) which renders the policy void or voidable, Clause 24(a) and (b) shall apply whether or not such use, occupation or possession is permitted under Clauses 32A or 32B of the Contract or is with the consent of the Contractor and the Employer shall have no claim against the Contractor for such damage or loss whether or not due to any negligence, omission, default or breach of statutory duty of the Contractor, Sub-Contractors (of any tier) or their servants or agents.[5]**

[5] Before using, occupying or taking possession of any part of the works for any purpose, however temporary or trivial, or appointing, pursuant to the provisions of Clause 32A, any independent contractor, artist, tradesman or others the Employer must ensure that full insurance cover remains in force for any loss of damage to or destruction of the Works or ancillary Items and also that he will be insured for any injury or damaged caused by such use, etc. The Architect should make certain that the necessary cover is provided either through the Contractor's policy, with any necessary adjustment agreed with the Contractor's insurers, or by special policies taken out by the Employer.

This is a new sub-clause and protects the Contractor from any claim made by the Employer in respect of any damage caused by the use, occupation or possession by the Employer of part of the Works. The Sub Clauses 24(a) and (b) referred to deal with the cost of damage due to excluded risks and to the possible determination of the employment of the Contractor as a result of such an event.

The foortnote 5 emphasises, if emphasis were needed, the importance of making certain that the proper insurance provisions are in place.

SF 88

32.15   There is no provision in the shorter form for partial possession.

32.16   A   ARCHITECT'S RESPONSIBILITIES UNDER CLAUSE 32
RIAI AND GDLA

1   Issue a certificate describing the 'relevant part' and 'relevant percentage'.

2   Issue a certificate of practical completion for the relevant part.

3   Issue a certificate of making good defects for the relevant part.

32.17   B   EMPLOYER'S RESPONSIBILITIES UNDER CLAUSE 32
RIAI AND GDLA

1   Obtain the Contractor's consent to partial possession.

2   Pay the Contractor any retention money due.

3   Make the appropriate insurance arrangements.

32.18   C   CONTRACTOR'S RESPONSIBILITIES UNDER CLAUSE 32
RIAI AND GDLA

1   Consent, if appropriate, to partial possession.

2   Liaise with the Employer with regard to insurance.

32.19   CASE REFERRED TO

*English Industrial Estates Corporation v George Wimpey
and Co Ltd* [1972] 7 BLR 122   par. 32.02

RIAI – Clause 33

DETERMINATION OF CONTRACT BY EMPLOYER

33.01   This clause deals with what is, in effect, a breach of contract by the Contractor. Just as a contract is brought into being by agreement between the parties (see par. Int.04) so also a contract can be discharged by the parties agreeing in advance as to the circumstances that would justify such discharge. The ordinary law holds that either party to a contract is entitled to repudiate the contract if the other party has committed what is called in modern judicial parlance a 'fundamental' breach, that is a breach that goes to the root of the contract. In *O'Donovan v O'Halloran Homes Ltd* [1983] High Court, unrep. 24th November, it was held that building a house in contravention of the planning permission was a fundamental breach and that the injured party was both entitled to rescind the contract and to receive damages. These fundamental matters are also referred to in contract law as 'conditions' to distinguish them from less important undertakings in the contract known as 'warranties'. These two words have a narrow contractual meaning and the use of the words in the standard building contract forms is different. All the clauses of the standard forms are described as 'conditions', but it is obvious that breaching some of them, such as Clause 15 – with reference to sub-letting – would not be of fundamental importance.

     Equally, the ordinary law holds that any breach of contract entitles the innocent party to damages, and this would normally require an action for damages with resulting delays and costs. The standard forms attempt to deal with both of these areas by firstly specifying what is a fundamental breach by listing the circumstances under which the contract might be discharged and, secondly, by stating how the cost to either party of the effects of the breach is to be dealt with. Clause 33 deals with determination by the Employer, and Clause 34 with determination by the Contractor. To 'determine' is to bring to an end, but it will be seen that the contract itself is not determined, but the employment of the Contractor. The contract must remain, or subsist, in order for all the provisions of the contract to come into force following the determination of the employment of the Contractor.

33.02   The clause itself is divided into four sub-clauses. These deal with (a) what might be described as 'building' reasons for determination, (b) bankruptcy, receivership, liquidation or examination, (c) the consequences of (a) and (b), and finally (d) the protection of the site after determination.

33.03   **(a) If the Contractor shall make default in any of the following respects, viz:**

i)   without reasonable cause shall wholly suspend the Works before completion

It was pointed out in par. 2.03 that the Contractor's prime responsibility is 'to carry out and complete the Works'. Failure to do this is clearly a fundamental breach of contract entitling the Employer to determine the Contractor's employment.

ii) shall fail to proceed with the Works with reasonable diligence

This again would come under the Contractor's overall responsibility, but it requires judgement on the part of the Architect as to what constitutes 'reasonable diligence'. If the Contractor suspends the Works, then the matter is clear-cut, but each case of 'reasonable diligence 'will have to be dealt with on the facts, with the Architect taking into account all the factors which might have affected the Contractor's progress.

iii) shall refuse or persistently neglect to comply with a notice in writing from the Architect requiring him to remove defective work or improper materials

The Architect, under Clause 2(c) and (e), is empowered to instruct the Contractor to remove or re-execute defective materials or work. Refusal by the Contractor to carry out such an instruction is a clear breach of contract. Even though the Employer is empowered by Clause 2, paragraph 5, to have any defective work or materials replaced by other at the Contractor's expense, it is clear that a 'persistent' neglect to comply with the Architect's instructions would leave the Architect no option but to invoke the provisions of Clause 33.

iv) shall fail to execute the Works in accordance with the Contract or shall in the opinion of the Architect be in serious breach of his obligations under the Contract

This is an overall provision and allows the Architect to decide whether or not the Contractor's conduct is such so as to justify the determination of his employment. It is a wide-ranging power, but would be invoked only if the Architect were satisfied that the interests of the Employer could be protected only by the invocation of the clause.

33.04   If any of the above four events occur, then the contract conditions provide for a mechanism to ensure that the Contractor is given an opportunity to remedy the breach and to allow the Employer to determine the Contractor's employment. The next paragraph deals with two separate matters. The first is the determination procedure itself, and the second is the effect of a determination notice on plant, materials, etc, on this site.

... then, if such default shall continue for ten working days after a notice by registered post or by letter delivered to the Contractor specifying the default has been given to the Contractor by the Architect, the Employer may, without prejudice to any other rights or remedies thereupon and at latest within ten working days by notice by registered post or letter delivered to the Contractor determine the employment of the Contractor under this Contract, provided that notice in pursuance of this clause shall not be given unreasonably or vexatiously and shall be void if the Employer is at the time of the notice in serious breach of this contract.

The timetable is important, because of the consequences of the action being undertaken and should be adhered to, as it is likely that a determination not complying with these requirements would be held to be invalid. The steps are:

1   The Architect sends a notice of default to the Contractor.

2   If the default continues for ten days after the notice, the Employer may within a further ten days, determine the employment of the Contractor. The Architect, not being a party to the Contract, has no power to determine; this action must be taken by the Employer.

It will be seen that this notice must not be given 'unreasonably or vexatiously'. Some architects have a tendency to threaten, and sometimes proceed with, determination procedures where the circumstances do not justify such a course of action, in order to achieve better progress on site. This temptation should be resisted because firstly, the Contractor may well regard it as a bluff, and secondly, the threat itself becomes less effective the more it is referred to. The Contractor will be aware that the balance of convenience will very often lie with allowing the contract to proceed, and the Architect must be aware of his duty towards the Employer of ensuring that extreme action be taken only when the circumstances clearly justify it.

The paragraph refers to 'other rights of remedies' which the Employer might have, and this is to protect any common law rights which would arise under ordinary contract law. The ordinary law holds that any breach of contract entitles the innocent party to damages.

The clause provides that any notice issued will be void if at the time of issue of the notice, the Employer himself is in serious breach of the contract; if, for instance he has not honoured certificates which are due.

33.05 **After such notice to the Contractor from the Architect shall have been given the Contractor shall not be at liberty to remove from the site or Works or from any ground contiguous thereto any plant, materials or goods belonging to him which shall have been placed thereon for the purpose of the Works and the Employer shall have a lien upon all such plant, materials or goods to subsist from the date of such notice being given until the notice shall have been complied with. Provided always that such lien shall not under any circum-stances subsist after the expiration of one calendar month from the date of such notice being given unless the Employer shall have entered upon and taken possession of the Works and site; and pro-vided also that such lien shall not apply to any plant, materials or goods belonging to any sub-contractor unless the value thereof shall have been included in a certificate of which the Contractor has received payment.**

This paragraph is to protect the Employer's ability to proceed with and complete the Works in the event of the determination of the employment of the Contractor. Under sub-clause (c)(i) of this clause the Employer is entitled to employ others to complete the Works, and to this end he will obviously require any plant, materials or goods which are on site at the time of determination. A 'lien' at law is defined as the right to hold the property of another as security for the performance of an obligation; in this case the obligation on the part of the Contractor to complete the Works. It will be seen that the lien lasts for one month only, unless the Employer moves onto the site, in which case the lien will remain until the completion of the Works. The lien does not apply to any plant or materials belonging to any sub-contractor, unless the Employer has paid for them by way of honouring a certificate in favour of the Contractor. This provision applies only to a nominated sub-contractor. This paragraph specifically refers to items 'belonging' to the Contractor, so the question of retention of title to goods does not arise (see par. 35.05).

33.06 **(b) If the Contractor commits an Act of Bankruptcy or being a com-pany enters into Liquidation whether compulsory or voluntary (except Liquidation for the purpose of reconstructions) or if a Receiver is appointed or if a petition to appoint an Examiner is pre-sented to the High Court, the Employer without prejudice to any other rights herein contained may send by registered post or have delivered to the Contractor a written notice determining the employ-ment of the Contractor under this Contract.**

There are now four kinds of financial difficulty that can arise as far as the Contractor is concerned. The first is if the Contractor is adjudged to be bankrupt, or as the contract says, commits an act of bankruptcy. Bankruptcy has been defined as 'a law for the benefit and the relief of creditors and their debtors in cases where the latter are unable or unwilling to pay their debts' (in *re Reiman* [1874] 20 Fed Cas 490). A person can be adjudged a bankrupt on the petition of the debtor himself, or on the petition of a creditor when the debtor has committed an act of bankruptcy. These acts are defined in the Bankruptcy Act 1988. In a case of bankruptcy, the debtor's affairs are taken over by the Official Assignee. Secondly, a Receiver may be appointed over the affairs of the Contractor, provided that the Contractor is trading as a company. A Receiver is a person appointed by the High Court, usually by the holder of a debenture such as a bank. His function is to discharge the debt and then return the company to the control of the directors. He has authority to terminate the company's contractual obligations (see *Ardmore Studios (Ireland) Ltd v Lynch* [1965] IR 1). The appointment of a Receiver often leads to the third kind of financial arrangement, the appointment of a Liquidator. A Liquidator is a person appointed to carry out the winding up of a company. His duties are to realise the assets of the company, settle its debts, and to distribute to the shareholders any surplus that remains. The Liquidator may be appointed voluntarily by the company, or on the order of the High Court, in which case he is known as an Official Liquidator. Fourthly, and finally, an Examiner may be appointed to a company. This is a new procedure, and is controlled by the Companies (Amendment) Act 1990. Again, the Examiner is appointed by the High Court but there is a considerable difference between an Examiner and either a Receiver or a Liquidator. The Examiner would take control of the affairs of a company when it appears to the court that the company cannot pay its debts. Once an Examiner is appointed no proceedings for the winding up of the company can be commenced. The purpose of appointing an Examiner is to see if it would be possible to restructure the company in such a way as to enable it to continue trading. The timetable is very short, and a period of three to four months would be normal for the entire process. The Goodman Group of companies was, in 1990, the first to have an Examiner appointed. It should be noted that an Examiner has power to rescind a contract.

33.07　It will be seen that whereas the four reasons for determination listed in par. 33.03 require a timetable to be implemented, in the case of bankruptcy, receivership, liquidation or examination, the Employer may immediately determine the employment of the Contractor. The Architect will obviously be directed by the Employer's Solicitor or Accountant in deciding whether a contractor is, or is not, in any of the financial positions referred to, but the Architect is probably better placed than most in observing the signs which suggest that a contractor is heading for financial difficulties, and he will keep the Employer up to date in this regard. The Architect will need to be very vigilant with regard to certification. When a contractor is heading for insolvency he will naturally try to inflate all claims so as to generate the largest possible cash flow, and the Architect must resist the temptation to keep the Contractor afloat by generous certification. An Architect has no power to act in this way, and will be personally responsible for any loss suffered by the Employer as a result of his certificates (see par. 35.03). On the other hand, the Architect must try not to aggravate the problem by under-certifying in an attempt to protect the Employer. The Architect must act fairly as between the parties, although he is not acting in any quasi-arbitral way.

33.08   Having established the grounds on which the Employer may determine the employment of the Contractor, the clause goes on to set out the consequences of such action.

The position will be very different depending on whether the employment of the Contractor has been determined under sub-clause (a) or sub-clause (b). In the former, the original contractor will still exist as a trading entity and the arrangements set out in sub-clause (c)(i) to (iv) can be conducted with him. In the case of the latter, the affairs of the Contractor will have been taken over by a Receiver, Liquidator or Examiner, and procedural difficulties might well ensue. The Employer will have to decide after consultation with the Architect and his other professional advisors, as to the best course of action as far as he is concerned. The following notes must be read in that light.

(c) In either of the above cases (a) or (b) the following shall apply, viz:

i)   The Employer may employ and pay a contractor or other person to carry out and complete the Works and he or they may enter upon the site and use all materials or goods, temporary buildings, plant and appliances thereon and may purchase all materials necessary for the purpose aforesaid.

This is a simple provision so as to entitle the Employer without any further notice to have the Works completed. The lien referred to in par. 33.05 comes into operation here to enable the Employer, or the new contractor on his behalf, to take over materials, etc, on site. The cost of this completion is dealt with in sub-clause (c)(iv).

ii)   The Contractor shall if so required by the Employer or Architect assign to the Employer without further payment the benefit of any contract for the supply of materials and/or Works intended for use under this Contract or for the execution of any works, and

the Employer shall pay the agreed price (if unpaid) for such materials or works supplied or executed after the said determination.

This provision is to allow as smooth a transition as is possible from the original Contractor to the new Contractor. The right to any contract for parts of the works, or for supplies which have been ordered should reduce the inevitable delays which will occur on determination.

iii) The Contractor shall during the execution or after completion of the Works under this clause as and when required remove from the site his temporary buildings, plant, appliances and any materials within such reasonable time as the Architect may specify in a written notice to him and in default the Employer may (without being responsible for any loss or damage) remove and sell the same holding the proceeds less all costs incurred to the credit of the Contractor.

The ordinary law will require the Employer, when removing temporary buildings, etc, to observe normal standards of such operations and the cost of any careless or negligent damage to property of the Contractor would be recoverable by the Contractor. Similarly, the Employer must obtain, as far as he can, a reasonable market price for any property of the Contractor.

iv) Until after completion of the work under this clause no payment shall be made to the Contractor under this Contract provided that upon completion as aforesaid, and the verification within a reasonable time for the accounts therefore the Architect shall certify the amount of expenses properly incurred by the Employer and if such amount added to the money paid to the Contractor before such determination exceeds the total amount which would have been payable on due completion the difference shall be a debt payable to the Employer by the Contractor and if the said amount added to the said money be less than the said total amount the difference shall be a debt payable to the Contractor by the Employer.

In other words, if it costs more to complete the Works after determination than the original Contract Sum, the Contractor must pay the extra. If it costs less, the Contractor gets the credit. If the determination has occurred under either sub-clause, the Contract Guarantee Bond, if one exists, will come into effect.

33.09   A bond is not required under the standard forms, and is not mentioned in the RIAI form. The GDLA form at Clause 28(a) refers to possible existence of a bond. A bond is, simply, an undertaking by a financial institution to re-imburse a party to a contract for any loss or damage which a court would award for breach of contract. The bond is normally given by a bank or insurance company. The party providing the bond is referred to as the 'bondsman'. The bondsman is not required to complete the works, and he will use his own judgement as to whether or not it would be better for the institution which he represents to compensate the Employer, or to complete the Works himself. The bond will stipulate a maximum amount, and this amount used, quite often, to be the Contract Sum. It came to be appreciated, however, that the cost to the Employer of a determination could never be the full Contract Sum, and lesser amounts are common to-day. An amount of 25% of the Contract Sum would be usual. The cost of the bond, included in the Contract, is usually in the region of 0.5% to 0.7% of the Contract Sum, but this can vary from contractor to contractor, and from other factors. A bond will often be refused if the bondsman is concerned that a contractor has quoted too low a price for a particular project. While the bond is for the protection of the Employer, it is obtained by the Contractor, but is paid for by the Employer. It is important that the Architect inform the bondsman during the course of the work as to any significant alterations, extras, or defects., Failure to do this might entitle the bondsman to repudiate the bond on the grounds that the contract which he had agreed to bond had been changed significantly without his knowledge. This was so held in the splendidly titled case of *The Wardens and Commonality of the Mystery of Mercers of the City of London v New Hampshire Insurance Company* [1991] 7 CLJ 130. Sub-contracts are often bonded, as well as the Contract itself (see par. 37.04).

33.10   **(d) Protection of Site**

i)   **When the Architect has issued a notice by registered post or by letter delivered to the Contractor specifying the default as provided for in sub-clause (a) or the Employer determines the employment of the Contractor as provided for in sub-clause (b) of this clause and if in the reasonable opinion of the Architect adequate site security to ensure protection of the Works and any materials placed on the site for the purpose of the Works has not already been provided the Employer may without prejudice to any other rights or remedies forthwith proceed to provide such site security.**

Early printing of the RIAI form omitted the words 'or the Employer determines the employment of the Contractor as provided for in sub-clause (b)' and care should be taken to see that this phrase is properly included. The sub-clause itself deals with the practicalities of protecting the site. When rumours, or the fact, of a contractor's bankruptcy or default became widespread it had been the practice for suppliers and sub-contractors to remove from the site any materials which had been delivered there, and for which they had not been paid. The actual ownership of such materials is dealt with in par. 35.05. This sub-clause is to prevent such abuses.

ii) **The cost of the provision by the Employer of such site security shall be paid by the Contractor or deducted from any money that becomes due to him or treated as a debt payable by him to the Employer save only that the Contractor shall not be liable for the cost of any security guard or watchman or any other recurring cost for a period of more than one calender month from the date of such notice or determination.**

The period of one month has been suggested as being too short. It is presumably set at that duration to correspond with the month allowed for the lien on materials in sub-clause (a). It should, however, encourage the Employer to decide as soon as possible on the course of action which he will take following on determination.

GDLA – Clause 33

33.11   There are a number of differences between the two longer forms. The four reasons for determination in sub-clause (a) of the RIAI form are added to as follows (the numbering of the sub-clauses changes as a result):

i) **Shall fail to commence the Works within ten (10) working days of getting possession of the site.**

This requires no comment.

vi) **Where a Trade Dispute arises between him and the workmen engaged by him on or in connection with the Works to whom a registered employment agreement applies shall in the opinion of the Architect fail, neglect, or refuse to comply with the settlement procedure set out in such agreement.**

A registered employment agreement, as has been pointed out in par. 1.03 is one that is made under the Industrial Relations Act 1946. Placing the responsibility for interpreting the settlement procedure upon the Architect seems to be extending the Architect's duties into an area where he should tread very carefully, and liaise very closely with the Employer.

There is no provision in the GDLA form for dealing with examination. It might be possible, however, for the Architect, in such a circumstance, to determine the Contract on the grounds that the Contractor was not proceeding with 'reasonable diligence'.

33.12 The provisions in sub-clause (a) in the RIAI form dealing with a lien on plant, materials, etc, on site are not included in the GDLA form. This matter is covered by the provision of GDLA Clause 14 (Vesting of materials and plant). Equally the provisions of RIAI sub-clause (d) are not included, as protection of the site is similarly covered by GDLA Clause 14.

33.13 Under the GDLA form there is a further ground for a determination of the employment of the Contractor by the Employer and this is contained in sub-clause 39(e). Clause 39 GDLA deals with Fair Wages legislation and sub-clause (e) of that clause make non-compliance with the provisions of the clause generally a ground for determination (see par. 39.01).

SF 88 – Clause 21

DETERMINATION BY EMPLOYER

33.14 **The Employer may, following seven days' notice by registered post or recorded delivery to the Contractor determine the employment of the Contractor under this Contract if the Contractor without reasonable cause fails to proceed diligently with the Works or wholly suspends the carrying-out of the Works before completion.**

In the event of the Employer determining the employment of the Contractor as aforesaid the Employer may without prejudice to any other of this rights or remedies employ other contractors to complete the Works and may charge the cost to the Contractor and deduct the same from any money due to the Contractor.

These provisions are a summary of some of the provisions of longer forms. While financial difficulty of any sort is not mentioned, this would clearly involve suspending the Works and so become a cause for determination.

33.15   A   ARCHITECT'S RESPONSIBILITIES UNDER CLAUSE 33
RIAI AND GDLA

1   Decide if the Contractor is in default, and issue the necessary notice.

2   Decide if any necessary assignments have been made.

3   Direct the removal of any necessary temporary buildings, plant, materials, etc.

4   Certify the cost (or saving) or the determination to the Employer.

5   Decide if site protection is necessary.

6   Decide if registered employment agreements are being observed (GDLA only).

33.16   B   EMPLOYER'S RESPONSIBILITIES UNDER CLAUSE 33
RIAI AND GDLA

1   Determine the employment of the Contractor, as advised by the Architect.

2   Employ other to complete the Works.

3   Decide on the removal and sale of the Contractor's property.

33.17   C   CONTRACTOR'S RESPONSIBILITIES UNDER CLAUSE 33
RIAI AND GDLA

1   Assign any necessary contracts.

2   Remove any property from the site as directed.

33.18   CASES REFERRED TO

Ardmore Studios (Ireland) Ltd v Lynch [1965] IR 1	par. 33.06
O'Donovan v O'Halloran Homes	
[1983] High Court, unrep. 24th November	par. 33.01
re Reiman [1874] 20 Fed Cas 4.90	par. 33.06
The Wardens and Commonality of the Mystery of	
Mercers of the City of London v New Hampshire	
Insurance Company [1991] 7 CLJ 130	par. 33.09

RIAI – Clause 34

DETERMINATION OF CONTRACT BY CONTRACTOR

There are two reasons given in the RIAI form why the Contractor may determine his own employment under the Contract. The first of these is if certificates are not honoured. The second is if the Employer becomes insolvent. Naturally enough, the GDLA form omits the second reason, presumably on the comforting ground that neither the State nor any body deriving its authority from the State will become insolvent.

34.01 **(a) If the Employer does not pay the Contractor within the period for honouring certificates named in Clause 35(a) the Contractor after five working days notice to the Employer may suspend the Works for a period of ten working days and on the expiry of this period unless payment shall have been made in the meantime determine his own employment under this Contact as from the date of such expiry. When work is suspended under this provision the time for completion shall be extended by two working days for each working day of such suspension.**

It was stated in par. 2.33 that the essence of the contract is that the Contractor shall build and the Employer shall pay. The contract requires the Employer, in Clause 35(a) to honour any certificate from the Architect within seven working days of receiving the certificate from the Contractor. Normally, the Architect would issue this certificate within five working days of receiving a statement from the Contractor. This means, in effect, that if the Contractor has not been paid within about one month after issuing a statement to the Architect, he may determine his own employment under the contract. Sometimes an Employer may decide to deduct amounts from the sum certified for, say, defective work and it is thought that the Contractor would not be entitled to determine if the Employer had a bona-fide reason for this deduction. An Employer would always be entitled to deduct damages as provided for in Clause 29. An extension of time must be granted as provided in this clause, and this extension would be in addition to any extension of time which the Contractor might claim under the provisions of Clause 30. The GDLA form makes specific provision in sub-clause 30(k) for such an extension of time, but the absence of this provision in the RIAI form does not deprive the Contractor of the remedy provided here (see par. 30.18).

34.02 **(b) If the Employer commits an Act of Bankruptcy or being a company enters into Liquidation whether compulsory or voluntary (except Liquidation for the purpose of reconstruction) or if a Receiver is appointed or if a petition to appoint an Examiner is presented to the Hight Court, the Contractor without prejudice to any other rights herein contained may send by registered post or have delivered to the Employer a written notice determining the employment of the Contractor under this Contract.**

This is similar to the clause that relates to the bankruptcy of the Contractor, and the notes (pars. 33.06 and 33.07) to that sub-clause apply in this instance. As with Clause 33, examination is now included as part of the 1996 revision.

34.03 Just as in Clause 33, this clause goes on to set out the procedure to be followed when determination is carried out by the Contractor.

Upon such determination under this provision then without prejudice to the accrued rights of either party their respective rights and liabilities shall be as follows:

The Contractor shall thereupon with all reasonable dispatch remove from the site all his goods, machinery and plant and shall also give facility for his sub-contractors so to do.

This sub-clause requires no comment.

34.04 **The Contractor shall thereupon be paid by the Employer:**

i) **the Contract value of the Work Completed at the date of such determination aforesaid subject to the provisions of Clause 13 of these Conditions.**

The rules for valuing work are set out in Clause 13 (Ascertainment of Prices for Variations). These same rules apply to this clause.

ii) **the value of the work commenced and executed but not completed at the date of such determination, the value being ascertained *mutatis mutandis* in accordance with the provisions of Clause 13 of these Conditions.**

Mutatis mutandis means the necessary changes being made. This sub-clause follows from sub-clause (i) and needs no comment.

iii) **the cost of materials or goods properly ordered and delivered for the Works actually paid for by the Contractor or of which he is**

legally bound to accept delivery and on such costs being paid to the Employer such materials or goods shall become the Employer's sole property

Obviously at any one time, materials will be on order, some will be in transit, others may be delivered but not yet fixed or incorporated into the Works, and some provision is required to set out the position with regard to ownership and payment in respect of these goods.

iv) The reasonable cost of removal as above provided.

The removal referred to is that set out in par. 34.03. The reasonable cost shall be determined by the Architect, and in consultation with the Quantity Surveyor where one is retained.

v) Any loss or damage caused to the Contractor owing to such determination as aforesaid.

Previous notes (pars. 2.26 and 2.27) dealt with loss or expense in relation to Architect's instructions. The same general position would apply here. Loss of the profit which the Contractor would have made had the contract proceeded would be a legitimate loss, as would agreements to hire plant, machinery, temporary buildings, etc. Contracts of employment might also be affected, and in all these matters the Contractor is entitled to recoup any expense or compensation.

Provided that in addition to all other remedies the Contractor upon the said determination may take possession of and shall have a lien upon all unfixed materials and goods intended for the Works which may have become the property of the Employer under this Contract until payment of all money due to the Contractor from the Employer.

This is a further safeguard for the Contractor. Ownership of unfixed goods is dealt with in par. 35.05. The purpose of this sub-clause is to ensure that a measure of protection is given to the Contractor by this lien, and that failing payment, the Contractor will have a right over the goods and materials. (See par. 33.05 for notes on 'lien'.)

GDLA – Clause 34

34.05   This is very similar to RIAI Clause 34, except that there is no mention of examination as a ground for determination and the possible bankruptcy of the Employer is also omitted on the reasonable assumption that the State will remain solvent.

Sub-clause (5) is re-worded as 'any loss of profit on the Contract suffered by the Contractor owing to such determination as aforesaid'. This is a narrower right than that set out in (v) in the RIAI form. The items mentioned in the notes to sub-clause (v) would probably be allowable in any case under the heading of damages for breach of contract.

SF 88 – Clause 22

DETERMINATION BY CONTRACTOR

34.06 **The Contractor may, following seven days notice in writing by registered post or recorded delivery to the Employer of his intention to determine under this clause, forthwith determine the employment of the Contractor under this Contract if the Employer shall make default in anyone or more of the following respects:**

i) **if the Employer fails to make any interim payment due within 14 days of such payment being due;**

ii) **if the Employer or any person for whom he is responsible materially interferes with or substantially obstructs the carrying out of the Works provided that the Employer shall have been requested in writing to withdraw or terminate such interference or obstruction and has failed to do so within a reasonable time;**

iii) **if the Employer suspends the carrying out of the Works for a continuous period in excess of one month.**

In the event of the Contractor determining his employment under this Contract as aforesaid the Employer shall pay to the Contractor such sum as shall in the opinion of the Architect expressed in writing be fair and reasonable for the value of the Work executed, material on site and the cost of removal of all plant, tools and equipment after taking into account amounts previously paid. Provided always that the right of determination shall be without prejudice to any other rights or remedies which the Contractor may possess.

The only new points in the SF 88 form which are not dealt with in the longer forms are the references at (ii) and (iii) to obstruction or suspension of the Works by the Employer. These provisions are presumably intended to deal mainly with alterations and extensions, where the co-operation of the Employer in providing access to various portions of a building would be necessary. Clearly the Contractor cannot proceed with the Works in the absence of such co-operation. It has, in any event, been questioned as to whether or not the Employer has any right to suspend the works.

34.07   B   EMPLOYER'S RESPONSIBILITIES UNDER CLAUSE 34
               RIAI AND GDLA

1   Pay the Contractor as provided in sub-clauses (i) to (v).

34.08   C   CONTRACTOR'S RESPONSIBILITIES UNDER CLAUSE 34
               RIAI AND GDLA

1   Determine his own employment if justified.

2   Remove all goods, machinery and plant from the site.

3   Take a lien on unfixed materials if necessary.

RIAI – Clause 35

CERTIFICATES AND PAYMENTS

35.01　This clause is the longest in the RIAI and GDLA forms, and is divided into thirteen sub-clauses. The most detailed of these sub-clauses are those dealing with the retention money, and the clause itself is a detailed setting out of the way in which the financial matters of the Contract are decided.

Considerable portions of the clause deal with procedural and 'timetable' matters. The Architect cannot be expected to be aware of the many grey areas of law which overshadow the whole area of certificates, either financial ones or otherwise, and the Architect's general awareness of the law should be as described in par. 2.13. However, if the Architect ensures that the procedural requirements with regard to payments are followed, he has carried out his duties under this clause. The sub-clauses deal with:

(a) (b) (c) and (d):	Certificates issued during the course of the work
(e) (f) and (g):	The Retention Fund
(h) (i) (j) and (l):	The Final Certificate
(k):	Conclusiveness of Certificates
(m):	Interest for non-payment of certificates

A very important point, as far as the Contractor (and the Nominated Sub-Contractors) is concerned is that it seems to be accepted law that a certificate must have been issued under the contract before the Contractor would be entitled for any payment for any work done (*Dunlop and Rankin Ltd v Hendall Steel Structures* [1957] 1 WLR 1022).

The following sub-clause was inserted as a result of the report issued by the Forum for the Construction Industry in February 2001. The report dealt with a number of different matters relating to procurement generally, including the appointment of consultants, health and safety, bonds etc. The sub-clause addresses a matter which had been of concern to the Construction Industry Federation for some years and that was the difficulty, in some cases of the Contractor obtaining payment towards the end of a contract. Some Employers no doubt might not be too happy about paying for work not yet done. The alternative of a bank guarantee might be more attractive for Employers.

(a) Upon issue of the letter of intent or the signing of the Contract, whichever is the earlier, the Employer shall pay an amount equal to two months average payments (calculated as the tender sum divided by the number of months in the contract period multiplied by two) into an account (hereinafter called the Guarantee Account) in the joint names of the Employer and the Contractor at the bank named in the appendix hereto.

The amount lodged in the Guarantee Account together with any interest accrued shall be used to pay the Contractor on presentation to the bank of the Architect's last interim and final certificates or any unpaid interim certificate pursuant to Clause 34(b). The surplus or the deficit of the Guarantee Account following payment to the Contractor shall accrue to or be suffered by the Employer.

Where money is paid into an account as provided above the bank shall be instructed that it is a Guarantee Account under Clause 35 of the RIAI Conditions of Contract and that disbursements shall be made to either party to the account only on the certificate of the Architect authorising such disbursements. The signature of neither the Employer nor the Contractor is necessary for such disbursements.

or alternatively

(a) The Employer shall provide a certificate from his bank which will confirm that sufficient funds will be available to him to meet the cash flow of the development and a guaranteed payment of any Architect's certificate presented by the Contractor which remains unpaid after the expiry of the period stipulated for honoring certificates.

35.02   **(b) At the period of Interim Certificates named in the Appendix the Contractor shall (subject to Clause 16(c) of these Conditions) on production of a detailed progress statement be entitled to receive in five working days unless otherwise stated in the Appendix a certificate from the Architect of the amount due to him from the Employer, which certificate shall include any amounts allowed in respect of subcontracts and the Architect shall specify and show separately the amount (if any) allowed in respect of each Nominated Sub-Contractor. Each certificate shall be honoured by the Employer within seven working days of presentation of same to him by the**

**Contractor. If the amount certified differs from the progress state-
ment submitted by the Contractor the Architect, on request, shall
give the Contractor an explanation of the difference.**

This sub-clause can be broken down into five separate parts:

1 Interim Certificates will be issued by the Architect at regular intervals.
The period will be agreed by the parties, either as a tender condition, or
on signing the contract. If no specific period is mentioned in the appendix, then Interim Certificates are to issue monthly.

2 The reference to sub-clause 16(c) is to allow the Architect to pay a
Nominated Sub-Contractor directly if the Contractor does not pay the
amounts specified on the Certificate (see par. 16.13).

3 The Interim Certificate must be issued within five working days of
receiving a statement, unless the parties have agreed, in the appendix, to
a different period.

4 The Employer must honour the Certificate within seven days of presentation. Failure to do so is a ground for the Contractor to issue a notice of
his intention to determine his own employment under the contract (see
par. 34.01).

5 The Contractor is entitled to an explanation if the amount certified differs from the amount which he has claimed. Apart from the question of
retention (see par. 35.06) the amounts, in practice, almost always
diverge. If no quantity surveyor is retained, the Architect will usually
certify what appears to him to be a reasonable figure in all the circumstances. In the absence of a Bill of Quantities, it is almost impossible for
the Architect to decide exactly how much might be due, and a sensible
working arrangement usually develops between the Architect and the
Contractor as to how much might be due at any one time. The Contractor
will often suggest a figure to the Architect, before applying in writing
for a certificate, and this, if agreed, will remove any causes for dispute.

In contracts where a quantity surveyor is retained, a detailed statement is
usually agreed between the Contractor's surveyors and the Quantity
Surveyor, and this figure is then issued to the Architect by the Quantity
Surveyor as a recommendation. Again, it would be usual for the Architect to
certify the amount recommended, but this does not, of course, relieve the
Architect of any responsibility for the accuracy of the certificate.

35.03 The Architect's responsibility for the accuracy of any certificate is considerable. It used to be thought, as a result of *Chambers v Goldthorpe* [1901] 1
KB 624, that where an Architect was bound to act impartially as between the

parties to the contract, he was in the position of an arbitrator, and he had a quasi-judicial role. In these circumstances he would not be liable for an action in negligence in the exercise of that particular function. Over the years however, this position changed. The case of *Wisbech UDC v Ward* [1927] 2 KB 556, decided that while the Architect might be protected as far as a final certificate was concerned, this was not the case where interim certificates were issued. The matter of interim certificates was also examined in the case of *Townsend v Stone Toms* [1984] 27 BLR 26 where it was held that an Architect was negligent in certifying defective work in an interim certificate, even where it would be possible to adjust the amount certified at the issue of the final certificate.

The conclusiveness of an interim certificate has been the subject of many court decisions over the years and it might be useful to refer to the general position, as reference is constantly being made to this problem. What was called the 'rule' in *Dawnays v Minter* (*Dawnays Ltd v FG Minter Ltd* [1971] 1 BLR 19) held that an Employer was not entitled to deduct money from an interim certificate because of defective work or over-valuation, even where there was a wide-ranging arbitration clause. It was decided that the Employer must wait until the conclusion of the arbitration itself. However, the case of *Gilbert-Ash (Northern) Ltd v Modern Engineering (Bristol) Ltd* [1974] 1 BLR 75 abolished this rule, holding that an Employer could deduct such monies. The position might well be academic, as the Contractor can seek arbitration during the course of the contract on the question of an interim certificate, but if he does not do so, it now appears that the Employer might not be entitled to withhold the money.

These matters were considered in a number of Irish cases. *In John Sisk and Son Ltd v Lawter Products BV* [1976] High Court, unrep. 15th November, the 'old' view was taken that the Employer was not entitled to deduct anything from the certificate. A different view was taken in *PJ Hegarty and Sons Ltd v Royal Liver Friendly Society* [1985] High Court, unrep. 11th October. It was held that an Employer was entitled to deduct monies and that 'an amount included in a certificate (whether interim or final) does not constitute a debt or a particular character and enjoys no special immunity from any cross-claim or right of set-off to which the debtor may be entitled.' One of the main reasons given by the court for this decision was the right of the parties to go to arbitration at any time on the question of certificates. This view, however, was not followed in *Rohan Construction Ltd v Antigen Ltd* [1989] ILRM 783. This case, which can now be taken as the law in Ireland, held that a right of set-off was clearly inconsistent with the terms of the RIAI form, although it is allowable in the GDLA form. The wording of the contract can be the key to set-off rights, and this was recently the argument in the case of *RM Douglas Construction Ltd v Bass Leisure Ltd* [1991] 7 CLJ

114 where-set-off was allowed because the wording of the contract form did not specifically exclude it. This could, presumably, now be argued against the decision in the *Rohan* case.

The case that settled the Architect's liability for certifying defective work was *Sutcliffe v Thackrah* [1974] 4 BLR 16. The House of Lords held that in certifying, an Architect was not acting in any arbitral or judicial capacity, and was liable for any negligence in certifying. To 'certify', after all, means that the certifier is 'certain'. It is vital for the Architect to be aware of the fact that he is to certify only for work which has been properly done, and that he will be liable if he acts otherwise. It would be clear though that defects which he could not have observed, or any fraudulent concealment, would not form the basis of any negligence claim (see par. 35.11).

35.04 **(c) The amount stated as due in an Interim Certificate shall be the total value of the work duly executed and of materials and goods delivered upon the site of the Works for use thereon up to the date upon which the Contractor shall have applied for the said certificate less an amount to be retained by the Employer (as hereinafter provided) and less any instalments previously certified under this clause. Provided that such certificate shall include only the value of the said materials and goods and from such time as they are, in the opinion of the Architect, reasonably, properly and not prematurely brought to or placed on the site of the Works and only if adequately stored and/or protected against weather or other casualties.**

Where in any certificate (of which the Contractor has received payment) the Architect has included the value of any unfixed materials or goods intended for or placed on or adjacent to the Works such materials or goods shall become the property of the Employer and they shall not be removed except for use upon the Works without the authority of the Architect in writing but the Contractor shall remain responsible for loss or damage to them.

There are two main points in this sub-clause:

1   An interim certificate shall be for the value of the work done and materials ordered since the previous valuation. The Architect is entitled to deduct the agreed percentage for retention as set out in the appendix (see par. 35.06) for the notes on the Retention Fund).

2   Goods which have been certified become the property of the Employer, but the Contractor remains responsible for them (see the notes to the next sub-clause, 35.05).

35.05 **(d) The amount stated as due on an Interim Certificate may at the discretion of the Architect include the value of any materials or goods before delivery thereof to the site of the Works provided that:**

i)   **such materials or goods are intended for inclusion in the Works.**

ii) **nothing remains to be done to such materials or goods to complete the same up to the point of their incorporation in the Works.**

iii) **such materials or goods have been and are set apart at the premises where they have been manufactured, or assembled or are stored and furthermore have been clearly and visibly marked individually or in sets either by letters or figures or by reference to a pre-determined code so as to identify**
   a) **where they are stored on premises of the Contractor, the Employer and other cases the person to whose order they are held, and**
   b) **their destination as being the Works.**

iv) **where such materials or goods were ordered from a supplier by the Contractor or a sub-contractor the contract for the supply is in writing and expressly provides that the property therein shall pass unconditionally to the Contractor or the sub-contractor (as the case may be) not later than the happening of the events set out in paragraphs (ii) and (iii) of this sub-clause.**

v)   **where such materials or goods were ordered from a supplier by a sub-contractor the relevant sub-contract is in writing and expressly provides that on the property in such materials or goods passing to a sub-contractor the same shall immediately thereon pass to the Contractor.**

vi) **where such materials or goods were manufactured or assembled by a sub-contractor the sub-contract is in writing and expressly provides that the property in such materials or goods shall pass unconditionally to the Contractor not later than the happening of the events set out in paragraph (ii) and (iii) of this sub-clause.**

vii) **the materials or goods are in accordance with the Contract and that insurance cover, in a form and with insurers satisfactory to the Employer, has been obtained by the Contractor in respect of any damage or loss of any such materials or goods.**

viii) **the Contractor furnishes to the Architect reasonable proof that the property in such materials or goods is vested in him and that the appropriate conditions set out in paragraph (i) to (vii) of this sub-clause have been complied with.**

In other words, materials and goods may be included in certificates before they are delivered to the site provided that they are ordered, complete, identifiable, and specified, and provided that the Employer is protected. The insurance requirement in sub-clause (d)(vii) was added in the 2001 Forum Revisions.

It will be obvious that considerable amounts of the various items needed for a building project will require substantial work carried out on them before they are delivered to the site. These might be items such as structural steelwork, precast concrete products, stone facings, mechanical service machinery, etc. The Contractor, or a Nominated Sub-Contractor will have to spend large amounts of money on these items long before they will be delivered to the site. In addition, substantial quantities of materials will have to be ordered and stored, and paid for. Some provisions are required, therefore, to enable the Contractor to be paid for these items before they reach the site. The Architect will decide, on inspection, if the items are intended for the Works, are complete, are identifiable, and are as specified.

It should be equally clear that standard or production items such as bricks, concrete blocks, etc, should not be included in certificates until they are incorporated into the works.

Paragraphs (iv), (v) and (vi) of this sub-clause deal with the provisions to ensure that the Employer is protected against loss where goods or materials have been certified and paid for before the items are delivered to the site and incorporated into the Works. The ordinary law dealing with title to goods is quite involved, but the Architect should be aware of the basic position. Many sales of goods now incorporate what is called a 'Retention of Title' Clause, which means that ownership of the goods will not pass to a buyer in possession until the goods have been paid for, and this retention can follow through a series of sales from manufacturer, to wholesaler, to retailer, to customer. The general rule in building contracts is that materials or items which have been included in the Architect's certificate, and paid for by the Employer, become the Employer's property, even where there is a retention of title clause. This would not be the case, though, if the Employer was aware of the existence of the retention of title clause, or as the law says if he had 'notice' of the clause. The Sale of Goods and Supply of Services Act 1980 says at section 12:

> 12(1) In every contract of sale, other than one to which subsection (2) applies, there is
>
> a)   an implied condition on the part of the seller that, in the case of a sale, he has a right to sell the goods and, in the case of an agreement

to sell, he will have a right to sell the goods at the time when the property is to pass, and

b) an implied warranty that the goods are free, and will remain free until the time when the property is to pass from any charge or encumbrance not disclosed to the buyer before the contract is made, and that the buyer will enjoy quiet possession of the goods except so far as it may be disturbed by the owner or other person entitled to the benefit of any charge or encumbrance so disclosed.

Subsection (2) of the section referred to in subsection (1) deals with situations where a charge or encumbrance is disclosed.

There have been many cases where the details of these various contractual provisions (and in England the details of the Sale of Goods Act 1979), have been examined. The English law differs from that in Ireland, but cases which are generally similar will be considered by the Irish Courts (see Preface). Two cases dealing with sub-contractors will show the difficulties. In *Dawbar Williamson Roofing Ltd v Humberside County Council* [1979] 14 BLR 70, a roofing contractor who had supplied slates to a site had not received payment from a contractor who had received payment, but who had become insolvent before passing on the payment. In *Archivent v Strathclyde Regional Council* [1984] 27 BLR 98, the position was identical, with the goods in question being ventilators. In each case the court had to decide who was to suffer: the Employer by having to pay twice, or the Sub-Contractor through not being paid at all. The results in the cases differed, the Sub-Contractor succeeding in *Dawbar Williamson*, but failing in *Archivent*.

The position in *Dawbar Williamson* was that the main contract (JCT/RIBA 63), just as in the RIAI form, provided that any goods unfixed on site which had been paid for by the Employer would become the Employer's property. While the sub-contract form which Dawbar Williamson had signed provided that the Sub-Contractor was deemed to have notice of the provisions of the main contract, it contained no express provision as to when property should pass to the main contractor, and the court held that no such property had, therefore passed. In *Archivent* the court held that good title had passed to the Employer because of the provisions of the Sale of Goods Act 1979 Section 25(1), whereas this particular section was held not to be relevant in the case of *Dawbar Williamson* primarily because Dawbor Williamson were sub-contractors, and Archivent were suppliers.

The two cases emphasise the difficulty of this area of law. It has been described in Building Law Reports as 'a minefield, a maze, and a quagmire' and the Architect must pay particular attention to those paragraphs of this sub-clause dealing with title, i.e. paragraphs (iv), (v), (vi) and (viii) and he must ensure that he has satisfied himself that, as far as he can under the contract, he has protected the Employer.

Where in any certificate (of which the Contractor has received payment) the Architect has included the value of any unfixed materials or goods intended for the Works such materials or goods shall become the property of the Employer and they shall not be removed except for use upon the Works without the authority of the Architect in writing, but the Contractor shall remain responsible for loss or damage to them, and for the cost of the storage, handling and insurance of the same until such time as they are delivered to the Works.

This wording is the same as the last paragraph of sub-clause (c) with the addition of the phrase 'and for the cost of storage, handling and insurance of the same until such time as they are delivered to the Works'.

35.06 **(e) The amount to be retained by the Employer (the 'Retention Fund') shall be such percentage of the value of the work and materials as aforesaid as is named in the Appendix as 'Percentage of Certified Value Retained'. The total amount to be retained shall not exceed the sum named in the Appendix as 'Limit of Retention Fund' if such limit obtains.**

After the total amount retained has reached the sum named in the appendix as limit of retention fund the full value of works and materials shall be certified by the architect.

The purpose of the Employer in retaining something of the value of the work completed is to protect himself in the case of defects appearing which the Contractor is unable or unwilling to remedy. Clause 2(c) authorises the Architect to order the removal of work or materials, presumably, although not stated, on the grounds that they do not conform with the contract requirements, and paragraph 5 of the same clause authorises the Employer to employ others to carry out work which the Contractor refuses to do. The Employer, in such a circumstance, will have the funds to have this work carried out. Similarly, if the Contractor becomes insolvent, or if his employment is determined, the Employer is protected. Retention amounts were traditionally 10% of the amount certified, with no upper limit, but as contracts grew and interest rates rose, it was soon as inequitable to retain very large sums, in some cases heading for millions of pounds. The position to-day is that the retention percentage will vary from 2% to 8% depending on the amount of the contract. There is a recommended sliding scale issued by the Construction Industry Federation. In addition, an upper limit or ceiling is imposed on the amount to be retained, and when this limit has been reached, the full value of the work is then certified.

The way in which the retention money is dealt with is covered in the notes to the next two sub-clauses at pars. 35.08and 35.09. The contract provides that either part of sub-clause (f) or sub-clause (g) be struck out depending on the wishes of the parties to the contract.

35.07 **(f)(1) After the issue of the Certificate of Practical Completion the Contractor shall provide a retention bond issued by a bonding agency, approved by the Architect, which approval shall not unreasonably be withheld in the format attached to these conditions and the Architect shall, upon receipt of the bond, issue an interim certificate releasing the retention fund in full.**

Sub-clause (f)(1) has been introduced as a result of the recommendations made by the Forum for the Construction Industry in a document dated 2001. Concern had been expressed over the years by contractors with regard to the difficulty in obtaining final payments. This retention bond proposal is being suggested by the Forum for a trial basis of three years. The remainder of the clause has not been changed.

The following sub-clause is to operate where the parties to the Contract do not intend to open a joint account for the Retention Fund. If they do so intend, sub-clause (g) will come into effect.

* (f)(2) The amount retained by virtue of sub-clause (e) of this clause shall be dealt with in the following manner:

i) **as and when such amount is so retained it shall be held upon trust by the Employer for the Contractor without obligation to invest subject to the right of the Employer to have recourse thereto from time to time for payment of any amount which he is entitled under the provisions of the Contract to deduct from any sum due or to become due to the Contractor.**

ii) **when the Architect certifies that the Works are practically complete he shall at the same time issue a certificate for payment of one moiety of the total amount then so retained and the Contractor shall be entitled to payment thereof within the period for honouring certificates.**

iii) **the residue of the amount then so retained shall be included in the Final Certificate as described in sub-clause (b) of this clause.**

It will be seen in paragraph (f)(2)(i) that the retention money is held in trust by the Employer for the Contractor. This can be a protection for the Contractor in the case of the Employer becoming insolvent, but only if the money retained can be identified or traced. As this seldom happens, the protection is seldom available. Unless sub-clause (g) operates the retention moneys remain part of the overall assets of the Employer and are not available in preference to other creditors who would outrank the Contractor. The paragraph also says that the Employer has no 'obligation to invest' the retention money. This is written into the contract to clarify the position, as ordinarily a trustee is obliged to invest money in approved securities, and pay the interest to the beneficiary, in this case the Contractor.

It has been pointed out in par. 29.04 that the Employer is entitled to use money in the retention fund where he has the right to liquidated damages even if the money is held 'in trust'. This is because of the wording: 'subject to the right of the Employer to have recourse thereto from time to time for payment of any amount which he is entitled under the provisions of this contract to deduct from any sum due or to become due to the Contractor'. This was so held in *Henry Boot Building v Croydon Hotel and Leisure* [1974] 36 BLR 41.

As has been seen in par. 31.01, half the retention money is certified to the Contractor when the certificate of Practical Completion is issued, and this is provided for in sub-paragraph (ii). The last sub-paragraph (iii) provides that the second half of the retention money will be included in the Final Certificate (see par. 35.10).

35.08 *** (g) The amount retained by virtue of sub-clause (e) of this clause shall be dealt with in the following manner:**

As and when such amount is so retained the Architect shall on the application of the Contractor certify payment of the amount and the Employer shall forthwith pay such amount into an account (hereinafter called the 'Joint Account') in the joint names of the Employer and the Contractor at the Bank named in the Appendix hereto.

The amount so retained and paid into the Joint Account shall be placed on deposit at interest or otherwise dealt with as may be agreed between the Employer and the Contractor, and the Employer shall stand possessed thereof upon the trusts following, that is to say·

i) **as and when such amount is so retained the principal and all accrued interest or property representing the same in accordance with any dealing agreed between the parties as aforesaid (here-**

inafter called the 'Joint Account Retention Fund') shall be held upon trust by the Employer for the Contractor subject to the right of the Employer to have recourse thereto from time to time for payment of any amount which is stated to be a debt payable by the Contractor to the Employer or which he is entitled under the provisions or for breach of this Contract to deduct from any sum due or to become due to the Contractor;

ii) on the issue of the Certificate of Practical Completion the Architect shall authorise forthwith the release of one moiety of the Joint Account Retention Fund.

iii) the release of the residue of the Joint Account Retention Fund shall be authorised by the Architect on the issue of the Final Certificate and the amount retained as aforesaid and paid by the Employer into the Joint Account shall be included in the sum paid to the Contractor for the purpose of Paragraph (i) of sub-clause (b) to the intent that the interest included in and any alteration in value of the Joint Account Retention Fund shall accrue to or be suffered by the Contractor.

The residue of the amount then so retained and not paid into the Joint Account shall be included in the Final Certificate as described in sub-clause (h) of this clause.

Provided always that if the Contractor shall duly determine this Contract the Joint Account Retention Fund shall be held upon trust for the Contractor and shall forthwith be paid to the Contractor (subject as aforesaid).

Where money is paid into a Joint Account as provided above the Bank shall be instructed that it is a Joint Account under Clause 35(f) of the RIAI Conditions of Contract and that disbursements from this account shall be made to either party to the account only on the Certificate of the Architect authorising such disbursements. The signature of neither the Employer nor the Contractor is necessary for such disbursements.

* NOTE: If sub-clause 35(f)(2) is being implemented then the entire of sub-clause 35(g) is to be struck out.

If the provisions of sub-clause 35(f)(1) or (2) have been implemented then the following sub-clause (g) should be struck out.

The provision of a joint account is a secure protection for the Contractor as far as the retention monies are concerned. The amount is held on trust, is separate and identifiable, and can be released only on the certificate of the Architect. Furthermore, the Contractor is entitled to any interest that accrues. In these circumstances, it is surprising that relatively few such joint accounts seem to be requested by contractors. The arrangements for dealing with the joint account and which are set out in sub-clause (f) are straight forward and need no comment.

35.09   **(h)(i) Within three calendar months of the date of Practical Completion of the Works the Contractor shall furnish the Architect with all documents necessary for the purposes of the Computations required by these Conditions including those relating to the account of Nominated Sub-Contractors and Nominated Suppliers.**

     ii) No Contractor's documents other than those furnished in accordance with Section (i) of this sub-clause shall be taken into consideration by the Architect in the computation of the amount of the Final Certificate save in circumstances which are adjudged by the Architect to be exceptional or save for any additional documents which the Architect may at any time seek from the Contractor.

     iii) On compliance by the Contractor with the requirement of Section (i) of this sub-clause the measurement and valuation of the Works shall proceed and shall be completed within the Period of Final Measurement stated in the Appendix to these Conditions and the Contractor shall be supplied with a copy of the priced bill of variations not later than the end of the said period and before the issue of the Final Certificate.

     iv) When due to exceptional circumstances the Contractor does not furnish the documents as required by Section (i) of this sub-clause the Architect at his discretion may extend the Period of Final Measurement and to the date for issue of the Final Certificate.

This sub-clause sets out the steps to be taken so as to enable the proposed final account figure to be obtained. If a quantity surveyor is retained, he will deal entirely with the matters set out in sections (i), (ii) and (iii) but acting always on the advice of and under the direction of the Architect. The procedure is simple. It is the Contractor's responsibility to provide all the necessary information so as to enable the final account figure to be calculated, and if he omits to claim or provide documents, he will stand the loss. The timetable suggested is more honoured in the breach than the observance and this is due, surprisingly, in many instances to the Contractor not providing the necessary information. The appendix suggests that the Period of Final Measurement be set at six months if no other period is preferred so that, in theory, a final account figure should be available not later than nine months after the issue of the Certificate of Practical Completion.

35.10 **(i) So soon as is practicable but before the end of ten working days from the end of the Defects Liability Period stated in the Appendix to these Conditions or from completion of making good defects under Clause 31 of these Conditions or from the completion of all items of work or supply outstanding at Practical Completion (see Clause 31) or from the Period of Final Measurement referred to in paragraph (ii) of sub-clause (g) of this clause whichever is the latest, the Architect shall give notice to the Contractor and to the Employer of his intention to issue the Final Certificate and unless the Architect receives notice of arbitration within ten working days or such other period as may be stated in the Appendix from the Employer or Contractor he shall issue the Final Certificate. The Final Certificate shall state:**

> **i) the sum of the amounts certified for payment under interim cer-tificates and the amount of the moiety of the retention money certified at time of Practical Completion.**
>
> **ii) the Contract Sum adjusted as necessary in accordance with the terms of these Conditions.**
>
> **iii) the difference (if any) between the two sums expressed as a bal-ance due to the Contractor from the Employer or to the Employer from the Contractor as the case may be. Subject to any deduc-tions authorised by these Conditions the said balance shall be, as of from the tenth working day after the issue of the said Final Certificate, a debt payable as the case may be by the Employer to the Contractor or by the Contractor to the Employer.**

This sub-clause might be described, like sub-clause (h), as a 'timetable' and 'regulatory' Clause. It provides that the Architect shall inform the parties to the Contract of his intention to issue a Final Certificate for a stated amount, ten days after the last of the following events:

1 the end of the Defects Liability Period;

2 the completion of making good defects;

3 the completion of items outstanding at Practical Completion; or

4 the end of the Period of Final Measurement.

If either of the parties to the Contract wishes to dispute the amount of the Final Certificate, they must ask for an Arbitrator to be appointed. The clause also states in paragraph (iii) that the difference between the amount certified in the interim certificates and the amount stated in the Final Certificate will be a debt owing either to the Employer or to the Contractor. It would be an unwise Architect who would allow a situation to develop where the Contractor is owed money, as this situation pre-supposes that the Architect has over-certified (see par. 35.03). The reference to Arbitration in this sub-clause allows the Contractor, or the Employer, to question the amount of the proposed Final Certificate. If arbitration is sought by either party, the issue of the Final Certificate will have to wait until the decision of the Arbitrator is made known (see Clause 38 – Disputes Resolution).

35.11 **(j) The said Final Certificates shall be conclusive in any proceedings arising out of this Contract (whether by Arbitration under Clause 38 of these Conditions of otherwise) that the Works have been properly carried out and completed in accordance with the terms of this Contract and that any necessary effect has been given to all terms of this Contract which require an adjustment to be made to the Contract Sum, except and insofar as any sum mentioned in the said Final Certificate is erroneous by reason of:**

i) **fraud, dishonesty, or fraudulent concealment relating to the Works or any part thereof or to any matter dealt with in the said Final Certificate; or**

ii) **any defect (including any omission) in the Works or any part thereof which reasonable inspection or examination at any rea-sonable time during the carrying out of the Works or before the issue of the said Final Certificate would not have disclosed.**

The issue of the Final Certificate is, in theory, the end of the Contract which was entered into when the parties signed the Articles of Agreement. In the normal course their liability to one another in any action arising under the contract would last for another six years in the case of a simple contract, and for another twelve years for a contract signed under seal. This is discussed in the notes to the Articles of Agreement (par. A.01 and par. Int.06). However, because of the uncertainty which has prevailed for many years, and in partic-ular since the notorious case of *Dutton v Bognor Regis UDC* [1972] 3 BLR 13, there is no clear break point as to when the parties cease to be liable to one another. This is fully discussed in the Introduction at par. Int.13.

The sub-clause, in effect, attempts to impose a 'finality' to the Final Certificate, but like many other such attempts, the Courts have decided that these will be subject to exceptions.

Over many years, a succession of cases has qualified the position and, as in many other areas of the contract, the situation is far from clear. The most recent attempt to interpret the finality of a certificate was a case which dealt with one of the JCT forms (*Colbart Ltd v Kumer* (1992) 7 BLISS 5). The wording of the JCT form in question (The Intermediate Form) is different from the RIAI forms but the conclusions of the judge were interesting and would seem to be applicable to the RIAI forms. The judge held that the final certificate should not be conclusive that the Works had been carried out in accordance with the Contract if, for instance, specified materials had been changed, but that it should be conclusive as regards matters which depended on the Architect's judgement. The certificate was conclusive as regards quality and standards. This would seem to be a fair interpretation of the intention of this sub-clause, and it emphasises the necessity for vigilance on the part of the Architect in issuing the final certificate.

The exceptions mentioned in the sub-clause itself, at paragraphs (i) and (ii) are clear. Any fraud, or concealment, or a latent defect (that is, one that has not yet appeared) can always be made the subject of a claim by the Employer after the issue of the Final Certificate, subject again to the interpretation by the Courts of the position under the Statute of Limitations 1957 (par. Int.06). The exceptions imposed by the Courts are concerned with the precise wording of various clauses in the Contract. The case of *Elliott v The Minister for Education* [1987] ILRM 710 decided that the Final Certificate was only conclusive, as far as the amount certified was concerned, in relation to any clause which referred to adjustment to the 'Contract Sum' and the High Court held that the Final Certificate did not prevent a claim under Clause 29(b) after the issue of the Final Certificate (see par. 29.06). This judgement would presumably apply to Clause 2 paragraph 5 where the same general wording is used. The case of *HW Neville (Sunblest) Ltd v William Press and Son Ltd* [1981] 20 BLR 78 decided that the issue of a final certificate did not prevent a subsequent case for breach of contract succeeding, and resulting in damages. The existence of an arbitration clause that can review any certificate of the architect has also caused the courts to question the finality of a 'final' certificate. The conclusiveness of an interim certificate is dealt with in par. 35.03.

This sub-clause refers to Arbitration, as does sub-clause (h) (see Clause 38 – Disputes Resolution).

35.12 **(k) Save as aforesaid no certificate of the Architect shall of itself be conclusive evidence that any works, materials, or goods to which it relates are in accordance with the Contract.**

It is not very clear as to what precisely this sub-clause intends to cover. The preceding sub-clause (j) refers to the final certificate being conclusive in any proceedings that 'the Works have been properly carried out and completed in accordance with the terms of this Contract'. It must be presumed that this clause refers to interim certificates, and would imply that interim certificates cannot be taken as evidence that the works being certified are approved. However, as was seen in par. 35.03 the courts have held (*Sutcliffe v Thackrah* [1974] 4 BLR 16 and *Townsend v Stone Toms* [1984] 27 BLR 26) that an Architect was negligent in certifying defective work in an interim certificate. It would be prudent for an architect only to certify work which meets his approval even where he would have the opportunity to correct matters in later certificates. This clause is not contained in the GDLA form.

35.13 **(l) If the Architect fails to issue a Final Certificate in accordance with sub-clause (h) of this clause then the Contractor shall be entitled to charge to the Employer interest on the amount of the Final Certificate at the current AA bank rate of interest on overdrafts until such time as the Final Certificate is issued.**

Sub-clause (h) lists the four events, after the latest of which the Architect is to issue the Final Certificate. If the Architect does not do so, and if Arbitration is not sought, then interest on the amount contained in the final account as being due to the Contractor, is payable by the Employer. The rate of interest shall be 'at the current AA bank rate'. Banks generally have different rates for personal (A), business (AA), and Government or other secured (AAA) overdrafts.

35.14 **(m) If the Employer does not pay to the Contractor any amount certified within the period stipulated for payment thereof the Contractor may, without prejudice to other rights and remedies, after seven working days from the latest date on which the certificate should have been honoured be entitled to charge interest to the Employer on the amount outstanding in respect of such certificate at the current AA bank rate of interest on overdrafts until such time as payment is made by the Employer.**

Whereas sub-clause (l) dealt with the position where the Architect did not issue the Final Certificate in time, this sub-clause provides for the situation where the Employer does not pay any certificate, either interim or final, in time. The reference in the sub-clause to 'other rights or remedies' would refer to the Contractor's rights under ordinary law, and in particular to his right to determination as set out in Clause 34 (see par. 34.01). The right to interest, either under sub-clause (l) or (m) could be affected if the dispute goes to arbitration. The position with regard to interest, as far as arbitration is concerned, is not totally clear. Under the Arbitration Acts, an Arbitrator is empowered to award interest at the same rate of a judgement debt, but only from the time of the publishing of the Arbitrator's award (Arbitration Act 1954 – Section 34). Under the Courts Act (1981), at Section 20(1) the Minister for Justice may make an order setting a rate of interest. The present rate of interest is 8%. There has been a considerable amount of case law dealing with the position which would apply to interest as a general rule, but the Architect, and eventually the Arbitrator, would be entitled to award interest at the rate agreed by both parties to the contract, where the right to interest arises from the implementation of the sub-clauses 35(l) and 35(m). If the interest is being claimed under headings not specified in the Contract, and for a period before the Award, most arbitrators take a commercial rather than a strict legal view and award what seems equitable.

GDLA – Clause 35

CERTIFICATES AND PAYMENTS

35.15   The clause is basically the same as the RIAI form. A new sub-clause 35(e)(ii) has been introduced as a result of the recommendations of February 2001 made by the Forum for the Construction Industry. The existing sub-clauses 35(e)(ii) and (iii) are to be moved down one place and renumbered as (iii) and (iv).

(e)(ii) After the Architect notifies the Employer and the Contractor that the Works are practically complete, the Contractor may at his own expense provide a retention bond in favour of the Employer issued by a financial institution approved by the Employer, which approval shall not be unreasonably withheld in the format set out in Supplement (B) of these conditions. The Architect, upon receipt by the Employer of such retention bond, shall issue a certificate for the release of the residue of the amounts still retained to the value of the retention bond and the Contractor shall be entitled to payment thereof within the period for horouring interim certificates.

NOTE: If the Employer decides that the retention bond option is not to be exercised, Clause 35(e)(ii) should be struck out.

This new clause echoes the new clause 35(f)(1) which has been inserted into the RIAI Standard Form with the exception that the Employer is given the specific option of striking out the clause.

There are other differences between the GDLA Clause 35 and the RIAI

Form which was issued in March 1993 as follows:

(The revisions are not yet reprinted in the contract form and are issued as a supplement. They are minor and refer only to the paragraph numbering.)

1   Sub-clause (a)(i): there are three differences:

   a)   The certificate referred to shall be 'subject to sub-clause 16(d) of these Conditions'. This is the sub-clause that requires proof of payment to sub-contractors, and that empowers the Employer to pay a nominated sub-contractor directly.

   b)   The period for honouring certificates is set at ten working days (as opposed to seven in the RIAI form) or at a period to be agreed and set out in the appendix. The RIAI form does not provide for altering the seven day period.

   c)   The issue of an interim certificate is dependent on the insurance which the Contractor is required to take out under Clause 21, 22, 25, or 26 of the Conditions being in force.

2   Sub-clause (a)(ii) and sub-clause (b): These sub-clauses are both contained in sub-clause (b) of the RIAI form. The overall wording of the sub-clauses is different in both forms but the intent is similar. The only item in the GDLA form that does not appear in the RIAI form, and is therefore not commented on, is a reference to sub-clause 36(f) in sub-clause 35(a)(ii) which deals with increases in wages, materials, sub-contracts, etc. The equivalent provision in the RIAI form at sub-clause 36(e) allows the inclusion of these items in interim certificates in a similar way.

3   Sub-clause (c)(i): The words 'and are stored in Ireland' are added to the provision that the value of materials and goods intended for inclusion in the Works may be included in interim certificates. In the absence of any other definition, 'Ireland' must be taken to be the area defined in the Constitution at Article 2, that is the 'whole island of Ireland'.

4   Sub-clause (c)(viii) requires the Contractor, in addition to proving that the ownership of goods covered by sub-clause (c) is vested in him, to establish that the goods are insured to the full value.

5   Sub-clause (d): The arrangements for the Retention Fund are different (see par. 35.06). In the RIAI form both the amount of the fund and the percentage retained are limited to 10%, though a lesser amount is nearly always agreed. In the GDLA form the percentage rate is limited to 10% but there is no provision for an overall limit on the fund. This is, presumably, because if a 10% rate is agreed, the overall fund is automatically limited to 10% of the Contract Sum.

6   Sub-clause (e): The Forum recommendation referred to earlier (see par. 2.30) includes the provision of a bond by the Contractor for dealing with retention. Clause 35(e)(ii) and (iii) are renumbered 35(e)(iii) and (iv) and a new sub-clause (ii) is inserted. This requires little comment but it should be noted that the Employer is given the right to strike out the sub-clause. It also differs in a number of other ways:

a) The first paragraph of the sub-clause in the RIAI form does not occur in the GDLA form. This is the requirement for the Employer to hold the retention money in trust for the Contractor. The omission was made, presumably, because of the assumption that the Employer will never become insolvent.

b) There is a provision at paragraph (iii) that the Employer can have recourse to the Retention Fund for payment of any amount which he is entitled to under the Contract, or under any other contract made between himself and the Contractor (the right to 'set-off' first provided for in Clause 2(c) – see par. 2.30). It is submitted that this was never the purpose of the Retention Fund as far as other contracts between the parties are concerned and the provision should be deleted from future editions of the form.

7   The GDLA form has no provision for a joint account in connection with the retention fund. As has been pointed out in the note to sub-clause (e) this is because the insolvency of the Employer is not contemplated. The entire of sub-clause 35(f) in the previous RIAI form is, therefore, omitted (i.e. the joint account). The numbering of the subsequent sub-clauses differs as a result.

8   The provisions for preparing the final account as set out in Clause 35(g) of the previous RIAI form are somewhat different in sub-clause 35(f) of the GDLA form. At 35(f)(iii) the Employer, in addition to the Architect, is to be supplied with a copy of the priced bills of final account. The period for preparing this account is set out in the appendix to both forms, but the time limit varies. In the RIAI form, if no time is stated, then six months is automatically allowed. In the GDLA form, if no time is stated, the period may not exceed the Period of Final Measurement.

9   The events, and the timetable, referred to in sub-clause (h) RIAI, are different in the comparable provision (g) in the GDLA form. The requirements are that within twenty-one working days after the latest of the following events:

a) the end of the Defects Liability Period (par. 31.06);

b) final Completion as defined in sub-clause 28(e) (see par. 28.04); or

c) forty working days after completion of final measurement and valuation of the Works (par. 35.09);

the Architect shall give notice to the Contractor and the Employer of his intention to issue a Final Certificate, and unless he receives notice of arbitration within thirty working days, he shall issue the final certificate.

10 The provisions of sub-clauses (i) and (j) relating to the conclusiveness, or otherwise, of the Final Certificate as set out in the RIAI form are omitted (see par. 35.11). Instead, the following sentence occurs: 'The said Final certificate shall be conclusive in any proceedings that the final cost of the Works has been properly computed in accordance with the terms of this Contract.' In other words, the Final Certificate is not being treated at all as being conclusive as far as the carrying out of the Works is concerned, and this is a recognition of the actual lack of finality of 'final' certificates discussed in pars. 35.03 and 35.11.

11 The sub-clauses (k) and (l) in the RIAI form are omitted and, under the contract provisions, the Contractor is not entitled to interest either because of non-payment of interim certificates or the withholding of the final certificate. An Arbitrator may, however, award interest on these grounds and will, presumably, do so (see par. 35.14).

SF 88 – Clause 12

PAYMENTS

35.16 **The Employer shall pay or allow to the Contractor the amounts certified as follows:**

The Architect shall on the application of the Contractor, at intervals of not less than four weeks, certify interim payments to the Contractor in respect of the value of the Works properly executed less a retention of 10% and less any previous amounts certified; and the Employer shall pay to the Contractor the amount so certified within 10 days of receipt of the Certificate.

This provision contains most of the elements relating to interim certificates that occur in the longer forms. The notes relating to interim payments (par. 35.02, 35.04, 35.05) and retention (par. 35.06) will be relevant.

SF 88 – Clause 13

PAYMENT ON PRACTICAL COMPLETION

35.17 **The Employer shall pay or allow to the Contractor the amount certi-fied as follows:**

The Architect shall within 14 days after the date of Practical Completion certify payment to the Contractor of 95% of the total amount to be paid to the Contractor under this Contract, so far as he can reasonably ascertain such amount save the value of any work not completed; and the Employer shall pay to the Contractor the amount so ccrtified within 10 days of receipt of that certificate.

The clause contains the 'Practical Completion' requirement to release half of the Retention Fund (see par. 35.07). The Contractor will have received, under Clause 12, 90% of the value of the work up to practical completion. At that point he is entitled to half the Retention Fund, i.e. a further 5%.

SF 88 – Clause 14

FINAL CERTIFICATE

35.18 **The Contractor shall within three months from the date of Practical Completion supply all documentation reasonably required for the Computation of the amount to be finally certified by the Architect. The Architect shall immediately following the end of the Defects Liability Period or when work arising out of the Contractor's obliga-tions under Clause 7 of these Conditions has been carried out, whichever date is later, give notice to both parties in writing of his intention to issue a Final Certificate stating the amount due. Save where notice of a dispute has been given pursuant to Clause 23 of these Conditions, the Architect shall after 14 days from the date of such notice forthwith issue a certificate for the total amount due less any previous amounts certified and the Employer shall pay to the Contractor the amount so certified within 14 days of the date of the Certificate. The Final certificate shall be conclusive in any proceed-ings that the final cost of the Works has been properly computed in accordance with the terms of this Contract.**

This Final Certificate provision contains many of the requirements relating to the matter in the longer forms:

1   All documents to be supplied (par. 35.09);

2   Defects Liability to be complied with (par. 35.10);

3   Notice of intention to issue the Final certificate (par. 35.10);

4   The conclusiveness of the Final Certificate. It is interesting to see that the wording of the GDLA form is followed here (par. 35.15.1) in preference to that of the RIAI form (par. 35.11), and this seems preferable in view of the uncertainty which prevails as far as the RIAI provisions are concerned.

35.19   A   ARCHITECT'S RESPONSIBILITIES UNDER CLAUSE 35 RIAI AND GDLA

1   Issue interim certificates at appropriate intervals, and deduct the appropriate retention.

2   Explain any differences, if so requested, between the Contractor's statement and the issued certificate.

3   Conform to the contractual requirements with regard to the certification of materials.

4   Agree and confirm retention arrangements.

5   Arrange, if requested, a joint account for the Retention Fund and administer that account (not in GDLA).

6   Give notice of, and issue, a Final Certificate.

35.20   B   EMPLOYER'S RESPONSIBILITIES UNDER CLAUSE 35 RIAI AND GDLA

1   Honour certificates when presented.

2   Hold retention money 'upon trust' (RIAI only).

3   Comply with the 'Joint Account' provisions (RIAI only).

35.21   C   CONTRACTOR'S RESPONSIBILITIES UNDER CLAUSE 35 RIAI AND GDLA

1   Furnish progress statements.

2   Be responsible for unfixed materials and goods.

3   Furnish proof that ownership in unfixed materials and goods is vested in him and (in GDLA only) establish that the goods are insured.

4   Comply with the 'Joint Account' provisions (RIAI only).

35.22   CASES REFERRED TO

Archivent v Strathclyde Regional Council [1984] 27 BLR 98 14 BLR 70	par. 35.05
Chambers v Goldthorpe [1901] 1 KB 624	par. 35.03
Colbart Ltd v Kumar [1992] 7 Bliss 5	par. 35.11
Dawbar Williamson Roofing Ltd v Humberside County Council [1974]	par. 35.05
Dawnays Ltd v FG Minter Ltd [1971] 1 BLR 19	par. 35.03
RM Douglas Construction ltd v Bass Leisure Ltd [1991] 7 CLJ 114	par. 35.03
Dunlop and Rankin Ltd v Hendall Steel Structures [1957] 1 NLR 1022	par. 35.01
Dutton v Bognor Regis UDC [1972] 3 BLR 13	par. 35.22
Elliott v The Minister for Education [1978] ILRM 710	par. 35.11
PJ Hegarty and Sons Ltd v Royal Liver Friendly Society [1985] High Court. unrep. 11th October	par. 35.03
Henry Boot Building v Croydon Hotel and Leisure [1974] 36 BLR 41	par. 35.07
Gilbert Ash (Northern) Ltd v Modern Engineering (Bristol) Ltd [1974] 1 BLR	par. 35.03
Rohan Construction Ltd v Antigen Ltd [1989] ILRM 783	par. 35.03
John Sisk and Sons Ltd v Lawlor Products BV [1976] High Court, unrep. 15th November	par. 35.03
HW Neville (Sunblest) Ltd v William Press and Son Ltd [1981] 20 BLR 78	par. 35.11
Sutcliffe v Thackrah [1974] 25 BLR 147	pars. 35.03, 35.12
Townsend v Stone Toms [1984] 27 BLR 26	pars. 35.03, 35.12
Wisbech UDC v Ward [1927] 2KB 624	par. 35.03

RIAI – Clause 36

WAGES AND PRICE VARIATIONS

36.01   It will be recalled that par. 1.01 defined the purpose of having a Designated
Date in the Conditions, so that a base could be set from which any variation
in the rates of wages or prices of materials which occurred during the course
of the contract could be measured. This clause regulates the way in which
these changes are valued. Certain words or phrases used in the clause are
defined in a Supplement which is issued from time to time by the three parties who form the Liaison Committee that interprets and drafts the standard
forms (with the agreement of the Department of Finance in the case of the
GDLA form). The Supplement forms part of the RIAI form, and is issued as
a separate document for the GDLA form (The full Supplement is set out in
the appendix). The wordings defined in the Supplement to the 1988 Edition
are as follows:

   – Work people
   – Wages
   – Expenses
   – Labour on costs necessarily payable.
   – Materials or goods necessary for the execution of the Works.

The provisions of the clause itself, and of the Supplement, are necessarily
quite involved because of the complex and varied customs and practices
which have grown up in the Construction Industry with regard to wages and
material costs. For many years attempts have been made to introduce a 'formula' clause which would state an index or percentage by which the wage
and price variations could be calculated. This would eliminate the time-consuming and costly procedures involved in calculating and producing written
evidence of the variations which might have occurred in the wages paid to all
the operatives, and the costs of all the materials, during the course of the
Works. In the 1980 Edition of the JCT/RIBA form this has been done in
Clause 40 and the formula which regulates those variations is updated
monthly by the Joint Contracts Tribunal (JCT). At the time of writing, a
Formula Fluctuations System has been agreed by the Liaison Committee and
is supported by the Forum. It is hoped that agreement can be arrived at shortly in order to allow a trial run to commence.

It is not proposed to comment in detail on the provisions of the clause as these are straightforward, but the following are the basic provisions:

1   The clause takes effect from the Designated Date.

2   The interpretation of the wordings shall not be changed during the contract, even if a revised supplement is issued.

3   The provisions of this clause apply to Nominated Sub-Contractors and also to any work which the Contractor has sub-let. The Contractor would be well advised to obtain the consent of the Architect as required under Clause 15 for any sub-letting, so as to ensure that payment for increases in those areas will be ensured.

4   The Contractor is required to give notice to the Architect as soon as he becomes aware of any increased cost of materials.

5   The increases (or decreases) shall be included in the next certificate due.

6   The actual increase in wages shall have an addition of 7.5%, and those of materials an addition of 12.5% The purpose in allowing a percentage addition to the actual costs is to permit the Contractor to recover some element of the profit content (for overheads, etc.) which would normally be included in any tender.

7   These provisions shall not apply to daywork rates [Clause 13(c)].

8   The cost of making good defects is a responsibility of the Contractor and is not affected by Clause 36.

The full clause reads as follows:

36.02   **(a) For the purpose of this clause:**

i)   the Contract Sum shall be deemed to have been calculated in the manner set out below and shall be subject to adjustment in the events specified hereunder;

ii) the Royal Institute of the Architects of Ireland in agreement with the Construction Industry Federation and the Society of Chartered Surveyors in the Republic of Ireland may publish from time to time a supplement to these Conditions setting out the meaning to be given to certain wordings of this clause.

The meanings contained in the Supplement last issued before the Designated Date shall take effect as if they were incorporated in this clause and shall not be changed during the currency of the Contract.

(b) The prices contained in the Bill of Quantities or Schedule of

Rates referred to in Clause 3 of these Conditions are deemed to be based on:

i)   the rates of wages and other emoluments and expenses payable by the Contractor at the Designated Date to work people engaged upon or in connection with the Works;

ii) such labour on-costs as are necessarily payable in addition there-to by the Contractor as an employer of labour at the Designated Date.

If the said rates of wages and other emoluments, expenses and/or labour on-costs are increased or decreased after the Designated Date the amount of such increases or decreases of such rates of wages, other emoluments, expenses and/or labour on-costs together with the percentage addition specified in sub-clause (f) of this clause on any increase shall be an addition to or a deduction from the Contract Sum as the case may be and shall be paid to or allowed by the Contractor accordingly.

(c)(i) The prices of the materials or goods necessary for the execution of the Works are deemed to be the market prices current at the Designated Date (hereinafter referred to as 'basic prices') and the Contractor shall, if required, submit to the Architect a list of the basic prices of such materials or goods;

ii) If during the progress of the Works the market price of any of the materials or goods specified as aforesaid varies from the basic price thereof then the difference between the basic price and the market price payable by the Contractor and current when any such goods or materials are invoiced to him together with the percentage addition specified in sub-clause (f) of this clause on any increase in price shall be an addition to or a deduc-tion from the Contract Sum as the case may be and shall be paid to or allowed by the Contractor accordingly.

(d) The Contractor shall within a reasonable time of his first becom-ing aware of any substantial increase in the price of any of the mate-rials or goods necessary for the execution of the Works or of any substantial increase in the sub-contract prices for any portion of the Works sub-let give written notice thereof to the Architect.

(e) The Contractor may include in any progress statement as provid-ed for by Clause 35(b) of these Conditions (or alternatively as part of the documentation to be furnished by him pursuant to section (i) of sub-clause 35(h)) a detailed statement of any increases or decreases in the rates of wages, emoluments, and/or labour on-costs as defined in sub-clause (b) of this clause in the prices of materials or goods necessary for the execution of the Works or in the price of any sub-contracts for any portion of the Works with the relevant percentage additions under sub-clause (f) of this clause. When the Architect has satisfied himself as to the correctness of the said statement such increases (together with the percentage additions applicable thereto) and/or such decreases shall be taken into account pursuant to Clause 35(c) in the next certificate for payment to which the Contractor may be entitled.

(f) The percentage addition to any increase in wages, emoluments, expenses and labour on-costs under sub-clause (b) of this clause shall be 7.5% and on any increased price under sub-clause (c)(ii) of this clause shall be 12.5%. These percentage additions shall be deemed to cover the cost of all items whatsoever not otherwise recoverable under this clause.

(g) The foregoing provisions of this clause shall not apply to work measured and valued at Daywork Prices in accordance with Clause 13(c).

(h) The foregoing provisions of this clause shall not apply to making good defects under Clause 31.

(i) The foregoing provision of this clause shall apply also to any sub-contract for any portion of the Works.

36.03   The importance of proper definitions of the various terms used (and as set out in the supplement, is evident from the case of *Irishenco v Dublin County Council* [1984] High Court, unrep. 21st March. The case also points to the dangers of altering a standard form. The parties to this contract deleted a standard price variation clause, and substituted one that was more restrictive. The judge held that increases sought for subsistence, travelling and site allowances would not be allowed because it was clear after looking at the deleted clause that it was the intention of the parties to restrict the clause in this way. He went on to say 'I am satisfied that, as a matter of law, this is a proper case in which when seeking the intentions of the parties, as indicated in the document of November 1977, I can have regard to the fact that the parties expressly deleted from their contract the provisions of the 1967 General Conditions. As a matter of law it seems that in interpreting the ambiguity that exists in the clause that has been inserted I am entitled to have regard to the provisions of the clause which the parties deleted and it will be seen immediately that the deleted clause expressly deals with the matters that are now in dispute.'

Another case dealing with increased costs was *Cooney Jennings Ltd v Dublin Corporation* [1984] unrep. 25th October. The Contractor in this case operated an incentive scheme which was based on standard rates of wages. During the course of the contract, basic wages increased, and the Contractor sought the increased costs of the bonus scheme in addition to the basic wages increases. The judge held that no such increase would be allowed because the incentive scheme had been adopted voluntarily by the Contractor. It followed that neither could he be allowed the increased cost of PRSI. as it related to the incentive scheme. In relation to various cases referred to during the hearing, the judge said: 'In relation to those authorities I think it is perfectly clear that each of them and the decision of the Court in each case turned upon the particular wording of the clauses used and the particular language used in the contracts so that they are not in any sense crucial in determining the issue which I have had to determine.' This comment would again reinforce the argument for using a standard form, without amendment.

GDLA – Clause 36

36.04   The latest GDLA form contains a note on the front page as follows: 'reprinted 31 March 2001 incorporating Public Sector amendments implemented by the Forum for the Construction Industry in Addendum 1'. One of the most significant of these changes is the subdivision of sub-clause 36 into three sections.

The sub-division of this clause into sections dealing with wage and price variations, formula fluctuations and non-fluctuation is to cater for the various options now available when dealing with inflationary matters.

The first option ('Wage and Price Variations') deals with the traditional method of calculating and, hopefully, agreeing wage and material variations as between the twoparties to the Contract. This method is very wasteful of resources and has led to theintroduction of the second option ('Formula Fluctuations'). This method is a calculation based on wage increases and a very wide range of materials and a percentage figure will be issued at regular intervals under rules published by the Forum for the Construction Industry. Considerable time and cost savings should be enjoyed by the industry as a result. The third option ('Non Fluctuation') is in fact to provide for a fixed price contract arrangement.

WAGES AND PRICE VARIATIONS [sub-clause 36(1)]

The first part of this clause is very similar to the RIAI form. A second (2) and third (3) was added to deal with formula fluctuations (see par. 36.05). A revision was issued to this clause in March 1993, but the contract form itself has not been reprinted. The changes are as follows:

1   Paragraph (a)(ii) has been changed by the omission of the words after 'Clause' in line 4.

2   Paragraph (b)(i)(1) has been altered by the omission of the reference to the National Joint Industrial Council for the Construction Industry, and by inserting a reference instead to the Construction Industry Federation and the appropriate Trade Unions.

3   Paragraph (b)(ii) has the same alteration as paragraph (b)(i)(1).

4   Two new paragraphs – (b)(iii) and (b)(iv) – refer to legislative enactments affecting wages and expenses.

5   Paragraph (d) is omitted and the lettering of subsequent paragraphs changes. The provision omitted at (d) is inserted now at paragraph (i)

The main differences between the RIAI and the GDLA are:

1   In paragraph (ii) of sub-clause (a), the approval of the Department of Finance is required for the publication of the Supplement.

2   In paragraph (i)(1) of sub-clause (b), the rates of wages shall be those agreed between the Construction Industry Federation and the appropriate Trades Union, and agreed by the Minister for Finance.

3   In paragraph (ii) of sub-clause (b), only the amount of an increase that is in accordance with the National Wage Agreement shall be allowed. If there is no National Wage Agreement, the increase must conform to Government guidelines. Any dispute as to whether or not an increase is in accordance with a National Wage Agreement shall be decided by the procedures set out in that agreement. While that decision is awaited, the increase may be paid, but only if approved by the Construction Industry Federation and the appropriate Trades Union. If the ultimate decision under the National Wage Agreement is that no increase should be paid, the Contractor must repay any increases which he has received. How simple a 'formula' as discussed in par. 36.01 would make all of this.

4   Sub-clause (h) of the GDLA form is not contained in the RIAI form and, this, it is submitted, makes sense.

Notwithstanding the foregoing provisions of this clause, the

Contractor shall not be entitled to payment for increases or additions provided for in the preceding sub-clauses of this clause insofar as they may come into being after the date set for practical completion in sub-clause 28(a) or, if such date is extended pursuant to Clause 30, then after such extended date, save only that if the Architect shall instruct the Contractor in writing under Clause 28 to postpone any work until after the said date or extended date for Practical Completion, the Contractor shall be entitled to payment for any of the said increases or additions arising from such work.

This sub-clause provides that the Contractor must bear the cost of any increases in wages or materials which occur after the contract ought to have been completed.

FORMULA FLUCTUATIONS [sub-clause 36(2)]

36.05   36(2)(a)(i) For the purpose of this clause the Contract Sum, which is deemed to be based on prices and costs ruling at the Base Date, shall be subject to adjustment in accordance with the provisions of the addition of 'Formula Fluctuations Rules for Building Contracts for Use with the GDLA Conditions of Contract' published by the Forum for the Construction Industry last issued before the Base Date and the aforesaid adjustment shall be conclusive in the matter of Wage and Price Variations.

(ii) If the use of the published indices in the application of Formula Fluctuation Rules would result in an increase claimed under this section being in whole or in part not in accordance with the terms of the relevant National Wage Agreement, the amount of such increase shall, to the extent that it is not in accordance with the National Wage Agreement, not be allowable to the Contractor. (In the absence of National Wage Agreements, wage increases claimed under this section will not be allowable if they do not conform with current Government guidelines on wages). Any question as to whether or not a particular increase is in accordance with the terms of the relevant National Wage Agreement shall be resolved on the basis of procedures provided for in that Agreement.

Pending the outcome of these procedures the increase sought, provided it has been approved by the Joint Industrial Council for the Construction Industry, shall be paid to the Contractor without prejudice to the right of the Employer to deduct the amount of the increase subsequently from monies due to the Contractor under this or any other clause in the event that the procedures referred to result in the increase sought being judged not to be in accordance with the terms of the relevant National Wage Agreement or to the extent that it is so declared not to be in accordance with the Agreement.

(b) The Architect shall ascertain in accordance with sub-clause 36(2)(a) the additions to and/or deductions from the Contract Sum pursuant to section (ii) sub-clause 35 (a) in the next certificate for payment to which the Contractor may be entitled.

(c) The foregoing provisions of this clause shall not apply to daywork valued in accordance with sub-clause 13(c) nor to making good defects under Clause 31.

(d) Notwithstanding the foregoing provisions of this clause the Contractor shall not be entitled to payment for increases or additions provided for in the preceding sub-clauses of this clause in so far as they may come into being after the date set for Practical Completion in sub-clause 28 (a) or, if such date is extended pursuant to clause 30, then after such extended date, save only that if the Architect shall instruct the Contractor in writing under Clause 28 to postpone any work until after the said date or extended date for Practical Completion the Contractor shall be entitled to payment for any of the said increases or additions arising from such work.

(e) The foregoing provisions of this clause shall apply also to any sub-contract for any portion of the Works.

or

36.06   NON FLUCTUATION [sub-clause 36(3)]

36(3)(a) For the purpose of this clause the Contract Sum shall not be adjusted to take account of any increases or decreases in the cost to the Contractor of any labour, materials, plant or other resources employed in carrying out the Works except for any increases or decreases arising under Clause 4.

(b) The foregoing provision of this clause shall apply also to any sub-contract for any portion of the Works unless decided otherwise by the Employer.

NOTE: Only Clause 36(1) or Clause 36(2) or Clause 36(3) will apply. The other two clauses shall be struck out.

SF 88 – Clause 15

FLUCTUATIONS

36.07 **No account shall be taken in any payment to the Contractor under this Contract of any increase or decrease in the cost to the Contractor of any labour, materials, plant or other resources employed in carrying out the Work except for any increase or decrease caused directly by Legislative Enactment, Statutory Instrument, or Ministerial Order.**

It was considered during the drafting of the shorter form that the nature of the contracts which it was envisaged would be covered by the form would be of such duration that no price variation clause would be justified. Variations due to legislative enactments were considered to be of a different nature (see pars. 4.01–4.03 dealing with the RIAI and GDLA forms).

36.08 A   ARCHITECT'S RESPONSIBILITIES UNDER CLAUSE 36

1   Certify, if satisfied, any monies due under Clause 36.

2   Strike out two of the three sub-clauses (GDLA only).

36.09 C   CONTRACTOR'S RESPONSIBILITIES UNDER CLAUSE 36

1   Submit, if required, a list of 'basic prices' to the Architect.

2   Order expeditiously the materials or goods required for the Works.

3   Inform the Architect of any imminent increases in materials or goods.

4   Include any increases in progress statements.

36.10 CASES REFERRED TO

Cooney Jennings Ltd v Dublin Corporation
    [1984] High Court, unrep. 25th October   par. 36.03
Irishenco v Dublin County Council
    [1984] High Court, unrep. 21st March   par. 36.03

RIAI – Clause 37

COLLATERAL AGREEMENTS

37.01 **Collateral agreements in the standard form published by the Royal Institute of the Architects of Ireland, the Construction Industry Federation, and the Society of Chartered Surveyors in the Republic of Ireland acting jointly and current at the Designated Date have been or may be executed between the Employer and Nominated Sub-Contractors. The terms of these Conditions are deemed to be amended and supplemented in all respects necessary to entitle the Employer vis-a-vis the Contractor to give effect to the terms of such collateral agreements.**

It will be recalled that in the notes to Clause 16 (Nominated Sub-Contractors) reference was made to the absence of any formal contractual relationship between the Employer and any of the Nominated Sub-Contractors. In some aspects this was useful as far as the Employer was concerned. It meant that the Employer had to deal with, and pay, only the one party, and that all the subsidiary contractors were dealt with, and paid by the Contractor. But there were disadvantages, and these were, chiefly, that the Employer had no direct rights against any sub-contractor for defective materials, workmanship or where design was concerned. As far as the Nominated Sub-Contractors were concerned, the main defect in the contract arrangement was that, in the absence of any contractual relationship he had no right to claim against the Employer if the Contractor became bankrupt. It was obvious, therefore, that some contractual relationship between the Employer and the nominated sub-contractor would be an advantage to both parties. This relationship is provided by the Collateral Agreement.

37.02 A collateral agreement or warranty is a contract. It is governed by the same contract law as any other contract is. It is called 'Collateral' – literally 'by the side of' – because it lies alongside another contract, called the Principal Contract, in this case the RIAI form. It is necessary because in contract law, the only parties who can get the benefit of, or be held responsible, are the parties to the contract, and a Nominated Sub-Contractor is not a party to the contract. The collateral agreement is sometimes referred to as a collateral warranty, because the sub-contractor warrants or undertakes to perform his work in a manner set out in the agreement.

The agreement referred to in Clause 37 as being a standard form is that of November 1st 1988 published by the three parties mentioned in the clause. The relevant portion as far as the basic agreement is concerned is as follows, giving firstly the sub-contractor's obligations.

A(1) The Sub-Contractor warrants that he has exercised and will exercise all reasonable skill and care in:

1   the design of the Sub-Contract Works insofar as the Sub-Contract Works have been or will be designed by the Sub-Contractor; and

2   the selection of materials and goods for the Sub-Contract Works insofar as such materials and goods have been or will be selected by the Sub-Contractor; and

3   the satisfaction of any performance specification or requirement insofar as such performance specification is included or referred to in the tender of the Sub-Contractor as part of the description of the Sub-Contract Works. This includes adhering to the Main Contractor's programme.

The case of *Norta Wallpapers (Ireland) Ltd v John Sisk and Sons (Dublin) Ltd* [1978] 14 BLR 49 which is dealt with in the notes to Clause 16 at par. 16.08 decided that the Contractor was responsible to the Employer for any defective materials or workmanship, provided by or carried out by a Nominated Sub-Contractor, so that sub-clauses (b) and (c) do not confer additional benefits on the Employer, apart from the right of a direct claim against the Sub-Contractor in the case of default on the part of the Contractor. Sub-clause (a), however, covers the gap which occurred after the *Norta* case, which decided, in addition, that the Contractor had no liability for the design of a Nominated Sub-Contractor where no opportunity was given to the Contractor to examine the proposals. Sub-clause (a), by giving direct responsibility to the sub-contractor in regard to the Employer, ensures that the Employer is adequately protected.

The Employer's obligations to the Sub-Contractor under the collateral agreement are similarly mandatory and are set out in Clause B of the agreement. This clause is discussed in par. 16.13 in the notes to Clause 16(c), but briefly they require the Employer to pay the Sub-Contractor directly, both as far as interim and final payments, if the Contractor defaults.

37.03   The collateral agreement goes on to provide that the Sub-Contractor will pay compensation to the Employer in the event of a determination of the sub-contract, including any additional costs in re-nomination, and also provides that the tender of the Sub-Contractor shall not contain any exclusions or limits to his liability to the Contractor. A problem arises if the employment of the Sub-Contractor is determined by reason of bankruptcy. In that case, there will be no point in seeking compensation, and this is why it is important for the Architect to ensure that the collateral agreement is bonded, or guaranteed.

A bond is an undertaking by a financial institution, often an insurance company, to reimburse the Employer for any loss or damage which results from breach of contract. The most frequent occasion when a bond is called in is in the case of bankruptcy. A bond can only exist where a contract exists, and this is why a collateral agreement is a pre-requisite to the obtaining of a bond. The amount of the bond will be agreed between the Employer and the financial institution (generally referred to as 'The Bondsman'). The bond used to be for the full contract amount, but nowadays the bond will only be required to cover from 10% to 25% of the contract sum. It is important to remember that the purpose of the bond is to reimburse the Employer, and that the Bondsman is under no obligation to complete the contract (see par. 33.09).

The main contract itself is very often bonded, and in the case of large contracts, invariably so. The GDLA form refers to the Contract Guarantee Bond in Clause 28(a) where the production of the bond may be a precondition for possession of the site.

GDLA and SF 88

37.04 Neither of these forms makes any provision for collateral agreements. This is somewhat surprising in the case of the GDLA form which tends to favour the Employer as against the Contractor. It would seem that a collateral agreement would confer more advantages on the Employer than on the Contractor and it would not be surprising if revisions of the GDLA form included such a clause. It can be assumed that one of the reasons why the draftsmen of the GDLA form considered that no such clause was necessary was because the Contractor is now responsible for the performance of the Sub-Contractor within the Contractor's programme. A collateral warranty, however, would protect the Employer from the consequences of design faults by a Nominated Sub-Contractor and would also, by way of a bond, protect the Employer from the extra costs of re-nomination.

37.05 A   ARCHITECT'S RESPONSIBILITY UNDER CLAUSE 37

1   Advise the Employer as to the desirability of obtaining a collateral agreement.

37.06   CASE REFERRED TO

Norta Wallpapers (Ireland) Ltd v John Sisk and Sons
    (Dublin) Ltd [1978] 14 BLR 49   par. 37.02

RIAI – Clause 38

(numbered 37 in GDLA form)

DISPUTES RESOLUTION

38.01 **(a) If a dispute arises between the parties with regard to any of the provisions of the contract such dispute shall be referred to conciliation in accordance with the Conciliation Procedures established by the Royal Institute of the Architects of Ireland in agreement with the Society of Chartered Surveyors and the Construction Industry Federation.**

In recent years there has been a spreading dissatisfaction with the process of litigation and with arbitration which is the form of dispute resolution most familiar to the construction industry. This is not the fault of the concept of arbitration itself but rather with the way it has developed into a mirror image of litigation. This has led to forms of alternative dispute resolution sometimes called mediation but more usually described in contract documents as conciliation.

Many engineering contracts had conciliation procedures, in addition to arbitration clauses, and these were invariably non-binding. The latest contract issued by the Institute of Engineers of Ireland contains a mandatory conciliation clause, but while recourse to conciliation was obligatory, acceptance of the recommendation was not. The standard form followed suit in 1996 and that contract document now requires the parties to conciliate in advance of arbitration.

Most commentators used to use the word mediation to describe the overall process, and they viewed conciliation as being part of that process. In recent years the word conciliation has been understood to include mediation rather than the other way around. The person conducting the process is now usually called the conciliator. The engineer himself in those engineering contracts such as the New Engineering Contract (issued by the Institution of Civil Engineers) acts as the conciliator. The basis of conciliation is aimed at correcting perceptions, reducing misunderstandings, and improving communication, so that rational bargaining can proceed. If the parties cannot agree to a solution, the conciliator will make a non-binding recommendation. This is often very useful as either party will be aware of what an independent person views as a reasonable solution of the dispute and this fact will greatly reduce the temptation to go further along the expensive arbitration route.

These descriptions cover what is now universally described as Alternative Dispute Resolution, or ADR. It is primarily an alternative to litigation and arbitration. When it is considered that there are over 10,000 cases listed every year in the High Court, that it takes two years on average for a case to come to hearing, and that the cost, of experts, witnesses, solicitors and counsel can run to £20,000 per day it is suggested that there must be a better way, particularly to resolve disputes of a specialist nature, such as insurances, property or construction disputes. The answer should be arbitration, but not only do all the costs mentioned before arise in an arbitration, the parties in dispute also have to pay for the hire of the room and for the arbitrator's fees, in addition to all the other costs. Another defect in both litigation and arbitration, and as far as some commercial areas are concerned, more of a disadvantage is the length of time taken. All of us are aware of commercial disputes that go on in various stages of litigation for five or even ten years, and arbitration can be as bad, indeed worse, as the arbitrators powers to deal with the relevant litigant are not as comprehensive as the Courts. *Jarndyce v Jarndyce* is not dead yet.

Conciliation has been defined as the intervention into a dispute, or negotiation, by an acceptable, impartial, and neutral third party who has no authoritative decision making power in order to assist disputing parties in voluntarily reaching their own mutually acceptable settlement of issues in dispute. The two most important parts of that definition is that the process is voluntary, and that the conciliator has no power to impose a solution, even though he makes a recommendation.

The voluntary aspect might seem a disadvantage in that the parties cannot be forced to take part, but that in itself carries a psychological advantage. If a party, without any contractual requirement, agrees to meet the other party to a dispute, the seeds of settlement are already sown and a disposition towards agreement exists.

There is no adversarial content to the process and this helps to ease the parties towards a settlement. In this way many business relationships can be preserved, and in certain areas of business in a small society like Ireland, this can be very important when firms or individuals tend to work with one another on many occasions.

While the process is voluntary and can be broken off at any time it is important to have some basic rules agreed which lay down the terms which will be in force for as long as the conciliation proceeds and standard conciliation procedures are now issued with the RIAI form. Parties to a conciliation pay their own costs, which in comparison to either litigation or arbitration will be very modest. It has been estimated that the costs in a conciliation will average around 10% of costs in the more formal processes. Obviously where the process is part of a contractual framework the costs will be minimal.

The agreement to a conciliation will contain a confidentiality clause, and will also make clear that no documents, or any evidence and facts, will be discoverable in subsequent proceedings if the conciliation fails.

The length of time taken to complete a conciliation can vary. The process very seldom lasts for more than two days, as it becomes obvious at an early stage whether or not a settlement is probable and a realistic mediator will stop the proceedings when he is satisfied that the process will not work. At the conclusion however, a degree of legal formality arises. The heads of agreement will be converted into a full agreement which will be signed by the parties and at this stage becomes an enforceable contract. It is important to have the agreement properly drafted as it could well be that, unlike documents produced during a conciliation, the agreement would be discoverable to a third party.

Of course conciliation is not always the most suitable method of proceeding. It may well be that it would be necessary to establish some form of precedent, and define a point of law, and clearly this must be done in Court. It must also be remembered that conciliation will, on occasion, fail and the dispute will then proceed to litigation or arbitration or indeed might revert to those processes because there is nothing to prevent parties to a dispute trying to conciliate even though they have already commenced formal proceedings.

38.02   The conciliation procedures referred to in Clause 38(a) are as follows:

1   This procedure shall apply to any conciliation requested under Clause 38(a) of the RIAI Form of Contract.

2   A party to the contract seeking conciliation shall notify the other party to that effect and shall at the same time specify the matter in dispute.

3   The parties shall agree on a conciliator, and failing agreement within 10 working days of notice under article 2, shall request the President of the RIAI to appoint a conciliator from a list of conciliators agreed between the RIAI, the SCS and the CIF.

4   The conciliator shall require the parties to submit, in advance of the hearing, a brief written opening statement and appending the necessary documentation not later than 10 working days after his appointment. The parties should at the same time notify the conciliator of the names of the persons appearing at the conciliation.

5   The conciliator shall within 10 working days after receipt of the statements and documentation establish the order of the proceedings and shall arrange a convenient time, date and place for the hearing.

6   The conciliator may consider and discuss such solutions to the dispute as he thinks appropriate or as may be suggested by either party. All information given to the conciliator is confidential and shall remain so unless authorised by the party who supplied the information.

7   The conciliator may, having informed the parties, consult independent third party experts.

8   The conciliator shall endeavour to commit the parties to reach a mutual settlement failing which he shall within 10 working days of the hearing, issue his recommendation. He shall not be required to give reasons. It shall remain confidential if rejected by either party.

9   If neither party rejects the recommendation within 10 working days after its issue, it shall be final and binding on the parties. If either party rejects the recommendation, a request for arbitration may be made under Clause 38(b) of the RIAI Form of Contract.

10 Each party to the conciliation shall pay their own costs. The parties shall be jointly and severally liable for the conciliator's costs in equal shares, unless the conciliator decides otherwise.

11 Conciliations are settlement negotiations and are without prejudice to the rights of the disputants. All statements, information and material made, given or exchanged, orally or in writing either during the conciliation or prior thereto or there after upon the request of the conciliator shall be inadmissible in any legal proceedings, in court or arbitration, to the maximum extent permitted by law. Evidence which is otherwise admissible in legal proceedings shall not be rendered inadmissible as a result of its use in the conciliation. The Disputants agree not to summon or otherwise require the conciliator to appear or testify or produce records, notes, or any other information or material in any legal proceedings, in court or arbitration, and no recordings or stenographic records will be made of the conciliation.

12 Any agreement reached by the disputants through the conciliation shall be set down in writing and duly executed by their authorised representative.

Very little comment is required on these provisions. The issue of a recommendation, a process not contained in all conciliation agreements, is regarded as a very useful way of concentrating the minds of the opposing parties, as it brings into existence a decision by an independent party which, even if not binding on the parties, will cause them to think deeply before proceeding to the costly process of arbitration.

38.03   **(b) Provided always that in case any dispute of difference shall arise between the Employer or the Architect on his behalf and the Contractor either during the progress of the Works or after the determination of the employment of the Contractor under the Contract or the abandonment or the breach of the Contract, as to the construction of the Contract or as to any matter or thing arising thereunder or as to the withholding by the Architect of any certificate to which the Contractor may claim to be entitled, then either party shall forthwith give to the other notice of such dispute or difference and such dispute or difference shall be and is hereby referred to the arbitration and final decision of such person as the parties hereunto may agree to appoint as Arbitrator or, failing agreement, as may be nominated on the request of either party by the President for the time being of the Royal Institute of the Architects of Ireland after consultation with the President of the Construction Industry Federation and the award of such Arbitrator shall be final and binding on the parties. Such reference, except on Article 3 or Article 4 of the Articles of Agreement or on the question of certificates shall not be opened until after the Practical Completion or alleged Practical Completion of the Works or determination or alleged determination of the Contractor's employment under this Contract unless with the written consent of the Employer or of the Architect on his behalf and the Contractor. The Arbitrator shall have power to open up, review and revise any opinion, decision, requisition or notice, and to determine all matters in dispute which shall be submitted to him and of which notice shall have been given as aforesaid in the same manner as if no such opinion, decision, requisition or notice had been given. Every or any such reference shall be deemed to be a submission to arbitration within the meaning of the Arbitration Act 1954 (number 26 of 1954), or the Arbitration Act (Northern Ireland) 1957 (as the case may be) or any act amending the same or either of them.**

The essence of arbitration as it affects the building contracts, is that the parties decide to refer any disputes which may arise to a tribunal of their own choosing, rather than to the Courts. But having done so, under any agreement that invokes the Arbitration Acts, the Courts are awarded immediate control of the arbitration process. The Acts in question are the Arbitration Act 1954, the Arbitration Act 1980 and the Arbitration (International Commercial) Act 1998. The provisions of these Acts will be examined later (pars. 38.08 and 38.09). The development of arbitration proceeds from the idea that certain technical areas, such as insurances, marine law, building, etc, would be better served if some method of resolving disputes could be found which would be under the control of a person having expertise in that particular field. In this way, engineers came to arbitrate in engineering disputes, architects in building disputes, and so on. The acceptance by the Courts of the resolution of technical disputes by those qualified in those areas was well put by a recent Chief Justice in an address to the Chartered Institute of Arbitrators: 'Anybody who would remove from me the diligent, and I hope, patient consideration of damp-proof courses, the depth of foundations, Armstrong junctions, and, I regret to say, even the quality of door-knobs on built-in wardrobes is my friend, not my enemy.' It is not necessary that these Arbitrators would have a legal background (though some do possess formal legal qualification), but they would be expected to be conversant with the law of arbitration. Whereas an Arbitrator can be dismissed for 'misconduct' or have his award 'set aside' (see par. 38.04) ignorance of the law is not normally a sufficient ground for this. Where the parties are concerned about matters of law, or where the Arbitrator himself seeks advice, he can under Section 35 of the 1954, ask the High Court to 'state a case', that is, say what the law is in regard to the question posed.

Those interested in reading more about the arbitration process would be recommended JAGO V SWILLERTON AND TOOMER, by HB Cresswell – the author of THE HONEYWOOD FILE (Orion Books, 1984), which is a fictional account of an arbitration written in a most entertaining way and containing, within the rather hilarious story, all the basic information about arbitration law and procedures.

38.04   Originally, the arbitration process was said to have three advantages over court actions. Firstly, it would be cheaper, secondly, it would be quicker, and thirdly, it would be confidential. The first two listed advantages, cost and speed, are obviously linked, and it must be said that arbitration seems to be moving closer all the time to the norms which prevail in the courts as far as these two areas are concerned. The main blame for this can be laid at the door of the 'reluctant litigant'. If a party to an arbitration, usually the defendant, or 'respondent' as he is known in an arbitration, wishes to delay proceedings so as to put off for as long as possible the day of judgement it it extremely difficult for an Arbitrator to overcome this strategy. The requirements of natural justice and the anxiety of an Arbitrator to avoid any action which might justify the overturning of his award makes this adoption of this tactic by a respondent usually successful. The ultimate sanction of a Court in this position would be to dismiss the action for want of prosecution. This remedy is not available to Arbitrators. In *Bremer Vulkan Schiffbau und Maschinenfabrick v South India Shipping Corporation* [1981] 1 AER 289, it was held that an Arbitrator had no power to strike out an arbitration for want of prosecution. Lord Searman said: 'The nearest he could get to a dismissal on grounds of delay would have been to fix a day for hearing and make an award on the merits based on whatever evidential material was then available to him.'

This was precisely the procedure adopted by the Arbitrator in an arbitration which was reviewed in *Grangeford Structures Ltd (In Liquidation) v SH Ltd* [1990] ILRM 277. In this case the respondent was guilty of what the Arbitrator considered were unreasonable delays and eventually set a date for the hearing of the arbitration. When the hearing opened the respondant's solicitor requested an adjournment on the grounds that he wished to submit a counterclaim. When the adjournment was refused by the Arbitrator, the respondent's solicitor withdrew, and the Arbitrator proceeded to hear evidence from the claimant. When the Arbitrator made his award, the respondent sought to have his decision set aside by the High Court on the grounds of misconduct. This was refused, and when the case was appealed to the Supreme Court, it was held that in the face of unreasonable delays an Arbitrator is entitled to proceed to hear evidence in the absence of one party and that his award is valid. It might be possible in future editions of the contract for a timetable to be suggested.

It seems, too, that in recent years arbitrations have tended to become more and more like formal court hearings, with an emphasis on procedure that might be inappropriate. An arbitration is, and must always be, a recognised legal procedure and as will be seen later (par. 38.08) an Arbitrator has the backing of the High Court as far as his powers are concerned, but it is up to an Arbitrator to ensure that procedures are in keeping with the scope of the arbitration and, by ensuring that evidence is relevant and concise, can minimise expense and delay. The Arbitrator can warn a party which is being over-zealous and detailed in evidence that he might take note of such behaviour in awarding costs.

The third advantage stated above, that of confidentiality, is of benefit. No person will be admitted to an arbitration hearing who is not either a party, a witness, or a legal representative and notetakers or reporters are only present when requested by the parties or the Arbitrator. In this way, no publicity results and this may be desired by the parties.

38.05   The Arbitrator is appointed by the parties to the contract. Where the President of the Royal Institute of Ireland is involved, he nominates a person to be Arbitrator, but the appointment is still made by the parties. One of the perceived disadvantages of arbitration is that a dispute in a building matter can often involve the Architect, and other professional advisors to the Employer. Under the terms of the building contract, the parties to that contract are obliged to arbitrate, but there is no process by which the Architect, or others, can be made join the proceedings. In a court action, the Court has the power to join third parties to an action, but the lack of the power to the Arbitrator often means that the Employer has to proceed on two separate, and often, consecutive actions as he will sometimes be unable to proceed against third parties until an Arbitrator has made an award and the Employer is aware of the amount of damage suffered.

38.06   In a contract that has an arbitration clause, and if that clause states that the arbitration will be governed by the Arbitration Acts, then the courts cannot hear any dispute under that contract. Under the 1954 Act, in Section 12(1) it provided that the Court '*may* make an order staying the proceedings' which might have been commenced by one of the parties in place of the arbitration proceedings. In the 1980 Act [Section 5(1)] the words are '*shall* make an order staying the proceedings'. It is important, however, that a party to an arbitration does not appear to acquiesce in the action of the other party if a court proceeding is initiated. The Act requires that any party seeking to have court proceedings stayed must make an application to that effect before delivering any pleadings, e.g. lodging a defence. The Courts themselves are reluctant to become involved in the arbitration process. In *Keenan v Shield Insurance Co Ltd* [1988] IR 89 it was commented: 'Arbitration is a significant feature of modern commercial life. It ill becomes the Courts to show any readiness to interfere with such a process; if policy considerations are appropriate, as I believe they are in a matter of this kind then every such consideration points to the desireability of making an arbitration award final in every sense of the term.'

The Arbitrator's decision is final, and there is no appeal. This is an aspect of arbitration that is disliked by some, although it does have the advantage of completing the legal process at an early stage. The 1954 Act at Section 27 says 'Unless a contrary is expressed therein, every arbitration agreement shall, where such provision is applicable to the reference be deemed to contain a provision that the award to be made by the Arbitrator or umpire shall be final and binding on the parties and persons claiming under them respectively.' The only way in which the Arbitrator's award can be upset is by an application to the High Court to have the Award 'set aside'. This may be done where the court decides that the Arbitrator has 'misconducted' himself. The term is mainly used to cover cases where there has been a breach of natural justice, and does not refer to moral turpitude. While awards have been set aside on other grounds, or have been 'remitted' or sent back by the Court to the Arbitrator for further consideration, it is only proposed to deal with the natural justice aspect here, as an Architect who is advising his client cannot be expected to have more than a basic knowledge of this part of the contract. The Arbitrator should always be even-handed. He should never take any action without informing both parties; he should always ensure that documents are circulated to both parties. 'When once they enter on an arbitration, arbitrators must not be guilty of any act which can possibly be construed as indicative of partiality or unfairness. It is not a question of the effect which misconduct on their part had in fact upon the result of the proceedings, but of what effect it might possibly have produced. It is not enough to show that, even if there was misconduct on their part, the award was unaffected by it, and was in reality just, arbitrators must not do anything which is not in itself fair and impartial' re *Brien and Brien* [1910] 2 IR 84. Human nature being what it is, Arbitrators behave like everyone else from time to time, and it has been held that an Arbitrator becoming 'completely intoxicated' at a dinner after the hearing was not misconducting himself (re *Hopper* [1967] 36 LJQB 97) but that an Arbitrator who charged excessive fees had (re *Pebble and Robinson* [1892] 2 QB 602).

Another aspect of arbitration which is disliked by many who get involved is that an Arbitrator is not obliged to give reasons for his decisions, unless he has agreed to this in his terms of appointment. The Arbitration Act 1979, in the UK requires Arbitrators to state reasons if asked. There are differing views as to whether or not an Arbitrator should give, or be made to give reasons, those approving saying that parties to an arbitration should have the right to know why they won or lost, and those disapproving saying that giving reasons will only enable dissatisfied parties to go to court over the result. Some provisions of the UK 1979 Act attempt to curtail this. In general, it is the practice in Ireland for an Arbitrator to give no reasons for his award. A recent case, *Vogelaar v Callaghan* [1996] 2 ILRM 226, held, in effect, that an arbitrator can only be required to give reasons when his appointment is made on that basis.

38.07   A party to the contract cannot ask for arbitration during the course of the Works except on three matters:

1   If the 'Architect' named in Article 3 of the Articles of Agreement is being replaced by the Employer the Contractor can object, and if an Arbitrator finds these reasons to be sufficient, thus the proposed new Architect may not be appointed by the Employer.

2   The same provisions apply to a replacement quantity surveyor, referred to Article 4 of the Articles of Agreement.

3   'On the question of certificates': Since this provision refers to interim certificates as well as to the final certificate, it means in effect that arbitration proceedings can be initiated at any stage of the contract, though it is normally left to the final certificate stages before such proceedings are sought. Differences over the final certificate are specifically catered for in Clause 35(h) par. 35.10.

38.08   An Arbitrator has power to 'open up, review and revise any opinion, decision, requisition or notice'. This is an extremely wide power which the Courts have not taken to themselves and a justification for it is given in a passage in *Northern Regional Health Authority v Derek Crouch Construction Co Ltd* [1984] 26 BLR 1:

> (The case, naturally, referred to a JCT/RIBA contract, but the wording is generally similar to the RIAI/GDLA forms.)

> Under the JCT contracts the Architect, who is the agent of the building owner is a key figure in deciding such matters as what extensions of time should be granted for the performance of the contract, whether and to what extent contractors and sub-contractors are responsible for delay, how much each should be paid and when they should be paid and whether and when the works have been completed. These are very personal decisions and, within limits, different architects might reach different conclusions. Despite the fact that the architect is subject to a duty to act fairly, these powers might be regarded as draconian and unacceptable if they were not subject to review and revision by a more independent individual. That process is provided for by the arbitration clause. It is, however, a rather special clause. Arbitration is usually no more and no less than litigation in the private sector. The Arbitrator is called upon to find the facts, apply the law and grant relief to one or other or both of the parties. Under a JCT arbitration clause (Clause 35) the Arbitrator has these powers but he also has power to 'open up, review and revise any certificates, opinions, decision, requirement or notice'. This goes further than merely entitling him to treat the Architect's certificates, opinions decisions requirements and notices as inconclusive in determining the rights of the parties. It enables, and in appropriate cases requires him to vary them and so create new rights, obligations and liabilities in the parties. This is not a power which is normally possessed by any court and again it has a strong element of personal judgement by an individual nominated in accordance with the agreement of the parties.

This judgement would seem to support the view that interim or final certificates can be reviewed, and therefore not regarded as final [see par. 35.03 (interim certificates) and 35.11 (final certificate)].

38.09   Some further provisions of the 1954 Act of which architects should be aware are:

1   The witnesses are to be examined on oath unless the agreement says otherwise (sec. 19).

2   Any party to an arbitration can seek an order of subpoena to compel witnesses to attend and to produce documents (sec. 20).

3   An Arbitrator may make an interim award (sec. 25).

4   The Arbitrator's decision can be enforced by an order of the High Court both here, and by virtue of various international conventions, in many other countries (sec. 41).

GDLA – Clause 37

DISPUTES RESOLUTION

38.10   The GDLA form differs from that of the RIAI in four respects. Until February 2001 there was no provision for conciliation in the GDLA Contract when, at that time, the Forum for the Construction Industry requested its inclusion. The conciliation provisions are very much the same as those in the RIAI Form and the procedures are identical. The procedures are referred to as Supplement C.

1   Any dispute arising under Clause 39 of the GDLA form (the Fair Wages clause) which is not in the RIAI form is precluded from the arbitration process (see par. 39.01).

2   The re-nomination of the Architect or Quantity Surveyor mentioned in Articles 3 and 4 of the Articles of Agreement is not subject to arbitration.

3   The nomination of the Arbitrator by the President of the Royal Institute of the Architects of Ireland is not carried out in consultation with the President of the Construction Industry Federation but is a sole function.

4   There is no reference to the Arbitration Act (1957) Northern Ireland.

SF 88 – Clause 23

38.11   This clause is virtually the same as that in the RIAI form. There is no reference to the arbitration being delayed until after practical completion, so the process can be initiated at any time. There is no provision for conciliation.

38.12   RESPONSIBILITIES OF THE PARTIES

The Architect has no specific responsibility under these clauses. It is up to the Employer or the Contractor to decide as to whether or not arbitration will be sought, though the Architect's advice will undoubtedly be sought by the Employer.

38.13   CASES REFERRED TO

Bremer Vulkan Schiffbau and Maschinenfabrik v
    South India Shipping Corporation [1981] 1 AER 289   par. 38.04
Grangeford Structures Ltd (In Liquidation) v SH Ltd
    [1990] ILRM 277   par. 38.04
Keegan v Shield Insurance Co Ltd [1988] IR 89   par. 38.06
Northern Regional Health Authority v Derek Crouch
    (Construction) Ltd [1984] 26 BLR 1   par. 38.08
re Brien and Brien [1910] 2 IR 84   par. 38.06
re Hopper [1867] 36 LjQB 97   par. 38.06
re Pebble and Robinson [1892] 2 QB 602   par. 38.06
Vogelaar v Callaghan [1996] 2 ILRM 226   par. 38.06

GDLA – Clause 38

COPIES OF DRAWINGS AND SPECIFICATION
THE EMPLOYER'S PROPERTY

38.14   **All copies of any Drawings and Specifications which shall have been furnished to the Contractor shall be the property of the Employer and shall, if so required by the Employer be returned to the Employer before payment is made on foot of the Final Certificate.**

This is much the same provision as is contained in the RIAI form at sub-clause 3(b), paragraph one. It is not clear why the clause is placed differently in the GDLA form (see par. 3.09).

GDLA – Clause 39

FAIR WAGES CLAUSE

39.01   a) In the execution of this Contract the Contractor shall pay rates of wages and observe hours of labour and conditions of employment not less favourable than those laid down by the National Joint Industrial Council for the Construction Industry. The Contractor shall be responsible to the Employer for the due observance by all Sub-Contractors of the provisions of this Clause.

(b) The Contractor shall cause a copy of the preceding sub-clause to be prominently exhibited for the information of his work-people on the premises where work is being executed under this Contract.

(c) The Contractor shall keep proper wages books and time sheets showing the wages paid and the time worked by the work-people in his employ in and about the execution of this Contract and such wages books and time sheets shall be produced whenever required for the inspection of any person authorised by the Employer.

(d) The Contractor shall pay to the workmen employed in or about the Works all wages and sums of money which shall be due and payable to them and in no instance shall the Contractor allow more than one (1) month's wages to be in arrears or unpaid and shall if required to do so in writing by the Employer within (5) working days after the receipt of such request submit to the Employer a statement showing the amount of wages due at the date of such request to each workman then employed in or about the Works.

(e) In the event of any infringement of the above sub-clauses (a) to (d) the Employer shall have power (without prejudice to any rights of the Employer under any other conditions of this Contract) by notice in writing given to the Contractor to determine this Contract provided that he first gives notice to the Contractor, to rectify such infringement and the Contractor has failed to do so within ten (10) working days of the receipt of such notice. The Contractor shall not be entitled to any compensation in consequence of such determination.

(f) Should any question arise as to the observance by the Contractor of the above sub-clauses (a) to (d) hereof, the matter shall be referred to the Architect whose decision as to whether an infringement of same has taken place shall be final and binding upon the Contractor and the Employer.

This clause, which does not occur in the RIAI form, is not unexpected in a contract form which will use Government funds, but it could be argued that it is trying to import into the contract matters which might be covered by legislation.

Any agreement to which a government department, or agency, or semi-state body would be a party would naturally be expected to be implemented in a contract to which the same parties would be bound.

39.02   The clause could be summarised as follows:

1   The recommendations of the National Joint Industrial Council for the Construction Industry shall be observed.

2   Sub-clause (a) shall be displayed on the Works.

3   The Contractor shall keep proper books.

4   No workman shall be over four weeks in arrears of pay.

5   The Employer may determine the Contract if a) to d) are not observed.

6   The Architect shall decide all disputes. No arbitration is allowed.

39.03   A   ARCHITECT'S RESPONSIBILITIES UNDER CLAUSE 39 GDLA

1   Decide on any question re the observance of this clause.

39.04   B   EMPLOYER'S RESPONSIBILITIES UNDER CLAUSE 39 GDLA

1   Request, if necessary, a statement of wages from the Contractor.

2   Give notice, in the event of infringement, of determination.

39.05   C   CONTRACTOR'S RESPONSIBILITIES UNDER CLAUSE 39 GDLA

1   Pay the correct wages, and at the appropriate time.

2   Display sub-clause (a) on the site.

3   Keep proper wage books.

GDLA – Clause 40

MINISTERS AND MINISTERS OF STATE

40.01 **No minister or Minister of State shall be admitted to any share or part of this Contract or to any benefit to arise therefrom.**

This clause needs no comment. Obviously, it is not contained in the RIAI form.

GDLA – Clause 41

RECEIPT OF NOTICES

41.01 **Any written notice, consent, instruction, order or other instrument given or made by the Employer pursuant to or arising out of this Contract (unless the Agreement provides that it shall be given or made by the Architect) may where appropriate be given or made on behalf of the Employer by an Officer so authorised under Section 23(2) of the State Property Act 1954 and shall be deemed to have been received by the Contractor if handed to him or his Agent personally or sent by registered post to his last known address or if a Company to the registered offices of the Company.**

This is merely a procedural requirement and covers the authorisation which might be required as far as the powers of the Employer are concerned under the GDLA form The State Property Act 1954, at Section 23(2) provides:

> Any contract or instrument which if entered into or executed by a person (not being a body corporate) would not require to be under seal may be entered into or executed on behalf of the Commissioners by any person generally or specially authorised by the Commissioners in that behalf.

The Commissioners referred to in the Act are the Commissioners of Public Works in Ireland. The authorisation would clearly extend to both the Architect and the Quantity Surveyor named in the contract, and, in turn, any person properly authorised by them.

Supplement (RIAI Version)

To the Schedule of Conditions of Building Contract issued by the Royal Institute of the Architects of Ireland in agreement with the Construction Industry Federation and the Society of Chartered Surveyors in the Republic of Ireland, 1996 Edition.

The following meanings shall be given to certain wordings in Clause 36.

A.   Meanings for Clause 36(b)

1   'Work people' means operatives such as craftsmen, semi-skilled labour, labourers, drivers and operators of mechanical plant and machinery, site time keepers and site clerks. General foremen, site agents, trade foremen and charge hands shall also be deemed to be work people. Increases for administrative and other supervisory staff who individually spend more than 15 hours from Monday to Friday on the site of the Works shall be recoupable for the full-time spend in connection with the project. Contract managers and other such senior management staff shall not be deemed to be work people. In all cases the increase shall be recouped *pro rata* to the increase in the operative's wages and emoluments as agreed by the Joint Industrial Council for the Construction Industry, or, failing this, by agreement between the Construction Industry Federation and the authorised Trade Unions.

2   a) 'Wages' means the cost of normal time at standard rates and of all overtime at standard overtime rates. Only the hours at work shall be taken into account. Not coming within this meaning are site bonuses, bonus payments under site agreements, productivity or incentive bonuses or payments, or payments over the standard rates for normal time or over the standard overtime rates.

     b) 'Expenses' means travelling and subsistence (meal) allowances, country money, tool money, contractor's contributions to the Construction Industry pension fund and sick pay scheme and any other payments not covered by paragraph (a) of this Section and which may be agreed from time to time by the Joint Industrial Council for the Construction Industry or, failing this, by agreement between the Construction Industry Federation and the authorised Trade Unions.

3   'Labour on-costs necessarily payable' means:

a) the relative percentages in respect of Wage Variation Claims set out in the document entitled 'Percentage Additions to Labour Costs to cover Insurances, Holidays, etc.' issued in agreement between the Society of Chartered Surveyors in the Republic of Ireland and the Construction Industry Federation, the percentages to be used in calculating increases or decreases in wages, other emoluments and expenses over any period being those listed in the edition of the document then effective.

The figure to which the percentage addition specified in Clause 36(f) is to be added in respect of wages, other emoluments and expenses shall be the allowable sum of the increases or decreases in wages, other emoluments and expenses themselves and the relative percentages in respect thereof.

Increases or decreases in the relative percentages themselves shall not be payable until taken into account in the edition of the aforesaid document next issued after their occurrence.

b) the Contractor's contributions to any social insurance of other premiums not related to wage variation claims and payable under a legislative enactment instrument rule or order. An increase or decrease in any such labour on-cost shall be payable from the date on which it takes effect.

4   Any expenses or labour on-cost not payable at the Designated Date but introduced thereafter as a result of a legislative enactment instrument rule or order or agreed thereafter by the Joint Industrial Council for the Construction Industry, or, failing this, by agreement between the Construction Industry Federation and the authorised Trade Unions and which the Contractor is obliged to pay or allow shall be deemed to be an increase/decrease.

B.   Meanings for Clause 36(c)

'Materials or goods necessary for the execution of the Works' means:

a)   materials or goods embodied in the Works together with unavoidable waste and surpluses on such materials or goods;

b)   materials or goods specifically purchased for temporary use in the construction and on the site of the Works provided that such materials or goods are not re-usable in similar form on another job and, when no longer required for the Works, have only scrap value.

c) fuels and electric power for plant and essential temporary lighting installations when such fuels and power are wholly consumed on the site of the Works.

Provided always that in the case (c) the liability of the Employer shall be limited to that part of any increase which is in excess of 10% of the price ruling at the Designated Date, with an equivalent limitation to the Contractor's liability in the case of any decrease.

The following for the purposes of Clause 36(c) are deemed not to be materials or goods necessary for the execution of the Works:

formwork or any other materials which can be used on another job when no longer required for the Works;

materials or goods for temporary work associated with but not embodied in the Works nor used in the construction of the Works (e.g. site huts, hoardings, temporary roads);

plant, tools and equipment.

Supplement (GDLA variations)

In March 1993 a revised supplement was issued for the GDLA Contract. The main differences are:

1   The first paragraph contains a provision requiring approval of the Department of Finance.

2   The definition of 'work people' differs considerably in par. A.1.

3   The agreement of expenses [par. A.2(b)] requires the approval of the Minister for Finance.

4   The second and third paragraphs in par. A.3(a), par. A.3(b) and par. A.4 are omitted.

5   In par. B, the second paragraph differs by including a reference to sub-par. B(b).

Sub-Contract Forms

There are two separate sub-contract forms issued jointly by the Construction Industry Federation and the Sub-Contractors and Specialists Association. One is for use with the RIAI, and the other for use with the GDLA form. They are very similar, but there are some differences and the following is a schedule, listing where the GDLA forms differs from the RIAI version:

1   Clause 6 – Variations, etc

    If a variation is likely to involve the Sub-Contractor in loss or expense not reasonably contemplated, the Sub-Contractor in the RIAI form shall 'forthwith' inform the Contractor. In the GDLA form a timetable is provided, so that the Sub-Contractor must inform the Contractor within three working days, and within a further twenty working days must give details of the loss or expense. This reflects the differences in Clause 2(c) of the Main Contract.

    The omissions which will allow a 10% payment to the Sub-Contractor must, as in Clause 13(e) of the Main Contract, exceed 20% of the Sub-Contract Sum before any allowance is due.

2   Clause 8 – Defects

    The time for remedying defects is given in the RIAI form as 'reasonable', that is the GDLA form as 'such time as shall be determined by the Architect'.

3   Clause 11

    Contractor to apply for certificates of payment; Interim payments to the Sub-Contractor – Retention.

    There is a provision in the RIAI form referring to the bankruptcy of the Employer. This does not appear in the GDLA form, and this reflects the differences in Clause 34 of the main contract.

    The GDLA form contains a provision that does not occur in the RIAI form. This is a sub-section that allows the Contractor to ask for arbitration where he feels that the Sub-Contractor is invoking the sanctions allowed by the section without having regard to the Contractor's own difficulty in obtaining payment.

The sub-clause 11(e)(1)(iii) allows the Sub-Contractor to charge interest to the Contractor, seven days in the case of GDLA, and 28 days in the case of the RIAI, after the Contractor himself has been paid.

Sub-clause 11(f) in the RIAI form is referenced as (ii)(g) in the GDLA form. This is because 11(f) in the GDLA form deals with 'Procedure after Determination' which sub-clause occurs at 20(d) in the RIAI form. There are some differences in the procedure after determination. The GDLA form requires that prior notice under Clause 33 of the Main Contract conditions has been served before any removal of plant is undertaken, and it further requires that any such removal must have the Employer's consent. Neither of these provisions occurs in the RIAI form.

4   Clause 20 – Determination by Contractor

The GDLA form lists three further grounds for determination of the employment of the Sub-Contractor over those given in the RIAI form:

i)   Where the Sub-Contractor fails to commence the Sub-Contract Works within a reasonable period of receiving an order in writing [sub-clause 20(a)(4)].

ii) Where the Sub-Contractor fails to execute the Works in accordance with his Sub-Contract [sub-clause 20(a)(5)].

iii) Where a trade dispute occurs, and is not resolved within the Registered Employment Agreement procedure [sub-clause 20(a)(6)].

5   Clause 23 – Wages and Conditions of Employment

The RIAI form has a general provision covering appropriate wages and conditions of employment 'as may be generally from time to time prevailing in the industry...' The GDLA form requires that the rates and conditions of the National Joint Industrial Council for the construction industry be observed. It further requires Clause 39 of the main GDLA form (Fair Wages Clause) to be observed.

6   Clause 25 – Wage and Price Variation

The clauses are very different in the two forms. The RIAI form sets out in four sub-clauses the various rules which shall apply to the variations. The GDLA form, perhaps more sensibly requires the provisions of Clause 36 of the main contract form (Wages and Price Variations) to be observed – *mutatis mutandis*, i.e. the necessary changes being made.

The Appendix – RIAI and GDLA

AP.01 The purpose of the appendix is to gather together the various items which might vary from contract to contract, and thereby to simplify the task of reference. The two forms of contract are largely similar in this respect, and the differences between them are set out item by item. The actual pages are reproduced at the end of this section. There are fifteen items in the RIAI form that require to be completed, but only eleven in the GDLA form. Each item has a clause reference.

1   *Designated Date*

This item occurs only in the RIAI form. It is defined in par. 1.01, and relates to Clause 1(a).

2   *Percentage for Professional Fees (if not stated, 12.5%)*

Clause 22(b) in both forms requires the percentage for professional fees, which might be incurred as a result of fire damage, to be defined. See par. 22.02.

3   *Cost of Site Clearance*

This again refers, in both forms, to Clause 22(b) and is commented on in par. 22.02. The item is to cover the cost of site clearance after fire damage.

4   *Minimum sum for Public Liability Insurance (if not stated, £200,000)*

The item occurs in both forms, but the GDLA form suggests the sum of £250,000. The clause in both forms which deals with this item is 23(e)(ii). The inadequacy of the amount suggested is commented on in pars. 21.07, 21.10 and 21.11.

5   *Date for Possession*

In the RIAI form there are two items, this one and the next, which enable to time for completing the Works to be calculated. In the GDLA form, this information is contained in a single item, set out as *Period for Practical Completion*. Clauses 28 and 29(a) in the RIAI form deal with this, and Clauses 28(a) and 29(a) are the corresponding GDLA clauses. The commentary on this part of the Contract is contained in pars. 28.01, 28.02, 28.03, 29.01 and 29.02.

6   *Date for Completion*

Again, as in Item 5, this only occurs in the RIAI form. See 5 above.

7   *Liquidated and Ascertained Damages*

Clause 29(a) in both forms deals with this item, and it is covered in pars. 29.01 seq. of the notes with regard to an appropriate figure.

8   *Defects Liability Period*

Both forms are again similar, but the references to the clauses differ slightly. The RIAI and GDLA forms both deal with this item at Clause 31, but the second reference in the RIAI form is Clause 35(h) but is 35(g) in the GDLA form. The factors which should be considered in arriving at this period are dealt with in par. 31.02.

9   *Period of Interim Certificates (if not stated, 4 weeks)*

This item is the same in both forms and refers to Clause 35(a). The notes deal with this matter at par. 35.02.

10 *Time for Issue of Interim Certificates by the Architect (if not stated, 5 working days)*

The wording of this item in the GDLA form is slightly different but the changes are of no effect. Clause 35(a) in both forms defines five days, unless the appendix alters this, as the period within which the architect must issue an interim Certificate after receiving the Contractor's statement. See par. 35.02.

11 *Time for honouring Certificate (if not stated, 10 working days)*

This item only occurs in the GDLA form. Clause 35(a) of that form allows the Employer ten days to honour a Certificate, unless the appendix shows a different period. The RIAI form has a fixed period of seven days. See par. 35.15.

12 *Percentage of Certified Value Retained (not to exceed 10%)*

Clause 35(d) of both forms deals with this item, which is identical in both forms. The appropriate amounts are discussed in par. 35.06.

13 *Limit of Retention Fund*

This item only occurs in the RIAI form, and is dealt with at Clause 35(d). The notes deal with this matter at pars. 35.06 and 35.15.

14 *Joint Account Retention Fund*

This item only occurs in the RIAI form, as there is no provision in the GDLA form for a joint account. Clause 35(f) deals with this, and the notes at par. 35.08 comment on the matter.

15 *Period of Final Measurement (if not stated, 6 months)*

This item occurs in both forms but the period is limited in differing ways. In the RIAI form (Clause 35(g)(iii) six months is suggested if no different period is proposed. The GDLA appendix says: (Not to exceed Defects Liability Period) and occurs at Clause 35(f)(iii) of the Contract Form. Pars. 35.09 and 35.15(h) comment on these matters.

16 *Period for Serving Notice of Arbitration (if not stated, 10 days)*

This item only occurs in the RIAI form. Early printings of the form gave a figure of 14 days. This period refers to the time within which arbitration on the proposed final account figure must be sought. Clause 35(h) refers. In the GDLA forms this period is fixed at 30 days [Clause 35(g)].

Index

Access — 3.09, 11.01–.06, 34.06

Addition — 2.06, 2.10, 2.37, 3.02, 12.03, 13.01, 14.02, 19.03, 20.04, 26.04, 30.07, 36.01–.04, Supplement

Agent — A.01, A.02, 2.04–.06, 2.35, 3.02, 8.03, 10.01, 10.02, 13.08, 16.08, 16.10, 16.11, 19.03, 20.06, 21.02, 32.01, 24.01, 25.01, 29.05, 30.01, 30.14, 30.15, 38.08, 41.01, Supplement

Agreed Rules of Measurement — 3.03

Alteration — 2.10, 2.37, 4.01, 26.01, 26.03, 26.04, 33.09, 34.06, 35.08

Ancillary — 22.01–.03, 24.01, 24.05, 25.01, 30.05, 30.14, 32.08

Appendix — A.03, 1.01, 1.05, 1.09, 16.10, 16.12–.14, 21.01, 21.02, 22.02, 22.06, 28.01–.04, 28.07, 29.01–.03, 29.09, 29.11, 30.15, 31.02, 32.12, 35.02, 35.04, 35.06, 35.08–.10, 35.15, 36.01, AP.01

Appointment — Int.11, A.02, 2.39, 12.01, 12.08, 12.10, 12.12, 24.03, 33.06, 38.03, 38.05–.07

Arbitration / Arbitrator — A.01, A.03, 2.08, 2.17, 2.18, 13.05, 16.08, 16.16, 24.03–.05, 24.08, 24.09, 29.05, 35.03, 35.10, 35.11, 35.13–.15, 38.01–.12, 39.02, Sub-Contract Forms, AP.01 (and see Quasi-Arbitrator)

Articles of Agreement — 1.05, 2.03, 2.13, 3.01, 3.03, 3.06, 3.08, 29.08, 30.18, 35.11, 38.03, 41.01

Artists — Int.04, Int.06, A.01–.03, 11.01, 28.03, 28.11, 30.06, 30.10, 32.01-05, 38.03

Ascertained Damages — 29.01, 29.03, 29.04, 29.10, 29.11, AP.01

Ascertainment — 2.25, 2.26, 2.43, 13.01–.12, 14.01, 14.03, 14.06, 18.01, 19.01, 24.05,

28.01, 28.09, 29.03, 29.05, 29.07, 29.09, 34.04, 35.17

Assignment — Int.18, Int.19, 2.06, 15.01–.08, 33.01, 33.15

Bankruptcy — 14.07, 16.05, 16.16, 16.17, 28.03, 30.15, 33.02, 33.06, 33.07, 33.10, 34.02, 37.01, 37.03, Sub-Contract Forms

Bill of Quantities — Int.01, A.01, A.03, 1.01, 2.03, 2.14, 3.01–.06, 3.08–.10, 3.12, 3.15, 3.17, 13.02, 13.04, 13.06, 18.01, 19.03, 29.01, 30.12, 35.02, 35.15, 36.02

Bill of Reductions — 3.02

Bond (Contract Guarantee) — 20.03, 28.03, 28.11, 33.08, 33.09, 37.03, 37.04

Breach — Int.12, Int.13, 2.03, 2.05, 2.17, 2.26, 6.08, 14.01, 16.10, 16.11, 16.16, 28.01, 28.03, 29.01, 29.02, 30.01, 30.15, 33.01, 33.03, 33.04, 33.09, 34.05, 35.08, 35.09, 35.11, 37.03, 38.03, 38.06

Building Regulations — 6.01, 6.02, 6.03, 6.04, 6.06, 8.02, 8.04

Bye-Laws — Int.07, 6.01–.08, 6.11

Carry Out — Int.02, Int.06, Int.10, Int.19, 2.01–.03, 2.07, 2.17, 2.24, 2.28, 2.31, 2.33, 2.36, 2.37, 2.38, 2.41, 2.43, 2.45, 3.01, 3.02, 6.01, 6.02, 6.04, 6.08, 7.02, 8.01, 8.02, 8.13, 8.15, 10.01, 10.03, 11.01–.03, 12.01, 12.03–.05, 13.03, 13.04, 13.06, 13.07, 14.01, 15.01, 15.04, 16.01–.03, 16.05, 16.10, 18.01, 19.01, 20.06, 24.05, 26.02, 28.04, 29.05, 30.04, 30.10, 31.01, 32.01, 32.02, 33.03, 33.06, 33.08, 33.14, 34.03, 34.06, 35.01, 35.05, 35.06, 35.11, 35.12, 35.15, 35.18, 36.06, 37.02, 38.10

Certificate (Conclusiveness) — A.01, A.02, 2.06, 2.18, 2.28, 2.32, 2.36, 2.39, 6.01, 6.03, 12.03, 13.03, 13.05, 19.01, 29.05, 32.07, 35.01–.03, 35.05, 35.10–.12,

35.15, 35.18, 38.03, 38.07, 38.08

Certificate (Final) — Int.06, 2.28, 28.04, 29.05, 31.02, 35.01, 35.03, 35.07–.15, 35.18, 35.19, 38.07, 38.08, 38.14

Certificate (Interim) — 13.03, 16.12–.14, 16.19, 19.01, 19.02, 22.03, 32.09–.12, 32.15, 33.04, 33.05, 33.07, 34.01, 35.01–.05, 35.07, 35.08, 35.10–.12, 35.14–.17, 35.19, 35.20, 36.01, 36.02, 38.07, 38.08

Clerk of Works — 2.06, 2.07, 2.38, 12.01–.06, 12.08, 12.10–.12, 13.07, Supplement

Collateral Warranty (Agreement) — Int.02, Int.18, 8.08, 16.13, 16.15–.17, 16.20, 17.01, 20.02, 25.03, 28.03, 37.01–.05

Commencement — Int.06, A.03, 2.19, 21.03, 23.09, 26.01, 26.02, 28.03, Sub-Contract Forms

Complete — Int.02, Int.10, A.01–.03, 2.01, 2.03, 2.11, 2.17, 2.23, 2.33, 2.45, 8.13, 9.01, 10.03, 14.07, 14.08, 15.01, 16.06, 16.07, 16.11, 16.14, 16.16, 22.03, 23.08, 24.09, 28.01–.03, 28.06, 28.07, 28.11, 29.01, 29.03–.05, 29.08, 29.09, 29.11, 30.01, 30.15, 30.18, 31.01, 31.05, 31.07, 31.08, 32.01, 32.06, 32.10, 33.03, 33.05, 33.08, 33.09, 33.14, 33.16, 34.04, 35.05–.07, 35.09, 35.11, 35.12, 35.17, 36.04, 37.03, 38.03, 38.08, AP.01

Completion (Final) — 2.06, 3.17, 13.02, 13.03, 14.07, 14.09, 14.12–.14, 16.14, 21.02, 23.14, 26.01, 28.01–.04, 28.06, 28.07, 28.11, 35.09–.12, 35.15, 35.18

Completion (Practical) — A.03, 2.06, 2.21, 2.23, 13.05, 16.06, 16.14, 22.02, 26.02, 26.04, 28.03–.09, 28.11, 29.01–.04, 29.08, 29.09, 30.01, 30.15, 30.17, 30.18, 30.20, 31.01, 31.02, 31.04, 31.06–.08, 32.06, 32.10, 32.12, 32.16, 33.03, 33.05, 35.07–.10, 35.17–.19, 36.04, 38.03, 38.11, AP.01

Conciliation — 38.01, 38.02

Conclusive — 2.28, 29.01, 29.05, 35.01, 35.03, 35.11, 35.12, 35.15, 35.18

Conditions — Int.04, Int.08–.10, Int.18, A.01,

A.03, 1.01, 1.02, 1.07, 2.07, 2.09, 2.12, 2.14, 2.21, 2.25, 2.32, 2.34, 2.36, 2.39, 3.03, 3.06, 3.08, 6.10, 8.02, 8.03, 8.07, 10.01, 11.01, 12.01, 12.03, 13.04, 13.05, 13.07, 16.14, 16.16, 17.01, 18.01, 20.01, 22.04, 23.03, 23.12, 24.03, 24.04, 25.01, 28.03, 29.01, 29.02, 29.05, 29.08, 30.05, 30.07, 33.01, 33.04, 34.04, 35.02, 35.05, 35.08–.11, 35.15, 35.18, 36.01–.03, 37.01, 37.03, 39.01, Supplement, Sub-Contract Forms

Confidentiality — A.01, 3.10, 3.12, 3.15, 38.04

Consultants — Int.03, Int.11, Int.19, 2.07, 3.08

Contract (Documents) — Int.01, Int.08, A.01, 1.01, 2.01, 2.03, 2.06, 2.13–.15, 2.17, 2.33, 3.01, 3.03, 3.06, 3.08, 3.12, 3.15–.17, 5.01, 5.02, 6.10, 8.01, 8.13, 8.15, 9.01, 9.02, 12.01, 13.02, 13.04, 16.01, 17.01, 18.01, 19.01–.03, 32.01, 32.02

Contract (Engineering) — Int.09, 2.08, 2.15, 2.41, 7.01, 12.06, 15.01, 17.01, 17.02, 19.01, 20.05, 23.05, 23.07, 31.03, Sub-Contract Forms

Contract (Guarantee) — see Bond

Contract (Oral) — Int.05

Contract (Simple) — Int.01, Int.06, A.01, 35.11

Contract (Standard Form of) — Int.01, Int.03, Int.06, Int.08–.09, A.01–.03, 2.08, 9.02, 12.08, 16.11, 17.01, 19.01, 20.01, 20.02, 20.05, 21.06, 22.03, 25.04, 28.02, 30.13, 31.07, 33.01, 33.06, 33.09, 36.01, 36.03, 37.01, 37.02

Contract (Sum) — A.01, 2.02, 2.23, 2.25, 2.26, 2.28, 2.38, 3.02, 3.03, 3.05, 3.06, 4.01, 4.04, 6.01, 6.10, 8.01, 8.14, 9.01, 13.02, 13.10, 14.01–.03, 15.01, 18.01, 18.03, 19.02, 19.03, 26.01, 28.03, 29.05, 32.01, 32.02, 32.07, 33.08–.11, 35.15, 36.02, 37.03, Sub-Contract Forms

Contract (Under Seal) — Int.06, Int.15, A.01, 35.11

Contract (Unenforceable) — Int.07, 6.04

Contract (Void) — Int.07, 3.04, 6.01, 6.02, 6.04

Contract (Voidable) — Int.07, 3.04

Contract (Written) — Int.05, 2.08, 2.09, 35.05

Copy (of Drawings, etc) — A.01, 3.06, 3.08–.10, 3.12, 3.15, 3.17, 6.10, 6.13, 13.03, 13.08, 13.10, 13.11, 35.09, 38.14, 39.01

Copyright — 3.13

Covered Up — 2.16, 9.01, 12.02

Damage — Int.12, Int.14–.17, 1.04, 2.05, 2.17, 2.27, 2.28, 3.13, 6.08, 8.05, 11.01, 14.01, 14.10, 16.04, 16.06, 16.08, 16.10, 16.16, 20.01–.06, 21.02, 21.03, 21.04, 22.02, 22.03, 22.05, 22.06, 22.08, 24.01–.05, 25.01–.03, 25.05, 25.06, 26.01, 26.02, 26.04, 27.01, 28.03, 29.01, 30.01, 30.05, 30.12–.15, 31.04, 32.07–.09, 33.01, 33.04, 33.08, 33.09, 34.01, 34.04, 34.05, 35.04, 35.05, 35.07, 35.11, 37.03, 38.05, AP.01

Damages –see Ascertained Damages; Liquidated Damages

Date (Extended) — 28.01, 29.01, 29.03, 29.04, 29.08, 29.11, 30.01, 30.12, 36.04

Date (for Completion) — A.03, 2.23, 16.06, 16.07, 28.01–.03, 28.07, 29.01–.04, 29.08, 29.09, 29.11, 30.01, 30.15, 30.18, 31.02, 31.04, 31.07, 32.10, 32.12, 35.09, 35.17, 35.18, 36.04, AP.01

Date (for Possession) — A.03, 28.01, 29.02, 29.09, 32.08, 32.09, AP.01

Daywork (Prices / Sheets) — 13.06, 13.07, 13.09, 13.10, 36.01, 36.02

Debt — 2.28, 15.02, 26.04, 33.06, 33.08, 33.10, 35.03, 35.08, 35.10, 35.14

Decennial — Int.19, 21.02

Defect — Int.06, Int.10, Int.15, Int.19, 2.17, 2.18, 2.21, 2.23, 2.39, 6.08, 8.03–.05, 8.08, 9.01, 9.02, 16.07, 16.08, 16.12, 16.14, 16.16, 17.01, 20.02, 22.02, 25.01, 25.03, 25.06, 26.01, 28.04, 28.07, 28.11, 31.01–.03, 31.05–.07, 31.09, 32.11, 32.12, 32.16, 33.03, 33.09, 34.01, 35.03, 35.06, 35.10, 35.11, 36.01, 36.02, 37.01,

37.02, Sub-Contract Forms, AP.01 (and see Latent Defect)

Defects Liability — 2.17, 2.21, 8.13, 16.14, 28.04, 28.07, AP.01

Defects Liability Period — 2.21, 16.14, 28.04, 28.07, 31.01, 31.02, 31.06, 31.07, 32.10, 32.12, 35.10, 35.15, 35.18, AP.01

Delay — 2.06, 2.13, 2.23, 2.27, 2.43, 9.01, 13.03, 13.10, 14.01, 16.04, 16.06, 20.02, 22.05, 23.05, 28.01, 28.03, 28.09, 28.11, 29.02, 29.04, 29.05, 29.07, 29.09, 29.11, 30.01, 30.02, 30.05, 30.08, 30.10–.12, 30.14, 30.15, 30.17, 30.19, 30.21, 33.01, 33.08, 38.04, 38.08

Delegate — 2.05, 2.07, 2.39, 12.07

Design — Int.10, Int.17–.19, 2.06, 2.41, 3.13, 8.07–.09, 11.03, 13.02, 16.01, 16.08, 16.13, 16.16, 17.01, 17.02, 24.01, 25.01–.06, 32.01, 32.02, 37.01, 37.02, 37.04

Designated Date — 1.01, 1.02, 1.05, 1.08, 1.09, 4.01, 13.08, 23.06, 36.01, 36.02, 37.01, Supplement, AP.01

Determination — 2.06, 14.09, 16.16, 16.17, 24.03–.05, 24.08, 24.09, 30.01, 33.01–.11, 33.13–.15, 34.04, 34.06, 35.14, 37.03, 38.03, Sub-Contract Forms

Determination (by the Contractor) — Int.06, 14.07, 16.16, 16.17, 24.04, 24.09, 30.17, 33.01, 34.01–.06, 34.08, 35.02, 35.08, 35.14, Sub-Contract Forms

Determination (by the Employer) — Int.06, 2.24, 14.07, 24.08, 33.01, 33.03–.08, 33.10, 33.13, 33.14, 33.16, 35.06, 39.02, 39.04

Dimensions — 2.14, 5.01, 5.02, 7.01

Directive (EC) — Int.17, 8.09, 8.10, 11.04

Discrepancy — 2.13, 2.14, 3.03, 5.01, 5.02, 5.04, 30.07

Dismissal — 2.20, 2.23, 2.42, 38.03, 38.04

Dispute Resolution — 2.18, 38.01

Documents — Int.01, Int.08, 2.37, 3.03, 3.08, 3.10–.12, 3.15, 5.01, 5.02, 28.01–.03, 29.01, 31.02, 32.06, 35.09, 35.18, 38.06, 38.09, AP.01 (and see Contract Documents)

Drawings — A.01, 2.01, 2.03, 2.14, 3.02, 3.06, 3.08, 3.09, 3.13, 3.15, 3.17, 7.01, 12.02, 32.07, 38.14

Duty — Int.10–.14, Int.18, A.01, 2.01, 2.06, 2.17, 2.39, 2.40, 4.01, 6.02, 6.03, 6.08, 11.01, 11.03, 12.01, 12.02, 12.04, 12.05, 12.07, 12.10, 13.07, 16.05, 16.07, 16.10, 16.11, 20.02, 22.03, 23.06, 26.01, 29.04, 31.03, 33.04, 33.06, 33.11, 35.01, 38.08

Economic Loss — Int.14

Employment Agreement — 1.02, 1.03, 1.07, 1.10, 2.40, 14.01, 16.16, 33.11, 33.15, 34.04

Enactment — 1.07, 4.01, 4.03, 6.03, 36.05, Supplement

Engineering Contracts — see Contract (Engineering); New Engineering Contract

Environmental Impact Assessment — 6.05

Error — 3.04, 7.01–.03, 25.01

European Community — Int.17, 8.09, 8.10, 11.04, 22.03

Examiner / Examination — 33.06, 33.07, 33.08, 33.11, 34.02, 34.05

Exchequer — Int.01, 3.12

Excluded Risks — 20.01, 20.02, 20.06, 22.02, 23.04, 23.13, 24.01–.03, 24.05–.07, 25.01, 25.02

Exempted Development — 6.01

Existing Structures — Int.15, A.01, 18.01, 20.01, 20.02, 20.04, 20.06, 21.02, 22.05, 26.01, 26.03, 26.04

Expense — 2.04, 2.11, 2.15, 2.19, 2.26, 2.27, 2.29, 2.43, 3.04, 7.02, 9.01, 9.02, 13.04, 14.01, 16.10, 19.03, 20.02, 25.01, 29.04, 29.10, 29.11, 30.08, 30.12, 30.17, 33.03, 34.04, 38.04, Sub-Contract Forms

Expenses — 2.13, 9.01, 14.01, 33.08, 36.01, 36.02, Supplement

Extension (of Time) — Int.08, Int.15, 1.03, 2.02, 2.06, 2.11, 2.12, 2.29, 6.10, 9.01, 16.04–.07, 22.04, 28.01, 28.03, 28.06, 29.01–.05, 29.07, 29.11, 30.01, 30.04–.07, 30.10, 30.12, 30.14–.20, 34.01, 35.09, 36.04, 38.08

Fair Wages — 33.13, 38.10, 39.01, Sub-Contract Forms

Final Completion (see Completion, Final)

Final Measurement (Period of) — 28.04, 31.01, 35.09, 35.10, 35.15, AP.01

Fitness For Purpose — Int.10, 8.02–.07, 8.09, 17.02

Fluctuations — 36.05

Fluctuations (Formula) — 1.06, 36.05

Force Majeure — 30.02

Foreman — 2.06, 10.01, 10.02, 12.04, 13.01, 13.08

Foundations — Int.10, 6.08, 9.01, 9.07, 38.03

Fraud — Int.05, Int.07, 35.03, 35.11

Fundamental — Int.04, Int.07, 3.04, 33.01, 33.03

Goods — Int.10, Int.17, 2.15, 8.02–.08, 14.07, 14.10, 14.11, 16.01, 16.12, 16.13, 16.16, 17.01, 17.02, 19.02, 19.03, 20.06, 21.02, 22.01, 22.03, 22.05, 33.05, 33.08, 34.03, 34.04, 34.08, 35.04, 35.05, 35.12, 35.15, 35.21, 36.01, 36.02, 36.07, 37.02, Supplement

Government Department — Int.01, Int.06, 3.12, 6.04, 8.10, 13.08, 13.10, 16.15, 29.04, 36.01, 36.04, 39.01

Guarantee Account — 35.02

Health and Safety at Work — 6.01, 6.05, 11.04

Holiday (Bank / Public / Statutory) — 1.02–.04, 1.07, Supplement

Illegality — Int.05, Int.07, 2.13, 3.04, 6.01, 6.02, 6.06

Implied Terms — Int.08, Int.10, 2.39, 6.03, 8.02–.06, 11.01, 12.01, 13.01, 16.05, 16.07, 16.08, 17.01, 17.02, 21.02, 35.05

Incompetent — 2.20, 2.42

Increases — 1.01, 1.06, 4.01–.04, 16.05, 16.16, 19.01, 35.15, 36.01–.05, 36.07, Supplement

Indemnity — 16.10, 16.21, 20.02, 20.06, 21.01, 21.09, 21.11, 25.01, 25.04, 32.01

Injunction — 1.04, 3.08, 3.13

Inspection — 2.16, 2.17, 2.39, 2.41, 3.14,

6.08, 9.01, 9.06, 9.07, 12.01, 12.05, 12.07, 12.09, 20.02, 23.12, 26.01, 30.07, 35.05, 35.11, 39.01

Instructions — Int.09, A.01, A.02, 2.01, 2.03–.08, 2.11, 2.12, 2.14, 2.17, 2.20, 2.22–.26, 2.28–.32, 2.36–.38, 2.41–.45, 3.05, 3.08, 3.14, 3.15, 6.10, 6.12, 6.13, 7.01, 9.01, 9.02, 9.07, 10.01, 11.02, 11.03, 12.02–.05, 12.07, 13.01, 13.02, 13.10, 16.02, 16.05–.07, 16.17, 18.01, 18.03, 19.02, 19.03, 28.01, 28.06, 28.07, 28.09, 30.05, 30.07, 30.08, 30.12, 31.02, 31.04, 31.08, 31.09, 33.03, 34.04, 35.08, 36.04, 41.01

Instructions (Oral) — 2.01, 2.03, 2.37, 12.04, 13.01, 13.02

Insurance (Contractor's All Risks) — 20.02, 22.01–.03, 22.05, 22.06, 22.08, 23.01, 23.02–.04, 24.01, 25.02, 26.01, 28.04, 28.05, 31.01, 32.03

Insurance (Decennial) — Int.19, 20.02

Insurance (by Employer) — 21.01, 22.02

Insurance (Employer's Liability) — 16.10, 21.01, 22.03, 23.01, 23.03–.05, 26.01, 28.04

Insurance (Exclusions) — Int.17, 8.04–.06, 16.10, 17.01, 20.01, 20.02, 22.02, 22.05, 23.04, 23.06, 24.01–.03, 24.05, 24.07, 25.01, 25.02, 27.01, 32.03, 37.03

Insurance (Non–Negligence) — 20.02

Insurance (Professional Indemnity) — 20.02, 25.01, 25.04, 26.01

Insurance (Public Liability) — 16.10, 20.06–.07, 22.03, 23.01, 23.02, 23.04, 23.05, 25.02, 26.01, 28.04, 28.07, AP.01

Interest (Bank) — 2.27, 19.03, 22.03, 22.04, 29.04, 35.01, 35.06–.08, 35.13–.15, Sub-Contract Forms

Invalidate — 2.02, 2.37, 28.06

Latent Defect — Int.19, 8.04, 8.05, 16.14, 35.11

Legislation — Int.05, Int.08, Int.10, Int.17, 8.02, 8.09, 33.13, 39.01

Legislature — 6.01, 6.03, 6.06

Letter of Intent — Int.05

Liability — Int.03, Int.10, Int.12–.19, 2.03, 2.05, 2.17, 2.21, 2.32, 2.41, 3.05, 6.07, 6.08, 7.01, 8.05, 8.07–.09, 8.13, 12.05, 14.01, 14.10, 15.02, 15.03, 16.05, 16.06, 16.08–.11, 16.14–.17, 17.01–.03, 20.02, 20.03, 21.01, 22.03, 23.07, 24.01, 25.02–.04, 26.01, 27.01, 28.04, 28.07, 31.01–.03, 31.06, 31.07, 32.07, 32.10, 32.12, 33.10, 34.03, 35.03, 35.10, 35.11, 35.15, 35.18, 37.02, 37.03, 38.08, Supplement, AP.01 (and see Defects Liability Period)

Liaison Committee — Int.09, 21.01, 36.01

Licence — 4.01, 6.06, 11.01

Lien — 14.07, 14.13, 33.05, 33.08, 33.10, 33.12, 34.04, 34.08

Limitation — Int.06, Int.10, Int.15, Int.17, 2.10, 6.01–.03, 8.07, 12.02, 16.12, 16.14, 21.01, 30.12, 31.02, 32.12, 35.06, 35.11, 35.15, 37.03, Supplement

Liquidated Damages — 16.06, 29.01, 29.03, 29.04, 29.08, 29.10, 29.11, 30.01, 30.15, 31.04, 35.07, AP.01

Liquidator — 16.05, 16.15, 33.06, 33.08

Local Authority — Int.01, Int.14, Int.16, 2.06, 3.02, 6.01–.04, 6.08, 30.10

Loss — Int.14, Int.16, Int.19, 2.11, 2.19, 2.26, 2.27, 2.29, 2.43, 3.01, 3.04, 6.08, 8.05, 13.04, 14.01–.03, 14.10, 16.02, 16.10, 17.01, 19.03, 20.01, 20.03, 20.05-.06, 21.01, 22.02, 22.03, 22.05, 24.01–.05, 25.02, 26.01, 26.02, 26.04, 28.01, 28.03, 28.09, 29.01, 29.02, 29.04, 29.05, 29.07, 29.09–.11, 30.05, 30.12–.14, 30.17, 31.02, 32.01, 32.08, 33.07–.09, 34.04, 34.05, 35.04, 35.05, 35.09, 37.03, Sub-Contract Forms

Loss (Direct) — 2.27, 29.04, 30.13

Materials — Int.09, Int.10, 1.01, 1.08, 2.06, 2.10, 2.15, 4.03, 8.01, 8.02, 8.04–.15, 12.02, 13.06, 13.07, 14.01, 14.07–.14, 16.01, 16.08, 16.12, 16.14–.16, 17.01, 19.01, 19.03, 20.02, 21.02, 22.01–.03, 22.05, 26.01, 27.01, 30.07, 30.09, 31.02, 31.03, 31.07, 33.03–.05, 33.08, 33.10, 33.12, 33.15, 34.04, 34.06, 34.08, 35.04–.06, 35.12, 35.15, 35.19, 36.01,

36.02, 36.04, 36.06, 36.07, 37.01, 37.02, Supplement

Merchantability — 8.03–.05, 17.02

Method of Measurement — Int.09, 3.03, 3.06, 13.04–.06, 13.09

Method of Work — 2.37, 2.41, 11.02, 11.03, 12.04

Ministers / Ministers of State — 1.08, 4.03, 6.05, 20.06, 35.14, 36.04, 36.06, 40.01

Misconduct — 2.20, 2.42, 38.03, 38.04, 38.06

National Wage Agreement — 36.04, 39.01, 39.02

Negligence — Int.02, Int.10, Int.13, Int.16, Int.18, 6.08, 16.10, 16.11, 20.02, 20.03, 20.06, 21.01, 22.02, 23.10, 24.01, 25.01, 26.01, 28.07, 30.14, 30.16, 31.06, 32.08, 33.08, 35.03

New Engineering Contract — Int.09, 21.05, 23.09, 23.13

Nominated Sub-Contractor — Int.02, Int.09, Int.12, Int.18, 1.01, 2.06, 3.08, 8.05, 8.07, 8.08, 11.01, 14.01, 16.01–.21, 17.01, 17.02, 18.01, 19.01–.03, 19.05, 20.02, 20.06, 22.01, 25.01, 25.03, 29.04, 30.09, 30.15, 32.01, 33.05, 33.10, 34.03, 35.01, 35.02, 35.05, 35.09, 35.15, 36.01, 37.01–.04, 38.08, 39.01, Sub-Contract Forms

Nominated Supplier — Int.02, Int.08, 1.01, 2.06, 8.04, 8.07, 11.01, 16.16, 17.01–.07, 18.01, 19.01–.03, 19.05, 25.01, 30.09, 35.05, 35.09, Sub-Contract Forms

Nomination — 2.06, 8.04, 16.01–.03, 16.05–.07, 16.09, 16.19–.21, 17.01–.03, 17.05, 17.06, 18.01, 38.03, 38.05, 38.08, 38.10

Non–Completion — 2.28, 29.01, 32.04

Notice — 1.02, 1.04, 1.10, 2.18, 2.28, 2.43, 6.01–.03, 6.10–.13, 8.03, 9.01, 10.01, 11.01, 15.01, 16.16, 24.03–.05, 28.03, 28.06, 28.09, 28.10, 29.01, 29.05, 29.07, 30.14, 30.17, 30.21, 31.07, 33.03–.06, 33.08, 33.10, 33.14, 33.15, 34.01, 34.02, 34.06, 35.02, 35.05, 35.10, 35.15, 35.18, 35.19, 36.01, 36.02, 38.03, 38.08, 39.01,

39.04, 41.01, Sub-Contract Forms, AP.01

Objection — A.01–.03, 8.07, 12.01, 12.08, 12.10, 15.01, 15.03, 16.02, 16.09, 16.19, 16.21, 17.02, 17.03, 17.07, 32.01, 32.02, 32.05, 38.07

Omission — Int.10, 2.06, 2.11, 2.37, 3.04, 12.05, 13.01, 13.04, 13.10, 13.11, 14.01–.05, 16.10, 18.01, 19.02, 20.06, 21.02, 21.03, 23.08, 25.01, 29.04, 30.14, 30.16, 32.01, 35.09, 35.11, Sub-Contract Forms

Opening Up — 2.06, 2.16, 8.01, 9.01, 9.05–.07, 30.07, 38.03, 38.08

Opinion — Int.07, Int.09, 2.01, 2.15, 2.17, 2.20, 2.36, 2.39–.42, 3.05, 6.02, 13.04, 13.06, 14.01, 28.05, 29.01, 29.03, 29.07, 30.01, 30.14, 31.01, 31.02, 31.07, 32.10, 32.11, 33.03, 33.10, 33.11, 34.06, 35.04, 38.03, 38.08

Overheads — 2.26, 2.27, 13.06, 14.02, 30.12, 36.01

Ownership — Int.04, Int.09, Int.18, Int.19, 14.07–.09, 20.02, 21.02, 22.01, 33.10, 34.04, 35.05, 35.15, 35.21, 38.08

Partial Possession — 22.03, 23.10, 23.11, 32.01–.04, 32.12, 32.13, 32.15, 32.17, 32.18

P.C. Sum — 2.06, 2.38, 14.02, 16.05, 16.07, 18.01, 19.01–.04

Penalty — 6.02, 24.02, 29.01

Plain Language Contract — Int.01, 20.05

Planning (Acts / Permission) — Int.05, Int.07, Int.10, 6.01–.04, 6.06, 6.07, 33.01

Possession — A.03, 11.01, 11.02, 23.10, 23.11, 28.01, 28.03, 28.09–.11, 29.02, 29.09, 30.03, 30.12, 31.01, 32.06–.09, 32.13, 33.05, 33.11, 34.04, 35.05, 37.03, AP.01

Postponement — 2.19, 28.01, 28.06, 28.07, 30.07, 31.04, 36.04

Power (of Architect) — Int.02, Int.05, Int.10, 2.01, 2.04, 2.06, 2.07, 2.11, 2.13, 2.15, 2.18, 2.19, 2.21, 2.22, 2.24, 2.39, 2.40, 9.01, 9.02, 12.03, 12.04, 12.07, 13.01,

14.11, 15.02, 15.04, 16.16, 31.02, 33.03, 33.04, 33.07, 38.08

Practical Completion — see Completion, Practical

Preliminaries — 2.26, 30.12

Price Variation — 1.01, 1.08, 2.02, 2.06, 2.11, 2.12, 2.25, 3.06, 6.10, 12.03, 13.02, 13.05, 13.06, 13.08, 14.02, 18.01, 19.03, 35.09, 36.01–.05, Supplement, Sub-Contract Forms

Prime Cost — see P.C. Sum

Privety of Contract — 16.02, 16.03, 16.11, 16.13, 17.01

Profit — 2.26, 2.27, 13.06, 14.02, 19.03, 30.12, 34.04, 34.05, 36.01

Provisional Sum — 2.06, 2.38, 3.14, 6.01, 6.09, 8.01, 12.02, 14.02, 16.03, 17.01, 18.01, 18.03, 18.04, 19.01, 19.02, 19.04

Quantity Surveyor — Int.02, Int.09, Int.11, A.01–.03, 2.14, 2.26, 2.32, 2.43, 3.02, 3.03, 3.09, 3.10, 8.01, 12.02, 13.03, 13.05, 13.10, 14.01, 18.01, 22.02, 22.05, 32.02, 34.04, 35.02, 35.09, 38.07, 38.10, 41.01 (and see Bill of Quantities)

Quasi-Arbitrator — 30.14, 33.07, 35.03

Receiver — 16.15, 16.16, 33.06, 33.08, 34.02

Rectification — 2.13, 3.02, 3.04, 7.03, 9.02, 28.04, 31.01, 31.02, 39.01

Re-Execution — 2.17, 2.23, 2.29, 9.02, 33.03

Relevant Part — 32.06–.08, 32.10–.12, 32.16

Removal — Int.09, Int.19, 2.15, 2.17, 2.23, 9.02, 14.07, 14.09, 14.12–.14, 16.16, 24.05, 30.07, 33.03, 33.05, 33.08, 33.10, 33.15–.17, 34.03, 34.04, 34.06, 34.08, 35.04–.06, Sub-Contract Forms

Re-Nomination — A.01–.03, 16.05–.07, 16.16, 16.17, 16.19, 16.21, 37.03, 37.04, 38.10

Resident Architect — 12.06–.08

Retention — 2.15, 16.12–.15, 22.03, 22.07, 28.04, 29.04, 31.01, 31.05, 32.07, 32.12, 35.01, 35.02, 35.04–.08, 35.10, 35.15–.17, 35.19, 35.20, Sub-Contract Forms, AP.01

Retention Bond — 2.30, 35.15

Safety — 2.41, 6.08, 8.09, 11.02–.05, 14.10, 21.02

Satisfaction — 1.04, 2.01, 2.03, 2.17, 2.33, 2.39, 6.03, 8.04–.06, 8.09, 9.01, 9.06, 16.01, 16.06, 16.10, 16.14, 22.03, 23.07, 29.07, 33.03, 35.05, 36.02, 36.03, 36.07, 37.02

Schedule of Rates — A.01, A.03, 1.01, 2.37, 3.01, 3.06, 3.08–.10, 3.12, 3.15, 3.17, 13.04, 13.06, 36.02

Set-Off — 2.31, 9.04, 29.08, 35.03, 35.15

Setting–Out — 7.01–.04

Site (Agent) — 10.01, 10.02, 13.08, Supplement

Site (Architect) — 2.07 (and see Resident Architect)

Site (Engineer) — 10.01

Site (Protection of) — 14.07, 33.02, 33.10, 33.12, 33.15

Site (Staff) — 2.17, 2.39, 9.01, 10.01, 12.07, 12.09, 32.01

Skill — Int.02, Int.10, Int.11, Int.13, 3.13, 8.03–.05, 8.08, 15.01, 16.08, 16.13, 17.02, 20.02, 30.14, 37.02

Specification — A.03, 2.03, 2.15, 2.18, 2.37, 3.06, 3.08, 3.09, 3.13, 3.15, 6.10, 8.01, 8.07, 8.10, 8.13, 12.02, 22.02, 23.04, 26.01, 32.01, 32.02, 32.04, 35.02, 35.05, 37.02, 38.14

Standard Form of Contract — see Contract, Standard Form of

Statute of Limitations — Int.15

Sub-Contract Forms — 16.01, 16.04, 16.10–.13, 16.15–.17, 19.01, 35.05, 36.02, Sub-Contract Forms

Sub-Contractor (Domestic) — 15.03, 16.02, 16.03, 25.01, 33.05, 33.10, 34.03, 35.05, 37.01, 39.01

Sub-Contractor — see Domestic Sub-Contractor; Nominated Sub-Contractor

Sub-Letting — 15.01, 15.03, 15.04, 15.06, 15.08, 16.01, 33.01, 36.01, 36.02

Subrogation — 20.03

Sum — Int.02, Int.04, A.01, 2.02, 2.06, 2.17, 2.23, 2.25, 2.26, 2.28, 2.34, 2.38, 3.02,

3.03, 3.05, 3.06, 3.14, 4.01, 4.04, 6.01,
6.09, 6.10, 8.01, 8.14, 9.01, 13.02, 13.10,
14.01–.03, 14.05, 15.01, 16.03–.05,
16.12–.14, 16.17, 17.01, 18.01, 18.03,
18.04, 19.01–.04, 20.03, 22.02, 22.03,
23.07, 26.01, 28.03, 29.01, 29.04, 29.05,
29.08, 32.01, 32.02, 32.07, 32.09, 32.12,
33.08, 33.09, 34.01, 34.06, 35.06–.08,
35.10, 35.11, 35.15, 36.02, 37.03, 39.01,
Supplement, Sub-Contract Forms, AP.01
(and see Contract Sum; P.C. Sum;
Provisional Sum)

Supervision — Int.10, Int.18, 2.17, 2.39–.41,
7.01, 10.03, 12.01, 12.08, Supplement

Supplement — 1.01, 23.04, 36.01–.04, 37.01,
Supplement

Supplier – see Nominated Supplier

Suspension (of Works) — 16.16, 30.17,
33.03, 33.14, 34.01, 34.06

Tariff — 4.01

Temporary Works — 2.40, 2.41, 11.04,
22.01, 33.08, 33.15, 34.03, Supplement

Tender — Int.04, Int.05, A.02, 1.01, 1.05,
2.17, 2.37, 3.02, 3.03, 3.06, 3.10, 5.01,
15.01, 16.03, 16.08, 17.01, 22.03,
28.01–.03, 28.10, 29.01, 29.02, 30.09,
31.02, 31.07, 32.06, 35.02, 36.01, 37.02,
37.03

Tests — Int.10, Int.18, 2.18, 8.01, 8.12, 8.14,
8.15, 31.02

Time — see Extention of Time

Tort — Int.06, Int.12–.14, Int.16, Int.18, 6.07,
7.01, 20.02

Trade Dispute — 16.16, 33.11, Sub-Contract
Forms

Tradesmen — 11.01, 13.06, 30.06, 30.10,
32.01–.05

Trust — 2.39, 16.15, 29.04, 35.07, 35.08,
35.15, 35.20

Variation (Wage and Price) — see Price
Variation

Variations — Int.04, Int.05, A.03, 2.02,
2.06–.08, 2.10–.12, 2.25, 2.26, 2.29,
3.01, 3.04–.06, 3.14, 4.03, 6.10, 12.04,
13.01–.12, 14.01, 14.02, 18.01, 22.03,

22.07, 24.05, 30.05, 34.04, 35.09, Sub-
Contract Forms

Vesting — Int.09, 4.01, 14.07–.09, 33.12,
35.05, 35.15, 35.21

Vitiate — 2.02, 3.04, 13.01

War Damage — 23.04, 23.05, 27.01

Warranty — Int.02, 2.05, 8.03–.05, 8.07,
8.08, 16.08, 16.13, 17.01, 25.03, 35.05,
37.01–.05 (and see Collateral Warranty)

Weather (Inclement) — 28.01, 30.04, 31.02,
35.04

Workmanlike — Int.02, Int.10, Int.18, 2.32,
8.02, 8.13, 10.03

Workmanship — 2.15, 8.01, 8.12, 8.14, 8.15,
16.08, 20.02, 21.02, 22.02, 31.02, 31.03,
31.07, 37.01, 37.02

Workmen — 2.40, 9.01, 9.08, 13.07, 16.16,
19.03, 30.06, 32.01, 33.11, 36.01, 36.02,
39.01, 39.02, Supplement

Works — Int.02, Int.04, Int.09, Int.10,
A.01–.03, 2.01–.03, 2.06, 2.08, 2.09,
2.11, 2.15, 2.17, 2.20, 2.23, 2.31, 2.33,
2.37, 2.38–.42, 3.03, 3.06, 3.09, 3.12,
5.01, 6.01, 6.02, 6.11, 8.02, 8.09, 8.13,
10.01, 10.03, 12.01, 12.04, 13.01–.05,
13.10, 14.01, 14.07–.09, 15.01, 15.04,
16.01, 16.02, 16.06, 16.07, 16.09, 16.10,
16.13–.16, 17.01, 18.01, 19.03, 20.01,
20.06-.07, 21.02, 21.03, 22.01–.03,
22.05, 22.06, 22.08, 23.07-.11, 24.01,
24.05, 24.09, 25.01, 26.01, 26.02, 26.04,
27.01, 28.01, 28.03–.07, 28.09–.11,
29.01, 29.03–.05, 29.07, 29.08, 29.11,
30.01, 30.02, 30.04–.06, 30.09–.11,
30.14, 30.15, 30.17, 30.18, 31.01, 31.05,
31.07, 31.08, 32.01, 32.06–.09, 33.03,
33.05, 33.08–.11, 33.14, 33.16, 34.01,
34.04, 34.06, 35.04–.07, 35.09, 35.11,
35.12, 35.15, 35.16, 35.18, 36.01, 36.02,
36.07, 37.02, 38.03, 38.07, 38.08, 39.01,
39.02, Supplement, Sub-Contract Forms,
AP.01 (and see Clerk of Works;
Suspension of Works; Temporary
Works)

Standard Documents

1   COLLATERAL AGREEMENT BETWEEN EMPLOYER
    AND NOMINATED SUB-CONTRACTOR   339

2   SUB-CONTRACT FORM – RIAI   345

3   SUB-CONTRACT FORM – GDLA   365

4   BUILDING CONTRACT (Plain Language Contract)   383

5   GDLA – SUPPLEMENT (A): Clause 36 – Definitions   395

6   GDLA – SUPPLEMENT (B): Retention Bond   397

7   GDLA – SUPPLEMENT (C): Conciliation Procedures   399

Date . . . . 19 . . . .

COLLATERAL AGREEMENT

between

EMPLOYER

and

NOMINATED

SUB-CONTRACTOR

Employer . . . .

Sub-Contractor . . . .

Issued by the Royal Institute of the Architects of Ireland in agreement with the Construction Industry Federation and the Society of Chartered Surveyors in the Republic of Ireland.

8 Merrion Square
Dublin 2

1988 Edition

(Copyright)

Date of Publication 1st November 1988

Collateral Agreement

made the .... day of .... 19 ....

between ✿ ....

of (or whose Registered Office is situated at) ....

....

....

(hereinafter called "the Employer") of the one part and ✿ ....

....

....

of (or whose Registered Office is situated at) ....

....

....

(hereinafter called "the Sub-Contractor) of the other part.

Whereas the Sub-Contractor has been invited to tender for the carrying out of certain Sub-Contract Works namely:

....

....

....

as a Nominated Sub-Contractor in accordance with the relevant clauses of the R.I.A.I. Schedule of Conditions of Building Contract, 1988 Edition, it being intended that the Sub-Contract Works form part of certain other works namely:

....

....

....

to be carried out by the Contractor (....

hereinafter called the Main Contractor) under the terms of a Contract (hereinafter called the Main Contract) with the Employer dated .... providing for payment by the Main Contractor of liquidated damages for delay in the amount of

IR£ .... per ....

And whereas the Sub-Contractor has made an estimate of the sum which he will require for carrying out the said Sub-Contract Works as shown on the tender bearing the date ....

Now It Is Agreed Between the Employer and the Sub-Contractor that if the Sub-Contractor is, at or after the date hereof, selected as a Nominated Sub-Contractor for the Sub-Contract Works the warranties and agreements set out below shall have effect.

A   (1)   The Sub-Contractor warrants that he has exercised and will exercise all reasonable skill and care in:-

        (a)   the design of the Sub-Contract Works insofar as the Sub-Contract Works have been or will be designed by the Sub-Contractor; and

        (b)   the selection of materials and goods for the Sub-Contract Works insofar as such materials and goods have been or will be selected by the Sub-Contractor; and

---

✿*Where any of the parties to this Agreement is a partnership, the parties shall be described as"*   *and*
    " *the names of the individual partners) trading as* "   *" (the partnership name) and all the partners shall sign the Agreement.*

(c)   the satisfaction of any performance specification or requirement insofar as such performance specification or requirement is included or referred to in the tender of the Sub-Contractor as part of the description of the Sub-Contract Works.

(2)   The Sub-Contractor will, save insofar as he is delayed by any of the events referred to in Sub-paragraphs (a) to (j) of Clause 30 of the Main Contract,

    (a)   so supply the Architect of Main Contractor with information as and when either may reasonably request same, and

    (b)   so perform the Sub-Contract Works.

(3)   If either the employment of the Sub-Contractor under the Sub-Contract with the Main Contractor or the Sub-Contract itself is determined (under the terms of the Sub-Contract or for repudiation) by reason of any breach of the Sub-Contract by the Sub-Contractor or of any act of bankruptcy or liquidation of the Sub-Contractor then the Sub-Contractor shall pay compensation to the Employer.

(4)   The compensation payable under the previous sub-clause shall be the sum of all damages, expenses and losses suffered by the Employer in consequence of such determination including any additional cost of employing the Main Contractor or a substitute Sub-Contractor to complete the Sub-Contract Works.

(5)   Nothing in the tender of the Sub-Contractor shall operate to exclude or limit his liability to the Employer for breach of this Agreement.

B   (1)   The Architect shall on a written request from the Sub-Contractor require the Main Contractor to furnish reasonable proof that he has duly discharged any sum in respect of the value of the work, goods or services executed or supplied by the Sub-Contractor which is included in the total of a Certificate issued by the Architect under the Main Contract.

    (2)   If in respect of the whole or part of such sum the Contractor fails for 5 working days from the Architect's requirement of proof of discharge either to furnish in writing such proof or to show in writing reasonable cause for withholding payment, the Architect shall within 10 working days thereafter issue to the Employer a Certificate stating the sum wrongly withheld and naming the Sub-Contractor. The Employer shall deduct the sum so certified from any amount payable or which shall become payable to the Main Contractor (or part of the sum to the extent that the amount payable is less than the whole sum) and pay the sum so deducted direct to the Sub-Contractor within 10 working days of the certificate or of the amount becoming payable to the Main Contractor (whichever is the later).

    (3)   Any payment on foot of any Certificate issued under this clause shall be deemed a payment to the Main Contractor under the Main Contract.

    (4)   If the Employer is bound to pay the Sub-Contractor and one or more other Sub-Contractors direct out of any amount payable to the Main Contractor which is not sufficient to pay each Sub-Contractor fully, the amounts payable direct shall be abated pro rata.

    (5)   When the Architect issues a Certificate to the Main Contractor which includes in the total any sum in respect of the value of the work, goods or services executed or supplied by the Sub-Contractor he shall endorse the Certificate accordingly and simultaneously inform the Sub-Contractor in writing that the Certificate has been issued and state the gross cumulative amount payable to the Sub-Contractor.

C   (1)   In this clause "the Sub-Contract Retention" means the original sum or sums retained by the Employer out of the Main Contract payments in respect of work, goods or services executed or supplied by the Sub-Contractor less the whole of any deduction or set-off from or against the Main Contract Retention Fund to which the Employer is entitled in consequence of any breach of the Sub-Contract.

(2) (Subject to Clause D) When in the opinion of the Architect the Sub-Contract Works have been practically completed before practical completion of the Main Contract Works and if the Sub-Contractor has satisfactorily indemnified the Contractor against any defects he shall forthwith issue to the Main Contractor a Certificate for Payment of one moiety of the Sub-Contract Retention. The other moiety of the Sub-Contract Retention shall similarly be paid on a further Certificate given by the Architect on the expiry of a period equal to the Defects Liability Period named in the Appendix to the Main Contract calculated from the former Certificae or the making good by the Sub-Contractor of all defects that have appeared in the Sub-Contract Works (whichever is later). If Retention Money has been paid into a Joint Account under the Main Contract the Architect shall arrange disbursements accordingly.

(3) Sums released under the previous sub-clause shall be paid by the Main Contractor to the Sub-Contractor in accordance with the Sub-Contract.

(4) Any payment on foot of any Certificate issued under this Clause shall be deemed to be payment to the Main Contractor under the Main Contract.

(1) If the employment of the Main Contractor is determined under Clause 33 of the Main Contract, then:

(a) Clause C shall cease to apply.

(b) If after making reasonable allowances for all contingencies, the Architect is of the opinion that a balance will become payable to the Main Contractor under Clause 33 of the Main Contract he shall issue a Certificate to the Employer to that effect and he shall in the Certificate estimate the balance that will be payable under the Main Contract; The Employer shall pay the Sub-Contractor direct (but only up to the amount of the estimated balance) in accordance with Clause B and before any amount becomes payable to the Main Contractor under the Main Contract and shall deduct the amount from any amount subsequently becoming payable to the Main Contractor.

(c) In addition to the provisions of Clause B and Clause D (1) (b) the Employer may (but is not bound to) pay the Sub-Contractor direct for any work, goods or services executed or supplied for the purpose of the Main Contract before the date of determination insofar as payment has not already been made by the Main Contractor (and whether or not payment therefor has already been made by the Main Contractor) and deduct any such payment from any sum payable or to become payable to the Main Contractor.

(1) If any dispute whatsoever arises between the Employer and Sub-Contractor in connection with the construction performance or breach of this Agreement or with the subject matter thereof then either party shall give to the other notice of such dispute which shall, subject to Sub-Clause E (2), be referred to the arbitration and final decision of a person agreed between the parties, or failing such agreement, as may be nominated on the request of either party by the President for the time being of the Royal Institute of the Architects of Ireland after consultation with the President of the Cnstruction Industry Federation

(2) If any dispute arises within Clause E (1) and the Employer is of the opinion that such dispute touches or concerns a dispute between the Employer and the Main Contractor then provided no pleading has been delivered in either dispute and the hearing (other than a preliminary hearing) of either dispute has not commenced before an arbitrator the . Employer may by notice in writing to the Sub-Contractor and Main Contractor require that both disputes shall be referred to the one arbitrator ("the Joint Arbitrator"). Such notice shall abrogate any previous reference of either such dispute to any arbitrator other than the joint arbitrator. In default of agreement between all parties the joint arbitrator shall be nominated upon the application of any party to the disputes by the President for the time being of the Royal Institute of the Architects of Ireland after consultation with the President of the Construction Industry Federation. A joint arbitrator may give such directions for the determination of the two disputes either concurrently or consecutively as he may think just and convenient.

In Witness Whereof the parties hereto have set their hands (or the Common Seals of the parties hereto have been affixed, or the Common Seal of the Employer has been affixed and the Sub-Contractor has set his hand hereto, or the Employer has set his hand and the Common Seal of the Sub-Contractor has been affixed hereto) the day and year first above written.

Signature of Employer . . . .

Signature of Sub-Contractor . . . .

Signed by the above-named Employer in the presence of:

Name . . . .

Address . . . .

Occupation . . . .

Signed by the above-named Sub-Contractor in the presence of:

Name . . . .

Address . . . .

Occupation . . . .

or

Common Seal of the above-named Employer: Common Seal of the above-named Employer
                                               affixed in the presence of:

                                               Director . . . .

                                               Director . . . .

                                               and

                                               Secretary . . . .

Common Seal of above-named Sub-Contractor: Common Seal of the above-named
                                               Sub-Contractor affixed in the presence of:

                                               Director . . . .

                                               Director . . . .

                                               and

                                               Secretary . . . .

FOR OFFICE USE

Title of Main Contract ....

....

Sub-Contract for ....

....

Dated .... 19 ....

SUB CONTRACT

(For Use with the RIAI Main Contract Form)

Between

....

....

and

....

....

Issued under the sanction of and approved by the Construction Industry Federation and the Sub-Contractors and Specialists Association.

5th EDITION
(COPYRIGHT)
October 1989

CONSTRUCTION HOUSE, CANAL ROAD, DUBLIN 6.

THIS SUB-CONTRACT is made the . . . . day of . . . . 19 . . . .

between . . . .

of (or, whose Registered Office is situated at) . . . .

. . . .

(hereinafter called "the Contractor") of the one part and . . . .

. . . .

of (or, whose Registered Office is situated at) . . . .

. . . .

(hereinafter called "the Sub-Contractor" of the other part:

SUPPLEMENTAL to an Agreement (hereinafter referred to as "the Main Contract")

made the . . . . day of . . . . ,19 . . . . . between

. . . . (hereinafter called "the Employer")

of the one part and the Contractor of the other part:

WHEREAS the Contractor desires to have executed the Works of which particulars are set out in PART 1 of the Appendix of this Sub-Contract (hereinafter referred to as "the Sub-Contract Works") and which form part of the works (hereinafter referred to as "the Main Contract Works") comprised in and to be executed in accordance with the Main Contract, and any authorised variations of the Sub-Contract Works;

AND WHEREAS the Sub-Contractor is entitled to assume that the Agreement and Schedule of Conditions of Building Contract into which the Contractor has entered is the latest edition of that document issued under the sanction of the Royal Institute of the Architects of Ireland in agreement with the Construction Industry Federation. In this Sub-Contract the "R.I.A.I. Conditions" means those conditions. If the Agreement and Conditions are not as aforesaid the Sub-Contractor shall be given prior notice of any alternations before the Sub-Contract document is executed. No additions or omissions to any part of this document shall be made by either signatory except by mutual agreement.

NOW IT IS HEREBY AGREED AND DECLARED as follows:—

Notice of the Main Contract to the Sub-Contractor

1. The Sub-Contractor shall be deemed to have notice of all the provisions of the Main Contract except the detailed prices of the Contractor included in Schedules and Bills of Quantities.

Execution of the Sub-Contract Works

2. The Sub-Contractor shall execute and complete the Sub-Contract Work subject to and in accordance with this Sub-Contract in all respects to the reasonable satisfaction of the Contractor and of the Architect/Engineer for the time being under the Main Contract (hereinafter called "the Architect/Engineer") and in conformity with the reasonable directions and requirements of the Contractor which shall be a programme agreed between the Contractor and the Sub-Contractor and approved by the Architect/Engineer, who in the case of default in carrying out the programme may himself direct the order in which the Sub-Contract Work shall be carried out.

Sub-Contractor's liability under incorporated Provisions of the Main Contract

3. The Sub-Contractor agrees:

   (a) To observe, perform and comply with all the provisions of the Main Contract on the part of the Contractor, to be observed, performed and complied with so far as they relate and apply to the Sub-Contract Works (or any portion of the same) and are not repugnant to or inconsistent with the express provisions of this Sub-Contract as if all the same were severally set out herein; and

(b) Subject to Clause 4 (b) (ii) to indemnify and save harmless the Contractor against and from:—

    (i) any claim, breach or non-observance or non-performance of the said provisions of the Main Contract or any of them due to any act, neglect or the default on the part of the Sub-Contractor only; and

    (ii) any act or omission of the Sub-Contractor, his servants or agents which involves the Contractor in any liability to the Employer under the Main Contract; and

    (iii) any damage, loss or expense due to or resulting from any negligence or breach of duty on the part of the Sub-Contractor, his servants or agents (inclusively of any wrongful use by him or them of the Contractor's property); and

    (iv) any claim by an employee of the Sub-Contractor under the Employers' Liability Acts or other Acts of the Oireachtas of a like nature, respectively, in force for the time being.

PROVIDED that nothing in the Sub-Contract contained shall impose any liability on the Sub-Contractor in respect of any negligence or breach of duty on the part of the Employer, the Contractor, his other Sub-Contractors or their respective servants or agents nor create any privity of contract between the Sub-Contractor and the Employer or any other Sub-Contractor.

Insurance by the Parties for Damage to Persons and to Property

4. (a) The Contractor shall take out before commencing the Works and maintain Public Liability and Employer's Liability Policies of Insurance in accordance with the Main Contract.

(b) The Sub-Contractor shall take out before commencing the Sub-Contract Works and maintain Public Liability and Employer's Liability Policies of Insurance as follows:—

    (i) The policies shall cover the Sub-Contractor's liability by statute and at common law and liability to indemnify the Contractor under Clause 3 of this Sub-Contract in each case against any liability, loss, claim or proceeding in respect of injury, death or disease of any person, and (subject to Clause 5) injury or damage to property arising out of or in the course of or by reason of the execution of the Sub-Contract Works.

    (ii) The Sub-Contractor may include in his policies under this clause the exclusions permitted by Clause 23 (e) para. (i) or (ii) (as relevant) of the R.I.A.I. Conditions. Without prejudice to the Sub-Contractor's liability at common law or by statute the Sub-Contractor shall not be bound to indemnify the Contractor under Clause 3 in respect of any liability, loss, claim or proceedings for injury, death, disease of any person or damage to property which arises otherwise than in connection with an accident or which is within a permitted exclusion and is not covered by an Employer's Liability or Public Liability Insurance Policy of the Sub-Contractor.

    (iii) The Public Liability Policy of the Sub-Contractor shall be for a sum not less than the sum stated in Part II of the Appendix to this Sub-Contract.

    (iv) The Sub-Contractor's policies under this clause shall be with insurers approved by the Contractor, which approval shall not be unreasonably withheld, and shall include provisions by which in the event of any claim in respect of which the Sub-Contractor would be entitled to receive indemnity under the policy being brought or made against the Contractor the insurers will indemnify the Contractor against such claims and any costs, charges and expenses in respect thereof.

All Risks Insurance

5. (a) In this Clause "Sub-Contract Ancillary Items" shall mean temporary works and all unfixed materials and goods delivered to and placed on or adjacent to and intended for the Sub-Contract Works except temporary buildings, plant, tools or equipment owned or hired by the Sub-Contractor or any Sub-Contractor of his.

(b) Subject to sub-clauses (c), (d) and (e) the Contractor shall for the benefit of himself and the Sub-Contractor keep in force in accordance with the requirements of the Main Contract an All Risks Policy of insurance covering the Works and Ancillary Items (including the Sub-Contract Works and the Sub-Contract Ancillary Items) which shall as regards loss or damage from any cause whatsoever be at the sole risk of the Contractor.

(c) In the case of any loss or damage to the Sub-Contract Works or Sub-Contract Ancillary Items falling within an exclusion permitted by Clause 23 (e) (iii) of the R.I.A.I. Conditions and included in the Contractor's All Risks Policy of Insurance then (without prejudice to any liability of the Sub-Contractor for negligence, omission or default and subject to sub-clause (d) of this Clause) the occurrence of such loss or damage shall be disregarded in computing any amounts payable to the Sub-Contractor and the reinstatement and making good of such loss or damage and (when required) removal and disposal of debris shall be deemed to be a variation ordered under Clause 6.

(d) In the case of any loss or damage to the Sub-Contract Works or Sub-Contract Ancillary Items due to any fault, or omission in design by the Sub-Contractor, his servants or agents (including his sub-contractors and suppliers, other than nominated sub-contractors or nominated suppliers) the Sub-Contractor shall proceed with due diligence to repair or make good the same at his own expense.

(e) Until not less than 80% of the contract value of the item is included in the amount of a certificate under the Main Contract and the item is fixed to the Main Contract Works the Sub-Contractor shall be liable for making good loss or damage due to theft or misappropriation of any Sub-Contract Ancillary Item (whether or not the theft or misappropriation is due to the negligence or default of the Contractor, his servants or agents). However, if the Contractor is in breach of Clause 16 of this Sub-Contract the Sub-Contractor may give written notice to the Contractor specifying the breach and seven days thereafter the Contractor shall become liable for theft or misappropriation of any Sub-Contract Ancillary Items until the breach is remedied and the Sub-Contractor is notified in writing.

(f) If the Main Contract is validly determined under Clause 24 (b) of the R.I.A.I. Conditions the Contractor may determine the Sub-Contract by written notice to the Sub-Contractor. The provisions of Clause 24 (b) of the Main Contract as to payment shall then apply mutatis mutandis to payment to the Sub-Contractor.

(g) The Sub-Contractor shall observe and comply with the conditions contained in the Contractor's policy of insurance under this Clause so far as compliance is within the control of the Sub-Contractor. The Sub-Contractor shall be entitled to inspect the Contractor's policy.

(h) The Sub-Contractor shall notify the Contractor by means of a notice in writing of at least 10 working days before commencing any operation that would constitute an abnormal hazard in building operations and that in the absence of notice to and acceptance by insurers renders void or voidable any of the policies of insurance under Clauses 4 or 5. The Sub-Contractor shall be liable for any additional insurance costs of the Contractor, or for which the Contractor is liable to the Employer due to any such operation, and if due to any such operation insurers will not accept any risk which the Contractor is required to insure the risk shall be insured by the Sub-Contractor at his own cost.

(i) The Sub-Contract shall be entitled to the benefit of Clauses 26 & 32 (b) of the R.I.A.I. Conditions. The Contractor shall ensure that the Employer under the Main Contract complies with those clauses where applicable.

Variations etc

6. In the event of the Contractor:—

(a) requiring or authorising in writing any variations of or omissions from the Sub-Contract Works; or

(b) Issuing in writing to the Sub-Contractor any instructions of the Architect/ Engineer in relation to the Sub-Contract Works (whether in regard to variations or otherwise howsoever); or

(c) issuing to the Sub-Contractor or his agent any verbal instructions or directions involving a variation, such instructions shall be confirmed in writing by the Sub-Contractor to the Contractor within five days and if not dissented from in writing by the Contractor to the Sub-Contractor within a further five days, shall be deemed to be a variation of the Sub-Contract Works;

then the Sub-Contractor shall forthwith comply with and carry out the same in all respects accordingly.

PROVIDED that if compliance with such instructions or directions involves the Sub-Contractor in loss or expense beyond that provided for in or reasonably contemplated by this Sub-Contract, then the Sub-Contractor shall forthwith notify the Contractor and the amount of such loss or expense shall be ascertained and added to the Contract Sum. Where a variation by way of omission is, as compared with the works included in the Sub-Contract in a character so extensive that in the opinion of the Architect the Sub-Contractor has sustained a loss by reason of, prior to the notification to him of such variation, having properly incurred expenses which in consequence of the variation have become wholly or in part unnecessary, there shall be added to the Sub-Contract Sum a sum to be ascertained by the Architect as being in all circumstances reasonable compensation for such loss.

If through variation and/or omission the final measurement shows a credit on the Sub-Contract Sum the Sub-Contractor shall be entitled, if agreed by the Architect, to an allowance of 10% on this credit. P.C. Sums, Provisional Sums, Provisional Works and Contingency Sums and the amount of any adjustment under Clause 24 of this Sub-Contract are not to be taken into account in arriving at the credit on which this allowance is based.

Save as aforesaid no variation of or omission from or other alteration or modification of the Sub-Contract shall be made or allowed by the Sub-Contractor.

Completion

7. (a) The Sub-Contractor shall commence the Sub-Contract works within a reasonable period of time after the receipt by him of an order in writing under this Sub-Contract from the Contractor to that effect and shall proceed with the same with due expedition.

The Sub-Contractor shall progress and complete the Sub-Contract Works and each section thereof within the period specified in Part III of the Appendix to this Sub-Contract.

If the Sub-Contractor fails to progress or complete the Sub-Contract works or any section thereof within the period specified or any extended period as hereinafter provided, he shall pay to the Contractor any loss or damage suffered or incurred by the Contractor and caused by the failure of the Sub-Contractor as aforesaid of which loss or damage the Contractor shall at the earliest opportunity give reasonable notice to the Sub-Contractor that the same is being or has been suffered or incurred.

(b) If the completion of the Sub-Contract Works or any section thereof be delayed and such delay

(i) shall be caused by or be due to any of the matters specified in Clauses 6 (a), (b) or (c) of this Sub-Contract or by or to any act or omission of the Contractor, his other Sub-Contractors, his or their respective servants or agents; or

(ii) shall be within any of the cases in which the Contractor could obtain an extension of the period or periods for completion under the Main Contract: (See NOTE).

then the Sub-Contractor shall immediately give notice thereof in writing to the Contractor and the Contractor shall grant or (where the Contractor has to apply to the Architect) he shall apply for a fair and reasonable extension of the said period or periods for completion of the Sub-Contract Works or each section thereof (as the case may require) and such extended period or periods shall be the period or periods for completion of the same respectively and this clause shall be read and construed accordingly.

If the Sub-Contractor be delayed in the commencement or completion of the Sub-Contract Works due to circumstances beyond his control he shall so inform the Contractor and he shall then be entitled to make a claim for any loss or damage incurred to the same extent as the main Contractor is entitled under the main Contract form.

NOTE:- Users of this Form of Sub-Contract should ascertain the provisions relating to Delay and Extension of Time contained in the Main Contract whatever its form. These provisions will, under Clause 7 (b) (ii), insure to the benefit of the parties to the Sub-Contract.

In the R.I.A.I. Standard Form of Contract these provisions are set out in Clause 30.

Defects

8. The Sub-Contractor shall within a reasonable time after receipt by him from the Contractor of the Architect's/Engineer's or agent's instructions or a copy thereof relating to the same, make good all defects, shrinkages or other faults in the Sub-Contract Works, due to faulty materials or bad workmanship which the Contractor (whether at his own cost or not) shall be liable to make good under the Main Contract.

PROVIDED that where the Contractor is liable to make good such defects, shrinkages or other faults, but not at his own cost, then the Contractor shall secure a similar benefit to the Sub-Contractor and shall account to the Sub-Contractor for any money actually received by him in respect of same.

Consequential damage to the Contractor

9. (a) If the Contractor (whether by himself or any other Sub-Contractor) shall execute any work (whether permanent or temporary) to the Main Contract Works or to any part of the same required by the Architect/Engineer or rendered necessary by reason of defects, shrinkages or other faults in the Sub-Contract Works due to materials or workmanship not being in accordance with this Sub-Contract or to frost occurring during, but before the completion of the Sub-Contract Works, then the Sub-Contractor shall pay to the Contractor the cost of the execution of such work.

PROVIDED that if the Contractor shall pay or allow to the Employer the value of, or other agreed sum (not exceeding such cost as aforesaid) in respect of, such work instead and in satisfaction of executing the same, then the Sub-Contractor shall pay to the Contractor such value or other agreed sum as aforesaid.

PROVIDED also that the Sub-Contractor shall not be required to pay the cost of any works to make good damage by frost which may appear after completion unless the Architect shall decide that such damage is due to injury which occurred before completion or of which the Contractor before commencing the same has not given reasonable notice to the Sub-Contractor.

Consequential damage to the Sub-Contractor

(b) If the Sub-Contractor shall execute any work to or in connection with the Sub-Contract Works (whether permanent or temporary) required by the Architect/Engineer or rendered necessary by reason of any defects, shrinkages or other faults in the Main Contract Works due to materials or workmanship not being in accordance with the Main Contract or to frost occurring before the completion of the Main Contract Works, then the Contractor shall pay to the Sub-Contractor the cost of the execution of such work provided that nothing contained in this Sub-Clause shall exclude the liability of the Sub-Contractor under Sub-Section (a) above.

PROVIDED that if instead of the Sub-Contractor actually executing such work and in satisfaction of the same the Contractor shall pay or allow to the Employer the value of, or other agreed sum (not exceeding such cost as aforesaid) in respect of, such work, then the Contractor shall indemnify the Sub-Contractor against any claim, damage or loss in respect of failure to execute such work.

PROVIDED also that the Contractor shall not be required to pay the cost of any work to make good damage by frost which may appear after completion unless the Architect/Engineer shall decide that such damage was due to injury which took place before completion or of which the Sub-Contractor before commencing the same has not given reasonable notice to the Contractor.

Sub-Contract Sum — Valuation of Variations

10. The price of the Sub-Contract Works (herein referred to as "the Sub-Contract Sum") shall be the sum named in Part IV or determined by the provisions of Part V of the Appendix to this Sub-Contract or such other sums as shall become payable by reason of any authorised variations. The value of all authorised variations shall be determined by the Surveyor for the time being under the Main Contract (or if none the Architect/Engineer) in accordance with the applicable provisions (relating to the ascertainment of prices for authorised variations) laid down in the Agreement and Schedule of Conditions of Building Contract currently issued under the sanction of the Royal Institute of the Architects of Ireland in agreement with the Construction Industry Federation; save that where the Sub-Contractor has with the agreement of the Contractor annexed to this Sub-Contract a

schedule of prices for measured work and/or a schedule of daywork prices, such prices shall be allowed to the Sub-Contractor in determining the value of authorised variations in substitution for any prices which would otherwise be applicable under this clause. (See NOTE).

NOTE – The Sub-Contractor should ascertain whether the Bills of Quantities (if any) prepared in connection with the Main Contract have been prepared in accordance with the principles of the Standard Method of Measurement of Building Works applicable to work in Ireland last before approved by the Royal Institution of Chartered Surveyors (Republic of Ireland Branch) and the Construction Industry Federation.

Contractor to
apply for
Certificates of
Payment

11. (a) The Contractor shall, subject to and in accordance with the Main Contract, from time to time and in any event, unless otherwise agreed, not later than 30 days after receipt of the Sub-Contractor's detailed progress statement make application (of which prior thereto the Contractor shall give to the Sub-Contractor at least seven days' notice unless otherwise agreed between the Contractor and the Sub-Contractor) to the Architect for Certificates of Payment and for inclusion therein of the amount which at the date thereof fairly represents the value of the Sub-Contract Works and any variations authorised under this Sub-Contract then executed and of the materials and goods delivered upon the site for use in the Sub-Contract Works.

PROVIDED that the application shall include only the value of the said materials and goods as and from such time as they are reasonably properly and not prematurely brought upon the site and then only if adequately stored and/or protected against weather and casualties.

The Contractor shall also embody in or annex to the said application any representations of the Sub-Contractor in regard to such value.

Interim Payments
to the
Sub-Contractor —
Retention Money

(b) Fourteen days after the receipt by the Contractor of any Certificate from the Architect/Engineer the amounts certified therein to be due in respect of the Sub-Contract Works shall be due by the Contractor to the Sub-Contractor, and the Contractor shall within said time notify in writing to the Sub-Contractor the amount certified in the said Certificate to be due to him, any authorised variations thereof less Retention Money, which shall mean in this Contract the proportion attributable to the Sub-Contract Works of the money retained by the Employer in accordance with the Main Contract and less a cash discount of 5% (if payment is made within seven days after the Contractor himself is paid and if provision is made in the main Contract for the allowance of such discount to the Contractor) provided always that the Sub-Contractor shall not take steps to enforce payment of such sum until the expiration of such period of seven days after the Contractor has received payment of such Certificate unless:—

    (i) the Contractor being a person or firm commits an act of Bankruptcy or being a company enters into liquidation whether compulsory or voluntary (except liquidation for the purpose of reconstruction), or—

    (ii) a Receiver has been appointed over the business or undertaking of the Contractor, or—

    (iii) a judgement has been obtained and registered against the Contractor or execution, whether legal or equitable, has been levied on the property of the Contractor, or—

    (iv) the Contractor has suspended work on the Main Contract or left the State, or—

    (v) the Contractor has not received payment of any Certificate within twenty-eight days of the date of its issue.

In the event that the Contractor considers that the Sub-Contractor is invoking this section inequitably, the Contractor may refer the matter to the President for the time being of the Construction Industry Federation who shall nominate a person to arbitrate on the matter. The arbitration award shall be issued within 10 working days from receipt of the complaint of the contractor and shall be deemed to be a submission to arbitration within the meaning of the Arbitration Act 1954 (number 26 of 1954) or the Arbitration Act (Northern Ireland) 1957 (as the case may be) or any act amending the same or either of them. Due to the time constraint for the arbitration process, it is agreed that there will be no legal representation.

This sub-clause (v) shall not apply in the event that the employer commits an act of bankruptcy or being a company enters into liquidation whether compulsory or voluntary (except liquidation for the purpose of reconstruction).

Contractor to furnish details of Certificates

(c) If the Contractor shall fail to notify the Sub-Contractor in accordance with the provisions of the foregoing sub-clause (b) then the Contractor shall on demand to him by the Sub-Contractor furnish to the Sub-Contractor details of all monies certified for the Sub-Contractor by the Architect/Engineer. If the Contractor shall not furnish such details within four days after such demand, the Sub-Contractor shall be entitled to obtain these from the Architect/Engineer.

Payments to Contractor in Trust for Sub-Contractor

(d) Payments made to the Contractor in respect of work done and materials used by the Sub-Contractor shall until received by the Sub-Contractor be deemed to be money or moneys worth held in trust but without obligation to invest by the Contractor for the Sub-Contractor to be applied in or towards payment of the Sub-Contractor's account, subject always to the right of adjustment by the Architect/Engineer in the event of his certifying that adjustment is necessary.

Non-Payment by Contractor

(e) (1) If the Contractor does not pay to the Sub-Contractor the amounts certified by any Certificate issued by the Architect/Engineer to be due to the Sub-Contractor within the period mentioned in sub-clause (b) hereof, then the Sub-Contractor—

(i) may (but without prejudice to any other right or remedy) apply directly to the Employer for and the Employer may make payment of the amounts certified to be due to the Sub-Contractor direct to the Sub-Contractor and the Employer may set off the amount of any payment or payments made by him to the Sub-Contractor against any moneys due or to become due to the Contractor.

Payment by the Employer to the Sub-Contractor direct shall be regarded as payment by the Contractor to the Sub-Contractor and shall annul the right of suspension under sub-paragraph (ii) of this paragraph (1), or

(ii) may, if payment has not been received within seven days after receipt of payment by the Contractor or within twenty-eight days of the date of issue of the Architect's/Engineer's Certificate covering the amount due in respect of the Sub-Contract Works, after seven days' notice to the Contractor, suspend the works for a period of fourteen days and upon the expiry of this period, unless payment shall have been made in the meantime by the Contractor or by the Employer direct, may determine the Sub-Contractor's employment under this Sub-Contract as from the date of such expiry.

When work is suspended under this provision, the time for completion shall be extended by two days for each day of such suspension which shall not be deemed a delay for which the Sub-Contractor is liable under this Sub-Contract, or

(iii) may, without prejudice to other rights or remedies after 28 days from the date of the issue of the Certificate by the Architect/Engineer to the Contractor covering the amount due in respect of the Sub-Contract Works, be entitled to charge interest to the Contractor on the amount included in such Certificate at current bank rate of interest on over-drafts until such time as payment is made by the Contractor, or by the Employer under sub-paragraph (i) of this paragraph (1).

Dispute as to Certificate

(f) If the Sub-Contractor shall feel aggrieved by the amount certified by the Architect/Engineer or by his failure to certify or failure by the Employer to honour his certificate in whole or in part within the time period stipulated in the main contract document, then, subject to the Sub-Contractor giving to the Contractor such indemnity and security as the Contractor shall reasonably require, the Contractor shall allow the Sub-Contractor to use the Contractor's name and if necessary will join the Sub-Contractor as claimant in any legal proceedings by the Sub-Contractor in respect of the said matters complained of by the Sub-Contractor. (See NOTE).

NOTE– Arbitration under this Sub-Clause would be governed by the provisions with regard to arbitration contained in the Main Contract. The Sub-Clause should be struck out when the Sub-Contractor is not nominated or selected by the Architect under the Main Contract.

Special
Interim
Payment

(g) If before the issue of a Final Certificate to the Contractor under the Main Contract a period of time equal to the Retention Period of the Main Contract has elapsed since practical completion of the Sub-Contract Works the subject of this Agreement then the Sub-Contractor may request the Contractor in writing to make application to the Architect/Engineer for Certificates certifying the value of the work executed upon the Sub-Contract Works, and the Contractor shall make such application. The provisions of this clause shall apply to such Certificates as if they were Certificates of Payment expressly provided for in the Main Contract.

Final Payment
to Sub-
Contractor

(h) If before the issue of a Final Certificate to the Contractor under the Main Contract the Architect/Engineer desires to secure final payment to the Sub-Contractor on completion of the Sub-Contract Works and in accordance with and subject to the provisions of the Main Contract relating to Prime Costs and Provisional Sums issues a Certificate to the Contractor including an amount to cover such final payment, then the Contractor shall on receipt of payment from the Employer pay to the Sub-Contractor the amount so certified by the Architect/Engineer as aforesaid, but such payment shall be made only if the Sub-Contractor indemnifies and secures the Contractor to the reasonable satisfaction of the Contractor against all latent defects in the Sub-Contract Works and if by such final payment the Contractor will be discharged under the Main Contract from all liabilities in respect of the Sub-Contract Works except for any latent defects.

(i) If and to the extent that the amount retained by the Employer in accordance with the Main Contract includes any Retention Money the Contractor's interest in such money shall be fiduciary as trustee without obligation to invest for the Sub-Contractor and if the Contractor attempts or purports to mortgage or otherwise charge such interest or his interest in the whole of the amount retained as aforesaid such mortgage or charge shall in so far as it relates to the Retention Money be void.

Sub-Contractor's
claim to
Rights and
Benefits of
Main Contract

12. The Contractor (so far as he lawfully can) will, at the request and cost of the Sub-Contractor, obtain for him any rights or benefits of the Main Contract so far as the same are applicable to the Sub-Contract Works, but not further or otherwise.

Contractor's
right to
Deduction
or Set Off

13. (1) The Contractor shall be entitled to deduct from any money (including any retention money) otherwise due under this sub-Contract any amount agreed by the Sub-Contractor as due to the Contractor, or finally awarded in arbitration or litigation in favour of the Contractor, and which arises out of or under this Sub-Contract.

(2) The Contractor shall be entitled to set-off against any money (including any retention money) otherwise due under this Sub-Contract the amount of any claim for loss and/or expense which has actually been incurred by the Contractor by reason of any breach of, or failure to observe the provisions of, this Sub-Contract by the Sub-Contractor, provided:-

(a) the amount of such set-off has been quantified in detail and with reasonable accuracy by the Contractor; and

(b) the Contractor has given to the Sub-Contractor notice in writing specifying his intention to set-off the amount quantified in accordance with proviso (a) of this sub-clause and the grounds on which such set-off is claimed to be made. Such notice shall be given not less than seventeen days before the money from which the amount is to be set-off becomes due and payable to the Sub-Contractor; provided that such written notice shall not be binding insofar as the Contractor may amend it in preparing his pleadings for any Arbitration pursuant to the notice of arbitration. The form of arbitration shall be as set out in Clause 11 (b) (v).

(3) Any amount set-off under the provisions of sub-clause (2) hereof is without prejudice to the rights of the Contractor or Sub-Contractor in any subsequent negotiations, arbitration proceedings or litigation to seek to vary the amount claimed and set-off by the Contractor under sub-clause (2) hereof, save where the issue has already been settled by arbitration in the form as set out in Clause 11 (b) (v).

(4) The rights of the parties to this Sub-Contract in respect of set-off are fully set out in these Conditions and no other rights whatsoever shall be implied as terms of this Sub-Contract relating to set-off.

Right of Access of Contractor and Architect/ Engineer

14. The Contractor and the Architect/Engineer or his Agent (and all persons duly authorised by them or either of them) shall at all reasonable times have access to any work which is being prepared for or will be utilised in the Sub-Contract Works, unless the Architect/Engineer shall certify in writing that the Sub-Contractor has reasonable grounds for refusing such access.

Sub-letting of Sub-Contract Works

15. The Sub-Contractor shall not assign this Sub-Contract nor sub-let the Sub-Contract Works or any portion of the same without the written consent of both the Contractor and the Architect/Engineer provided that the consent of the Contractor shall not be unreasonably withheld, and that in case of any difference of opinion between the Contractor and the Architect/Engineer the opinion of the Architect/Engineer shall prevail.

Provision of Water etc. and Temporary Works, etc. for Sub-Contract Works

16. (a) If and so far as provided in the Main Contract (but not otherwise) the Contractor shall supply at his own costs all necessary water, lighting, watching and attendance for the purposes of the Sub-Contract Works. Subject as aforesaid, the Sub-Contractor shall make all necessary provision in regard to the said matters and each of them.

(b) If and so far as provided by the Main Contract (but not otherwise) the Contractor shall provide all reasonable facilities to the Sub-Contractor for such workshop and storage accommodation as may be reasonably required.

Sub-Contractor's User of Contractor's Scaffolding

17. The Sub-Contractor, his employees and workmen in common with all other persons having the like right shall for the purposes of the Sub-Contract Works (but not further or otherwise) be entitled to use any scaffolding belonging to or provided by the Contractor, while it remains so erected upon the site.

PROVIDED that such other user as aforesaid shall be on the express condition that no warranty or other liability on the part of the Contractor or of his other sub-contractors shall be created or implied in regard to the fitness, condition or suitability of the said scaffolding.

Contractor and Sub-Contractor not to make Wrongful User of or interference with the property of the other

18. Save as hereinbefore expressly provided, the Contractor and the Sub-Contractor respectively, their respective servants or agents shall not make any wrongful user of or interfere with the plant, ways, scaffolding, temporary works, appliances or other property, respectively, belonging to or provided by the other of them or be guilty of any act or omission which shall constitute a breach or infringement of any statute or of any legally binding bye-law, regulation, order or rule made under the same or by any local or other public or competent authority.

PROVIDED that nothing herein contained shall prejudice or limit the rights of the Contractor or the Sub-Contractor in the carrying out of their respective statutory duties or contractual duties hereunder or under the Main Contract.

Plant, etc. of Sub-Contractor to be at his sole risk

19. The plant, tools, equipment, or other property belonging to or provided by the Sub-Contractor, his servants or agents (other than materials and goods properly on the site for use in the Sub-Contract Works) shall be at the sole risk of the Sub-Contractor, and any loss or damage to the same or caused by the same shall be the sole liability of the Sub-Contractor who shall indemnify the Contractor against any loss, claim or proceedings in respect thereof. Any insurance against any such loss or claim shall be the sole concern of the Sub-Contractor.

Determination by Contractor

20. (a) DEFAULT

If the Sub-Contractor shall make default in any of the following respects, viz.:

(1) without reasonable cause shall wholly suspend the works before completion, otherwise than in accordance with Clause 11 (e) hereof;

(2) shall fail to proceed with the works with reasonable diligence;

(3) refuses or persistently neglects after notice in writing from the Contractor to remove defective work or improper materials;

then if such default shall continue for fourteen days after a written notice to the Sub-Contractor from the Contractor specifying the same served on the Sub-Contractor personally or by registered post, the Contractor may (without prejudice to any other rights herein contained) thereupon by written notice served on the Sub-Contractor personally or by registered post, determine the employment of the Sub-Contractor.

PROVIDED that notice hereunder shall not be given unreasonably or vexatiously and such notice shall be void if the Contractor is at the time of the notice in breach of this Contract.

After such first mentioned notice shall have been given, the Sub-Contractor shall not be at liberty to remove from the site or works, or from any ground contiguous thereto, any plant or materials belonging to him which shall have been placed thereon for the purposes of the works; and the Contractor shall have a lien upon all such plant and materials, to subsist from the date of such notice being given until the notice shall have been complied with.

PROVIDED always that such lien shall not, under any circumstances, subsist after the expiration of thirty-one days from the date of such notice being given, unless the Contractor shall have entered upon and taken possession of the works.

(b) BANKRUPTCY OF SUB-CONTRACTOR

If the Sub-Contractor commits an act of Bankruptcy or being a company enters into liquidation whether compulsory or voluntary (except liquidation for the purpose of reconstruction) or a Receiver is appointed in respect of the Company", or has suspended work on the Sub-Contract or left the State, the Contractor without prejudice to any other rights herein contained may send by registered post to the Sub-Contractor a written notice determining the employment of the Sub-Contractor under this Contract.

In either of the above cases (a) or (b) the following shall apply:-

(1) the Contractor may employ and pay a Sub-Contractor or other person or persons to carry out and complete the works and he or they may enter upon the site and use all materials, temporary buildings, plant and appliances thereon, and may purchase all materials necessary for the purposes aforesaid;

(2) the Sub-Contractor shall if so required by the Contractor or Architect/ Engineer assign to the Contractor without further payment the benefit of any contract for the supply of materials and/or works intended for use under this Sub-Contract or for the execution of any works, and the Contractor shall pay the agreed price (if unpaid) for such materials or works supplied or executed after the said determination;

(3) the Sub-Contractor shall during the execution or after completion of the works under this clause, as and when required, remove from the site his temporary buildings, plant, appliances, and any materials within such reasonable time as the Contractor may specify in a written notice to him, and in default the Contractor may (without being responsible for loss or damage) remove and sell the same, holding the proceeds less all costs incurred to the credit of the Sub-Contractor;

(4) until after completion of the works under this clause no payment shall be made to the Sub-Contractor under this contract, provided that upon completion as aforesaid and the verification within a reasonable time of the accounts therefor the Architect/Engineer shall certify the amount of expenses properly incurred by the Contractor, and if such amount added to the moneys paid to the Sub-Contractor before such determination exceeds the total amount which would have been payable on due completion, the difference shall be a debt payable to the Contractor by the Sub-Contractor; and if the said amount added to the said moneys be less than the said total amount, the differences shall be a debt payable to the Sub-Contractor by the Contractor.

Determination
by
Sub-Contractor

(c) If—

(i) the Contractor being a person or firm commits an act of Bankruptcy or being a company enters into liquidation whether compulsory or voluntary (except liquidation for the purpose of reconstruction) or—

(ii) a Receiver has been appointed over the business or undertaking of the Contractor or—

    (iii) a judgement has been obtained and registered against the Contractor or execution, whether legal or equitable, has been levied on the property of the Contractor, or—

    (iv) the Contractor has suspended work on the Main Contract or Sub-Contract, or has unreasonably delayed the commencement of the Sub-Contract or left the State, then the Sub-Contractor may by written notice sent by registered post to the last known address of the Contractor or served personally on the Contractor determine the employment of the Sub-Contractor under this Sub-Contract from the date of such notice.

Procedure after Determination

(d) Upon such determination under the foregoing sub-clause (e) then without prejudice to the accrued rights of either party their respective rights and liabilities shall be as follows:—

the Sub-Contractor shall thereupon with all reasonable despatch and in such manner and with such precautions as will prevent injury or damage to persons or property, remove from the site all his temporary buildings, plant and machinery, appliances, goods and materials but subject always to the provisions of paragraph (iii) hereunder.

The Sub-Contractor shall thereupon be paid by the Contractor:—

    (i) the value of the Sub-Contract Works completed at the date of such determination such value to be determined by the Architect/Engineer at the request of the Sub-Contractor in accordance with Clause 10 and the Architect/Engineer shall give credit for the amounts already paid to the Sub-Contractor;

    (ii) the value of the Sub-Contract Works commenced and executed but not completed at the date of such determination such value to be determined by the Architect/Engineer at the request of the Sub-Contractor in accordance with Clause 10;

    (iii) the cost of materials or goods properly ordered for the Sub-Contract Works for which the Sub-Contractor shall have paid or of which the Sub-Contractor is legally bound to accept delivery and such cost shall be determined by the Architect/Engineer at the request of the Sub-Contractor and on payment for the same to the Sub-Contractor any materials or goods so paid for shall become the property of the Contractor;

    (iv) the reasonable cost of the removal of the temporary buildings, plant, machinery, appliances, goods and materials, such reasonable cost to be determined by the Architect/Engineer;

    (v) such loss or damage sustained by the Sub-Contractor and caused by such determination as the Architect/Engineer may consider reasonable and the amount whereof shall be certified by him.

PROVIDED that in addition to all other remedies the Sub-Contractor may upon such determination take possession of and have a lien upon all materials and goods ordered for the Sub-Contract Works which shall not have been fixed to the Main Contract Works until payment of all moneys due to the Sub-Contractor by the Contractor.

Determination of Main Contract

21. If for any reason the employment of the Contractor under the Main Contract is determined (whether by the Contractor or by the Employer) and whether by reason of—

    (a) any act, neglect or default of the Contract, or

    (b) the Contractor being a person or firm commits an act of Bankruptcy or being a company enters into liquidation whether compulsory or voluntary (except liquidation for the purpose of reconstruction), or

    (c) a Receiver being appointed over the business or undertaking of the Contractor, or

    (d) a Judgement being obtained and registered against him or execution whether legal or equitable being levied on his property, or

    (e) his suspending work on the Main Contract or leaving the State, then the employment of the Sub-Contractor under this Sub-Contract shall automatically determine and the Sub-Contractor shall be entitled to be paid by the Employer directly such sums as he would have been entitled to be paid by the Contractor under Clause 11 sub-clause (f) hereof had his employment under this Sub-Contract been determined under Clause 11 sub-clause (e) hereof.

Construction of Sub-Contract in relation to Main Contract

22.   Nothing in this Sub-Contract contained shall be deemed to limit or prejudice the right of the Contractor to determine the Main Contract subject to and in accordance with the terms of the same or to limit or prejudice the right of the Contractor (save as in this Sub-Contract expressly provided) to execute and carry out the Main Contract Works in accordance with its terms and the exercise of any such rights or of such right of determination of his employment by the Contractor as aforesaid shall not be or be deemed to be a breach by the Contractor of this Sub-Contract, and in the event of the Contractor determining his employment under the Main Contract as aforesaid, then the employment of the Sub-Contractor under this Sub-Contract shall thereupon also determine without right or claim on the part of the Sub-Contractor to damages or for loss or expense or otherwise but the Sub-Contractor shall be entitled to be paid by the Contractor the Value of the Sub-Contract Works and any authorised variations thereof and/or parts thereof actually executed by the Sub-Contractor and not paid for at the date of such determination, such value to be calculated in accordance with Clause 10 hereof.

Save as aforesaid, in the event of the provisions of the Main Contract (so far as they are applicable to the Sub-Contract Works) being repugnant to or inconsistent with this Sub-Contract, the provisions of this Sub-Contract shall prevail and this Sub-Contract shall be read and construed accordingly.

Wages and Conditions of Employment

23.   (a)   PROVIDED always that this Sub-Contract is upon this express condition that during its continuance the wages and conditions of employment of the employees of the Contractor and Sub-Contractor respectively engaged on the Main Countract Works and the Sub-Contract Works shall be such as may from time to time be prescribed by competent authority in the industry or trade to which such employees belong, and the Contractor observe the same accordingly.

PROVIDED that in default of such wages and/or conditions of employment being prescribed as aforesaid, the Contractor and Sub-Contractor as a condition of this Sub-Contract shall pay such wages and/or observe such conditions of employment as may be generally from time to time prevailing in industries or trades of a similar or comparable nature in the districts in which their said respective employees are engaged.

(b)   If either party shall commit a breach of this clause, then the other party shall be entitled (without prejudice to any other right or remedy) to be indemnified by the party so in breach against any loss or damage accruing from or arising out of or connected with such breach.

Variations arising from Legislative enactments

24.   Where after the Designated Date the cost of the performance of this Sub-Contract has been increased or decreased as the result of any legislative enactments, instruments, rules or orders or the exercise by the Government of powers vested in it, whether by way of the imposition of new duties or tariffs or the alteration of existing duties or tariffs, or restriction of licences for the importation of any commodity, or by way of affecting the cost of labour, or otherwise, the amount of such increase or decrease as certified by the Architect shall be borne by or shall accrue to the Contractor, as the case may be, and the Sub-Contract sum shall be varied accordingly.

Wage and Price Variation

25.   The Sub-Contract Sum shall be deemed to have been calculated in the manner set out below and shall be subject to adjustment in the events specified hereunder.

(1)   (a)   The Sub-Contract Sum is based upon the rate of wages and other emoluments and expenses (including the cost of insurances or other premiums dependent thereon) payable by the Sub-Contractor to work people engaged upon or in connection with the Sub-Contract Works in accordance with any rules or decisions of the recognised wage fixing body of the trade concerned applicable to the Sub-Contract Work and current at the Designated Date. In this clause wages, emoluments and expenses of work people engaged upon or in connection with the Works include wages, emoluments and expenses of only such members of the Sub-Contractor's administrative and supervisory staff who individually spend more than 15 hours from Monday to Friday of any week on the site of the Works and only in respect of or attributable to such a week or such weeks so spent.

(b) In the said rates of wages and other emoluments and expenses (including) the cost of insurance or other premiums dependent thereon) shall be increased or decreased by reason of any alteration in any such rules or decisions made after the said Designated Date, the amount of such increase or decrease of such rates of wages, other emoluments and expenses (including the cost of insurance or other premiums dependent thereon) together with the percentage addition specified in Sub-Clause (4) of this Clause on any increase shall be an addition to or a deduction from the Sub-Contract Sum as the case may be and shall be paid to or allowed by the Sub-Contractor accordingly.

(2) (a) The value of the Sub-Contract Works is based on the market prices of materials and goods current at the Designated Date and the Sub-Contractor shall, if required, submit to the Contractor a list of basic prices of such materials and goods.

(b) If after the Designated Date the market price of any of the materials or goods specified as aforesaid varies from the basic price thereof, then the difference between the basic price and the market price payable by the Sub-Contractor and current when any such goods or materials are bought together with the percentage addition specified in Sub-Clause (4) of this Clause on any increase in price shall be an addition to or a deduction from the Sub-Contract sum as the case may be and shall be paid to or allowed by the Sub-Contractor accordingly.

(3) (a) If the Sub-contractor shall decide subject to Clause 15 of this Sub-Contract to sub-let any portion of the Sub-Contract Works he shall incorporate in any such agreement for sub-letting the provisions contained in Sub-Clauses (1) and (2) of this Clause if and so far as the same may be relevant and applicable.

(b) If the price payable under any agreement for sub-letting which includes the provisions contained in Sub-Clauses (1) and (2) of this Clause is decreased below the price stated in that agreement by reason of the operation of the provisions of this Clause, then the net amount of such decrease shall be deducted from the Sub-Contract Sum and if the price payable under that agreement shall be increased above that stated in that agreement by reason of the operation of the provisions of this Clause, then the net amount of the increases shall be added to the Sub-Contract Sum.

The Sub-Contractor shall within a reasonable time give written notice to the Contractor of the happening of any of the events referred to in paragraph (b) of Sub-Clause (1) of this Clause and of any increase or decrease in the basic prices of any of the materials or goods specified under paragraph (b) of Sub-Clause (2) of this Clause and of any reduction or increase in the prices payable under any agreement for sub-letting any portion of the Sub-Contract Works.

No addition to or deduction from the Sub-contract Sum made by virtue of this Clause shall alter in any way the amount of profit of the Sub Contractor included in the Sub-Contract Sum.

The Contractor shall at the request of the Sub-Contractor include in any Progress Statements as provided for by Clause 35 of the Main contract or alternatively in the Contractor's Memorandum of Variations, a detailed statement of any increases or decreases in the rates of wages and other emoluments and expenses, as defined in paragraph (a) of Sub-Clause (1) of this Clause, in the prices of goods and materials necessary for the execution of the work, or in the price payable under any agreement for sub-letting which includes the provisions contained in Sub-Clauses (1) and (2) of this Clause and the Architect/Engineer, having satisfied himself as to the correctness of the said amounts, shall add or deduct to the amount of the next Certificate to which the Contractor may be entitled under the Main Contract a sum equal to the amount of such increases or decreases and he shall specify and show separately the amount allowed in respect of the Sub-Contract Works.

(4) The percentage addition to any increase in wages, emoluments or expenses (including the cost of insurance or other premiums dependent thereon) under Sub-Clause (1) (b) of this Clause shall be 7½% and on any increased price under Sub-Clause (2) (b) of this Clause shall be 12½%. These percentage additions shall be deemed to cover the cost of all items whatsoever not otherwise recoverable under this Clause.

14

(5)   The "Designated Date" for the purpose of this Clause shall mean the date ten days prior to the latest date set for receipt of tenders or the latest revision of such date. Where no date is set for receipt of tenders the Designated Date shall mean the date of receipt of the tender.

The Designated Date for the tender of the Sub-Contractor is set out in Part VII of the Appendix.

Arbitration

26.   In the event of any dispute or difference between the Contractor and the Sub-Contractor, whether arising during the execution or after the completion or abandonment of the Sub-Contract Works or after the determination of the employment of the Sub-Contractor under this Sub-Contract (whether by breach or in any other manner), in regard to any matter or thing of whatsoever nature arising out of this Sub-Contract or in connection therewith, then either party shall give to the other notice in writing of such dispute or difference and such dispute or difference shall be and is hereby referred to the arbitration of such person as the parties hereto may agree to appoint as Arbitrator or failing such agreements as may be appointed on the request of either party by the President for the time being of the Construction Industry Federation and in either case the Award of such Arbitrator shall be final and binding on the parties.

PROVIDED that such Arbitrator shall not without the written consent of the Architect/ Engineer or the Contractor and in any case of the Sub-Contractor enter on the arbitration until after the completion or abandonment of the Main Contract Works, except to arbitrate upon the question, whether or not a certificate has been improperly withheld or is not in accordance with the terms of the Main Contract or upon the question as to whether a notice of determination has been properly issued in accordance in Clauses 11 or 12 of the Sub-Contract document.

AND provided further that in any such arbitration as is provided for in this Clause any decision of the Architect/Engineer which is final and binding on the Contractor under the Main Contract shall also be and be deemed to be final and binding between and upon the Contractor and Sub-Contractor.

Every or any such reference shall be deemed to be a submission to arbitration within the meaning of the Arbitration Acts, 1954 (Number 26 of 1954) or the Arbitration Act (Northern Ireland), 1957 (as the case may be) or any act amending the same or either of them.

Strike out (A)
or (B) as
required

★   (A) IN WITNESS WHEREOF the parties hereto have hereunto set their hands the day and year first above written.

★   (B) IN WITNESS WHEREOF the Common Seals of the parties hereto have hereunto been affixed the day and year first above written.

APPENDIX

PART 1

FIRST RECITAL. Particulars of the Works (being a part of the Works comprised in the Main Contract) in this Sub-Contract referred to as "the Sub-Contract Works", viz:

....

....

....

....

....

(NOTE — It is to be clearly stated whether scaffolding is to be supplied by the Contractor or the Sub-Contractor).

PART II

CLAUSE 4. Minimum Sum for Sub-Contractor's Public Liability Insurance (If

not stated £200,000) ....

PART III

CLAUSE 7.

Description of Work	Completion period or periods of the Sub-Contract Works or respective Section thereof	
	Commencement Date	Completion Date
....	....	
....	....	
....	....	
....	....	

PART IV

CLAUSE 10. Value of the Sub-Contract Works ....

....

....

....

....

....

£_____

PART V

CLAUSE 10. Special Daywork Rates and method of determining value of Extras, Omissions and Variations.

. . . .

. . . .

. . . .

. . . .

. . . .

. . . .

. . .   .

PART VI

CLAUSE 11. Terms of Payment.

(a)   Period for honouring Certificates
      (if none stated 14 days)   . . . .

(b)   Discount Term   . . . .

(c)   Period of Interim Payments   . . . .

(d)   Retention   . . . .

      (i) First Moiety . . . .

      (ii) Second Moiety . . . .

(NOTE: If no other time is stated the first moiety of Retention Money shall be released upon practical completion of the Sub-Contract Works to the satisfaction of the Contractor and of the Architect/Engineer).

PART VII

CLAUSE 25. Designated Date . . . .

(A) SIGNED by the above-named Contractor
     in the presence of:

                    —or—

(B) THE COMMON SEAL of the above-named   )
     Contractor was hereunto affixed in the   }
     presence of   )   (C.S.)

                    —or—

(C) SIGNED, SEALED AND DELIVERED by   )
     the above-named Contractor in the   }
     presence of:)   (Seal)

(A) SIGNED by the above named Sub-Contractor   )
     in the presence of: }
)
                    —or—

(B) THE COMMON SEAL of the above-named   )
     Sub-Contractor was hereunto affixed in the }
     presence of:)   (C.S.)

                    —or—

(C) SIGNED, SEALED AND DELIVERED by   )
     the above-named Sub-Contractor in the   }
     presence of:)   (Seal)

FOOTNOTE – Where the Sub-Contract is executed under hand the parties should sign in the
spaces provided in alternative (A).
     Where the Sub-Contract is executed under seal alternative (B) should be used by a party
which is a limited company or other corporation, and alternative (C) by a party which is
not a corporation. A fifty pence stamp must be impressed within thirty days of the date of
execution of the original where it is under seal, and a twenty-five pence stamp on the counter-part
(if any).
     In the case of each party the two alternatives which do not apply should be struck out.

Title of Main Contract . . . .

. . . .

Sub-Contract for . . . .

. . . .

Dated . . . . .19 . . . .

SUB CONTRACT

(For Use with the GDLA Main Contract Form)

Between

. . . .

. . . .

and

. . . .

. . . .

Issued under the sanction of and approved by the Construction Industry Federation and the Sub-Contractors and Specialists Association.

*2nd EDITION
(COPYRIGHT)
October 1989*

CONSTRUCTION HOUSE, CANAL ROAD, DUBLIN 6.

THIS SUB-CONTRACT is made the . . . . day of . . . . .19 . . . .

between . . . .

of (or, whose Registered Office is situated at) . . . .

. . . .

(hereinafter called "the Contractor") of the one part and . . . .

. . . .

of (or, whose Registered Office is situated at) . . . .

. . . .

(hereinafter called "the Sub-Contractor" of the other part:

SUPPLEMENTAL to an Agreement (hereinafter referred to as "the Main Contract")

made the . . . . day of . . . . ,19 . . . . . between

. . . . (hereinafter called "the Employer")

of the one part and the Contractor of the other part:

WHEREAS the Contractor desires to have executed the Works of which particulars are set out in PART 1 of the Appendix of this Sub-Contract (hereinafter referred to as "the Sub-Contract Works") and which form part of the works (hereinafter referred to as "the Main Contract Works") comprised in and to be executed in accordance with the Main Contract, and any authorised variations of the Sub-Contract Works;

AND WHEREAS the Sub-Contractor is entitled to assume that the Agreement and Conditions of Contract for building work into which the Contractor has entered is the latest edition of that document issued for use by Government Departments and Local Authorities and by other bodies the placing of whose contracts is subject to approval by a Government Department or Local Authority when work is to be paid for wholly or partly from Exchequer Funds. In this Sub-Contract the "Main Conditions" means those conditions. If the Agreement and Conditions are not as aforesaid the Sub-Contractor shall be given prior notice of any alternations before the Sub-Contract document is executed. No additions or omissions to any part of this document shall be made by either signatory except by mutual agreement.

NOW IT IS HEREBY AGREED AND DECLARED as follows:—

Notice of the Main Contract to the Sub-Contractor

1. The Sub-Contractor shall be deemed to have notice of all the provisions of the Main Contract except the detailed prices of the Contractor included in Schedules and Bills of Quantities.

Execution of the Sub-Contract Works

2. The Sub-Contractor shall execute and complete the Sub-Contract Work subject to and in accordance with this Sub-Contract in all respects to the reasonable satisfaction of the Contractor and of the Architect/Engineer for the time being under the Main Contract (hereinafter called "the Architect/Engineer") and in conformity with the reasonable directions and requirements of the Contractor which shall be a programme agreed between the Contractor and Sub-Contractor and approved by the Architect/Engineer, who in the case of default in carrying out the programme may himself direct the order in which the Sub-Contract Work shall be carried out.

Sub-Contractor's liability under incorporated Provisions of the Main Contract

3. The Sub-Contractor agrees:

(a) To observe, perform and comply with all the provisions of the Main Contract on the part of the Contractor, to be observed, performed and complied with so far as they relate and apply to the Sub-Contract Works (or any portion of the same) and are not repugnant to or inconsistent with the express provisions of this Sub-Contract as if all the same were severally set out herein; and

(b) Subject to Clause 4 (b) (ii) to indemnify and save harmless the Contractor against and from:—

(i)   any claim, breach or non-observance or non-performance of the said provisions of the Main Contract or any of them due to any act, neglect or the default on the part of the Sub-Contractor only; and

(ii)   any act or omission of the Sub-Contractor, his servants or agents which involves the Contractor in any liability to the Employer under the Main Contract; and

(iii)   any damage, loss or expense due to or resulting from any negligence or breach of duty on the part of the Sub-Contractor, his servants or agents (inclusively of any wrongful use by him or them of the Contractor's property); and

(iv)   any claim by an employee of the Sub-Contractor under the Employers' Liability Acts or other Acts of the Oireachtas of a like nature, respectively, in force for the time being.

PROVIDED that nothing in the Sub-Contract contained shall impose any liability on the Sub-Contractor in respect of any negligence or breach of duty on the part of the Employer, the Contractor, his other Sub-Contractors or their respective servants or agents nor create any privity of contract between the Sub-Contractor and the Employer or any other Sub-Contractor.

Insurance by the Parties for Damage to Persons and to Property

4.   (a) The Contractor shall take out before commencing the Works and maintain Public Liability and Employer's Liability Policies of Insurance in accordance with the Main Contract.

(b) The Sub-Contractor shall take out before commencing the Sub-Contract Works and maintain Public Liability and Employer's Liability Policies of Insurance as follows:—

(i)   The policies shall cover the Sub-Contractor's liability by statute and at common law and liability to indemnify the Contractor under Clause 3 of this Sub-Contract in each case against any liability, loss, claim or proceeding in respect of injury, death or disease of any person, and (subject to Clause 5) injury or damage to property arising out of or in the course of or by reason of the execution of the Sub-Contract Works.

(ii)   The Sub-Contractor may include in his policies under this clause the exclusions permitted by Clause 23 (e) para. (i) or (ii) (as relevant of the Main Contract Conditions. Without prejudice to the Sub-Contractor's liability at common law or by statute the Sub-Contractor shall not be bound to indemnify the Contractor under Clause 3 in respect of any liability, loss, claim or proceedings for injury, death, disease of any person or damage to property which arises otherwise than in connection with an accident or which is within a permitted exclusion and is not covered by an Employer's Liability or Public Liability Insurance Policy of the Sub-Contractor.

(iii)   The Public Liability Policy of the Sub-Contractor shall be for a sum not less than the sum stated in Part II of the Appendix to this Sub-Contract.

(iv)   The Sub-Contractor's policies under this clause shall be with insurers approved by the Contractor, which approval shall not be unreasonably withheld, and shall include provisions by which in the event of any claim in respect of which the Sub-Contractor would be entitled to receive indemnity under the policy being brought or made against the Contractor the insurers will indemnify the Contractor against such claims and any costs, charges and expenses in respect thereof.

All Risks Insurance

5.   (a) In this Clause "Sub-Contract Ancillary Items" shall mean temporary works and all unfixed materials and goods delivered to and placed on or adjacent to and intended for the Sub-Contract Works except temporary buildings, plant, tools or equipment owned or hired by the Sub-Contractor or any Sub-Contractor of his.

(b) Subject to sub-clauses (c), (d) and (e) the Contractor shall for the benefit of himself and the Sub-Contractor keep in force in accordance with the requirements of the Main Contract an All Risks Policy of insurance covering the Works and Ancillary Items (including the Sub-Contract Works and the Sub-Contract Ancillary Items) which shall as regards loss or damage from any cause whatsoever be at the sole risk of the Contractor.

(c) In the case of any loss or damage to the Sub-Contract Works or Sub-Contract Ancillary Items falling within an exclusion permitted by Clause 23 (e) (iii) of the Main Contract Conditions and included in the Contractor's All Risks Policy of Insurance then (without prejudice to any liability of the Sub-Contractor for negligence, omission or default and subject to sub-clause (d) of this Clause) the occurrence of such loss or damage shall be disregarded in computing any amounts payable to the Sub-Contractor and the reinstatement and making good of such loss or damage and (when required) removal and disposal of debris shall be deemed to be a variation ordered under Clause 6.

(d) In the case of any loss or damage to the Sub-Contract Works or Sub-Contract Ancillary Items due to any fault, or omission in design by the Sub-Contractor, his servants or agents (including his sub-contractors and suppliers, other than nominated sub-contractors or nominated suppliers) the Sub-Contractor shall proceed with due diligence to repair or make good the same at his own expense.

(e) Until not less than 80% of the contract value of the item is included in the amount of a certificate under the Main Contract and the item is fixed to the Main Contract Works the Sub-Contractor shall be liable for making good loss or damage due to theft or misappropriation of any Sub-Contract Ancillary Item (whether or not the theft or misappropriation is due to the negligence or default of the Contractor, his servants or agents). However, if the Contractor is in breach of Clause 16 of this Sub-Contract the Sub-Contractor may give written notice to the Contractor specifying the breach and seven days thereafter the Contractor shall become liable for theft or misappropriation of any Sub-Contract Ancillary Items until the breach is remedied and the Sub-Contractor is notified in writing.

(f) If the Main Contract is validly determined under Clause 24 (b) of the Conditions the Contractor may determine the Sub-Contract by written notice to the Sub-Contractor. The provisions of Clause 24 (b) of the Main Contract as to payment shall then apply mutatis mutandis to payment to the Sub-Contractor.

(g) The Sub-Contractor shall observe and comply with the conditions contained in the Contractor's policy of insurance under this Clause so far as compliance is within the control of the Sub-Contractor. The Sub-Contractor shall be entitled to inspect the Contractor's policy.

(h) The Sub-Contractor shall notify the Contractor by means of a notice in writing of at least 10 working days before commencing any operation that would constitute an abnormal hazard in building operations and that in the absence of notice to and acceptance by insurers renders void or voidable any of the policies of insurance under Clauses 4 or 5. The Sub-Contractor shall be liable for any additional insurance costs of the Contractor, or for which the Contractor is liable to the Employer due to any such operation, and if due to any such operation insurers will not accept any risk which the Contractor is required to insure the risk shall be insured by the Sub-Contractor at his own cost.

(i) The Sub-Contract shall be entitled to the benefit of Clauses 26 & 32 (b) of the Main Contract Conditions. The Contractor shall ensure that the Employer under the Main Contract complies with those clauses where applicable.

Variations etc.

6. In the event of the Contractor:—

(a) requiring or authorising in writing any variations of or omissions from the Sub-Contract Works; or

(b) Issuing in writing to the Sub-Contractor any instructions of the Architect/ Engineer in relation to the Sub-Contract Works (whether in regard to variations or otherwise howsoever); or

(c) issuing to the Sub-Contractor or his agent any verbal instructions or directions involving a variation, such instructions shall be confirmed in writing by the Sub-Contractor to the Contractor. within 3 days and if not dissented from in writing by the Contractor to the Sub-Contractor within a further 10 days, shall be deemed to be a variation of the Sub-Contract Works;

then the Sub-Contractor shall forthwith comply with and carry out the same in all respects accordingly.

PROVIDED that if compliance with such instructions or directions will or is likely to involve the Sub-Contractor in loss of expense beyond that provided for in or reasonably contemplated by this Sub-Contract, then the Sub-Contractor shall so inform the Contractor in writing specifying within 3 working days of receipt of the instruction or direction the nature of the loss or expense and within a further 20 working days the estimated value of such loss or expense then unless such instructions or directions were issued by reason of some breach of the Sub-Contract by the Sub-Contractor the amount of such loss or expense shall be ascertained and added to the Sub-Contract Sum. Where a variation by way of omission is, as compared with the works included in the Sub-Contract in a character so extensive that in the opinion of the Architect the Sub-Contractor has sustained a loss by reason of, prior to the notification to him of such variation, having properly incurred expenses which in consequence of the variation have become wholly or in part unnecessary, there shall be added to the Sub-Contract Sum a sum to be ascertained by the Architect as being in all circumstances reasonable compensation for such loss.

If through variation and/or omission the final measurement shows a credit on the Sub-Contract Sum of 20% or more the Sub-Contractor shall be entitled, if agreed by the Architect, to an allowance of 10% on this credit.

P.C. Sums, Provisional Sums, Provisional Works and Contingency Sums and the amount of any adjustment under Clause 24 of this Sub-Contract are not to be taken into account in arriving at the credit on which this allowance is based.

Save as aforesaid no variation of or omission from or other alteration or modification of the Sub-Contract shall be made or allowed by the Sub-Contractor.

Completion

7. (a) The Sub-Contractor shall commence the Sub-Contract works within a reasonable period of time after the receipt by him of an order in writing under this Sub-Contract from the Contractor to that effect and shall proceed with the same with due expedition.

The Sub-Contractor shall progress and complete the Sub-Contract Works and each section thereof within the period specified in Part III of the Appendix to this Sub-Contract.

If the Sub-Contractor fails to progress or complete the Sub-Contract works or any section thereof within the period specified or any extended period as hereinafter provided, he shall pay to the Contractor any loss or damage suffered or incurred by the Contractor and caused by the failure of the Sub-Contractor as aforesaid of which loss or damage the Contractor shall at the earliest opportunity give reasonable notice to the Sub-Contractor that the same is being or has been suffered or incurred.

(b) If the completion of the Sub-Contract Works or any section thereof be delayed and such delay

(i) shall be caused by or be due to any of the matters specified in Clauses 6 (a), (b) or (c) of this Sub-Contract or by or to any act or omission of the Contractor, his other Sub-Contractors, his or their respective servants or agents; or

(ii) shall be within any of the cases in which the Contractor could obtain an extension of the period or periods for completion under the Main Contract: (See NOTE).

then the Sub-Contractor shall immediately give notice thereof in writing to the Contractor and the Contractor shall grant or (where the Contractor has to apply to the Architect) he shall apply for a fair and reasonable extension of the said period or periods for completion of the Sub-Contract Works or each section thereof (as the case may require) and such extended period or periods shall be the period or periods of completion of the same respectively and this clause shall be read and construed accordingly.

If the Sub-Contractor be delayed in the commencement or completion of the Sub-Contract Works due to circumstances beyond his control he shall so inform the Contractor and he shall then be entitled to make a claim for any loss or damage incurred to the same extent as the main Contractor is entitled under the main Contract form.

NOTE:– Users of this Form of Sub-Contract should ascertain the provisions relating to Delay and Extension of Time contained in the Main Contract whatever its form. These provisions will, under Clause 7 (b) (ii), inure to the benefit of the parties to the Sub-Contract.

In the Main Contract Conditions these provisions are set out in Clause 30.

Defects

8.   The Sub-Contractor shall within such time as shall be determined by the Architect, or in the absence of such a determination, a reasonable time after receipt by him from the Contractor of the Architect's/Engineer's or agent's instructions or a copy thereof relating to the same, make good all defects, shrinkages or other faults in the Sub-Contract Works, due to faulty materials or bad workmanship which the Contractor (whether at his own cost or not) shall be liable to make good under the Main Contract.

PROVIDED that where the Contractor is liable to make good such defects, shrinkages of other faults, but not at his own cost, then the Contractor shall secure a similar benefit to the Sub-Contractor and shall account to the Sub-Contractor for any money actually received by him in respect of same.

Consequential damage to the Contractor

9.   (a) If the Contractor (whether by himself or any other Sub-Contractor) shall execute any work (whether permanent or temporary) to the Main Contract Works or to any part of the same required by the Architect/Engineer or rendered necessary by reason of defects, shrinkages or other faults in the Sub-Contract Works due to materials or workmanship not being in accordance with this Sub-Contract or to frost occurring during, but before the completion of the Main Contract Works, then the Sub-Contractor shall pay to the Contractor the cost of the execution of such works.

PROVIDED that if the Contractor shall pay or allow to the Employer the value of, or other agreed sum (not exceeding such cost as aforesaid) in respect of, such work instead and in satisfaction of executing the same, then the Sub-Contractor shall pay to the Contractor such value or other agreed sum as aforesaid.

PROVIDED also that the Sub-Contractor shall not be required to pay the cost of any works to make good damage by frost which may appear after completion of the Main Contract Works unless the Architect shall decide that such damage is due to injury which occurred before completion of the Main Contract Works or of which the Contractor before commencing the same has not given reasonable notice to the Sub-Contractor.

Consequential damage to the Sub-Contractor

(b) If the Sub-Contractor shall execute any work to or in connection with the Sub-Contract Works (whether permanent or temporary) required by the Architect/Engineer or rendered necessary by reason of any defects, shrinkages or other faults in the Main Contract Works due to materials or workmanship not being in accordance with the Main Contract or to frost occurring before the completion of the Main Contract Works, then the Contractor shall pay to the Sub-Contractor the cost of the execution of such work provided that nothing contained in this Sub-Clause shall exclude the liability of the Sub-Contractor under Sub-Section (a) above.

PROVIDED that if instead of the Sub-Contractor actually executing such work and in satisfaction of the same the Contractor shall pay or allow to the Employer the value of, or other agreed sum (not exceeding such cost as aforesaid) in respect of, such work, then the Contractor shall indemnify the Sub-Contractor against any claim, damage or loss in respect of failure to execute such work.

PROVIDED also that the Contractor shall not be required to pay the cost of any work to make good damage by frost which may appear after completion of the Main Contract Works unless the Architect/Engineer shall decide that such damage was due to injury which took place before completion of the Main Contract Works or of which the Sub-Contractor before commencing the same has not given reasonable notice to the Contractor.

Sub-Contract Sum – Valuation of Variations

10.   The price of the Sub-Contractor Works (herein referred to as "the Sub-Contract Sum") shall be the sum named in Part IV or determined by the provisions of Part V of the Appendix to this Sub-Contract or such other sums as shall become payable by reason of any authorised variations. The value of all authorised variations shall be determined by the Surveyor for the time being under the Main Contract (or if none the Architect/Engineer) in accordance with the applicable provisions (relating to the ascertainment of prices for authorised variations) laid down in the Main Contract Conditions save that where the

Sub-Contractor has with the Agreement of the Contractor annexed to this Sub-Contract a schedule of prices for measured work and/or a schedule of daywork prices, such prices shall be allowed to the Sub-Contractor in determining the value of authorised variations in substitution for any prices which would otherwise be applicable under this clause. (See NOTE).

NOTE – The Sub-Contractor should ascertain whether the Bills of Quantities (if any) prepared in connection with the Main Contract have been prepared in accordance with the principles of the Standard Method of Measurement of Building Works applicable to work in Ireland last before approved by the Royal Institution of Chartered Surveyors (Republic of Ireland Branch) and the Construction Industry Federation.

Contractor to apply for Certificate of Payment

11. (a) The Contractor shall, subject to and in accordance with the Main Contract, from time to time and in any event, unless otherwise agreed, not later than 30 days after receipt of the Sub-Contractor's detailed progress statement make application (of which prior thereto the Contractor shall give to the Sub-Contractor at least seven days' notice unless otherwise agreed between the Contractor and the Sub-Contractor) to the Architect for Certificates of Payment and for inclusion therein of the amount which at the date thereof fairly represents the value of the Sub-Contract Works and any variations authorised under this Sub-Contract then executed and of the materials and goods delivered upon the site for use in the Sub-Contract Works.

PROVIDED that the application shall include only the value of the said materials and goods as and from time as they are reasonably properly and not prematurely brought upon the site and then only if adequately stored and/or protected against weather and casualties.

The Contractor shall also embody in or annex to the said application any representations of the Sub-Contractor in regard to such value.

Interim Payments to the Sub-Contractor– Retention

(b) Fourteen days after the receipt by the Contractor of any Certificate from the Architect/Engineer the amounts certified therein to be due in respect of the Sub-Contract Works shall be due by the Contractor to the Sub-Contractor, and the Contractor shall within said time notify in writing to the Sub-Contractor the amount certified in the said Certificate to be due to him, any authorised variations thereof less Retention Money, which shall mean in this Contract the proportion attributable to the Sub-Contract Works of the money retained by the Employer in accordance with the Main Contract and less a cash discount of 5% (if payment is made within seven days after the Contractor himself is paid and if provision is made in the main Contract for the allowance of such discount to the Contractor) provided always that the Sub-Contractor shall not take steps to enforce payment of such sum until the expiration of such period of seven days after the Contractor has received payment of such Certificate unless:—

(i) the Contractor being a person or firm commits an act of Bankruptcy or being a company enters into liquidation whether compulsory or voluntary (except liquidation for the purpose of reconstruction), or—

(ii) a Receiver has been appointed over the business or undertaking of the Contractor, or—

(iii) a judgement has been obtained and registered against the Contractor or execution, whether legal or equitable, has been levied on the property of the Contractor, or—

(iv) the Contractor has suspended work on the Main Contract or left the State, or—

(v) the Contractor has not received payment of any Certificate within twenty-eight days of the date of its issue.

This sub-clause (v) shall not apply in the event that the employer commits an act of bankruptcy or being a company enters into liquidation whether compulsory or voluntary (except liquidation for the purpose of reconstruction).

In the event that the Contractor considers that the Sub-Contractor is invoking this section without regard to the Contractor's difficulty in obtaining payment, the Contractor may refer the matter to the President for the time being of the Construction Industry Federation who shall nominate a person to arbitrate on the matter. The arbitration award shall be issued within 10 working days from receipt of the complaint of the Contractor and shall be deemed to be a submission to arbitration within the meaning of the Arbitration Act 1954 (number 26 of 1954) or the Arbitration Act (Northern Ireland) 1957 (as the case may be) or any act amending the same or either of them. Due to the time constraint for the arbitration process, it is agreed that there will be no legal representative.

In the event that the Contractor considers that the Sub-Contractor is invoking this section inequitably, the Contractor may refer the matter to the President for the time being of the Construction Industry Federation who shall nominate a person to arbitrate on the matter. The arbitration award shall be issued within 10 working days from receipt of the complaint of the contractor and shall be deemed to be a submission to arbitration within the meaning of the Arbitration Act 1954 (number 26 of 1954) or the Arbitration Act (Northern Ireland) 1957 (as the case may be) or any act amending the same or either of them. Due to the time constraint for the arbitration process, it is agreed that there will be no legal representation.

Contractor to furnish details of Certificates

(c) If the Contractor shall fail to notify the Sub-Contractor in accordance with the provisions of the foregoing sub-clause (b) then the Contractor shall on demand to him by the Sub-Contractor furnish to the Sub-Contractor details of all monies certified for the Sub-Contractor by the Architect/Engineer. If the Contractor shall not furnish such details within four days after such demand, the Sub-Contractor shall be entitled to obtain these from the Architect/Engineer.

Payments to Contractor in Trust for Sub-Contractor

(d) Payments made to the Contractor in respect of work done and materials used by the Sub-Contractor shall until received by the Sub-Contractor be deemed to be money or moneys worth held in trust but without obligation to invest by the Contractor for the Sub-Contractor to be applied in or towards payment of the Sub-Contractor's account, subject always to the right of adjustment by the Architect/Engineer in the event of his certifying that adjustment is necessary.

Non-Payment by Contractor

(e) (1) If the Contractor does not pay to the Sub-Contractor the amounts certified by any Certificate issued by the Architect/Engineer to be due to the Sub-Contractor within the period mentioned in sub-clause (b) hereof, then the Sub-Contractor—

(i) may (but without prejudice to any other right or remedy) apply directly to the Employer for and the Employer may make payment of the amounts certified to be due to the Sub-Contractor direct to the Sub-Contractor and the Employer may set off the amount of any payment or payments made by him to the Sub-Contractor against any moneys due or to become due to the Contractor.

Payment by the Employer to the Sub-Contractor direct shall be regarded as payment by the Contractor to the Sub-Contractor and shall annul the right of suspension under sub-paragraph (ii) of this paragraph (1), or

(ii) may, if payment has not been received within seven days after receipt of payment by the Contractor or within twenty-eight days of the date of issue of the Architect's/Engineer's Certificate covering the amount due in respect of the Sub-Contract Works, after seven days' notice to the Contractor, suspend the works for a period of fourteen days and upon the expiry of this period, unless payment shall have been made in the meantime by the Contractor or by the Employer direct, may determine the Sub-Contractor's employment under this Sub-Contract as from the date of such expiry.

When work is suspended under this provision, the time for completion shall be extended by two days for each day of such suspension which shall not be deemed a delay for which the Sub-Contractor is liable under this Sub-Contract, or

(iii) may, without prejudice to other rights or remedies after seven days from the receipt of payment by the contractor covering the amount due in respect of the Sub-Contract Works, be entitled to charge interest to the Contractor on the amount included in such

Certificate at current bank rate of interest on overdrafts until such time as payment is made by the Contractor, or by the Employer under sub-paragraph (i) of this paragraph (1).

Determination by Sub-Contractor

(2) If—

    (i) the Contractor being a person or firm commits an act of Bankruptcy or being a company enters into liquidation whether compulsory or voluntary (except liquidation for the purpose of reconstruction) or—

    (ii) a Receiver has been appointed over the business or undertaking of the Contractor or—

    (iii) a judgement has been obtained and registered against the Contractor or execution, whether legal or equitable, has been levied on the property of the Contractor, or—

    (iv) the Contractor has suspended work on the Main Contract or Sub-Contract, or has unreasonably delayed the commencement of the Sub-Contract or left the State, then the Sub-Contractor may by written notice sent by registered post to the last known address of the Contractor or served personally on the Contractor determine the employment of the Sub-Contractor under this Sub-Contract from the date of such notice.

Procedure after Determination

(f) Upon such determination under the foregoing sub-clause (e) then without prejudice to the accrued rights of either party their respective rights and liabilities shall be as follows:—

Subject to no prior notice of default or determination under the provisions of clause 33 of the Main Contract Conditions having been served the Sub-Contractor shall thereupon with all reasonable despatch and in such manner and with such precautions as will prevent injury or damage to persons or property, remove from the site all his temporary buildings, plant and machinery, appliances, goods and materials but subject always to the provisions of paragraph (iii) hereunder. In the event of prior notice of default or determination having been served under the Main Contract Conditions the Sub-Contractor shall only remove from the site buildings plant, machinery, appliances, goods and materials with the consent of the Employer.

The Sub-Contractor shall thereupon be paid by the Contractor:—

    (i) the value of the Sub-Contract Works completed at the date of such determination such value to be determined by the Architect/Engineer at the request of the Sub-Contractor in accordance with Clause 10 and the Architect/Engineer shall give credit for the amounts already paid to the Sub-Contractor;

    (ii) the value of the Sub-Contract Works commenced and executed but not completed at the date of such determination such value to be determined by the Architect/Engineer at the request of the Sub-Cntractor in accordance with Clause 10;

    (iii) the cost of materials or goods properly ordered for the Sub-Contract Works for which the Sub-Contractor shall have paid or of which the Sub-Contractor is legally bound to accept delivery and such cost shall be determined by the Architect/Engineer at the request of the Sub-Contractor and on payment for the same to the Sub-Contractor any materials or goods so paid for shall become the property of the Contractor;

    (iv) the reasonable cost of the removal of the temporary buildings, plant, machinery, appliances, goods and materials, such reasonable cost to be determined by the Architect/Engineer;

    (v) such loss or damage sustained by the Sub-Contractor and caused by such determination as the Architect/Engineer may consider reasonable and the amount whereof shall be certified by him.

PROVIDED that in addition to all other remedies and subject to the Architect not having served prior notice of default or the Employer prior notice of

Sub-Contractor may upon such determination take possession of and have a lien upon all materials and goods ordered for the Sub-Contract Works which shall not have been fixed to the Main Contract Works until payment of all moneys due to the Sub-Contractor by the Contractor

Dispute as to Certificate

(g) If the Sub-Contractor shall feel aggrieved by the amount certified by the Architect/Engineer or by his failure to certify or failure by the Employer to honour his certificate in whole or in part within the time period stipulated in the main contract document, then, subject to the Sub-Contractor giving to the Contractor such indemnity and security as the Contractor shall reasonably require, the Contractor shall allow the Sub-Contractor to use the Contractor's name and if necessary will join the Sub-Contractor as claimant in the legal proceedings by the Sub-Contractor in respect of the said matters complained of by the Sub-Contractor. (See NOTE).

NOTE– Arbitration under this Sub-Clause would be governed by the provisions with regard to arbitration contained in the Main Contract. The Sub-Clause should be struck out when the Sub-Contractor is not nominated or selected by the Architect under the Main Contract.

Special Interim Payment

(h) If before the issue of a Final Certificate to the Contractor under the Main Contract a period of time equal to the Retention Period of the Main Contract has elapsed since practical completion of the Sub-Contract Works the subject of this Agreement then the Sub-Contractor may request the Contractor in writing to make application to the Architect/Engineer for Certificates certifying the value of the work executed upon the Sub-Contract Works, and the Contractor shall make such application. The provisions of this clause shall apply to such Certificates as if they were Certificates of Payment expressly provided for in the Main Contract.

Final Payment to Sub-Contractor

(i) If before the issue of a Final Certificate to the Contractor under the Main Contract the Architect/Engineer desires to secure final payment to the Sub-Contractor on completion of the Sub-Contract Works and in accordance with and subject to the provisions of the Main Contract relating to Prime Costs and Provisional Sums issues a Certificate to the Contractor including an amount to cover such final payment, then the Contractor shall on receipt of payment from the Employer pay to the Sub-Contractor the amount so certified by the Architect/Engineer as aforesaid, but such payment shall be made only if the Sub-Contractor indemnifies and secures the Contractor to the reasonable satisfaction of the Contractor against all latent defects in the Sub-Contract Works and if by such final payment the Contractor will be discharged under the Main Contract from all liabilities in respect of the Sub-Contract Works except for any latent defects.

(j) If and to the extent that the amount retained by the Employer in accordance with the Main Contract includes any Retention Money the Contractor's interest in such money shall be fiduciary as trustee without obligation to invest for the Sub-Contractor and if the Contractor attempts or purports to mortgage or otherwise charge such interest or his interest in the whole of the amount retained as aforesaid such mortgage or charge shall in so far as it relates to the Retention Money be void.

Sub-Contractor's claim to Rights and Benefits of Main Contract

12. The Contractor (so far as he lawfully can) will, at the request and cost of the Sub-Contractor, obtain for him any rights or benefits of the Main Contract so far as the same are applicable to the Sub-Contract Works, but not further or otherwise.

Contractor's Right to Deduction or Set Off

13. (1) The Contractor shall be entitled to deduct from any money (including any retention money) otherwise due under this sub-Contract any amount agreed by the Sub-Contractor as due to the Contractor, or finally awarded in arbitration or litigation in favour of the Contractor, and which arises out of or under this Sub-Contract.

(2) The Contractor shall be entitled to set-off against any money (including any retention money) otherwise due under this Sub-Contract the amount of any claim for loss and/or expense which has actually been incurred by the Contractor by reason of any breach of, or failure to observe the provisions of, this Sub-Contract by the Sub-Contractor, provided:-

(a) the amount of such set-off has been quantified in detail and with reasonable accuracy by the Contractor; and

(b) the Contractor has given to the Sub-Contractor notice in writing specifying his intention to set-off the amount quantified in accordance with proviso (a) of this sub-clause and the grounds on which such set-off is claimed to be made. Such notice shall be given not less than seventeen days before the money from which the amount is to be set-off becomes. due and payable to the Sub-Contractor; provided that such written notice shall not be binding insofar as the Contractor may amend it in preparing his pleadings for any Arbitration pursuant to the notice of arbitration. The form of arbitration shall be as set out in Clause 11(b)(v).

(3) Any amount set-off under the provisions of sub-clause (2) hereof is without prejudice to the rights of the Contractor or Sub-Contractor in any subsequent negotiations, arbitration proceedings or litigation to seek to vary the amount claimed and set-off by the Contractor under sub-clause (2) hereof.

(4) The rights of the parties to this Sub-Contract in respect of set-off are fully set out in these Conditions and no other rights whatsoever shall be implied as terms of this Sub-Contract relating to set-off.

A similar arbitration procedure to that suggested for 11 (b) (v) might be inserted in the event that the Sub-Contractor disagrees with the set off.

Right of Access of Contractor and Architect/Engineer

14. The Contractor and the Architect/Engineer or his Agent (and all persons duly authorised by them or either of them) shall at all reasonable times have access to any work which is being prepared for or will be utilised in the Sub-Contract Works, unless the Architect/Engineer shall certify in writing that the Sub-Contractor has reasonable grounds for refusing such access.

Sub-letting of Sub-Contract Works

15. The Sub-Contractor shall not assign this Sub-Contract nor sub-let the Sub-Contract Works or any portion of the same without the written consent of both the Contractor and the Architect/Engineer provided that the consent of the Contractor shall not be unreasonably withheld, and that in case of any difference of opinion between the Contractor and the Architect/Engineer the opinion of the Architect/Engineer shall prevail.

Provision of Water, etc. and Temporary Works, etc. for Sub-Contract Works

16. (a) If and so far as provided in the Main Contract (but not otherwise) the Contractor shall supply at his own costs all necessary water, lighting, watching and attendance for the purposes of the Sub-Contract Works. Subject as aforesaid, the Sub-Contractor shall make all necessary provision in regard to the said matters and each of them.

(b) If and so far as provided by the Main Contract (but not otherwise) the Contractor shall provide all reasonable facilities to the Sub-Contractor for such workshop and storage accommodation as may be reasonably required.

Sub-Contractor's User of Contractor's Scaffolding

17. The Sub-Contractor, his employees and workmen in common with all other persons having the like right shall for the purposes of the Sub-Contract Works (but not further or otherwise) be entitled to use any scaffolding belonging to or provided by the Contractor, while it remains so erected upon the site.

PROVIDED that such other user as aforesaid shall be on the express condition that no warranty or other liability on the part of the Contractor or of his other sub-contractors shall be created or implied in regard to the fitness, condition or suitability of the said scaffolding.

Contractor and Sub-Contractor not to make Wrongful User of or interference with the property of the other

18. Save as hereinbefore expressly provided, the Contractor and the Sub-Contractor respectively, their respective servants or agents shall not make any wrongful user of or interfere with the plant, ways, scaffolding, temporary works, appliances or other property, respectively, belonging to or provided by the other of them or be guilty of any act or omission which shall constitute a breach or infringement of any statute or of any legally binding bye-law, regulation, order or rule made under the same or by any local or other public or competent authority.

PROVIDED that nothing herein contained shall prejudice or limit the rights of the Contractor or the Sub-Contractor in the carrying out of their respective statutory duties or contractual duties hereunder or under the Main Contract.

Plant etc. of Sub-Contractor to be at his sole risk

19. The plant, tools, equipment, or other property belonging to or provided by the Sub-Contractor, his servants or agents (other than materials and goods properly on the site for use in the Sub-Contract Works) shall be at the sole risk of the Sub-Contractor, and any loss or damage to the same or caused by the same shall be the sole liability of the Sub-Contractor who shall indemnify the Contractor against any loss, claim or proceedings in respect thereof. Any insurance against any such loss or claim shall be the sole concern of the Sub-Contractor.

20. (a) DEFAULT

If the Sub-Contractor shall make default in any of the following respects, viz.:

(1) without reasonable cause shall wholly suspend the works before completion, otherwise than in accordance with Clause 11 (e) hereof;

(2) shall fail to proceed with the works with reasonable diligence;

(3) refuses or persistently neglects after notice in writing from the Contractor to remove defective work or improper materials;

(4) shall fail to commence the Sub-Contract Works within a reasonable period after receipt by him of an order in writing;

(5) shall fail to execute the Sub-Contract Works in accordance with the Sub-Contract or shall be in serious breach of his obligations under the Sub-Contract;

(6) where a trade dispute arises between the Sub-Contractor and the workmen engaged by him on or in connection with the Sub-Contract Works to whom a Registered Employment Agreement applies shall fail, neglect or refuse to comply with the settlement procedures set out in such Agreement.

then if such default shall continue for fourteen days after a written notice to the Sub-Contractor from the Contractor specifying the same served on the Sub-Contractor personally or by registered post, the Contractor may (without prejudice to any other rights herein contained) thereupon by written notice served on the Sub-Contractor personally or by registered post, determine the employment of the Sub-Contractor.

PROVIDED that notice hereunder shall not be given unreasonably or vexatiously and such notice shall be void if the Contractor is at the time of the notice in breach of this Contract.

After such first mentioned notice shall have been given, the Sub-Contractor shall not be at liberty to remove from the site or works, or from any ground contiguous thereto, any plant or materials belonging to him which shall have been placed thereon for the purposes of the works; and the Contractor shall have a lien upon all such plant and materials, to subsist from the date of such notice being given until the notice shall have been complied with.

PROVIDED always that such lien shall not, under any circumstances, subsist after the expiration of thirty-one days from the date of such notice being given, unless the Contractor shall have entered upon and taken possession of the works.

(b) BANKRUPTCY OF SUB-CONTRACTOR

If the Sub-Contractor commits an act of Bankruptcy or being a company enters into liquidation whether compulsory or voluntary (except liquidation for the purpose of reconstruction) or has a Receiver appointed to it or has suspended work on the Sub-Contract or left the State, the Contractor without prejudice to any other rights herein contained may send by registered post to the Sub-Contractor a written notice determining the employment of the Sub-Contractor under this Contract.

In either of the above cases (a) or (b) the following shall apply:—

(1) the Contractor may employ and pay a Sub-Contractor or other person or persons to carry out and complete the works and he or they may enter upon the site and use all materials, temporary buildings, plant and appliances thereon, and may purchase all materials necessary for the purposes aforesaid;

(2) the Sub-Contractor shall if so required by the Contractor or Architect/ Engineer assign to the Contractor without further payment the benefit of any contract for the supply of materials and/or works intended for use under this Sub-Contract or for the execution of any works, and the Contractor shall pay the agreed price (if unpaid) for such materials or works supplied or executed after the said determination;

(3) the Sub-Contractor shall during the execution or after completion of the works under this clause, as and when required, remove from the site his temporary buildings, plant, appliances, and any materials within such reasonable time as the Contractor may specify in a written notice to him, and in default the Contractor may (without being responsible for loss or damage) remove and sell the same, holding the proceeds less all costs incurred to the credit of the Sub-Contractor;

(4) until after completion of the works under this clause no payment shall be made to the Sub-Contractor under this contract, provided that upon completion as aforesaid and the verification within a reasonable time of the accounts therefor the Architect/Engineer shall certify the amount of expenses properly incurred by the Contractor, and if such amount added to the moneys paid to the Sub-Contractor before such determination exceeds the total amount which would have been payable on due completion, the difference shall be a debt payable to the Contractor by the Sub-Contractor; and if the said amount added to the said moneys be less than the said total amount, the differences shall be a debt payable to the Sub-Contractor by the Contractor.

Determination of Main Contract

21. If for any reason the employment of the Contractor under the Main Contract is determined (whether by the Contractor or by the Employer) and whether by reason of—

(a) any act, neglect or default of the Contractor, or

(b) the Contractor being a person or firm commits an act of Bankruptcy or being a company enters into liquidation whether compulsory or voluntary (except liquidation for the purpose of reconstruction), or

(c) a Receiver being appointed over the business or undertaking of the Contractor, or

(d) a Judgement being obtained and registered against him or execution whether legal or equitable being levied on his property, or

(e) his suspending work on the Main Contract or leaving the State,

then the employment of the Sub-Contractor under this Sub-Contract shall automatically determine and the Sub-Contractor shall be entitled to be paid by the Employer directly such sums as he would have been entitled to be paid by the Contractor under Clause 11 sub-clause (f) hereof had his employment under this Sub-Contract been determined under Clause 11 sub-clause (e) hereof.

Construction of Sub-Contract in relation to Main Contract

22. Nothing in this Sub-Contract contained shall be deemed to limit or prejudice the right of the Contractor to determine the Main Contract subject to and in accordance with the terms of the same or to limit or prejudice the right of the Contractor (save as in this Sub-Contract expressly provided) to execute and carry out the Main Contract Works in accordance with its terms and the exercise of any such rights or of such right of determination of his employment by the Contractor as aforesaid shall not be or be deemed to be a breach by the Contractor of this Sub-Contract, and in the event of the Contractor determining his employment under the Main Contract as aforesaid, then the employment of the Sub-Contractor under this Sub-Contract shall thereupon also determine without right or claim on the part of the Sub-Contractor to damages or for loss or expense or otherwise, but the Sub-Contractor shall be entitled to be paid by the Contractor the Value of the Sub-Contract Works and any authorised variations thereof and/or parts thereof actually executed by the Sub-Contractor and not paid for at the date of such determination, such value to be calculated in accordance with Clause 10 hereof.

Wages and Conditions of Employment

23. (a) In the execution of the Sub-Contract Works the Sub-Contractor shall pay rates of wages and observe hours of labour and conditions of employment not less favourable than those laid down by the National Joint Industrial Council for the construction industry. The Sub-Contractor shall be responsible to the Contractor for the due observance by all Sub-Contractors of the provisions of this clause.

(b) The Sub-Contractors shall observe, form and comply with the provisions of clause 39 of the Main Contract Conditions on the part of the Contractor to be observed, performed and complied with so far as they relate and apply to the Sub-Contract Works.

Variations arising from Legislative enactments

24. Where after the Designated Date the cost of the performance of this Sub-Contract has been increased or decreased as the result of any legislative enactments, instruments, rules or orders or the exercise by the Government of powers vested in it imposing new

duties or tariffs or the alteration of existing duties or tariffs or restricting the importation of a commodity by licence, the amount of such increase or decrease as certified by the Architect shall be borne by or shall accrue to the Contractor, as the case may be, and the Sub-Contract sum shall be varied accordingly. Such increases or decreases shall not be recoverable under this clause if they come within the scope of clause 25 of this Sub-Contract.

Wage and Price Variation

25. The Sub-Contract Sum shall be deemed to have been calculated in the manner set out below and shall be subject to adjustment in the events specified hereunder.

(a) The provisions of clause 36 of the Main Contract Conditions shall as they apply to the Contractor and to the Main Contract Works be applied mutatis mutandis to the Sub-Contractor and the Sub-Contract Works.

(b) The designated date for the Sub-Contract Works shall be determined in the manner described in clause 1 of the Main Contract Conditions.

Arbitration

26. In the event of any dispute or difference between the Contractor and the Sub-Contractor, whether arising during the execution or after the completion or abandonment of the Sub-Contract Works or after the determination of the employment of the Sub-Contractor under this Sub-Contract (whether by breach or in any other manner), in regard to any matter or thing of whatsoever nature arising out of this Sub-Contract or in connection therewith, then either party shall give to the other notice in writing of such dispute or difference and such dispute or difference shall be and is hereby referred to the arbitration of such person as the parties hereto may agree to appoint as Arbitrator or failing such agreements as may be appointed on the request of either party by the President for the time being of the Construction Industry Federation and in either case the Award of such Arbitrator shall be final and binding on the parties.

PROVIDED that such Arbitrator shall not without the written consent of the Architect/ Engineer or the Contractor and in any case of the Sub-Contractor enter on the arbitration until after the completion or abandonment of the Main Contract Works, except to arbitrate upon the question, whether or not a certificate has been improperly withheld or is not in accordance with the terms of the Main Contract or upon the question as to whether a notice of determination has been properly issued in accordance in Clauses 11 or 12 of the Sub-Contract document.

AND provided further that in any such arbitration as is provided for in this Clause any decision of the Architect/Engineer which is final and binding on the Contractor under the Main Contract shall also be and be deemed to be final and binding between and upon the Contractor and Sub-Contractor.

Every of any such reference shall be deemed to be a submission to arbitration within the meaning of the Arbitration Acts, 1954 and 1980 (Number 26 of 1954) or the Arbitration Act (Northern Ireland), 1957 (as the case may be) or any act amending the same or either of them.

Strike out (A) or (B) as required

* (A) IN WITNESS WHEREOF the parties hereto have hereunto set their hands the day and year first above written.

* (B) IN WITNESS WHEREOF the Common Seals of the parties hereto have hereunto been affixed the day and year first above written.

APPENDIX

PART 1

FIRST RECITAL. Particulars of the Works (being a part of the Works comprised in the Main Contract) in this Sub-Contract referred to as "the Sub-Contract Works", viz:

. . . .

. . . .

. . . .

. . . .

. . . .

(NOTE – It is to be clearly stated whether scaffolding is to be supplied by the Contractor or the Sub-Contractor).

PART II

CLAUSE 4. Minimum Sum for Sub-Contractor's Public Liability Insurance (If

not stated £200,000) . . . .

PART III

CLAUSE 7.

Description of work	Completion period or periods of the Sub-Contract Works or respective Section thereof	
	Commencement Date	Completion Date
. . . .	. . . .	
. . . .	. . . .	
. . . .	. . . .	
. . . .	. . . .	

PART IV

CLAUSE 10. Value of the Sub-Contractor Works . . . .

. . . .

. . . .

. . . .

. . . .

£ _____

PART V

CLAUSE 10. Special Daywork Rates and method of determining value of Extras, Omissions and Variations

. . . .

. . . .

. . . .

. . . .

. . . .

. . . .

. . . .

PART VI

CLAUSE 11. Terms of Payment.

    (a) Period for honouring Certificates
        (if none stated 14 days)   . . . .

    (b) Discount Term   . . . .

    (c) Period of Interim Payments   . . . .

    (d) Retention   . . . .

        (i) First Moiety . . . .

        (ii) Second Moiety . . . .

(NOTE: If no other time is stated the first moiety of Retention Money shall be released upon practical completion of the Sub-Contract Works to the satisfaction of the Contractor and of the Architect/Engineer).

PART VII

CLAUSE 25. Designated Date . . . .

(A) SIGNED by the above-named Contractor
    in the present of: }

– or –

(B) THE COMMON SEAL of the above-named   }   (C.S.)
    Contractor was hereunto affixed in the
    presence of

– or –

(C) SIGNED, SEALED AND DELIVERED by   }   (Seal)
    the above-named Contractor in the
    presence of:

(A) SIGNED by the above named Sub-Contractor   }
    in the presence of:

– or –

(B) THE COMMON SEAL of the above-named   }   (C.S.)
    Sub-Contactor was hereunto affixed in the
    presence of:

– or –

(C) SIGNED, SEALED AND DELIVERED by   }   (Seal)
    the above-named Sub-Contractor in the
    presence of:

FOOTNOTE - *Where the Sub-Contract is executed under hand the parties should sign in the spaces provided in alternative (A).*

Where the Sub-Contract is executed under seal alternative (B) should be used by a party which is a limited company or other corporation, and alternative (C) by a party which is not a corporation. A fifty pence stamp must be impressed within thirty days of the date of execution of the original where it is under seal, and a twenty-five pence stamp on the counterpart (if any).

In the case of each party the two alternatives which do not apply should be struck out.

Building Contract

Employer: ....

Contractor: ....

Architect: ....

Works: ....

Date: ....

· FOUNDED 1839 ·

Published by the Royal Institute of the Architects of Ireland.

© Copyright: The Royal Institute of the Architects of Ireland,
8 Merrion Square,
Dublin 2.

Ph: 01-676 1703
Fax: 01-676 0940
e-mail: info@riai.ie
www: http://www.riai.ie

May 1997. Print One.

1

The Contractor agrees to complete the Works and the Employer agrees to pay the final contract sum.

Contract Details:

The Employer:

Name: ....

Address: ....

....

Signed: .... Seal:

The Contractor:

Name: ....

Address: ....

....

Signed: .... Seal:

The Architect:

Name: ....

Address: ....

....

R.I.A.I. Membership Number ....

The Quantity Surveyor:

Name: ....

Address: ....

....

The Works:

Site Address: ....

....

Description: ....

....

2

The Contract Sum: £: ....

The Contract
Document: Drawings: ....

                      Specifications: ....

                      Bill of Quantities: ....

Contract Information   **Clause No.**

3.1   The Agreed Date:...

3.2   The Starting Date:...

3.2   The Finishing Date:..

2.5   Liquidated Damages: £............................per..

2.6.1   Interval for Certificate Issue: ....

2.6.3   Retention Percentage:...

2.6.3   Retention Limit:...

2.6.4   Location of Joint Account:...

2.6.5   Defects Period:..

5.1.1   Minimum Sum for Public
             Liability Insurance:..

---

(3)

The following clauses are the terms and conditions applying to this Contract entered into by the Employer and the Contractor to build the works for the Contract Sum.

Works   1

1.1 Contract Control

The Works shall be built in accordance with the Contract Documents, (all of which are signed and identifiable) which are deemed to contain any items which might be reasonably inferred as being included even if not specifically described. The Architect shall decide on the correct interpretation of any omission or discrepancy in these documents.

All materials and workmanship shall be as described in the Contract. Documents and the Contractor may be required to confirm that this is so by documentation. Any tests required shall be carried out by the Contractor who shall be paid unless the cost is included in the Contract or if the test fails.

The Contractor shall open up, at the Architect's request, any work which has been covered and the Architect shall carry out an inspection as soon as is practicable. If the work has been covered up after a direction not to or if the work uncovered is not in accordance with the Contract Documents, then the Contractor shall pay the cost; otherwise the Employer shall pay the cost.

The Architect, as agent of the Employer, may issue instructions in regard to:

1.1.1. Varying the design, quality or quantity of the Works. These are described as variations.

1.1.2. Opening up work for inspection.

1.1.3. Postponing any work.

1.1.4. Rectifying any works, which in his opinion, do not conform with the Contract Documents.

1.1.5. Any other matter concerning the Contract, but not the varying of the terms and conditions of the Contract itself.

The Contractor shall carry out any instruction issued by the Architect. Any variation which results will be valued in accordance with Clause 2.2. Any oral instruction shall be confirmed in writing by the Contractor to the Architect within five days, and if not questioned by the Architect after a further five days shall be taken as confirmed. Where the instruction is in writing and the Contractor does not start to implement the instruction within five days the Employer may have the work referred to in the instruction carried out by others and any additional cost will be at the Contractor's expense.

An Architect's instruction which is of a kind which might not have been reasonably expected in the Contract will entitle the Contractor to compensation to be agreed by the Architect.

1.2 Contract Documents:

1.2.1. If a Bill of Quantities has been prepared and is a Contract Document the quality and quantity of the work described in it shall, taken with the other Contract Documents, constitute the Works. The Bill, unless expressly stated otherwise, shall be prepared in accordance with the latest Agreed Rules of Measurement prepared by the Society of Chartered Surveyors and the Construction Industry Federation and agreed by the Royal Institute of the Architects of Ireland.

Any error in the Bill of Quantities shall be dealt with as a variation. The cost of any remeasurement asked for by the Contractor under this sub-clause and found not to be justified shall be charged to the Contractor.

1.2.2. If a Bill of Quantities has been prepared and is not a Contract Document the quality and quantity of the Works shall be as described in the drawings and specification. The rates in the

Bill of Quantities shall be used for valuing variations.

1.2.3. If no Bill of Quantities has been prepared the Contractor shall provide a Schedule of Rates.

1.2.4. The Contract Documents shall be kept by the Architect and will be available to the Contractor if required. The Contractor shall receive two copies of the Contract Documents and any further drawings issued without charge. A copy of all drawings and the specification shall be available on site.

1.2.5. The Contractor and the Quantity Surveyor shall be entitled to make one copy of the Bill of Quantities or the Schedule of Rates and the originals of both shall remain the property of the Contractor, shall be confidential and shall be returned to the Contractor on completion if requested.

1.3 Statutory Notices:

The Contractor shall comply with the requirements of any Act, Statutory Instrument, Local Authority or Public Service Company and any fees paid by the Contractor shall be repaid by the Employer.

1.4 Setting Out:

The Architect shall provide the Contractor with sufficient information to set out the Works accurately. The Contractor shall be responsible for setting out the Works.

1.5 Site Staff

The Contractor shall employ adequate site staff to control and manage the project and any instruction given to them by the architect shall be a valid one.

The Employer may employ site staff who shall act at all times under the direction of the Architect.

The Architect, or anyone authorised by him, is entitled to access to the works and any place where work is being prepared before delivery to the site.

1.6 Sub-Contracts

The Contractor may not assign this contract or sub-let any of it without the Architect's consent. If the Contractor, or a Nominated Sub-Contractor, sub-contracts work they remain responsible as if they had not sub-contracted. Where the contract documents provide for it, the Architect may nominate a Sub-Contractor.

1.6.1. Nominated Sub-Contractors can only be objected to by the Contractor on grounds which the Architect considers reasonable, or where the Nominated Sub-Contractor will not agree to sign the standard form of appointment published by the Construction Industry Federation. Any collateral agreement between the Employer and the Nominated Sub-Contractor shall be in the standard form published by the Royal Institute of the Architects of Ireland, the Society of Chartered Surveyors and the Construction Industry Federation, and it is assumed that the conditions of the main contract form can be amended to accept the collateral agreement.

If the Nominated Sub-Contractor does not sign a collateral agreement then the Employer shall not be liable in any way to the Nominated Sub-Contractor and the Contractor shall be responsible for any work carried out and materials supplied by the Sub-Contractor, but the Contractor shall not be responsible for any design work carried out by the Sub-Contractor.

If the Nominated Sub-Contractor does not complete his work under the terms of this contract, and if another Sub-Contractor is nominated promptly by the Architect, then the Contractor will be liable for any delay in completing the Works but shall not be liable for any increase in cost.

1.6.2. The Contractor must pay the Nominated Sub-Contractor any certified sum within five days of his being paid by the Employer. The Contractor may deduct retention money and any agreed cash discount.

The Architect may ask the Contractor for confirmation that the Nominated Sub-Contractor has been paid any previous amount certified and if the Architect is not satisfied with regard to these payments he may certify these amounts directly.

If any Nominated Sub-Contractor finishes his work and is entitled to final payment before the issue of the final certificate, the Architect can certify a final payment subject to an indemnity being received by the Contractor from the Sub-Contractor with regard to latent defects. In this case the retention fund may be reduced as appropriate and the Contractor will be free from any liability for the Sub-Contractor's work with the exception of any latent defects.

1.6.3. If the Architect specifies particular materials or goods from a supplier then this firm becomes a Nominated Supplier.

1.7 Artists or Specialists

The Employer may engage artists or other specialists to carry out work which would not normally be part of a building contract. The Contractor shall be paid for any extra which might arise from this work and which was not included in the Contract and shall be entitled to payment for any assistance given. The cost of the work itself shall be paid by the Employer.

Contract Sum 2

2.1 Legislation

If, after the agreed date, any legislative decision affects the cost of the Works then the Contract Sum shall be adjusted as required.

2.2 Variations

2.2.1. Variations shall be valued by the Architect or Quantity Surveyor in the presence, if requested, of the Contractor or his representative. The Contractor shall be given a copy of the valuation before the issue of the next certificate.

2.2.2. The value of variations shall be calculated as follows:-

a) The rates in the Bill of Quantities or in the Schedule of Rates shall be used where the work involved in the variation is of the same character to which the rates apply. If the omission of any work affects the nature of subsequent work then paragraph b) will apply.

b) Where the work, or the conditions under which it is carried out, is different from that envisaged in the Bill or Schedule then these rates shall be used as far as possible. If this cannot be done the valuation shall be based on rates for similar work in the same locality.

c) If the Architect decides that neither a) nor b) can apply then the Contractor will be allowed day- work rates as listed in the Bill of Quantities or Schedule of Rates. If no rates are listed then those rates agreed by the Society of Chartered Surveyors and the Construction Industry Federation and approved by the Royal Institute of the Architects of Ireland shall apply.

6

In the case of Nominated Sub-Contractors the rates shall be those agreed between the Society of Chartered Surveyors and the appropriate body representing the Sub-Contractor.

The Architect shall be entitled on a weekly basis to details of the workmen and the materials involved in any variation work.

2.3 Omitted Work

If a variation involves the omission of any work which is so extensive as to cause the Contractor loss or expense with regard to work carried out before he was notified of the variation, then the Architect shall add an appropriate amount to the contract sum.

If the final account shows a credit on the contract sum, the Contractor shall be entitled to 10% of that credit. Adjustments arising from provisional or contingency items, or arising under the price variation clause, shall not form part of this calculation.

2.4 Provisional Sums

Sums which are included in the contract sum to deal with Nominated Sub-Contractors, Nominated Suppliers, or other specified items shall be spent at the direction of the Architect.

Any discounts shall be credited to the Employer except for any discount for prompt payment by the Contractor to a Nominated Sub-Contractor or Supplier.

2.5 Late Finishing

If the Works are not practically complete by the stated finishing date, or any date extended under Clause 3.2, and if the Architect is satisfied that the works should have been completed, then the Architect will inform the Employer that he is entitled to liquidated damages as set out in this Contract until such time as the Architect certifies that the Works are practically complete, and the Employer may set these damages off against any sum due under the Contract.

If any delay is caused by the Employer, and the Contractor gives prompt notice of this delay, the Contractor will be entitled to any loss directly caused by this delay.

2.6 Payment

2.6.1. At the agreed periods the Contractor may apply to the Architect for payment and shall be entitled to a certificate within five days. The certificate shall state the amount due to any Nominated Sub-Contractor or Nominated Supplier. The Employer shall pay the amount certified within seven days. The Contractor can ask for an explanation if the amount certified is less than the amount claimed.

2.6.2. Interim certificates shall be for the total value of the work which, in the Architect's opinion has been properly executed, together with the cost of any items either delivered to the site or prepared specifically for the Works. These items become the property of the Employer when payment has been made, including items that have been ordered from a supplier or a sub-contractor, and the Architect shall be notified of any restrictions regarding retention of title. The Contractor remains responsible for the safety of these items.

If the Architect decides to include any items in an interim certificate before they are delivered to the site, the Architect must be satisfied that these items are complete, identifiable and traceable and are specifically prepared for the Works.

2.6.3 Interim certificates shall be reduced by the agreed retention percentage until the retention limit is reached, after which certificates shall be for the full amount of the work properly completed.

The money retained shall either be held in trust by the Employer for the Contractor but without any obligation to invest it, or it shall be paid into a joint account as later described. When the Architect certifies that the Works are practically complete the Contractor is entitled to receive half the retention fund, but at any time during the course of the Contract the Employer shall be entitled to use the retention money in accordance with these Contract Conditions. The final certificate shall include the remainder of the retention money.

2.6.4 If the parties agree to the retention money being paid into a joint account under the joint names of the Employer and the Contractor at an agreed bank, the interest due on the account shall be payable to the Contractor.

Payments from the joint account shall be made to either party to the Contract only at the direction of the Architect. The provisions of clause 2.6.3 shall apply to this joint retention account.

2.6.5 When the Architect issues the Certificate of Practical Completion, the Contractor shall provide all the necessary documents required to calculate the final account within three months, and only these documents shall be used for these calculations. The Architect shall proceed to complete the final account within six months of receiving the necessary documents.

When, at the end of the defects period, the defects listed by the Architect have been made good, the Architect shall notify the parties to the Contract of the proposed final Contract Sum and unless the parties request that the matter be referred to arbitration, the final certificate shall be issued within ten days of the first notice.

2.6.6 The final certificate shall be conclusive evidence that the final cost of Works has been properly calculated.

2.6.7 In the case of either an interim or a final certificate the Contractor shall be entitled to interest on any amount outstanding after seven working days after the issue of the certificate at the Dublin Interbank Overnight Rate.

2.7 Price Variations

Any changes after the agreed date in the price of materials or in wage rates shall be dealt with in accordance with the Formula Fluctuations Agreement issued by the Liaison Committee.

3.1   Agreed Date and "Days"

After the tender has been accepted an agreed date shall be set from which to calculate any variations which might arise under Clause 2.7.

Days mentioned in this Contract shall be working days as is normal in the Construction Industry.

3.2   Starting and Finishing

The starting date and the finishing date shall be agreed by the parties to the Contract.

The finishing date may be extended by the Architect, taking all relevant factors into account, if the Architect is satisfied that the Contractor has been delayed because:

3.2.1. Of circumstances beyond the control of the parties.

3.2.2. The site was not available at the starting date.

3.2.3. The weather was unusually bad.

3.2.4. Of damage covered by insurance.

3.2.5. Of industrial disputes.

3.2.6. Of Architect's instructions, late instructions or actions of the Employer.

3.2.7. Of delay caused by parties outside the Contract.

The Contractor shall notify the Architect immediately of any delay and the reasons for it. If the delay is caused by the events listed in 3.2.2, 3.2.6 or 3.2.7, the Contractor shall be entitled to cost as well as time.

3.3   Completion

When the Architect is satisfied that the building can be used for the purpose for which it was built then he shall issue a certificate of practical completion.

When this certificate is issued the following occurs:

3.3.1. The defects period commences.

3.3.2. The Employer becomes responsible for insurance.

3.3.3. Half of the retention fund is paid to the Contractor.

3.3.4. The time programme for the calculation of the final account shall commence.

The Architect shall issue a list of defects either during the defects period or not later than twenty days after the end of the defects period. These defects shall be repaired by the Contractor at his own cost.

If the Works are to be completed in phases then the Architect can certify the appropriate phase as being complete and any clause referring to completion in full shall then refer to partial completion in proportion.

4.1. Termination

4.1.1. The Employer will be entitled to terminate the Contract, after reasonable notice, if in the opinion of the Architect the Contractor is not complying with the Architect's instructions or the conditions of this contract. The Architect shall inform the Contractor and the Employer shall be entitled to the use of any plant and materials on site for which a certificate has provided payment.

4.1.2. If the Contractor becomes bankrupt, or if a receiver, liquidator or examiner is appointed the Employer shall be entitled to terminate the contract.

4.1.3. In the case of any termination the Employer shall be entitled to complete the works using any materials and plant on the site and after completion the Architect will certify any amounts due to the Employer for expenses incurred in the termination or due to the Contractor from the sale of any plant or materials.

4.1.4. When the Contract has been terminated by the Employer the Architect may secure the site, any materials and plant and the cost of doing this shall be a charge to the Contractor.

4.1.5. The Contractor shall be entitled to terminate the Contract if he is not paid within twenty days of the issue of any certificate and the finishing date shall be extended after termination by the Architect for a period of twice the length of time taken to honour the certificate.

4.1.6. The Contractor shall be entitled to terminate the Contract if the Employer becomes bankrupt or if a receiver, liquidator or examiner is appointed. The Contractor shall be entitled to any costs or damages arising from this termination and the Architect shall certify the amount.

4.2   Dispute Resolution

4.2.1. Conciliation: In the case of a dispute between the parties the matter shall be referred to conciliation in accordance with the procedures agreed between the Royal Institute of the Architects of Ireland, the Society of Chartered Surveyors and the Construction Industry Federation.

4.2.2. Arbitration: If conciliation fails to resolve a dispute it shall be referred to Arbitration. Any matter in dispute between the parties which arises from this Contract (including the replacement of the Architect or the Quantity Surveyor) can be referred to Arbitration. If the parties cannot agree to an arbitrator, they may request the President of the Royal Institute of the Architects of Ireland to nominate an Arbitrator after consultation with the President of The Construction Industry Federation. The Arbitration shall be governed by the Arbitration Acts.

5.1   Liability of the Parties

The Insurers or Insurance Brokers to both the Employer and the Contractor shall agree on the insurance provisions and shall advise the parties of any proposals to depart from the provisions of Clauses 5.1 to 5.3.

5.1.1 Loss or damage to physical property and of personal injury and death which arise in connection with the Contract, except those as set out in 5.1.2 is the responsibility of the Contractor, and the Contractor shall maintain appropriate insurance cover from the starting date until the issue of the Final Certificate.

5.1.2 Claims arising from the following shall be the responsibility of the Employer:

a) Loss or damage to property (excluding the Works), nuisance or interference with the occupation of the site which is the unavoidable result of the Contractor's operations or negligence or breach of any statutory duty by the Employer or any of his agents.

b) Damage to the Works, plant or materials which arises from faulty design by the Employer.

c) Damage to existing structures caused by the Contractor's operations in the case of alterations or extensions to those structures.

5.2. The Works

The Contractor shall be responsible for insuring the Works from the starting date until the issue of the Certificate of Practical Completion. The Contractor shall clear the site, repair any damage caused to the Works and pay any fees under the Insurance Policy and shall be paid for this work from the money received under the Policy which is to be lodged in a joint bank account in the names of the Employer and Contractor and released on Certificates of the Architect.

5.3 Insurance Policies

5.3.1. Each party is liable for and indemnifies the other against claims, proceedings, compensation and costs for loss of or damage to physical property (excluding the Works), personal injury and death caused by the risks carried by each party, adjusted to the extent that the other contributed to the loss or damage.

5.3.2. The Contractor shall submit the Policies and Certificates to the Architect before the starting date for his approval. If the Contractor does not do so, the Employer can arrange the necessary insurance and deduct the premium from any money due to the Contractor.

5.3.3. The Contractor's Insurance Policies shall specify any exclusions. If any damage occurs as a result of events arising from the exclusions, the costs shall not be taken into account when calculating amounts payable to the Contractor under the Contract. If, as a result of damage arising from an excluded risk, it appears appropriate to the Employer, the Contract may be determined and in the case of a dispute, either party may request a conciliation or arbitration.

SUPPLEMENT (A)

to the Conditions of Contract for Building Work for use by Government Departments, Local Authorities and Other Bodies

Issue No. 1 (R)   **effective from 12 May 1992**

The Royal Institute of the Architects of Ireland with the approval of the Department of Finance after consultation with the Construction Industry Federation, and the Society of Chartered Surveyors in the Republic of Ireland acting pursuant to Clause 36 of the Conditions of Contract publishes hereunder the meanings to be given to certain wordings in that Clause.

A. MEANINGS FOR CLAUSE 36(B)

1. "Work People" means operatives such as craftsmen, semi-skilled labour, labourers, drivers and operators of mechanical plant and machinery, site time keepers and site clerks. Trade foremen and charge hands shall also be deemed to be work people.

    Not to be counted as work people are general foremen wholly engaged on supervisory work, site agents and administrative or supervisory staff such as managers and surveyors.

    Insofar as general foremen not engaged whole-time on supervisory work, trade foremen, charge hands or any other work people have part-time administrative or supervisory duties they shall be treated for the purposes of Clause 36 as operatives at the operatives' rates appropriate to their trades, the hours to be charged being the full number of hours worked each day.

2. (a) "Wages" means the cost of normal time at standard rate and all overtime at standard overtime rates. Only the hours at work shall be taken into account. Not coming within this meaning are site bonuses, bonus payments under site agreements, productivity or incentive bonuses or payments or payments over the standard rates for normal time or over the standard overtime rates.

    (b) "Expenses" means travelling and subsistence (meal) allowances, country money, tool money, contractor's contributions to the Construction Industry pension fund and any other payments not covered in paragraph (a) of this Section and which may be agreed from time to time by the Minister for Finance.

3. "Labour on-costs necessarily payable" means

    (a) The relative percentages in respect of Wage Variation Claims set out in the document entitled "Percentage additions to Labour Costs to cover Insurances, Holidays etc" issued in agreement between the Royal Institution of Chartered Surveyors and the Construction Industry Federation, the percentages to be used in calculating increases or decreases in wages and expenses over any period being those listed in the edition of the document then effective.

    Increases or decreases in the relative percentages themselves shall not be payable until taken into account in the edition of the aforesaid document next issued after their occurrence.

B.   **MEANINGS FOR CLAUSE 36(C)**

"Materials and goods necessary for the execution of the Works" means

(a)   materials and goods embodied in the Works together with unavoidable waste and surpluses on such materials and goods;

(b)   materials and goods specifically purchased for temporary use in the construction and on the site of the Works provided that such materials and goods are not re-usable in similar form on another job and, when no longer required for the Works, have only scrap value;

(c)   fuels and electric power for plant and essential temporary lighting installations when such fuels and power are wholly consumed on the site of the Works provided always that in cases (b) and (c) the liability of the Employer shall be limited to that part of any increase which is in excess of 10% of the price ruling of the Designated Date, with an equivalent limitation to the Contractor's liability in the case of any decrease.

The following for the purposes of Sub-Clause 36(c) are deemed not to be goods and materials necessary for the execution of the Works:

Formwork of any other materials which can be used on another job when no longer required for the Works;

Materials and goods for temporary work associated with but not embodied in the Works nor used in the construction of the Works (e.g. site-huts, hoardings, temporary roads); plants, tools and equipment.

End of Supplement (A)

SUPPLEMENT (B)

of the Conditions of Contract for Building Work for use by Government Departments, Local Authorities and Other Bodies

Note: Supplement (A) relates to the 1992 Revision of the Price Variation Clause

effective from 31 March, 2001

RETENTION BOND

The Royal Institute of the Architects of Ireland with the approval of the Department of Finance after consultation with the Construction Industry Federation, and the Society of Chartered Surveyors in the Republic of Ireland acting pursuant to Sub-Clause 35(e)(ii) of the Conditions of Contract publishes hereunder the Retention Bond form to be used when operating Sub-Clause 35(e)(ii).

We,...understand that under the terms of your Contract No ....('the Contract') with..(hereinafter called the

Applicant),   of..................................for

the..

you.. at..are retaining the sum of £/€ ....being..................of the Contract value by way of retention monies ('the Retention Monies') and that you are prepared to release the said Retention Monies (less retention monies held on nominated subcontractors not bound by a Retention Bond agreement) against a guarantee.

In consideration of your releasing the sum of £/€ .... to the Applicant

we,..hereby guarantee the repayment to you on demand

of up to £/€...........................(say..) in the event

of the Applicant failing to fulfil his obligations under the said Contract, provided that your claim hereunder is received in writing at this office accompanied by your signed statement that:-

1)   the Applicant has failed to fulfil his obligations under the terms of the Contract,

and

2)   the Applicant has been advised in a written notice issued by the Architect, simultaneously copied to this office, in accordance with Clause 2(c)(iii) of the Conditions of Contract, of your intention to claim payment under this guarantee in the event of any of the obligations notified remaining unfulfilled fifteen (15) working days after the date of issue of the notice.

397

This guarantee shall remain valid until close of business at this office on the date of issue of the Final Certificate or until the expiry of 15 months after practical completion whichever is the earlier ('Expiry'), subject to any matter of claim in dispute with the Applicant notified to this office before Expiry. Any claim hereunder must be received in writing at this office before Expiry (subject to the notification referred to above) accompanied by your signed statement as aforesaid, and such claim and statement shall be accepted as conclusive evidence that the amount claimed is due to you under this guarantee.

Claims and statements as aforesaid must bear the dated confirmation of your bankers' in the case of Government Departments and Offices confirmation of an official not below the rank of Principal Officer that the signatories thereon are authorised so to sign.

This guarantee shall become operative upon receipt of the Retention Monies (less retention monies held on nominated subcontractors not bound by the retention bond agreement) by the Applicant.

Upon Expiry, this guarantee shall become null and void, whether returned to us for cancellation or not and any claim or statement received after expiry (subject to the notification referred to above) shall be ineffective.

This guarantee is personal to yourselves and is not transferable or assignable, except by agreement which agreement shall not be unreasonably witheld.

This guarantee shall be governed by and construed in accordance with the Laws of Ireland and shall be subject to the exclusive jurisdiction of the Irish Courts.

Arbitration clause

If either party to this bond shall be aggrieved regarding matters covered by this guarantee the party so aggrieved shall forthwith by notice in writing to the other refer such dispute or difference to arbitration of a person to be agreed upon between the parties or (if the parties fail to appoint an arbitrator within one calendar month of service of the notice as aforesaid) a person to be appointed on application of either party by the President for the time being of the Royal Institute of the Architects of Ireland and such arbitrator shall forthwith and with all due expedition enter upon the reference and make an award thereon which award shall be final and conclusive. If the arbitrator declines the appointment or after appointment is removed by order of a competent Court or is incapable of acting or dies and the parties do not within one calendar month of the vacancy arising fill the vacancy then the President for the time being of the Royal Institute of the Architects of Ireland may on application of either party appoint an arbitrator to fill the vacancy. In any case where the President for the time being of the Royal Institute of the Architects of Ireland is not able to exercise the aforesaid functions conferred upon him the said function may be exercised on his behalf by the Vice President for the time being of the Royal Institute of the Architects of Ireland.

Executed as a Deed this.........................day of.......................2001

The common Seal of
was hereunder affixed by
....

**of the Conditions of Contract for Building Work for use by Government
Departments, Local Authorities and Other Bodies**

effective from 31 March, 2001

CONCILIATION PROCEDURES

The Royal Institute of the Architects of Ireland with the approval of the Department of Finance after consultation with the Construction Industry Federation, and the Society of Chartered Surveyors in the Republic of Ireland acting pursuant to Sub-Clause 37(a) of the Conditions of Contract publishes hereunder the Conciliation Procedures which are to be followed when operating Sub-Clause 37(a).

1. This procedure shall apply to any conciliation requested under Clause 37(a) of the GDLA ('82) Form of Contract.

2. A party to the contract seeking conciliation shall notify the other party in writing to that effect and shall at the same time specify the matter in dispute.

3. The parties shall agree on a conciliator, and failing agreement within 10 working days of notice served under 2 above, shall request the President of the RIAI to appoint a conciliator from a list of conciliators agreed between the RIAI, the SCS and the CIF.

4. The conciliator shall require the parties to submit, in advance of the hearing, a brief written opening statement and appending the necessary documentation not later than 10 working days after his appointment. The parties should at the same time notify the conciliator of the names of the persons appearing at the conciliation.

5. The conciliator shall within 10 working days after receipt of the statements and documentation establish the order of the proceedings and shall arrange a convenient time, date and place for the hearing.

6. The conciliator may consider and discuss such solutions to the dispute as he thinks appropriate or as may be suggested by either party. All information given to the conciliator is confidential and shall remain so unless authorised by the party who supplied the information.

7. The conciliator may, having informed the parties, consult independent third party experts.

8. The conciliator shall endeavour to commit the parties to reach a mutual settlement failing which he shall within 10 working days of the hearing, issue his recommendation. He shall not be required to give reasons. It shall remain confidential if rejected by either party.

9. If neither party rejects the recommendation within 10 working days after its issue, it shall be final and binding on the parties. If either party rejects the recommendation, a request for arbitration may be made under Clause 37(b) of the GDLA ('82) Form of Contract.

10. Each party to the conciliation shall pay their own costs. The parties shall be jointly and severally liable for the conciliator's costs in equal shares, unless the conciliator decides otherwise.

11. Conciliations are settlement negotiations and are without prejudice to the rights of the disputants. All statements, information and material, made, given or exchanged, orally or in writing, either during the conciliation or prior thereto or thereafter, upon the request of the conciliator shall be inadmissible in any legal proceedings, in court or arbitration, to the maximum extent permitted by law. Evidence which is otherwise admissible in legal proceedings shall not be rendered inadmissible as a result of its use in the conciliation. The disputants agree not to summon or otherwise require the conciliator to appear or testify or produce records, notes or any other information or material in any legal proceedings, in court or arbitration, and no recording or stenographic records will be made of the conciliation.

12. Any agreement reached by the disputants through the conciliation shall be set down in writing and duly executed by their authorised representative.